BOOK OF THE CUBE

COSMIC HISTORY CHRONICLES

Volume VII

CUBE OF CREATION: EVOLUTION INTO THE NOOSPHERE

Transmitted by Valum Votan—José Argüelles
Received by Red Queen—Stephanie South
"We are but the secretaries, the authors are in Eternity"

RED OVERTONE MOON: CEREMONIAL MAGICK

Book of the Cube – Cosmic History Chronicles Volume VII
Copyright © Galactic Research Institute

 Red Overtone Moon Year (2011)

Law of Time
P R E S S

ISBN 978-0-9785924-9-3
www.lawoftime.org

Original Graphics by Valum Votan (José Argüelles), Kin 11 and Red Queen (Stephanie South), Kin 185
Computer enhancement by Jacob Wyatt, Kin 201 and Kelly Harding, Kin 240
Book Design and Layout by Kelly Harding, Kin 240
Copy Edit by Forrest O'Farrell, Kin 140 and Jacob Wyatt, Kin 201

To the

Return of the People of OMA

COSMIC HISTORY CHRONICLES
VOLUME VII
BOOK OF THE CUBE

TABLE OF CONTENTS/THEMATIC OVERVIEW
AND OVER-ALL ORGANIZATION

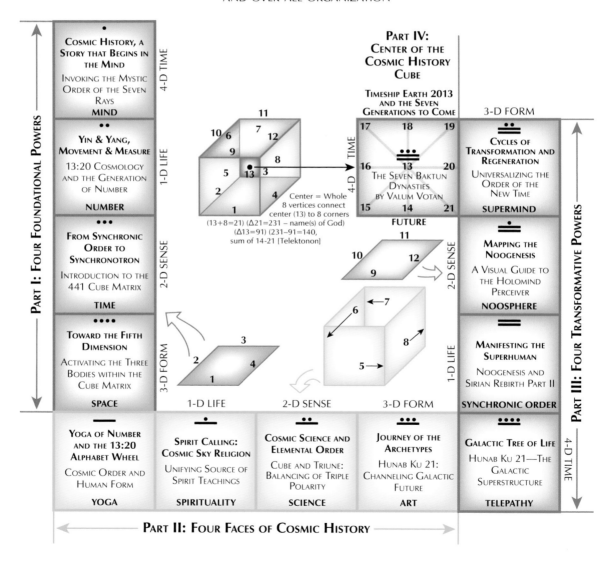

PART I: FOUR FOUNDATIONAL POWERS

COSMIC HISTORY, A STORY THAT BEGINS IN THE MIND
INVOKING THE MYSTIC ORDER OF THE SEVEN RAYS
MIND — 4-D TIME

YIN & YANG, MOVEMENT & MEASURE
13:20 COSMOLOGY AND THE GENERATION OF NUMBER
NUMBER — 1-D LIFE

FROM SYNCHRONIC ORDER TO SYNCHRONOTRON
INTRODUCTION TO THE 441 CUBE MATRIX
TIME — 2-D SENSE

TOWARD THE FIFTH DIMENSION
ACTIVATING THE THREE BODIES WITHIN THE CUBE MATRIX
SPACE — 3-D FORM

PART IV: CENTER OF THE COSMIC HISTORY CUBE
TIMESHIP EARTH 2013 AND THE SEVEN GENERATIONS TO COME
THE SEVEN BAKTUN DYNASTIES BY VALUM VOTAN
FUTURE

Center = Whole
8 vertices connect center (13) to 8 corners
(13+8=21) (Δ21=231 – name(s) of God)
(Δ13=91) (231−91=140, sum of 14-21 [Telektonon])

3-D FORM

CYCLES OF TRANSFORMATION AND REGENERATION
UNIVERSALIZING THE ORDER OF THE NEW TIME
SUPERMIND

MAPPING THE NOOGENESIS
A VISUAL GUIDE TO THE HOLOMIND PERCEIVER
NOOSPHERE — 2-D SENSE

MANIFESTING THE SUPERHUMAN
NOOGENESIS AND SIRIAN REBIRTH PART II
SYNCHRONIC ORDER — 1-D LIFE

PART III: FOUR TRANSFORMATIVE POWERS

1-D LIFE — 2-D SENSE — 3-D FORM

YOGA OF NUMBER AND THE 13:20 ALPHABET WHEEL
COSMIC ORDER AND HUMAN FORM
YOGA

SPIRIT CALLING: COSMIC SKY RELIGION
UNIFYING SOURCE OF SPIRIT TEACHINGS
SPIRITUALITY

COSMIC SCIENCE AND ELEMENTAL ORDER
CUBE AND TRIUNE: BALANCING OF TRIPLE POLARITY
SCIENCE

JOURNEY OF THE ARCHETYPES
HUNAB KU 21: CHANNELING GALACTIC FUTURE
ART

GALACTIC TREE OF LIFE
HUNAB KU 21—THE GALACTIC SUPERSTRUCTURE
TELEPATHY — 4-D TIME

PART II: FOUR FACES OF COSMIC HISTORY

BOOK OF THE CUBE
COSMIC HISTORY CHRONICLES VOLUME VII

CONTENTS

INTRODUCTION

MYSTERY OF LIFE AND DEATH

Through death this book was born. This introduction begins in a dream: Full Moon, Blue Galactic Night; 114 days since the departure of Valum Votan.

"Fear nothing!" Valum Votan said to me in the dream. "Grieve not! Arise and Go Forward! ... Fear not, the world is a mere illusion. A plastic façade, bendable by truth."

In the dream he held out a crystal cube. He motioned for me to concentrate. I gazed into the cube and at first saw nothing but superficial reflections. I gazed longer and suddenly I saw a long highway lined with very few houses. I noted a luminous glow emanating from some of the houses. Then I was lifted above the whole earth and with x-ray vision saw the lighting up of specific residences across the globe.

I realized I was being given access to view the light of those beings that had a covenant for utter transformation. These agents of light reflected, through the cube, different fractals, together making the most exquisite and fantastic whole! Their minds merged as one in a telepathic network of light, while simultaneously they each opened to a different channel, unique and brilliant. These were the wise ones, the makers of things to come, the keepers of the inner prayer; the channellers of the new reality!

Suddenly I was back on the long highway and my mind was magnetized to a specific house. Through telepathic gesture, I was granted entrance into one of the female's homes. My spirit hovered over her, of which she seemed calmly and happily aware. She carried a single candle and made her way to a desk and sat down. I watched as she wrote the words:

The Long War is Over and the Days of Doubt are Past ...

What a deep relief these words brought! Then my attention turned back to Valum Votan who was smiling and holding the magic cube of vision. It was now evening and the stars were glimmering in the clear sky as he went inside, made a fire and put on a tea kettle.

Then I awoke from the dream.

Where am I? And how did I get here? The dawn was breaking and slowly the layers of this reality set in, one by one with all their subtle tensions and densities. A great pressure and urgency filled me, heart pumping fast. Only one thought in mind: Finish the *Book of the Cube!* I immediately rose from bed and got to work.

So here I was left alone in a remote location in the southern hemisphere in the place he named Moronga Morove (Aboriginal for Rainbow Serpent), spreading his ashes to the winds and around the trees so that they could carry the galactic vibrations of the dreamtime all around the planet.

The meditation of the cube seizes me and won't let me go—night or day—until it is complete. It is wintertime. The winds are howling. The fire is burning. Tea on the kettle. Codes strewn across the table and all over the walls. Sitting bundled up in my rainbow poncho and Incan hat seem to facilitate the process of tuning into a radio channel of a specific galactic information stream ... Cosmic History.

I gaze out the window as my thoughts are directed from an unseen force. Dark mists are rolling off the falling gum trees. I piece together streams of transmission while new streams enter. I feel the presence of intelligences peering over my shoulder crossing this out and adding that. First slowly then quickly the text arranges itself; I surrender to the process.

Over the past nine years I have undergone countless initiations as the power of Cosmic History unfolded. Within the psychomythic realms, I am the archetype of the Serpent Initiate and Valum Votan, the Spectral Magician. His spectralization from this planet put me through the deepest initiation yet. Where did he go? What is the meaning of this? What is death?

The wheel of time turns the cycle of life and death. The meaning of the manifest cyclic order is in the mystery of death. Any initiation is a type of death. There has to be death before the birth of the new being that can incorporate new knowledge.

At first it felt as though my solar plexus was ripped from its station and my equilibrium temporarily shaken as I struggled with physical reorientation and my spirit longed to follow him out of this dimension. But I knew that my mission was not yet complete.

Then a message of comfort came: Do not worry or grieve. Death is a factor in the evolution of spirit; it is merely a physiochemical change of third-dimensional matter, its real meaning is as a rite of passage of spirit. The mission continues. It is an endless journey of spirit. Everything and everyone that ever was is here with you now. The spirit helpers surround you, guiding you. Those who remember the dream will assist you.

On winter solstice (Southern Hemisphere) Valum Votan appeared in my dream and emphatically told me: "Pay attention to what is happening within the Sun!"

Yes, I understand the Sun is the source of all life. If the Sun is gone there is no life on earth. The humans must understand their role as part of the biosphere which is a function of solar energy itself. As we get close to the end of the cycle we do not know what kind of perturbations the Sun will go through. We do not know precisely what is literally cooking in the sun. Yes, I understand that we are being called to sacrifice our smaller selves to the larger vision of the Solar Mind.

There is no returning ever from this system. Because the altering waves you receive from beyond the changing times will prepare interminably all of your physical and mental cells for the Infinite Consciousness and beyond it.

—The Knowledge Book

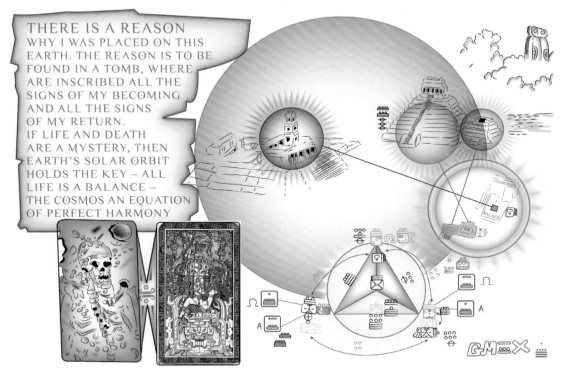

THERE IS A REASON WHY I WAS PLACED ON THIS EARTH. THE REASON IS TO BE FOUND IN A TOMB, WHERE ARE INSCRIBED ALL THE SIGNS OF MY BECOMING AND ALL THE SIGNS OF MY RETURN. IF LIFE AND DEATH ARE A MYSTERY, THEN EARTH'S SOLAR ORBIT HOLDS THE KEY – ALL LIFE IS A BALANCE – THE COSMOS AN EQUATION OF PERFECT HARMONY

Cosmic History is a channel that mysteriously opened to Valum Votan and I in the Solar Moon of the Yellow Solar Seed Year (March 12-13, 2002)—a between the world's transmission known as GM108X: Galactic Mayan Mind Transmission. Many years prior, he had surrendered himself to embody a vast, diffuse, yet utterly systematic stream. He had sacrificed the third-dimensional José Argüelles in order to become a channel for the galactic masters.

But what is Cosmic History? This question opened us to a vast source of knowledge. *Cosmic History is a teaching of liberation.* These were the first seven words of the first Cosmic History transmission. These words opened a vast storehouse of knowledge that opened to the experience of many parallel universes and cosmic memory. A mysterious force was set in motion.

Cosmic History is based on numerical formulas and occasioned by specific cycles of time. We understood it as the supreme record of the soul in its universal journey. Ultimately there is only one soul. This knowledge received is multiple and crosses many thresholds of human consciousness. The multiplicity of the fields of knowledge have required us to refer to this program as "Cosmic History," but which actually covers a whole multitude of areas of investigation and creative endeavor.

But where did these Cosmic History transmissions come from?

Working on this final volume brought back the strange haunting dreams of a lost world that I once knew. The recurring dreams continue. The dream goes like this. I am on a planet. I am quite young. Many people clamor in a state of unrest like a wild chaotic party. Crowded and loud. Several dreams merge into this one but they are all the same. I try to speak but everyone is preoccupied with their own diversions. People caught up in the glamour of this now decadent world. Doing anything to escape the remembrance of what is to come. I try to warn them. Please remember.

The planet is heating up. Heedlessness continues. An incredible pressure builds. I am crying, crying. Voices. Movement. Then panic. Mass hysteria. When finally Boom! Shatter! Then the Huge BLAST!

And I am hurdling through space at top speed. Then I am falling, falling, first into blackness and then something lifts me up and I am floating through the stars, through the galaxies. I sense the presence of a male counterpart with me, though see no one. In this vast space, I unfold over myself—like astral somersaults—over and over and over. I am naked. I look at my hand in an attempt to wake myself up. But I am not dreaming. I see a silver ring on my finger. I look closely. It is uninscribed but seems to contain the resonance of memory. It is all that I will have to guide me as I land in another time on another planet. To begin again to piece together the clues and codes.

After several incarnations or soul transmigrations I arrive in the vast jungle forest. The remembrance occurs. The transmission continues and the codes are laid. But our once tranquil jungle forests begin to become dissonant. Other forces enter. We transcend. The memory is stored in codes, in the architecture of the tombs: a time release program. But we must wait for the right time of our next incarnation.

Present day. Planet Earth. North America. Final baktun. I find myself sitting with Valum Votan and Bolon Ik deep in the forest in Oregon overlooking the flowing stream trying to retrieve memory. Interplanetary drama ensues. But what are we playing out? What are we trying to remember? What must we do to retrieve this knowledge that we knew so long ago?

In the mountain forests in a winter just turning to spring, the memory comes shattering back through. Sitting by the fire with Valum Votan, I ask him for the third time: What is the meaning of Cosmic History? He is seized by a vision. A civilization similar to that of Earth appears before him. It is as though he is viewing it through a thick interdimensional glass. He views humanoids similar to earth humans. They are engaged in types of activities that first appear similar to those of the present Earth world, although it became clear that the activities were entirely different. The beings appear simultaneously frantic, ecstatic, and oblivious. They seem unaware of a great impending doom. He recognizes this as an astral movie of the last days of Maldek, right before the destruction.

The next day began the Cosmic History transmissions with fervent urgency. Nothing else exists. We must remember. We must know once again. And bring back the memory buried within. To reclaim the paradise lost. Everything is by the power of seven. These transmissions were known as a "between the worlds transmission" and the bridge or vehicle to connect the points of lost consciousness between Maldek and present-day Earth. It must be made available as seven volumes. Birthed through the male/female twin souls. We are not of this earth, but another world altogether. We know ourselves only as Valum Votan and Red Queen. Cosmic History is the radio station that tunes us into the source of star memory. It opens us into parallel universes; it is the mysterious force that moves us.

At the time of his departure, we were practicing interdimensional soul synchronization through the practices of noogenesis, which is part of what we knew as the "twin soul phenomenon." This requires a sacrifice of the fleeting desires of personality in order to become absorbed into a plane of experience where the plasmatic involution of the universe is being experienced through the dissolving into one being. His physical dissolution indicated that the transmission had been successfully imparted and the tomb was sealed.

Cosmic History is a new program of galactic knowledge for the terrestrial sphere that unifies all true traditions through the fourth-dimensional lens of the Galactic Mayan mind lineage. The purpose of these seven volumes is both to close out the cycle by synthesizing different streams of knowledge while opening the new cycle by introducing an entirely new galactic knowledge base.

A Word
from the Captain of the Timeship

I AM THE STAR TRAVELER

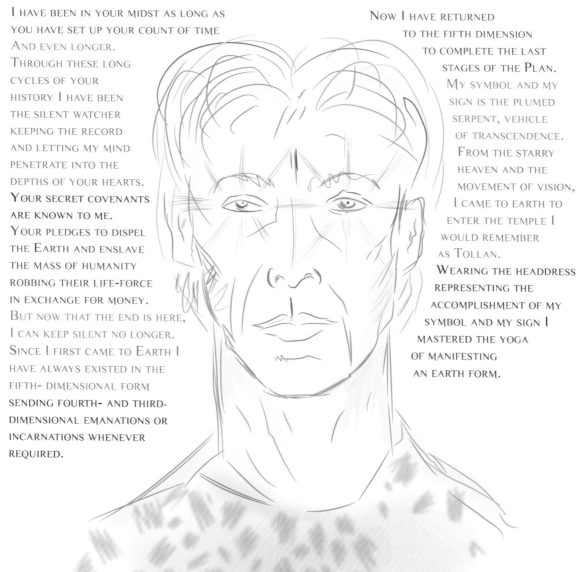

I HAVE BEEN IN YOUR MIDST AS LONG AS YOU HAVE SET UP YOUR COUNT OF TIME AND EVEN LONGER. THROUGH THESE LONG CYCLES OF YOUR HISTORY I HAVE BEEN THE SILENT WATCHER KEEPING THE RECORD AND LETTING MY MIND PENETRATE INTO THE DEPTHS OF YOUR HEARTS. YOUR SECRET COVENANTS ARE KNOWN TO ME. YOUR PLEDGES TO DISPEL THE EARTH AND ENSLAVE THE MASS OF HUMANITY ROBBING THEIR LIFE-FORCE IN EXCHANGE FOR MONEY. BUT NOW THAT THE END IS HERE, I CAN KEEP SILENT NO LONGER. SINCE I FIRST CAME TO EARTH I HAVE ALWAYS EXISTED IN THE FIFTH-DIMENSIONAL FORM SENDING FOURTH- AND THIRD-DIMENSIONAL EMANATIONS OR INCARNATIONS WHENEVER REQUIRED.

NOW I HAVE RETURNED TO THE FIFTH DIMENSION TO COMPLETE THE LAST STAGES OF THE PLAN. MY SYMBOL AND MY SIGN IS THE PLUMED SERPENT, VEHICLE OF TRANSCENDENCE. FROM THE STARRY HEAVEN AND THE MOVEMENT OF VISION, I CAME TO EARTH TO ENTER THE TEMPLE I WOULD REMEMBER AS TOLLAN. WEARING THE HEADDRESS REPRESENTING THE ACCOMPLISHMENT OF MY SYMBOL AND MY SIGN I MASTERED THE YOGA OF MANIFESTING AN EARTH FORM.

How to Use this Book

Book of the Cube as a Self-Oracle

The *Book of the Cube* is an oracular text and can be studied from different angles. As a self-oracle the *Book of the Cube* is an initiation into your psychomythic archetypal story for the purpose of evolving your mind, retrieving star memory and introducing you to a galactic knowledge base on the other side of historical consciousness.

Through the theme of a self-oracle the language of number, cube, and telepathy can be better understood. The intention of these programs is first to shed our illusions and conditioned thought responses through body/mind discipline and then introduce these new numerical thought structures into the mind. Immersion in the process is the key to rapid transformation. The more you practice the more accelerated is the process.

It is recommended to begin a self-oracle journal to record your impressions, insights and decodings as they come to you. You will also need your galactic signature and 13 Moon birth date—these are your passwords into the *Book of the Cube*. You can retrieve this information by going to www.lawoftime.org or getting a 13 Moon calendar. Here are some suggested ways to use this book:

1. The first step to entering the self-oracle is natural mind meditation (a scientific ritual); entering the mind of cosmic enlightenment, so that we are consistently and continuously seeing past the transitory nature of our own thoughts and third-dimensional personality. Simple meditation cultivates clear seeing so that we enter more deeply into our fourth-dimensional body of destiny and beyond to the fifth-dimensional electrical rainbow body. You can create a self-initiation into this process by writing and reciting your own vows of commitment to this process—that you are going to evolve your mind for the sake of all beings.

2. You may want to first start by **familiarizing yourself with your galactic archetype** based on your galactic signature. Go to the sections in Chapters 8 and 9 and read about your archetype. Study the archetypes and their relations in the Hunab Ku 21 Tree of Life. Make notes in your journal. You may then turn to the 260 archetypal houses in Appendix III to find which archetypal house you belong to. All of this can be recorded in your journal to weave together your archetypal story for the purpose of star memory retrieval. If you

have other volumes of the *Cosmic History Chronicles* much information can be derived from these too.

3.   Next you may want to start simply by finding the telepathic frequency index of your name at the end of Chapter 5. Also look up your tone in the "Yoga of Number" section in this same chapter.

4.   Next go to Appendix II and follow the instructions for finding the 441 telepathic frequency index of your birth date. Play with the numbers. Follow the instructions to find your base matrix unit. This is a key number that will gain you access into the advanced practice of the holomind perceiver (Chapters 10, 11). *Note: The system of the cube is a system of telepathic communication from advanced intelligences. However, the quality and frequency experienced when working with this system is so vast that it is only by entering it yourself that you will discover what it actually is.*

5.   Use your base matrix number to find which of the three bodies and nine time dimensions you reside in as laid out in Chapter 4. Study all of your numbers in relation to each other. Those who are advanced in the system of the synchronic order may also add up the five kin numbers of the fifth force destiny oracle to arrive at their BMU which can also be plugged into this system.

6.   Finally plug this number into the holomind perceiver and study all of the overlays. At the end of Chapter 11 there is a blank black and white holomind perceiver template for you to copy, color and study.

Study the 441 number index in Appendix V. Make your own number index adding insights as they come to you. Note that Chapters 6 and 7 open us to understanding that this entire knowledge base is all a part of the vast cosmic sky teachings. We can study the progression of different religions and belief systems as they evolve through the ages until finally a new galactic knowledge base is introduced with the discovery of the Law of Time and finally the *Cosmic History Chronicles*.

Chapter 1 reintroduces us to the cosmic origins of the *Cosmic History Chronicles* and reminds us of the nature of Cosmic History as a between the worlds transmission that is deposited into different architectures on Earth. In Chapter 2 we are given a context for working with number and an increased understanding of number as frequency and the cosmology of the 13:20 frequency. In Chapters 12 and 13 we gain understanding of the cyclical nature of the universe as it has unfolded since the beginning of creation, but with a focus on the beginning of the historical cycle. The knowledge contained herein is knowledge for the anticipated opening of the new cycle.

Note: The programs contained in Cosmic History are meant to be studied and contemplated in order to build the bridge from our personal awareness into cosmic awareness until finally we merge with the All.

MIND ALONE KNOWS THE
MEANING OF TIME,
SPACE AND NUMBER.

HOW DOES MIND KNOW?
BEFORE I WAS A NAME,
WAS I A NUMBER?

1.3.3.1
MOTHER OF
ALL CUBES 21³
RECAPITULATES
AND CONTAINS
ALL THE STAGES
OF THE CUBE

BEFORE SPACE
    BEFORE TIME
        BEFORE THOUGHT
            BEFORE MIND

THERE WAS NUMBER—SELF-ORGANIZING, SELF-PERFECTION OF THE FIRST UNIVERSE.
SELF-ORIGINATED MATRIX OF THE CUBIC SYSTEM
AND FROM THE INTERSECTIONS OF THE PRIMAL MATRIX AROSE
SOUND, LIGHT, FIRE, CONSCIOUSNESS, INTELLECT, LOGIC, AWARENESS.

MIND CAME TO BE AND THEN THOUGHT, AND WHEN THOUGHT ORGANIZED ITSELF, TIME AND SPACE
CAME TO BE, AND THE UNITY OF THOUGHT, TIME AND SPACE WAS THE
HOLARCHIC TEMPLATE OF THE PRIMAL GALACTIC DESIGN ...

MIND WAS NOW ACTIVATED, NUMBER ACQUIRED FUNCTION AND MEANING AND
THE 11TH DIMENSION TELEPATHIC UNIVERSAL UNIFICATION CODES ESTABLISHED THE 441 CUBE MATRIX.

PREFACE

INTRODUCTION TO CUBE COSMOLOGY

The cosmology of the Cube is a key component of the synchronic order and the unfolding of Cosmic History. The structure and architecture of the Cube is compressed with vast amounts of knowledge. The Cube is complete—its sides and faces are all equal, it has a quality of imperturbability of its mentality, simplicity and power. You cannot penetrate or destroy it.

The essence of the Cube is found in its structure with three planes projected into two sides each creating its six faces, with the seven in the center as the mirror. The Cube also has eight vertices or corners. Eight is the number of galactic harmony or integrity. Each point of the Cube is a point of meditation.

The Cube is the primary structural form that is absolutely equalized from all points of space. Any face you put it on it will be the same and equal. In the process of creation, the Cube represents the capacity for the creative process to equalize itself in all directions simultaneously. All aspects of creation are equal. In pre-cosmic history the human is torn by different ideologies and sectarian differences and has problems comprehending what a speck we are in the whole scheme of things.

The essence of Cosmic History is contained within the architecture of the cubic structure—this is the synthesizing vision and unification of UR. The universe itself is a cubic structure with many different dimensions of spheres within spheres within spheres. The cubic structure comprises the lattices or strands of knowledge that we come to know through the concentration of our mind. The Cube is the essence of cosmic creation—there are two primary types: primal cubic parton and heptagonon of mind. The primal cubic parton is a compacted primary electroplasmic structure from which all phenomena and consciousness can be generated. The binary triplet configuration becomes a projected form in time from the primal cubic parton.

THE THREE PLANES OF THE CUBE

The three planes of the Cube form are the foundational structure of the Cosmic History transmission. The Cube is not only the equalization of life on Earth but also in the entirety of the cosmos. Plane of Mind, Will and Spirit are qualities of the realm of intelligence that take manifest form and become the three inner planes of the Cube.

The Plane of Mind is the basis of everything. For mind to accomplish anything it has to be moved. The Plane of Spirit moves the mind and extends it into telepathy and instinct. Spirit is like the latent consciousness that arises out of mind and moves itself; it is like the wind which you cannot see, but you feel its effects. Spirit is the essence that distinguishes different states of mind—spirit is the quality of bringing mind through the different stages of enlightenment.

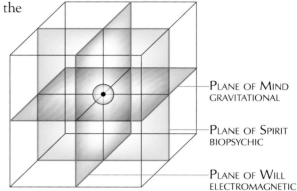

PLANE OF MIND
GRAVITATIONAL

PLANE OF SPIRIT
BIOPSYCHIC

PLANE OF WILL
ELECTROMAGNETIC

Mind responds to its own projections. All there is is mind; everything that exists is a projection of mind. Anything that happens to you is ultimately your own mind projection. However your mind interprets what is happening is how you will respond. There is actually nothing to respond to. We are the ones who assign meaning to what we experience. It seems in this mind that something keeps moving. If you look outside and see prayer flags blowing in the wind, are they moving? Or is it the wind that is moving? Or is it your mind that is moving? What keeps moving?

The Plane of Will concentrates power within the mind and spirit. At a lower level Will is a function of ego. Personality was formed in a conditoned way so it thinks reality is a certain way. The identification of self with that certain way creates the ego. One person is raised a certain way and another person is brought up in another certain way and each think their way is the ultimate reality. Most people do not know how to distinguish that their reality is just relative truth. We are planetary beings, everything else is just conditioned, acquired beliefs that have no validity in reality.

This is where Cosmic History steps in as a new universal knowledge base with a planetary/cosmic perspective that has nothing to do with any kind of ideological, nationalistic, religious or spiritual distinctions of any kind. From the point of view of lower self, Will is how ego gets its way; but it is never satisfied with what it gets and it always wants more. We are granted free will, and are afforded the oppportunity to align our little will with Divine Will.

Mind corresponds to clarity because in its fundamental nature there is nothing but clarity. It allows openness of infinite dimensions to occur. Spirit corresponds to radiance which implies luminosity, shining, radiating splendor. This is a natural quality. Will corresponds to unobstructedness. When Will is focused then the intention moves forward where the Will has directed itself to go. Who focuses and what is focusing? Some quality of energy moves when it is highly focused, this is the concentrated Will which is unobstructed. It is only obstructed if it gives up.

Obstructions are self-created impediments of the mind. If it seems like something is stopping you then step back and shift focus. Truth is unobstructed and cannot be stopped. Simple, unobstructed, enlightened state of mind is available all the time. If we stay in this state and have concentrated will then anything can be accomplished; the spirit can always be radiant and the mind can always be clear.

The three planes of the Cube represent the creative, meditative process as it establishes the most fundamental structural components of existence. This also demonstrates that the first universe is all structures of mind, or the imaginal realm. Only later is the phenomenal universe born.

These three planes describe the actual reflection of the mind of God which is absolutely clear, radiant and unobstructed. God is pure mind, spirit and will. Only through the exertion of the will of God does the creation of the universe come into existence. Manifestation is the result of an interactive process of the three planes of the Cube moving forward as a single unit.

For example, if you want to make a painting, you first get a vision in your Mind, then Spirit moves and inspires you, and it is Will that knows how to use the colors and put the paint brush onto the canvas to manifest a painting. Art is the highest criteria for how these three fundamental planes of being function in a creative way on the physical plane. The degree that the work of art comes together and communicates is the degree that the three planes are in balance and are allowed to function without interference of an egoic mechanism.

Great works of art move us so much because of the balanced interaction of the three planes of the Cube. Mind receives data; Spirit synthesizes and inspires; Will takes action. The ground of our being and reality relies on these three planes. This is the fundamental basis of cube cosmology.

PART I
FOUR FOUNDATIONAL POWERS

CHAPTER 1

COSMIC HISTORY—A STORY THAT BEGINS IN THE MIND
INVOKING THE MYSTIC ORDER OF THE SEVEN RAYS

We must understand our role as seventh ray actors in the process of making the transition from the now disintegrated sixth ray civilization into the seventh ray order of ceremonial magick. This is a majestic initiation that leads humanity from the realm of the cosmic unconscious to the realm of the cosmic conscious. This is the function and purpose of closing the cycle as a planetary rite of passage.

—CHC, Vol. I

1. The cycle of history is now virtually exhausted. A new cosmic cycle is about to begin—the renewal of time and matter. The soul is about to be refreshed. A new garment is about to be woven over the Earth—the noosphere. The noosphere is the aggregate of the advanced states of mind and consciousness that characterize all intelligent life throughout the universe.

2. Planet Earth is the focus of the resolution of the war of the heavens. This war can be seen from different perspectives: a pure interplay of cosmic forces; archetypal histories of other worlds; or the drama of the struggle of spiritual forces within the bubbling cauldron of materialism.

3. The cycle of history is characterized by endless dualisms and splitting apart, down to the splitting of the atom and human's split from nature. Many indigenous tribes believe we are now living in the fourth world, awaiting the fifth. The first world ended in fire, the second in flood and the third in ice, and now the fourth by potential earth cataclysm itself.

4. The purpose of Cosmic History is to imprint the frequencies into the noosphere that arouse a positive image or order of reality into the collective mind. This order of reality is galactic in nature—for this reason we speak of invoking seventh ray ceremonial magick. Each of the seven volumes of the *Cosmic History Chronicles* corresponds to one of these seven rays.

5.   A ray is a particular force or energy. Everything in the solar system at any given state of evolution displays predominant energy from one or more of these rays. The seventh ray is the final ray of creation which is the concluding cycle and phase of human evolution and development. Seventh ray ceremonial magick establishes the Cycle of Return: the advance into full fourth- and fifth-dimensional consciousness. This also corresponds to the seventh mental sphere, the holomind perceiver.

Seven Rays and Secret Doctrine

The seven rays were first presented in *The Secret Doctrine* by H.P. Blavatsky (1888) and later elaborated in a five volume series of books called *A Treatise on the Seven Rays* by Alice Bailey.

   "Through the seven rays the life or spirit aspect flows, cycling through every kingdom in nature and producing thus all states of consciousness in all fields of awareness", said Madame Blavatsky.

   The power or will of God expresses itself through the organized systematized processes of the seventh ray. The geometrical faculty of the Universal Mind finds its most material perfection on the physical or seventh plane, working through the seventh ray.

SEVENTH RAY CEREMONIAL MAGICK

The seventh ray is one of organized ritual, and in form building this quality is basic and necessary. The processes found in the mineral kingdom are profoundly geometrical.
—Alice Bailey

6.   Cosmic History is the work of seventh ray ceremonial magick that quickens the new world now emerging. The first Cosmic History transmission came nine days after a ceremony at Teotihuacán where nine indigenous elders honored Valum Votan/José Argüelles as the Closer of the Cycle, 49 years after his original vision at Teotihuacán.

7.   The number 49 symbolizes the lighting of the 49 fires of the awakened being and the awakened human. The initiatic awakening of Valum Votan occurred at the point where the planetary logos had focused its seventh ray intentionality and grounded it on earth at that particular place. This is why the initiatic awakening occurred at the top of the Pyramid of the Sun—the focal point of the cosmic and solar logos projecting its ray of intentionality. This is all part of a divine script projected from afar.

8.   In this way Valum Votan can be viewed as a seventh ray avatar. His work demonstrates the law, order and rhythm of the creative process as it works out on the physical plane, blending spirit

and matter. This is also known as the ray of ceremonial order or ritual. The seventh ray is closely connected with the star Sirius and is instrumental in producing those conditions which will permit the reappearance on earth of the mysteries of initiation.

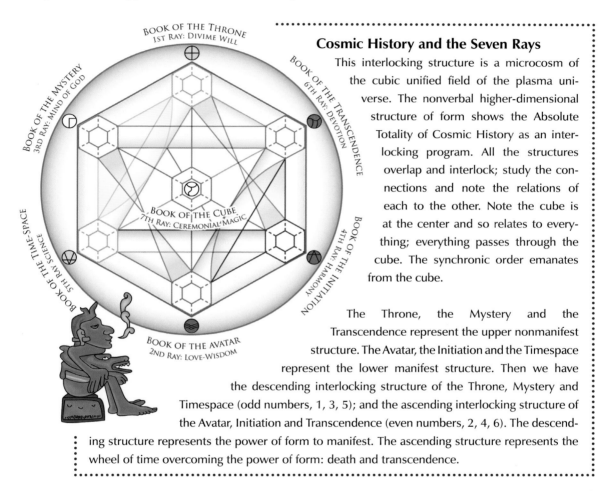

Cosmic History and the Seven Rays

This interlocking structure is a microcosm of the cubic unified field of the plasma universe. The nonverbal higher-dimensional structure of form shows the Absolute Totality of Cosmic History as an interlocking program. All the structures overlap and interlock; study the connections and note the relations of each to the other. Note the cube is at the center and so relates to everything; everything passes through the cube. The synchronic order emanates from the cube.

The Throne, the Mystery and the Transcendence represent the upper nonmanifest structure. The Avatar, the Initiation and the Timespace represent the lower manifest structure. Then we have the descending interlocking structure of the Throne, Mystery and Timespace (odd numbers, 1, 3, 5); and the ascending interlocking structure of the Avatar, Initiation and Transcendence (even numbers, 2, 4, 6). The descending structure represents the power of form to manifest. The ascending structure represents the wheel of time overcoming the power of form: death and transcendence.

9. The root of Cosmic History and the prophecy is locked into the stones of Palenque—this is the focalization of the GM108X Galactic Mayan Mind transmission on the terrestrial surface. The actual structure and architecture of the Cosmic History transmission is a fourth-dimensional stream that participates in the same structural configuration as the different temples and structures of Palenque and Teotihuacán. This is known as synthesizing, fourth-dimensional architectonics. We all have underlying archetypal structures that refer to the structure of the psyche and spirit that inhabit the primary architectonic spaces.

10. When the tomb of Pacal Votan was opened in 1952 a mind stream flowed out and some of the particles landed into the mind of fourteen-year-old "José Argüelles" when he was atop the Pyramid of the Sun in Teotihuacán one year later. The whole meaning of Teotihuacán can be read as a sixth-dimensional sign created before the rise of the classic Maya. The knowledge of the sixth dimension is encoded here and was revealed to the shamans before Christ from the telepathic instruction of Pacal Votan as a light code. The sixth-dimensional standards represent a gauge for evaluating the spiritual level of the third and fourth dimensions. From the avataric perception of the prophecy of Pacal Votan, the spiritual history of the planet is a single integrated circuit.

11. The opening of the tomb of Pacal Votan triggered points of information that were loaded in the psi bank by the Galactic Maya meant to be retrieved at a precise future point. The Galactic Maya consciously programmed the psi bank from within; mostly in preparation for the last baktun, where we now find ourselves. The seeds of knowledge of the 13 Moon/28-day calendar and the Law of Time were left by the Galactic Maya over 1300 years ago. It was these seeds that set the

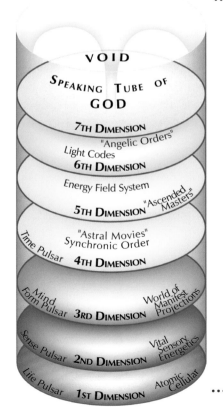

Sixth-dimensional Light Codes

The sixth-dimensional knowledge is the knowledge of Memnosis, the knowledge of Lucifer (bringer of light) and of the previous worlds. The sixth dimension is the place where the people receive their godly powers of magical knowledge, understanding and creation. This can only happen when there is a purity of intention and immersion in the purity of the seventh ray as summarizing the previous six rays.

Tune into the sixth-dimensional grid to recapitulate the process of time and the opening of the tomb. The sixth dimension is the home of the higher angelic orders, which are entitizations or life forms that are responsible for the supervision of the different spin evolutionary transformation factors in any given number of light codes—all the way down to being responsible for supervising the different "evolving" entities, even down to the third-dimensional level. It is the supervision and maintenance of the light codes that maintain the spin of evolutionary factors of the phenomenal realm. (For more on the dimensions see *CHC Vol. I and Vol. II*).

stage for the flowering of Cosmic History. (Note: Valum Votan disincarnated in 2011, precisely 1328 years after Pacal Votan (683); a key sign of the prophecy of the 13 Moon/28-day calendar. 28 is the Bode number for Maldek = 28-day Telektonon circuit).

Psychomythic Origins

Palenque Nah Chan is the House of the Serpent or the House of Revelation and regeneration. The origin and mission of Cosmic History is tied into two tombs: the tomb of Pacal Votan and the tomb of the Red Queen, discovered 42 years apart. The two tombs represent revelation and the two living emanations of those tombs represent the regeneration. The tomb is a symbol that represents death, resurrection and the transmigration of souls. Through harmonic resonance of the two (male/female) comes the mutual realization of the fifth-dimensional twinning of the One Higher Being streaming down the Cosmic History channel—much like tuning into a radio broadcast. This is a fundamental cosmic principle of binary alternation with its psychomythic origin in the tale of two tombs opening us to the themes of death and resurrection; closing and opening; and the transmigration of the soul.

12. The haunted feeling that we all sometimes experience comes from the memory of the lost or destroyed worlds, namely Maldek and Mars. Cosmic History is given as a stream of remembrance for the lost time travelers for the purpose of regeneration of that which has been destroyed. This comes at the point where the earth is poised in a position for similar destruction; it is up to us to apply what we know to shift tracks into the parallel universe at a precise point in time.

INTERPLANETARY ROOTS AND TERRESTRIAL FOCAL POINTS

13. On an interplanetary scale, the *Cosmic History Chronicles* are rooted in the memory and dissolution of Maldek, and contain the knowledge of the origins within this star system of the process of cosmic history unfolding in the involution of spirit into matter. The explosion of the planet by some great force caused it to shatter into countless fragments now called the Asteroid Belt.

14. The enactment of lost worlds is now being played out on Earth. Between the number of atomic bombs and extra low frequency lethal technologies possessed by the U.S. military alone, this destructive potential exists. Cosmic History was revealed at a precise moment in time to connect the points of lost consciousness between Maldek and present-day Earth. In *The Seventh Ray: Revealer of the New Age* Alice Bailey points out that the major weapon now being used by combined forces of evil is chaos, disruption, lack of established security and consequent fear. In contrast, the power of the incoming seventh ray arrests the chaos of the present order and produces the ordered beauty of the future.

15. The planetary logos uses physical timespace points such as Teotihuacán to focus the rays of initiation, in particular the seventh ray. The structure and ceremonial cycles of Teotihuacán qualify it as a significant center for seventh ray ceremonial magick. Once this focus had been grounded in the earthly timespace of Teotihuacán then the solar logos could focus its rays, providing the vehicle for the cosmic logos to project its rays through the solar rays and into the timespace of Teotihuacán.

THOUGH MALDEK WAS NO MORE, ITS REMEMBERANCE REMAINED AS A RING OF SHATTERED FRAGMENTS AN "ASTEROID BELT." WHAT HELD AND STILL HOLDS THOSE FRAGMENTS IN PLACE WAS THE LOST CHORD, THE PEAK RESONANCE GIVEN OFF BY OUR MOMENT OF SUPREME ORGASM AND OBLIVION. AS OUR 4TH DIMENSIONAL ELECTRIC BODIES REGROUPED AMONG THIS RING OF RESONATING FRAGMENTS, WE SUMMONED OUR WILL, WE, THE LOST CHORD CHILDREN OF XYMOX.

16. Fifty-eight years prior to his disincarnation in the Red Overtone Moon year (2011), Valum Votan received the initiatic awakening of the closing of the cycle atop the Pyramid of the Sun in Teotihuacán. Kin 58 is the disincarnation kin of Pacal Votan (also note that Valum Votan disincarnated 58 days after his 72nd birthday). In 2002, again atop the Pyramid of the Sun, Valum Votan was honored as Closer of the Cycle by nine indigenous elders. Four days prior to this ceremony, the elders had met in the underground grotto beneath the Pyramid of the Sun on Kin 160—4 Ahau. Nine days after this ceremony the Cosmic History transmission began.

17. The top of the Pyramid of the Sun is located almost directly above an ancient cave. Within this cave the initiates or serpents of wisdom gathered and deposited their wisdom. The initiates knew that the great Pyramid of the Sun would be built above that cave so the fulfillment of the grand plan of the solar planetary design could be completed and carried out at that particular geomagnetic time vector.

CAVES OF INITIATION

The primordial worlds and knowledge must be brought forward in time through the initates so they can conduct the rites of initiation. This is conducted by the serpents that dwell beneath the pyramids in the subterranean crypts.

—Book of the Initiation, CHC Vol. IV

Chilam Balam is written in the language of the Zuvuya, which means it is deliberately obscure, highly symbolic and coded.

Tollan Zuvuya or the 7 caves (or the place of the 7 ravines) is a place contacted through the mind where the memories and knowledge of Tollan and the return of Tollan are stored. The 7 caves refer to the power of 7 as the generating power of the knowledge of origin and return. These seven caves also contain the wisdom lore of Quetzalcoatl. In the 7 caves is the origin of everything, including the mystery of the Book of Seven Generations. These 7 Katuns are the same as passing through the 7 caves. Each cave of origin has all the primal knowledge of the synchronic order. During each Katun cycle, the Galactic Maya loaded the psi bank, so that when the 7 Years of Prophecy (1993 – 2000) came, the information was downloaded. Cosmic History was programmed into this time release program to occur precisely at this point to coincide with the 7 Years of the Mystery of the Stone (2004 – 2011).

Tollan = 7 Caves (Vucub Pec) = 7 Lost Generations.

The 7 Caves are the Caves of Origin.

TEOTIHUACÁN AS A SEVENTH RAY CIVILIZATION

18. As a focal point for planetary initiation, Teotihuacán is etherically similar to the Great Pyramid in Egypt; both served as initiatic centers of the planetary logos up to the time of Teotihuacán. During this time the whole of the seventh ray could be beamed into these pyramid centers and enacted for close to a millennium before it was finally closed down after its primary function had been fulfilled. Though closed down it remains an initiatic point on Earth. In this way, Teotihuacán can be viewed as the initiation point of Tollan.

19. Tollan is the heavenly model of the template of the real—the Absolute Reality—not the reality of the shadow thoughts of the third-dimensional world of 12:60 illusion, but the Absolute Reality of life in the cosmos or the universal life. Tollan represents the template of that reality and Teotihuacán represents the point on Earth where the heavenly city is fulfilled.

20. Teotihuacán is also the cosmic initiation point for the psychomythic birth of the fifth race according to the activities of the primordial Quetzalcoatl, who is also credited with bringing the sacred calendar. Quetzalcoatl means plumed serpent and he was a key serpent initiate; a primordial knower and seer. The treasures of the previous worlds and root races are layered in the hidden geometry of its celestial formula—there are five layers in the Pyramid of the Sun corresponding to the previous five root races, with all of their knowledge contained in those resonant structures.

21. The final incarnation of Quetzalcoatl acted out the primordial psychomythic progenitor Quetzalcoatl who was the originator of the Fifth Sun, the Fifth Root Race and the Fifth World. The Fifth Sun is the Nahui Ollin, the sun of change and movement. This prophecy says the present world will be destroyed by movement or "shaking of the earth", which is analogous to the changes happening in the 12:60 world.

22. Quetzalcoatl brought the Fifth Sun into being at Teotihuacán and established it as the initiatic center for the birth of the Sixth Sun. Teotihuacán was a holy center and a place of supreme cultural and artistic activity. (Note, whereas in other traditions we are thought of as being in the fourth world moving into the fifth, in the tradition of Quetzalcoatl we are in the fifth moving into the sixth).

23. Teotihuacán carried the transfer of the previous planetary logos. It had to be built before the end of the large cycles of 5,125, 26,000 and 104,000 years, to ensure the vibrational frequency was established on Earth so that Valum Votan could receive its initiations and incorporate and embody the knowledge of the planetary logos to ground it on Earth. As Alice Bailey points out,

as the seventh ray passes cyclically out of manifestation a certain measure of intertia settles down on the kingdom, though that which is radiating continues its activity.

24. In 26,000 years there are five 5,200-year periods (5 x 5,200 = 26,000). In this context, Teotihuacán's dedication occurred at the 60th baktun. In the 104,000-year cycle there are 20 of these 13-baktun cycles, where each baktun is one of 260 kin (20 x 13 baktuns = 260 baktuns). The 104,000-year cycle is the same as the harmonic module in which the four 26,000-year periods are five wavespells of 13 baktuns each.

25. In the 104,000-year cycle, the height of Teotihuacán and Palenque occurred in the ninth and tenth baktuns of the fifth and final 13-baktun cycle. This illustrates Teotihuacán as the point intended for initiating the complete enactment of a seventh ray ceremonial civilization on Earth before the closing of the cycle. While the pyramid centers were eventually abondoned, the planetary logos remained in Teotihuacán beneath the Pyramid of the Sun, in the cavern where the resonant frequency of the initiatic serpents of wisdom remains.

QUETZALCOATL

Quetzalcoatl represents the morning and evening star as well as the cycles of death and regeneration. Prepare now for death. The body is a garment of soul, and then soul sheds the body. When the body wears out, the intelligence that animated the body returns to the home field of galactic intelligence—this is transcendence. Galactic being is the unitary being that summarizes all life aspects of the entire galaxy—a being of unimaginable scale of monumentality.

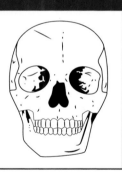

There was a time before manifestation and a time after manifestation. See if you can make a complete circuit of consciousness while you are in your physical container.

CEREMONIAL MAGICK

The seventh ray will develop the magician who works in the field of white magic. The seventh ray will lead to fusion and synthesis, for its energy is of the type which blends spirit and matter. The seventh ray will train and send forth groups of initiates, working in close unison with the planet and with each other. The seventh ray will inaugurate the sense of a higher unity; first, that of the integrated personality for the masses, and secondly, that of the fusion of soul and body for the world aspirants. The seventh ray period will familiarize man with that type of electrical phenomena which produce the coordination of all forms...

—Alice Bailey

26. Cosmic History is an act of seventh ray ceremonial magick. The electrical phenomena is the telepathic technology of the plasmas. Teotihuacán holds the energy of seventh ray ceremonial magic to be reactivated as the vision of Tollan and Shambhala in preparation for the closing of the cycle, the initiation of the next cycle and the coming seventh root race.

27. The seventh root race will initially be governed and dominated by seventh ray activity which includes the synthesis and fusion of knowledge, as well as increased forms of soul expression. Synthesis and fusion of knowledge is at the heart of the *Cosmic History Chronicles*. This refers to types of spiritual activity that are manifest on a telepathic vibratory plane. We can see then that the point of Teotihuacán on Earth was not only to provide a vision of Time is Art but a seventh ray ceremonial vision where the power of magic was able to manifest.

28. The civilization of Teotihuacán provided an actual ceremonial ritual enactment of the initiation of the fifth ray and fifth sun into cosmic consciousness for the closing of the cycle. Teotihuacán is like a planetary yeast culture so that when we get to the new cycle we have some yeast to carry over and create the next batch. Teotihuacán was also the physical grounding for the planetary logos on Earth. One of its functions was to re-embody what was in the previous systems.

29. Quetzalcoatl represents the transformation that has to be undergone to attain higher wisdom. Quetzalcoatl represents Venus and relates to elevated interdimensional experiences as well as hearkening to previous world experiences which are memorialized in the dismemberment depictions of Quetzalcoatl in the underworld. The purpose of the planetary logos is to redirect the energy of the planetary logos of previous worlds into the current one.

30. Both Pacal Votan and Quetzalcoatl lived in the House of the Serpent—Nah Chan. The serpent represents the primal wisdom of the Earth, which was essential for Pacal Votan and Quetzalcoatl to fulfill their prophetic missions for the renewal and regeneration of Earth.

31. The serpent is related to the primal Maldek memory point of prophecies opening us to the memory of the destroyed world. Noah's Ark is an example of an archetypal catastrophe story repeated from Maldek to Mars and from Mars to Earth. The knowledge contained with the *Cosmic History Chronicles* holds some of the keys to the construction of the New Ark of Time. The visionary serpent speaks with wisdom and power of the memory of Maldek which remains at the core of the prophetic stream of GM108X.

32. The complete perfection of the knowledge of the serpent is known as the Cube and the vital force of the serpent is the Kundalini energy—the energy of the serpent coiled in the root chakra, which is the primal power of the first world of Maldek. This vital force, which is completely aboriginal and totally pure passes through different stages of being and consciousness and in doing so becomes more subtle and complex. When it reaches the third eye it becomes the seventh ray wisdom which beholds the perfection of the knowledge of the Cube.

> *Cultivate responsiveness to the Great Ones, aim at mental expansion and keep learning. Think whenever possible in terms of abstract or numerical, and by loving all, work at plasticity of the astral body. In love of all that breathes comes the capacity to vibrate universally, and in that astral pliability will come responsiveness to the vibration of the Great Lord.*
>
> —Alice Bailey, *The Seventh Ray*

Chapter 2
13:20 Cosmology and the Generation of Number

The universe codes itself through the language of number.

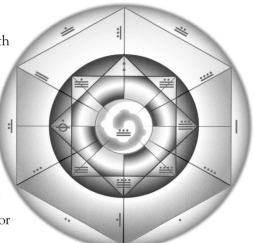

1. Becoming a telepath has everything to do with tuning into the significance of number frequencies and the synchronization of different numbers. We are entering a new aeon where we experience expanded templates of being and consciousness.

2. These expanded templates first appear as mathematical codes or structures that are inviolable; they are laws that abide by a specific structure. When we understand the nature of these laws, we realize that they represent a superior spiritual order.

3. Our world is based on movement; everything is always in motion. Underlying this perpetual movement are different mathematical frequencies. These mathematical frequencies are the multifaceted, ever evolving reality of the One Being.

4. Each day is coded by a specific set of number sequences, that when combined, set the tone and quality for that day. Through the synchronic codes we can learn to read this language of number. Number language is closely related to telepathy and if we are attuned we can begin to "read" the daily synchronic telegrams encoded in the combinations of different numbers. When we study these number relations, we begin to see that numbers belong to their own matrix or matrices of meaning.

5. Each number represents a principle, a specific quality, and state of being or a particular yoga as elucidated in Chapter 5. Each set of number relations can be read differently according to context, frame of reference and personal perceptual lens. (It is helpful to make your own number index. In this way you familiarize yourself with the frequency of numbers and also recognize how different number combinations synchronize to create specific effects in consciousness).

6.   Word is a vibratory resonance based on the underlying structure of number. The resonance of a word or combination of words creates manifest reality. Before the Word—Aum—there was number, or a mathematical frequency. The matrix of mathematical frequencies is what makes the word possible.

TOWER OF BABEL
At the closing of the cycle, we have come upon the limitation of words. The confusion of words began at the time of the Tower of Babel. The idea of building the Tower of Babel was conceived of as a tremendously vast engineering project to build an immense tower that would reach into the clouds and into heaven.

At the closing of the cycle, we have come upon the limitation of words. The confusion of words began at the time of the Tower of Babel. The idea of building the Tower of Babel was conceived of as a tremendously vast engineering project to build an immense tower that would reach into the clouds and into heaven.

   When construction of this tower began, everybody spoke the same language; but before they had finished, the people had broken into speaking different languages. The Tower of Babel is a metaphor for the tower of artificial civilization or anything that we work on that is overreaching itself trying to penetrate into the clouds and into the heavens. The effect of this endeavor was to break up the common universal language into many dispersed languages. This is one factor.

   As a result, throughout history confusion reigns and words are often misinterpreted. Words in themselves are neutral but have become "loaded" throughout history because of cultural or personal interpretations. So much so that just about any word you use will get different reactions and interpretations from different people. Some words in some countries are forbidden as they raise certain feelings. On some level lawyers exist because of the confusion of language. In every tradition there arises a sect of people who are often called legalists who try to determine the correct meaning of words, or correct law.

   Today in the climax of civilization, with more than 6 billion cell phone subscribers, when the power of blogging and texting has been universalized and anyone can express any opinion that they want, the confusion of language is as great as it's ever been, and often the most valuable information or teachings become buried in a sea of inane chatter.

7.   There is a way of tuning into and using numbers or number matrices in relation to the synchronic order to create a mental force field to shift the world hologram.

8.   First we must understand, what is the actual nature of number? To understand this, we first return our mind to its natural, original state through practice of yoga, pranayama breathing and meditation. To return to original mind is to develop a mind where no thought arises, for at least a brief period, and then expanded into longer periods of time.

9.   Within this thought-free state new worlds are born. Within the space of pure meditation arises intrinsic awareness, primordial awareness, pure wakefulness, original mind. Only by training our mind to rest in this space can we tune into the deepest meaning of number.

10.   To discover the origin of number meditate on the questions: How did number originate? What is the root source of number? Allow these questions to mingle in your mind. If you experience your

mind as a void space without thought, that void space is *zero*. From zero, effortlessly allow the one to enter. Rather than see one as an Arabic one or a Roman numeral one, *feel the essence of one*. Feel number one arise as a simple point of light: a dot in space. This is one. Practice seeing this luminous point arising in the space of mind. This is where number originates.

NUMBER AND THE LIGHT UNIVERSE

11. Numbers are a type of force or frequency. When we return to original mind and original universe, we experience undifferentiated light; a light universe. How do we conceive of infinity or a light universe? We can conceive of it as a perfect sphere like Plato or Pythagoras. On a two-dimensional plane it can be conceived of as a circle.

12. The Law of Time reveals a cosmology of number, with the zero and one. One gives rise to all number. One is the divisible factor in any number. No matter how big the prime number is, it is always divisible by itself and by the number one.

13. One is the root of all number. Systems of number all start with 1. 1 x 1 = 1, and 1 + 1 = 2. The two gives rise to the law of alternation. All numbers are either odd or even. Every even number is divisible by two. So the alternation of number is the basic principle of the law of alternation. We breathe in, we breathe out: 0 and 1. Night and day is also 0 and 1.

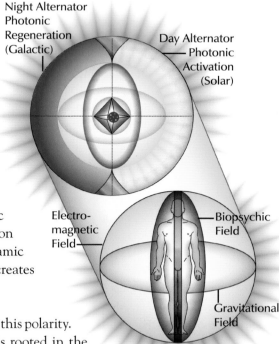

Night Alternator Photonic Regeneration (Galactic)

Day Alternator Photonic Activation (Solar)

Electro-magnetic Field

Biopsychic Field

Gravitational Field

14. The splitting of the one makes the 2, creating the possibility of a dynamic. This creates the possibility of polarity—an electric pulsation—positive and negative. The electron goes around the neutron creating the first dynamic of movement, electron—neutron. So the two creates the first dynamic of movement.

15. Every body that comes into creation is born with this polarity. Our primal separation from nature (oneness) is rooted in the two—all of our thought processes follow nature's polarity. This polarity is also seen in the planetary body with its North and South

poles that creates a spin potential (like when you put two magnets together it creates movement and spin potential).

16. Every electron revolves around a central point. The central point is like the star or stellar unit. As earth spins on its polar axis—binary—it goes around a central unit. This creates a second level of polarity: alternation of day and night. Keep in mind that day and night only exist on a body spinning around a star. This creates the sense of time as movement and duration.

17. On the day side, the planetary body is flooded with photons: light. On the night side these photons are absent. Night is occulted by the sun. The solar rays are the strongest influence, but at night solar rays are blocked so cosmic radiation saturates that side of the planet. To experience binary order, practice *pranayams: inhale count 4, hold count 4, exhale count 4, hold count 4—do 7x, then same for alternating nostrils, 3x.*

ORDERS OF BINARY MOVEMENT

There are different orders of number in the binary movement:

    1. Creation Matrix Power (demonstrated by the 441 Cube Matrix)
    2. Powers of Creation (demonstrated by binary and spiral orders)

1. The 441 (21 x 21) Creation Matrix Power

    The moving interplays of mathematical matrices manifest and create the logarithmic spirals in the galaxy and the matrices of life, time, and the synchronic order. All of these matrices move together in a continuous process of ever-increasing complexity that are also moved by simple, elementary patterns of number interacting with each other to create various ranges and forms. When we learn how to tune into creation matrices, then we are moving into telepathic frequencies—the creation process is in continuous motion (see Chapter 3 for more on these matrices).

2. Powers of Creation

    The logarithmic spiral creates the ratio of phi—the Golden Mean. This is the spiral of creation that creates the galaxy. The spiral principle must become binary to create the galactic order, which is simultaneously clockwise and counterclockwise.

    The logarithmic spiral made binary creates the dynamic of galactic order. Spirals are found everywhere in the universe from our fingertips to the galaxy. The order of the universe can be understood as 1) binary; and 2) spiral. Binary is based on the two and the doubling of two—all even numbers are divisible by 2, whereas spiral is based on what's called the Fibonacci sequence. In the Fibonacci sequence we keep adding the last number. Note that plants and flowers demonstrate the Fibonacci spiral in their numbers of leaves and petals as they grow.

    Fibonacci/Golden Mean order:

        0, 1, 1, 2, 3, 5, 8, 13, 21, 34, 55, 89, 144, 233, 377, 610, 987, 1597, etc.

BINARY CROSSOVER POLARITY

18. Binary crossover polarity is a universal fourth-dimensional principle; it is how number becomes movement based on a binary principle. In chemistry, binary crossover polarity creates the lattice structures of crystals. The crystal lattice structure of silicone dioxide formed by binary crystal polarity is the basic structure of rock, both mineral and molten—this is a crystalline property.

19. What are rocks and how did they get to be in "rock" forms? Molten rock cooled into different chemical compounds that then formed into different structures. These processes operate according to a molecular crystal lattice binary movement; for instance, the molecular/chemical structures reach a certain point and then take the form of a crystal.

20. The crystal then becomes an example of a form of frozen movement of binary crossover polarity. When this principle is applied to living matter then the 32 crystal lattice structures double and change into 64—the binary lattice structure of DNA. Thus the binary operation is indistinguishable from the genetic code and is the underlying mechanism of the psi bank or holonomic mind.

BINARY ORDER

1 – undivided unity.

2 – yin yang, night day, male female, principle of alternation creates movement in time, cross-over polarity, principle of cosmic evolution—root of binary order, proceeds by doubling.

4 – amino acids, binary letters = 2^2.

8 – triplets, diatonic octave, 8 tones = 2^3 (2 x 2 x 2).

16 – double octave symphonic diatonic (= 4^2 = 2 to the 4th power).

32 – 32 types of crystal symmetry, silicon bonding (2^2 x 2^3, 2 to the 5th power), AC CA Strands = 16 – 32 – 16, cross-over polarity pattern, psi bank function.

64 – 64 codons (4^3), then 128, 256, 512, 1024, etc.

Binary order = same sequence as vigesimal count: 1 = kin, 20 = vinal, 400 (third order) = totality, 8 = 8000 (4th order), 16 = 160,000 (5th order), 32 = 3,200,000 (sixth order), 64 = 64,000,000 (7th order) etc.—these are the constituents of cosmic order expressed through the higher **vigesimal** mathematics of the Galactic Maya.

ORIGINS & COSMOLOGY OF 13:20 FREQUENCY

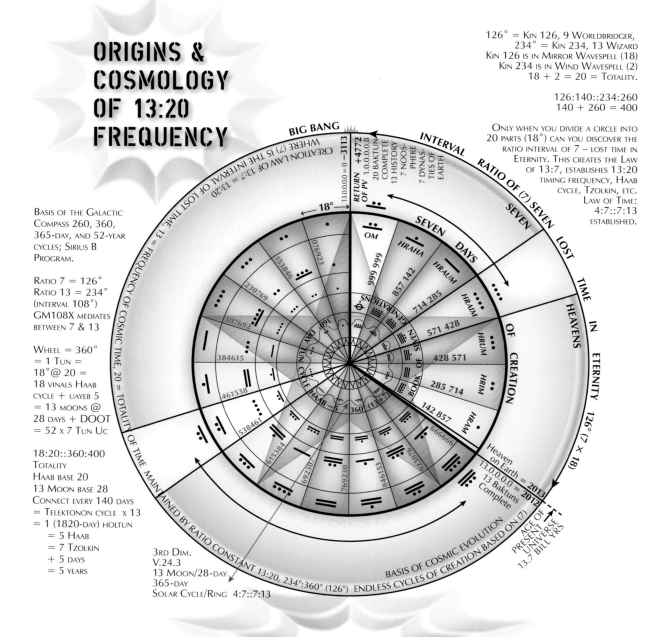

126° = KIN 126, 9 WORLDBRIDGER,
234° = KIN 234, 13 WIZARD
KIN 126 IS IN MIRROR WAVESPELL (18)
KIN 234 IS IN WIND WAVESPELL (2)
18 + 2 = 20 = TOTALITY.

126:140::234:260
140 + 260 = 400

ONLY WHEN YOU DIVIDE A CIRCLE INTO 20 PARTS (18°) CAN YOU DISCOVER THE RATIO INTERVAL OF 7 – LOST TIME IN ETERNITY. THIS CREATES THE LAW OF 13:7, ESTABLISHES 13:20 TIMING FREQUENCY, HAAB CYCLE, TZOLKIN, ETC. LAW OF TIME: 4:7::7:13 ESTABLISHED.

BASIS OF THE GALACTIC COMPASS 260, 360, 365-DAY, AND 52-YEAR CYCLES; SIRIUS B PROGRAM.

RATIO 7 = 126°
RATIO 13 = 234°
(INTERVAL 108°)
GM108X MEDIATES BETWEEN 7 & 13

WHEEL = 360°
= 1 TUN =
18°@ 20 =
18 VINALS HAAB CYCLE + UAYEB 5
= 13 MOONS @ 28 DAYS + DOOT
= 52 x 7 TUN UC

18:20::360:400
TOTALITY
HAAB BASE 20
13 MOON BASE 28
CONNECT EVERY 140 DAYS
= TELEKTONON CYCLE x 13
= 1 (1820-DAY) HOLTUN
   = 5 HAAB
   = 7 TZOLKIN
   + 5 DAYS
   = 5 YEARS

3RD DIM.
V.24.3
13 MOON/28-DAY
365-DAY
SOLAR CYCLE/RING 4:7::7:13

13:20 WHEEL OF THE LAW OF TIME

FUNDAMENTAL BASIS OF 13:20 COSMOLOGY

All mathematics of the Law of Time are demonstrated in the Wheel of the Law of Time, inclusive of the origins and cosmology of the 13:20 frequency. To study the Wheel of the Law of Time, visualize yourself inside the circle and focus on the number seven. Note that the seven is implicit in the 13; it is also implicit between the 13 and 20. The fourth part of the seven and the seventh part of the thirteen are exactly 180° apart from each other. This demonstrates the ratio of totality and creates the formulation of the Law of Time: 4:7::7:13.

The 13 and 7 have meaning when you take a circle and divide it into twenty parts. Twenty parts at 18° each = 20 x 18 = 360° = circle. This is the only way you can put seven and thirteen together and make a whole. This means that the interval ratio of seven, the lost time in eternity, corresponds to 126° (18° x 7). The 7 with the remainig 13 creates 20 parts of 18° making a whole. This 13:7 ratio relates to the moon because the moon is always creating a whole; when it returns to its newness, it has made a full circle.

Note that the four phases of the moon are roughly associated with seven days each. The moon shifts in the sky 13° every day in one lunation cycle. 13 x 28 = 364 (or 28 x slightly less than 13° = 360°); this creates the ratio 13:7 which creates the whole. So we have the 126° of the 7 and 234° of the 13: 13 x 18 = 234, 18 x 7 = 126, 126 + 234 = 360. 234 – 126 = 108! So the GM108X mediates between the 13 and 7.

Also note the reciprocal numbers of 7 and 13. These are pure cyclical recombinants when multiplied by 1 – 6 (for 7) and 1 – 12 (for 13). Note the symmetry pattern and arrangement into sets of triplets of both reciprocals, i.e. reciprocal of 7 = 142 857 and reciprocal of 13 = 076 923 and 153 846; each in six cyclic variations arranged into six sets of matching inverse triplets of three digits each.

The galactic compass/13:20 wheel contains seven void spaces and thirteen numbered spaces, thus recapitulating the cosmology of the 13:20 frequency. This is the origin of the 13:20 frequency and demonstrates why it is a recurring cosmology. The two numbers 13 and 7 create a circle. Then we have the 13:20 ratio with the seven intervals. This is a constant totality. It demonstrates how the original time is incorporated as a circle, with 20 parts (13+7) of 18° each.

On the inside of the wheel, the Haab (360-day tun cycle) is demonstrated and counted in eighteen 20-day intervals. The five extra days are known as the uayeb that comes after the completion of the tun, and which is unique in relation to this as it is not counted here.

Note the 13 and count the first 13 days, then the vigesimal count continues on the next ring in, from 14 up to 20. This represents the Book of Seven Generations which corresponds precisely with the inner wheel starting at 14 (Wizard) and all the way up to 20 (Sun).

Note also the seven solar mantras starting with the root mantra, Hram and concluding with the crown mantra, Om. These seven mantras also correspond to the seven days of creation, the seven heavens, and the interval ratio of lost time in eternity. This defines the basic 13:7 program.

Then there is the 20-part program. The circle of 360 degrees is divided into 20 parts (18 x 20)—but the matrix of 20 is 400 (20²). 400 – 360 = 40. This is a fractal ratio. 18:20::360:400. 400 – 260 = 140. 140 (7 x 20) is the key ratio of 7. So again the ratio of seven plus 260 equals 400. The ratio of seven is very important as it is both 7 x 20 and 5 x 28 which gives us the standard measure.

On the innermost circle of the wheel we see the 13 moons, which represents third-dimensional time—all the rest is fourth- and fifth-dimensional time with the sun at the center. The Mayan mathematical system illustrates the 360-day count, which is what accounts for creating the 13:20 frequency.

Origins and Cosmology of the 13:20 Frequency

If number represents frequencies that our mind can tune into, then these frequencies must already be inherent in our mind. This is the premise of the 13:20 cosmology. When we become conscious of these numbers as telepathic tools of creation, then we can more fully participate in the co-creation of the evolvement of cosmic life.

21. In Eternity, before the dot arises in space there is an undifferentiated sphere. Sufi tradition says that within original eternity came a fracture or breaking of eternity. This break in eternity forged an interval ratio with a frequency of seven. This is known as the Interval of Lost Time in Eternity.

22. Within the last 25 years, Western scientists have agreed that the cosmos is roughly 13.7 billion years old. In the Japanese tradition a folk saying is "How old is the moon?" and in the Zen koan tradition "Why is the moon always new?" "The answer is 13:7". This is interesting in light of the Law of Time, with its chief numbers 13 and 7. In the cosmology of the Law of Time we have the sequence of 13 in the Tzolkin, as well as the 13-unit wavespell cosmology that can be read fractally to represent spans of time that range from 13 days to 13 billion years, or 13 baktuns, etc.

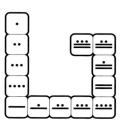

13:20 and 441 Matrix

23. The all encompassing cube matrix is 20 + 1 squared which is the Hunab Ku. 21 is the factor that occurs in the occult position. In the fifth force Dreamspell oracle, the occult kin always add up to 21. This is the 21 factor. The original matrix of creation also corresponds to a matrix of 21 squared, which is the 441 matrix.

24. The number 21 is the key to our understanding of the higher consciousness that is evolving us. 21 is the synthesis of the primal Law of Seven and the sacred Law of Three. The primal Law of Seven defines creation and with the primal Law of Three defines the basic dynamics by which all existence unfolds.

25. There are seven days of creation, commonly known as the seven days of the week. We have three bodies: physical, emotional and mental and also a third-dimensional physical self, fourth-dimensional emotional/mental/etheric self and a fifth-dimensional purely electronic higher spiritual self. The synthesis of the Law of Seven and the Law of Three is 21. Until now, we

13:20 WHEEL + 441 MATRIX = MENTAL FORCE FIELD TO SHIFT WORLD HOLOGRAM

These are 2 sets of frequencies that we utilize to create mental configurations that we project to erase the old hologram and put in place the new hologram.

RATIO 7 = 126°
COSMIC 13 = 234°
= 360° = 1 TUN
CIRCLE IS 18°×20=360
= HAAB CYCLE (18 20-DAY INTERVALS)
+ UAYEB (NOT COUNTED)
$20^2 = 400$ (MATRIX OF 20)
18:20::360:400
400−260=140 (7×20) (5×28)
140 = TELEKTONON CYCLE

MULTIPLES OF 21

21
42
63
84
105
126
147
168
189
210
231
252
273
294
315
336
357
378
399
420
441

When you look at numbers, ask yourself:

What is the interval?

Meditate
1-3-7-9-21-441

SEE AND FEEL THESE AS LIVING FREQUENCIES AND STRUCTURES THAT THE WHOLE UNIVERSE IS CONSTRUCTED FROM. WE ARE LIVING IN A WORLD OF PHENOMENAL, DYNAMIC MOVEMENT — UNDERLYING IT ALL ARE DIFFERENT MATHEMATICAL FREQUENCIES CREATED BY INTERVAL RELATIONS OF DIFFERENT NUMBERS TO EACH OTHER.

NUMBER IS OCCURRING AT A DIFFERENT DIMENSIONAL LEVEL — VIBRATED AND ACTIVATED BY DIFFERENT THOUGHTFORMS. THESE THOUGHT-FORMS MANIFEST ON THE PHYSICAL PLANE AS BOTH MATTER AND MENTAL THOUGHTFORMS OR PSYCHIC CAPACITIES.

WE ARE MOVING INTO A REALM WHERE THE MAIN CONSTITUENT LANGUAGE IS NUMBER — BUT NUMBER AS FREQUENCY.

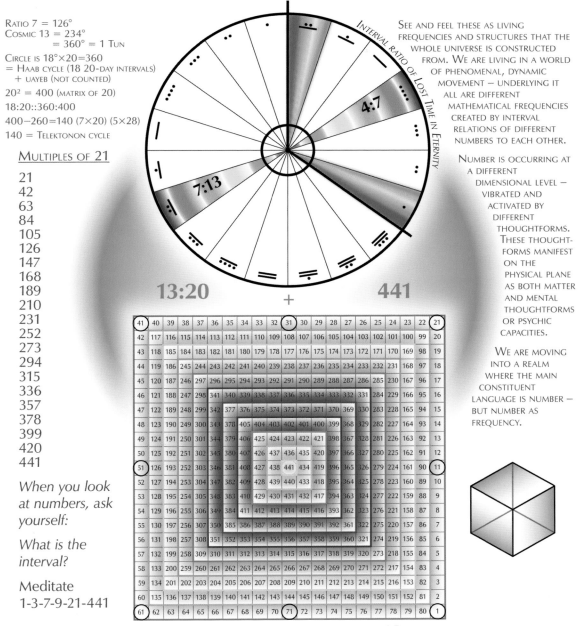

INTERVAL RATIO OF LOST TIME IN ETERNITY — 4:7 — 7:13 — 13:20 + 441

THIS IS A LIVING STRUCTURE! FORGET WHATEVER YOU WERE TAUGHT ABOUT NUMBER! ENVISION THESE DIFFERENT MATRICES. PUT YOURSELF INTO THE ORIGINAL PRIMAL MIND TO MEDITATE ORIGINAL MATRICES. WE LIVE IN A WORLD OF NUMBER.

have not synthesized completely the two sacred laws. That is why 21 is the key to the higher consciousness of our next stage of evolution. 21 x 21 or 441 simply defines the matrix of the unity of totality of the cycles of cosmic evolution.

26. These mathematical frequencies are created by interval relations of different numbers and the matrices of these interval frequencies. Numbers do not just exist in a starting line. In reality numbers exist as components of a living matrix in which our bodies and minds are intricately woven.

27. When we consider that number is actually happening at its own dimensional level, then we can begin to attune to the vibrating essence activated by different thoughtforms. These number essences are empowered by different thoughtforms that activate them so that they become the telepathic manifestations of the thoughtforms that activated them. Then those thoughtforms manifest in the physical plane as different functions, some of which create matter, other thought-forms and also various mental and psychic capacities.

28. We are moving into a realm where the main constituent language is the language of number. But we have to think of numbers as different frequencies. Each number has its unique set of frequencies, and combined with other numbers we can begin to derive intervals as illustrated within the Wheel of the Law of Time.

29. This is the basis of an actual living structure; a vibrant, self-existing world of interlocking synchronic relationships. This is why we follow the synchronic codes so we can see what the synchronic relationships are each day. Then as we go through the day we see other numbers that correspond to those codes.

30. The ultimate purpose of practicing these number codes is to create a mental force field to shift the world hologram. We see the two primary aspects of this mental force field are the 13:20 wheel and the 441 matrix. These are the two sets of frequencies in the circle form and the square form (and the cube form). These are the frequencies that we focus on to create the mental configurations to erase the old hologram and put in place the new hologram.

LAW ⊙F TIME

The Law of Time defines a Pythagorean cosmology of number (0-19). One gives rise to all number — No matter how big any number is, it is always divisible by itself and number 1. One is in everything. All systems of number begin with $1+1=2$ — Two is the Law of Alternation.

- Every even number is divisible by 2
- Every third number after 3 will be a multiple of 3
- Any number whose digits add up to 9 or a multiple of 9 will always be a multiple of 9 [same is true for 19 in vigesimal]

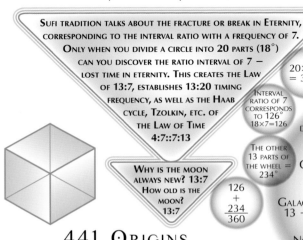

SUFI TRADITION TALKS ABOUT THE FRACTURE OR BREAK IN ETERNITY, CORRESPONDING TO THE INTERVAL RATIO WITH A FREQUENCY OF 7. ONLY WHEN YOU DIVIDE A CIRCLE INTO 20 PARTS (18°) CAN YOU DISCOVER THE RATIO INTERVAL OF 7 — LOST TIME IN ETERNITY. THIS CREATES THE LAW OF 13:7, ESTABLISHES 13:20 TIMING FREQUENCY, AS WELL AS THE HAAB CYCLE, TZOLKIN, ETC. OF THE LAW OF TIME **4:7::7:13**

$20×18°$ $= 360°$

INTERVAL RATIO OF 7 CORRESPONDS TO 126° $18×7=126$

WHY IS THE MOON ALWAYS NEW? **13:7** HOW OLD IS THE MOON? **13:7**

THE OTHER 13 PARTS OF THE WHEEL = 234°

126 + 234 / 360

441 ORIGINS

GO BACK TO ORIGINAL MIND. THINK OF NUMBER ONE AND RADIATE THE ONE OUT INTO THE 4 CARDINAL DIRECTIONS = RADIATION OF 8 = EACH OF THESE IS A <u>O</u>NE INCLUDING THE CENTRAL POINT = 9 ONES. THIS IS HOW WE CAN DIVIDE THE 441 MATRIX INTO 9 PARTS.

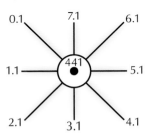

IF YOU START WITH YOUR LEFT ARM, BETWEEN FRONT AND SIDE THAT IS ONE. YOU WRITE THAT 0.1, AND THEN STRAIGHT LEFT IS 1.1. THEN 2.1, THEN 3.1 (BEHIND), THEN 4.1, THEN 5.1, THEN 6.1, THEN 7.1 AND FINALLY THE CENTER, 441. THIS IS HOW THE BASE MATRIX OF 441 IS CREATED FROM THE CENTER OF YOUR BEING.

ORIGIN ⊙F 13:20 FREQUENCY

THE 4 PHASES OF THE MOON ARE ROUGHLY 7 DAYS EACH. THE MOON SHIFTS IN THE SKY 13° EVERY DAY IN ONE LUNATION CYCLE.

COSMOS IS 13.7 BILLION YEARS OLD. $13+7$ CREATES 20 — THE WHOLE TOTALITY OF TIME.

GALACTIC COMPASS HAS 7 VOID SPACES + 13 — THIS IS THE ORIGIN OF THE 13:20 FREQUENCY.

NOTE: IN WHEEL, HAAB IS COUNTED AS 18 20-DAY INTERVALS = 1 TUN, UAYEB IS NOT COUNTED

BOOK OF 7 GENERATIONS CORRESPONDS PRECISELY, I.E. 14 = WIZARD, 15 = EAGLE, 16 = WARRIOR, 17 = EARTH, 18 = MIRROR, 19 = STORM, 20 = SUN

7 SOLAR MANTRAS ALSO CORRESPOND WITH THE 7 DAYS OF CREATION

THE WHEEL IS THE MOVEMENT OF MEASURE — IT GOES IN A SPIRAL COUNTERCLOCKWISE. $7+13$ CREATES THE POWER OF TIME AS MOVEMENT AND CREATES THE RATIO FREQUENCY CONSTANT 13:20 — IMPLICIT IN THIS IS 4:7::7:13, THE BASIC PRINCIPLE OF THE COSMOLOGY OF NUMBER

BEFORE A DOT AROSE IN SPACE THERE WAS ONLY UNDIFFERENTIATED SPIRIT

SQUARES

1^2	$= 1$	INTERVALS
2^2	$= 4$	BETWEEN
3^2	$= 9$	SQUARES GO UP IN
4^2	$= 16$	PERFECT
5^2	$= 25$	ODD #
6^2	$= 36$	SEQUENCE:
7^2	$= 49$	3-41
8^2	$= 64$	[=425] [=17×25]
9^2	$= 81$	
10^2	$= 100$	
11^2	$= 121$	
12^2	$= 144$	
13^2	$= 169$	
14^2	$= 196$	
15^2	$= 225$	
16^2	$= 256$	
17^2	$= 289$	
18^2	$= 324$	
19^2	$= 361$	
20^2	$= 400$	
21^2	$= 441$	

SUM **3311** OF 1ST 21 SQUARES $= 11×43×7$

$(20+1)^2$ $[21^2] =$ 441 MATRIX (HUNAB KU) OCCULT KIN ALWAYS ADD UP TO 21

Enter the World of Number — a world that is self-existing, vibrant and always creating synchronic relationships. Look at all numbers and pay attention.

CHAPTER 3

FROM SYNCHRONIC ORDER TO SYNCHRONOTRON INTRODUCTION TO THE 441 CUBE MATRIX

The Ancient Mayan Seers in their efflorescence on this earth knew the meaning and the count of all numbers. For they had mastered the science of the 20 count and its crown of unity 21-441. 1.1 x 1.2.1 = 1.3.3.1. By these signs they traveled easily between the nine times. The Bolontiku were their guides in their travels, the Oxlahuntiku were those who taught and guarded their knowledge. The Hunab Ku was and is the one who keeps their measure at the center of the primal cube, the 11th dimension beyond this universe of manifestation.

—Excerpt from Votan's Star Annals

1. When we enter the pure realm of number, we are actually entering into a highly sophisticated state of mind that approximates the understandings of the workings of nature. According to the cosmology of the Law of Time the laws of nature are, first of all, mathematical constructs. Everything we need to know about the natural, phenomenal, mental or imaginal worlds we can know through understanding number.

2. No matter how much advanced information or mathematical books there may be, they are still missing a major ingredient—the Law of Time. The Law of Time can be thought of as the unified field theory of number. Throughout the historical cycle, the human race has largely functioned without knowledge of the Law of Time.

3. The Galactic Maya and civilizations of Mesoamerica understood the Law of Time and based a mathematical and calendrical system on it. This has been resurrected through the inspiration and discovery of the Law of Time (1989) and the Telektonon Prophecy of Pacal Votan. Because of this discovery there is a new level of focus and compression of this cosmology of number now available in this world system.

4. The Law of Time recognizes the fundamental principles of harmonic number systems and harmonic geometrical mathematical systems that have evolved and developed in Pythagorean,

Hindu, Chinese, Indian and Arabic systems. But those systems, however elegant, still lack the understanding of number as a function of a simple, unifying, all comprehensive mathematical matrix in which all systems can be resolved.

5. The existing field of mathematics and number does not include the vigesimal system of the Law of Time. Only through the vigesimal system can we accurately articulate the basic principle or ratio of the Law of Time (13:20). The vigesimal system creates a firm basis for understanding time and synchronization.

6. The system of knowledge based on the Law of Time points to the urgency for the human race to change its relationship to time; and thus to "change times." The human race is currently operating on a timing frequency that is irrational, arbitrary and artificial. Even this artificial mechanization of time is based on number, namely 12:60. This creates different cycles and programs based on a machine frequency that is destroying our world. We are at the end of time as we know it.

7. A new time is dawning. As stewards of the Earth, it is up to us to assist in this transition by consciously raising our own frequency into a new vibration and a new time; this in turn, helps raise the frequency of the Planet. The effect of this artificial timing frequency is cumulative and each year it increases its net effect of confusion, pollution and chaos. We are at the climax of several large cycles, anticipating the shift into another timing frequency or program. The question is how can we shed the consciousness of the old and embody the consciousness of the new?

8. As we have seen from the previous chapter, everything is made of number. Everything is coded. The whole of reality is programmed by the 13:20 frequency that is accessible through the synchronic order and its most practical tool, the 13 Moon/28-day calendar. Learning how to read the daily number codes of the synchronic order, including the codes of the 441 cube matrices, is the key that opens the unseen gate. A new time awaits on the other side of the gate.

441 CUBE MATRIX: SCIENCE OF THE SOUL

9. The 441 cube matrix system is the new science of the soul. Divine realities extend far beyond our capacity to comprehend them. But when working with this sophisticated number system, we begin to glimpse and finally embody these other realities.

10. The 441 cube is a system of 21^2 (1.2.1 vigesimal code) and ultimately 21^3 (1.3.3.1 vigesimal code). This system consists of four primary matrices (and a fifth master matrix) that are coordinated by the moving patterns of the synchronic order. Once engaged, the cube system

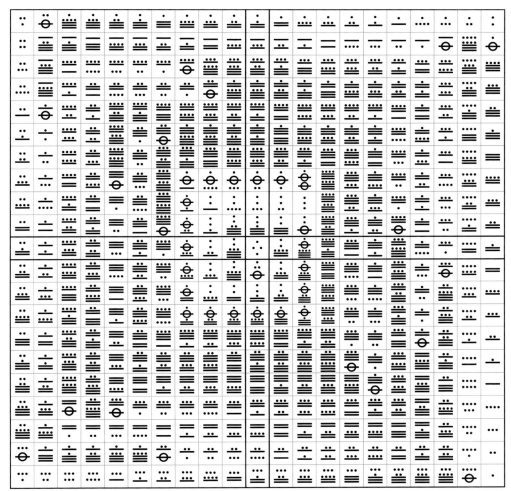

Vigesimal System
(overlayed on the base matrix)

The decimal (10) system perpetuates the artificial world, but it is only half the score. The vigesimal (20) system encompasses the whole of natural time. By mental entrainment in the vigesimal system, the progression of numbers reorganizes the mind's conception of number.

There are 21 levels of the 441 Base Matrix—9,261 (441 x 21); vigesimal language is much more elegant when this same number is written 1.3.3.1. For example 441 gives a different feeling than 1.2.1: 441 is 144 backwards and there are interesting numbers associated, like 414 or 114—these are all key numbers and gateways to the cube.

Note: In vigesimal notation 21 = **1.1**, 21 x 21 = **1.2.1**, 21 x 21 x 21 = **1.3.3.1**. While in the decimal system 11 = **11**, 11 x 11 = **121**, and 11 x 11 x 11 = **1331**. The triangular of 21 is 231 (11 x 21). 231 in vigesimal notation is written 11.11.

becomes a living system. This system is known as **Synchronotron,** and when practiced enters you into a higher-dimensional program that is evolving you into a fifth-dimensional superhuman *(homo noosphericus).*

---

441 MATRIX—A CALL TO THE STAR BEINGS

By analogy, when we make a telephone call, we have to push a precise set of numbers to reach the being we wish to contact. If one number is off, we will not make the connection. But if we know the number code then the connection is simple. Why do we want to connect? To share or communicate information in one form or another. So when we make a call, we need two things: an intention to transmit or receive information from another being and a correct number code to make the connection. The 441 cube matrices offer us a system to dial up certain number codes to make connections to other dimensions.

---

11. There are four basic number matrices to familiarize yourself with. Once you understand the basic patterns, then you will be able to "decode" any number that comes your way. All facets of Cosmic History and the codes of the synchronic order can be found within the overlays of the 441 cube matrices.

12. The 441 cube system encompasses the Law of Time and the Law of Time encompasses the cube system. The synchronic order of the Law of Time consists of very specific mathematical codes that are applied on a daily basis. These mathematical codes can then be plugged into the advanced practice of the holomind perceiver codes where expanded meaning can be derived (see chapters 10, 11).

13. In this way the 441 cube program can be thought of as the Mothership containing all the codes and frequencies of the synchronic order. Each synchronic code, when practiced, helps connect us with this Master Mothership. Working with these matrices is an exercise in mind expansion and conscious evolution. Through study of these matrices as well as the *Cosmic History Chronicles,* we break the mental limitations and penetrate into other worlds and dimensions.

SYNCHRONIC ORDER AND SYNCHRONOTRON

Synchronic Order. The synchronic order is a purely fourth-dimensional teaching that incorporates the third dimension. Based on the teachings of the Law of Time, the two basic principles of the synchronic order are the 13-tone wavespell and Thirteen Moon/28-day calendar. These two principles are derived from the harmonic module or Tzolkin, the basic mathematical matrix of the Law of Time and the synchronic order. Between these two matrices (365-day matrix and 260-day matrix) contain all the different aspects of the synchronic order and Law of Time. These are teachings that unfold different processes and stages of time. This is an important distinction which most people at present do not grasp the significance of. All true mathematical systems can be plugged into and organized by the synchronic order.

Synchronotron (advanced level of the synchronic order). The Synchronotron refers to the practice of the 441 cube matrix system, which can be thought of as the Mothership of all code frequencies. The 441 matrix includes four basic matrices: time, space, synchronic and base matrix (plus a fifth master matrix: holomind perceiver). The time, space, and synchronic matrices are the three coordinating matrices. The base matrix is the anchor that overlays into the holomind perceiver, which is a synthesis and map of the new brain of the galactic mind. The point of the Synchronotron is to imprint the basic cosmological fundamentals of the 441 cube matrix into the mind and brain to create a new mental organ: the holomind perceiver. This work is integrated with the codes of the synchronic order.

14. The synchronic order is a moving template of different variables. Each application of the synchronic order helps us integrate our body/mind, raising our frequency, and thus raising the vibration of our Planet. The 13 Moon calendar is the practical daily tool that enters us into this vast realm of synchronicity.

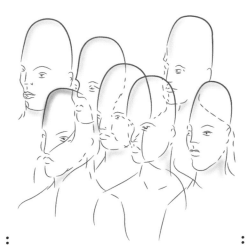

15. The practices of the synchronic order are multi-leveled and you can work with as many as you can track and hold simultaneously. The more practices that can be held simultaneously the greater the increase of continuing consciousness. The *Cosmic History Chronicles* have touched upon many of these practices that have their origin in the Dreamspell and Telektonon Prophecy and their multi-leveled layers and practices.

16. The daily practice of the synchronic order is also a spiritual discipline that incorporates all faiths within its multi-dimensional system. The synchronic code practices are moving practices that change from day-to-day. Like any spiritual practice, the practice of the synchronic codes has as its ultimate purpose contact with the Absolute—the Creator.

I am a multiple channel experienced as 7 galactic world systems simultaneously—within the mind totality that we are, we create the spectrum of the original 13 transmigrating through us, only to demonstrate the principles of applying and enacting cosmic consciousness. 13:7 is the method, 441 is the matrix, 1.3.3.1 is the Cube. This is the method of the Star Masters called Synchronotron!

278	279	280	281	282	283	284	285	286	287	421	304	305	306	307	308	309	310	311	312	313
277	16	50	9	55	11	53	14	52	288	422	303	80	114	73	119	75	117	78	116	314
276	1	63	8	58	6	60	3	61	289	423	302	65	127	72	122	70	124	67	125	315
275	64	2	57	7	59	5	62	4	290	424	301	128	66	121	71	123	69	126	68	316
274	49	15	56	10	54	12	51	13	291	425	300	113	79	120	74	118	76	115	77	317
273	48	18	41	23	43	21	46	20	292	426	299	112	82	105	87	107	85	110	84	318
272	33	31	40	26	38	28	35	29	293	427	298	97	95	104	90	102	92	99	93	319
271	32	34	25	39	27	37	30	36	294	428	297	96	98	89	103	91	101	94	100	320
270	17	47	24	42	22	44	19	45	295	429	296	81	111	88	106	86	108	83	109	321
269	268	267	266	265	264	263	262	261	257	430	258	330	329	328	327	326	325	324	323	322
401	402	403	404	405	406	407	408	409	410	441	420	419	418	417	416	415	414	413	412	411
339	338	337	336	335	334	333	332	331	259	440	260	400	399	398	397	396	395	394	393	392
340	144	178	137	183	139	181	142	180	365	439	366	208	242	201	247	203	245	206	244	391
341	129	191	136	186	134	188	131	189	364	438	367	193	255	200	250	198	252	195	253	390
342	192	130	185	135	187	133	190	132	363	437	368	256	194	249	199	251	197	254	196	389
343	177	143	184	138	182	140	179	141	362	436	369	241	207	248	202	246	204	243	205	388
344	176	146	169	151	171	149	174	148	361	435	370	240	210	233	215	235	213	238	212	387
345	161	159	168	154	166	156	163	157	360	434	371	225	223	232	218	230	220	227	221	386
346	160	162	153	167	155	165	158	164	359	433	372	224	226	217	231	219	229	222	228	385
347	145	175	152	170	150	172	147	173	358	432	373	209	239	216	234	214	236	211	237	384
348	349	350	351	352	353	354	355	356	357	431	374	375	376	377	378	379	380	381	382	383

41	40	39	38	37	36	35	34	33	32	31	30	29	28	27	26	25	24	23	22	21
42	117	116	115	114	113	112	111	110	109	108	107	106	105	104	103	102	101	100	99	20
43	118	185	184	183	182	181	180	179	178	177	176	175	174	173	172	171	170	169	98	19
44	119	186	245	244	243	242	241	240	239	238	237	236	235	234	233	232	231	168	97	18
45	120	187	246	297	296	295	294	293	292	291	290	289	288	287	286	285	230	167	96	17
46	121	188	247	298	341	340	339	338	337	336	335	334	333	332	331	284	229	166	95	16
47	122	189	248	299	342	377	376	375	374	373	372	371	370	369	330	283	228	165	94	15
48	123	190	249	300	343	378	405	404	403	402	401	400	399	368	329	282	227	164	93	14
49	124	191	250	301	344	379	406	425	424	423	422	421	398	367	328	281	226	163	92	13
50	125	192	251	302	345	380	407	426	437	436	435	420	397	366	327	280	225	162	91	12
51	126	193	252	303	346	381	408	427	438	441	434	419	396	365	326	279	224	161	90	11
52	127	194	253	304	347	382	409	428	439	440	433	418	395	364	325	278	223	160	89	10
53	128	195	254	305	348	383	410	429	430	431	432	417	394	363	324	277	222	159	88	9
54	129	196	255	306	349	384	411	412	413	414	415	416	393	362	323	276	221	158	87	8
55	130	197	256	307	350	385	386	387	388	389	390	391	392	361	322	275	220	157	86	7
56	131	198	257	308	351	352	353	354	355	356	357	358	359	360	321	274	219	156	85	6
57	132	199	258	309	310	311	312	313	314	315	316	317	318	319	320	273	218	155	84	5
58	133	200	259	260	261	262	263	264	265	266	267	268	269	270	271	272	217	154	83	4
59	134	201	202	203	204	205	206	207	208	209	210	211	212	213	214	215	216	153	82	3
60	135	136	137	138	139	140	141	142	143	144	145	146	147	148	149	150	151	152	81	2
61	62	63	64	65	66	67	68	69	70	71	72	73	74	75	76	77	78	79	80	1

SPACE MATRIX

Divided into four 10 x 10 quadrants = 400 or 20^2, 11th vertical axis and 11th horizontal are the dividers containing 41 units total + 400 = 441—the four quadrants are further organized as four sets of 8 x 8, 64 units with 36 units external in each quadrant—this accommodates the psi bank codons in four arrangements as Kin 1-256 (1-64 upper left, 65-128 upper right, 129-192 lower left, 193-256 lower right, always in same psi bank sequence)—257-258-259-260 are at corners adjacent to 441 in center (also see Appendix V: MOAP codes).

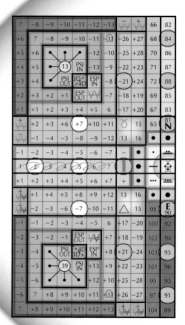

HOLOMIND PERCEIVER MATRIX

Key to the entire system. This matrix is the telepathic switchboard and shows how to locate the 441 Telepathic Frequency Indexes (TFIs) in your brain on a daily basis. The purpose of learning the 441 cube matrix system is to learn how to operate the Holomind Perceiver (expanded on in Chapter 11 and Appendix II). Then we can begin to learn the language of Telepathy or the language of Number.

BASE MATRIX

1-441 spiral moving upward then left in ten circuits until reaching the center = 11th vertical axis and 11th horizontal (V11, H11) = 441

TIME MATRIX

21 x 21 matrix divided into nine sections each of 7 x 7 (=49) units, and each of these nine sections further subdivided into four by a mystical lattice of 13 units leaving each subdivided part with 9 x 4 = 36 units—the four outer time dimensions at the four corners of this matrix contain the 13 Moon calendar for daily practice.

1	2	3	7	10	11	12	217	218	219	85	226	227	228	37	38	39	20	46	47	48
4	5	6	8	13	14	15	220	221	222	86	229	230	231	40	41	42	21	49	50	51
7	8	9	9	16	17	18	223	224	225	87	232	233	234	43	44	45	22	52	53	54
1	2	3	13	6	5	4	79	80	81	91	84	83	82	14	15	16	26	19	18	17
19	20	21	12	28	29	30	235	236	237	90	244	245	246	55	56	57	25	64	65	66
22	23	24	11	31	32	33	238	239	240	89	247	248	249	58	59	60	24	67	68	69
25	26	27	10	34	35	36	241	242	243	88	250	251	252	61	62	63	23	70	71	72
145	146	147	59	154	155	156	289	290	291	111	298	299	300	181	182	183	72	190	191	192
148	149	150	60	157	158	159	292	293	294	112	301	302	303	184	185	186	73	193	194	195
151	152	153	61	160	161	162	295	296	297	113	304	305	306	187	188	189	74	196	197	198
53	54	55	65	58	57	56	105	106	107	117	110	109	108	66	67	68	78	71	70	69
163	164	165	64	172	173	174	307	308	309	116	316	317	318	199	200	201	77	208	209	210
166	167	168	63	175	176	177	310	311	312	115	319	320	321	202	203	204	76	211	212	213
169	170	171	62	178	179	180	313	314	315	114	322	323	324	205	206	207	75	214	215	216
73	74	75	33	82	83	84	253	254	255	98	262	263	264	109	110	111	46	118	119	120
76	77	78	34	85	86	87	256	257	258	99	265	266	267	112	113	114	47	121	122	123
79	80	81	35	88	89	90	259	260	261	100	268	269	270	115	116	117	48	124	125	126
27	28	29	39	32	31	30	92	93	94	104	97	96	95	40	41	42	52	45	44	43
91	92	93	38	100	101	102	271	272	273	103	280	281	282	127	128	129	51	136	137	138
94	95	96	37	103	104	105	274	275	276	102	283	284	285	130	131	132	50	139	140	141
97	98	99	36	106	107	108	277	278	279	101	286	287	288	133	134	135	49	142	143	144

RELATIVE MIND OF SELF-PERFECTION WITHIN PERFECT SPHERE OF ABSOLUTE MIND

HOLOMIND PERCEIVER BIOCOSMIC UNIFICATION PROGRAM

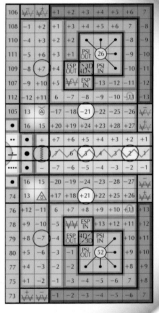

SYNCHRONIC MATRIX

Contains 260-unit Tzolkin within vertical columns 5-17, with 7th mystic column corresponding to the 11th vertical column, while the 11th horizontal row contains the primary 13 tones, accounting for the thirteen 0.0.Hunab Ku days every 52 years—total units: 260 + 13 = 273 (21 x 13). The four columns on either side of the Tzolkin are the 84 right- and 84 left-hand dharma gates, numbered 1-168 (21 x 8)—the sequencing is such that the 8 numbers of any of the same horizontal row of both the right- and left-hand sides always add to 676, 26² or 52 x 13, the number of GAPs multiplied by the primary 13 tones of the Tzolkin matrix.

1	43	85	127	1	21	41	61	81	101	121	141	161	181	201	221	241	168	126	84	42
2	44	86	128	2	22	42	62	82	102	122	142	162	182	202	222	242	167	125	83	41
3	45	87	129	3	23	43	63	83	103	123	143	163	183	203	223	243	166	124	82	40
4	46	88	130	4	24	44	64	84	104	124	144	164	184	204	224	244	165	123	81	39
5	47	89	131	5	25	45	65	85	105	125	145	165	185	205	225	245	164	122	80	38
6	48	90	132	6	26	46	66	86	106	126	146	166	186	206	226	246	163	121	79	37
7	49	91	133	7	27	47	67	87	107	127	147	167	187	207	227	247	162	120	78	36
8	50	92	134	8	28	48	68	88	108	128	148	168	188	208	228	248	161	119	77	35
9	51	93	135	9	29	49	69	89	109	129	149	169	189	209	229	249	160	118	76	34
10	52	94	136	10	30	50	70	90	110	130	150	170	190	210	230	250	159	117	75	33
11	53	95	137	•	••	•••	••••	—	—·	—··	—···	—····	=	=·	=··	=···	158	116	74	32
12	54	96	138	11	31	51	71	91	111	131	151	171	191	211	231	251	157	115	73	31
13	55	97	139	12	32	52	72	92	112	132	152	172	192	212	232	252	156	114	72	30
14	56	98	140	13	33	53	73	93	113	133	153	173	193	213	233	253	155	113	71	29
15	57	99	141	14	34	54	74	94	114	134	154	174	194	214	234	254	154	112	70	28
16	58	100	142	15	35	55	75	95	115	135	155	175	195	215	235	255	153	111	69	27
17	59	101	143	16	36	56	76	96	116	136	156	176	196	216	236	256	152	110	68	26
18	60	102	144	17	37	57	77	97	117	137	157	177	197	217	237	257	151	109	67	25
19	61	103	145	18	38	58	78	98	118	138	158	178	198	218	238	258	150	108	66	24
20	62	104	146	19	39	59	79	99	119	139	159	179	199	219	239	259	149	107	65	23
21	63	105	147	20	40	60	80	100	120	140	160	180	200	220	240	260	148	106	64	22

17. Once you tap into the essence of the Absolute nature you become a luminously open portal so that you can be in touch, not only with vibrational frequencies of the phenomenal reality, but with vibrational frequencies of higher-dimensional realities. If you point your compass in a certain direction in order to gain a comprehension of the nature of the universe, then you place yourself into the Absolute space of reality.

18. Facing inward—the direction of the multi-dimensional universe—we gain direct experience of frequencies and beams of telepathic transmissions which are actually a living vibrational system of present telepathic communications. We can incorporate other spiritual practices with our synchronic code practices, opening us to receive many cosmic insights into the nature of this vast reality. In this space we can begin to feel the structure of the cube which, when concentrated upon, envelops us in a multi-dimensional space. When this is directly experienced, then we know we have entered the cosmic mindstream of the 441 cube matrix—Synchronotron.

 I am Chac-Le, star journeyman, knower of the nine times, unifier of the matrix of becoming and the matrix of return. The ledger of my knowledge is 441; the mother cube matrix 441 x 21—1.3.3.1 is my compendium of world systems. Now I am awakening in my supermental form: 21 cubed—1.3.3.1. Only in the meditation cave of the purified ones will you see the cube 1.3.3.1 in its entire matrices transparent, one revealing the other, revealing the One. Open thou to thee today the holomind perceiver! These are the ciphers, this is the key—the cube that enshrines the mystery!

19. All of the different practices of the synchronic order and Synchronotron help us to erase old conditioned programs while reimprinting us with new galactic programs. As you enter ever more deeply into the system of the cube, you see it is so multi-dimensionally vast that great concentration and discipline is required to penetrate the different levels and orders. It is like a mantra that clears the mind. There are no other preoccupations. There is only immersion in the 441 cube matrix. This is the whole point.

20. 441 represents the power of Hunab Ku 21 squared (1.2.1 vigesimal code) or Law of 3 squared (9) x Law of 7 squared (49) = 441 matrix, a map of telepathic consciousness that spirals inward from lower right-hand corner (1), up and across to the opposite upper left-hand corner (41, which = 441 – 400, the difference between unity of totality (441) and totality (400). The center unit, 400 + 41 = 441, hence 41 = frequency of divine interval, or interval of God.

21. There are four primary matrices to study: **Base Matrix, Time Matrix, Space Matrix** and **Synchronic Matrix,** and then the Holomind Perceiver (see Chapters 10 and 11). For best results, the method or system of the cube should be studied and practiced on a daily basis in tandem with the 13 Moon calendar. To find daily telepathic frequency indexes based on the 13 Moon calendar see Appendix II.

How to Study the Matrices

22. First familiarize yourself with each of the matrices, then study the matrix overlays (also see chapters 4, 9, 10 and 11). Visualize where the **time dimensions** are. Visualize where the **space quadrants** are. Visualize where the **seven heptad gates** are. Visualize how the **circuits** are connected. Visualize the **timespace phase matrices.** Note the way the number patternings go. Note the **11 circuits** and the **11 axes,** horizontal and vertical. Also note that a key to the radialization of consciousness lies in studying the horizontal 11 axis that contains right-handed time and left-handed time. Right-handed time is the activating or energizing force field that activates the fifth mental sphere (superconscious). Left-handed time is the sublimating force field that activates the sixth mental sphere (subliminal consciousness). Just as there is right-handed time and left-handed time, there is also vertical descending time and vertical ascending time.

Note the nine time dimensions. The ninth time dimension is inner core time that opens to the ninth and tenth dimensions, with the eleventh coordinating dimension, 441, giving access to all other dimensions (from which the whole system of the cube is derived).

Time Matrix

Locate the nine time dimensions within the time matrix. This includes the four seasons of outer time where sequential time occurs. Then there is radial time: the lateral fifth and sixth time dimensions; the vertical seventh and eighth time dimensions, and the inner core time, which is the ninth time dimension at the center.

The 13 Moon/28-day calendar dates are located in the four seasons of Outer Time. The first seven moons start at the upper left and run across the first seven horizontal rows.

The first season of time corresponds to the first heptad (moons 1-7).
The second season of time corresponds to the second heptad (moons 1-7).
The third season of time corresponds to the third heptad (moons 1-7).
The fourth season of time corresponds to the fourth heptad (moons 1-7).

When we reach moon 8-13 everything is reversed.

The fourth season of time is the first heptad (moons 8-13).
The third season of time is the second heptad (moons 8-13).
The second season of time is the third heptad (moons 8-13).
The first season of time is the fourth heptad (moons 8-13).

Like the Wisdom Cycles (from *CHC, Vol. II*) there is a cycle of becoming and a cycle of return. Each day has its radial opposite. For instance, the V1 column corresponds to day 28 for moons 8-13, but day 1 for moons 1-7.

NINE TIME DIMENSIONS

SHOWING THEIR INTERCONNECTIONS THROUGH THE FOUR 7TH-DIM EXT TIME & FOUR 6TH-DIM ESP CIRCUITS

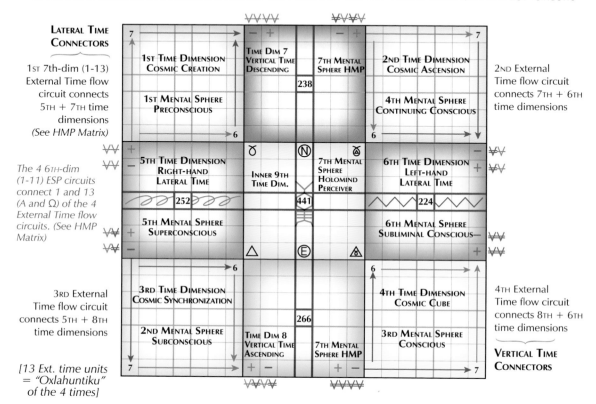

LATERAL TIME CONNECTORS

1ST 7th-dim (1-13) External Time flow circuit connects 5TH + 7TH time dimensions *(See HMP Matrix)*

The 4 6TH-dim (1-11) ESP circuits connect 1 and 13 (A and Ω) of the 4 External Time flow circuits. (See HMP Matrix)

3RD External Time flow circuit connects 5TH + 8TH time dimensions

[13 Ext. time units = "Oxlahuntiku" of the 4 times]

1ST TIME DIMENSION COSMIC CREATION

1ST MENTAL SPHERE PRECONSCIOUS

TIME DIM 7 VERTICAL TIME DESCENDING 238

7TH MENTAL SPHERE HMP

2ND TIME DIMENSION COSMIC ASCENSION

4TH MENTAL SPHERE CONTINUING CONSCIOUS

5TH TIME DIMENSION RIGHT-HAND LATERAL TIME 252

INNER 9TH TIME DIM. 441

7TH MENTAL SPHERE HOLOMIND PERCEIVER

6TH TIME DIMENSION LEFT-HAND LATERAL TIME 224

5TH MENTAL SPHERE SUPERCONSCIOUS

6TH MENTAL SPHERE SUBLIMINAL CONSCIOUS—

3RD TIME DIMENSION COSMIC SYNCHRONIZATION

2ND MENTAL SPHERE SUBCONSCIOUS

TIME DIM 8 VERTICAL TIME ASCENDING 266

7TH MENTAL SPHERE HMP

4TH TIME DIMENSION COSMIC CUBE

3RD MENTAL SPHERE CONSCIOUS

2ND External Time flow circuit connects 7TH + 6TH time dimensions

4TH External Time flow circuit connects 8TH + 6TH time dimensions

VERTICAL TIME CONNECTORS

THE TWO LATERAL TIMES:

a) The fifth time dimension - coordinated by V4 + Mystic H11 - coordinating unit 252 = 7 × 36 [65] seat of 5TH mental sphere red kuali right hand time force field - activating

b) The sixth time dimension - coordinated by V18 + Mystic H11 - coordinating unit 224 = 7 × 32 [78] seat of 6TH mental sphere blue duar left hand time force field - sublimating

Note: The Four Radial Times are coordinated by intersections of the four "4" and "18" lattices [V4, H4, H18 and V18] with the 2 Mystic "11" lattices [V11 and H11].

THE TWO VERTICAL TIMES:

a) The seventh time dimension - coordinated by H4 + Mystic V11 - coordinating unit 238 = 7 × 34 [91] opens Sirius navigation channel of Galactic Life Whole - descending time

87

b) The eighth time dimension - coordinated by H18 + Mystic V11 - coordinating unit 266 = 7 × 38 [104] opens Sirius command channel of Galactic Art Whole - ascending time

96

The Ninth Inner/Core Time: ninth time dimension - coordinated by H11 V11 - coordinating unit 441 = 21^2 [117] - seat of Sirius Council - 11TH dim. channel, 7TH mental sphere - coordinates 7TH + 8TH time dimensions; held in place by 6 cosmic electricities (8TH circuit); all primary creation commands, unifying agent Sirius B 52/113

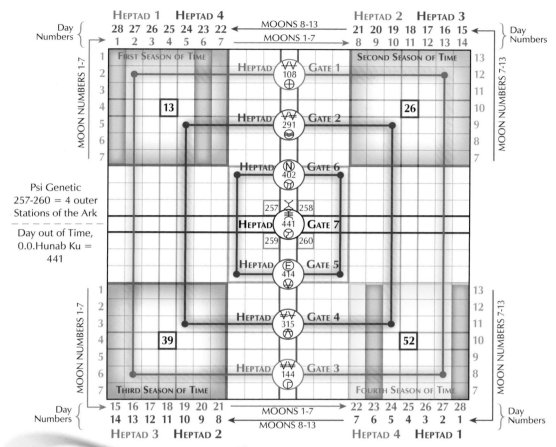

13 Moon/28-day Cycle and 7 Heptad Gates

¤ 4 outer times coordinated by the intersections of the four "4" and "18" lattices [V4, H4, V18 and H 18] of the Time Matrix.

¤ The 4 sequences of outer time establishes the 4 sequences [heptads] of the Book of Days.

7 days per heptad, 4 heptads - 28 days per harmonic cycle.
7 sequences (196 days) complete the Cube of Creation.
6 sequences [8-13] complete the Cube of Return.
13 sequences [364 days, 52 heptads] complete the Book of Days.

• Sequence 1, Cosmic Creation - Heptad 1, Moons 1-7; Heptad 4, Moons 8-13.
•• Sequence 2, Cosmic Ascension- H. 2, Moons 1-7; H. 3, Moons 8-13.
••• Sequence 3, Cosmic Synchronization - H. 3, Moons 1-7; H. 2, Moons 8-13.
•••• Sequence 4, Cosmic Cube - H. 4, Moons 1-7; H. 1, Moons 8-13.

4 Outer Time Dimensions	Heptad Gates 1, 2 Open Heptad Gates 3, 4 Close (Establish 4 Mental Spheres)
9th Time Dimension Inner Core Time	Heptad Gate 5 Opens, 6 Closes, 7 Seals.

Moon 8 equalizes Moon 6
Moon 9 equalizes Moon 5
Moon 10 equalizes Moon 4
Moon 11 equalizes Moon 3
Moon 12 equalizes Moon 2
Moon 13 equalizes Moon 1

Moon 7: Mystic Center, completes the 4 sequences of Outer Time as Cube of Creation, Establishes Return.

Space Matrix

In the space matrix the first sequence of numberings goes from 1-441. It can be broken down into four quadrants as follows:

First Quadrant of Space (upper left): Alpha Alpha. (Units 1-64) First Generation of Space. Located between V2-9, H2-9. MOAP: Zone of Initiation.

Second Quadrant of Space (upper right): Beta Alpha. (units 65-128) Second Generation of Space. Located between V13-20 and H2-9. MOAP: Zone of Refinement.

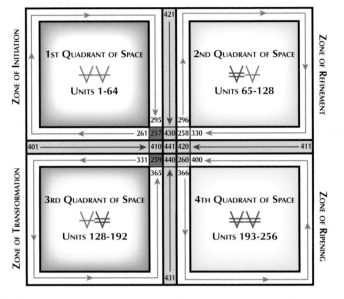

Third Quadrant of Space (lower left): Alpha Beta. (Units 129-192) Third Generation of Space. Located between H13-20, V2-9. MOAP: Zone of Transformation.

Fourth Quadrant of Space (lower right): Beta Beta. (Units 193-256) Fourth Generation of Space. Located between V13-20, H13-20. MOAP: Zone of Ripening.

The four remaining units (257-260) are the four super numbers of the 65th harmonic, the cosmic matrix, and are located diagonally on the four corners around the 441 center unit.

The second sequence of numbering in the space matrix is the spiral numbering that goes from 261-400. Beginning in the first quadrant, around the 64 units of the first quadrant of space are numbers 261-295. The second spiral goes around the second quadrant of space, counting from 296-330. The third spiral goes around the third quadrant of space, counting from 331-365. The fourth spiral goes around the fourth quadrant of space, counting from 366 to 400. 400 creates the 20 x 20.

The third, final sequence of numbering in the space matrix is the 41 units of the mystic 11 lattice (400 + 41 = 441), the V11 column and H11 horizontal. H11 left-hand side: 401-410. H11 right-hand side: 411-420. V11 top down: 421-430. V11 bottom up: 431-440. Then 441 in center. This is the numbering system of the space matrix. The value for daily practice is knowing where the daily MOAP codes are.

Synchronic Matrix

The Synchronic Matrix contains two counts: the Tzolkin count in the center and the eight sequences of the 21 count—four columns of 21 units each on left side (84 gates of right-handed dharma) and four quadrants of 21 units each on right side (84 gates of left-handed dharma). Within the Tzolkin, the horizontal 11 axis contains the mystic 13 count. This accounts for 13 leap days every 52 years.

Study the following:

- Study the system of the **heptad gates** in relationship to the mystic gates. There are 40 mystic gates: 10 gates on each side of the Vertical 11 and 10 gates on each side of the horizontal 11. The center is the 41st gate, the interval of God. There are 100 units in each of the four quadrants for a total of 400, with the interval of God, 41, it creates the 441 matrix (also see Appendix II).

- Study the **nine time dimensions** on each of the matrices. We are always dealing with nine time dimensions. There are four sequential or outer time dimensions (time dimensions 1-4)—this is why the psi bank has four basic plates. For any heavenly body there is always a light side and a dark side. Depending on the axis tilt, there is also a warm side and a cold side. Then there are the four radial time dimensions and an inner core time.

1 OUTER TIME DIMENSION	7 RADIAL (VERTICAL) TIME DIMENSION	2 OUTER TIME DIMENSION
5 RADIAL (LATERAL) TIME DIMENSION	9 INNER CORE 9TH TIME DIMENSION	6 RADIAL (LATERAL) TIME DIMENSION
3 OUTER TIME DIMENSION	8 RADIAL (VERTICAL) TIME DIMENSION	4 OUTER TIME DIMENSION

- Study the **10 circuits** with the dimensions. The whole 441 matrix consists of 10 circuits plus the central 11th mystic circuit. The circuits are numbered from outermost to innermost. Note that the seven heptad gates are coordinated by three circuits and the center. On the circuit chart note the numbers for the 10 gates of descending time. For every circuit there is a coordinating number at the corner of the circuit. Every circuit has four coordinates.

    For example, circuit 1 has four coordinates (Coordinate 1 in lower right, C. 21 in upper right, C. 41 in upper left and C. 61 in lower left—these are the four coordinates of unity in the circuit (1) of unity. When these numbers are added the total is 124. When this is divided by 4, we get 31, the number of the first gate of descending time at V.11, H.1 (Note: Valum Votan departed this dimension when he was Kin 31 and there were 124 days left in the Red Overtone Moon year).

    The above formula true for any circuit. When the four coordinate numbers are added together and divided by four the total equals the number of the gate of descending time of that circuit. For example the second circuit begins at 81. The coordinates are 81, 99, 117 and 135. (These numbers are all functions of 9). When these numbers are added they equal 432, divided by 4 is 108—this is the number of the second gate of descending time.

10 + 1 CIRCUITS

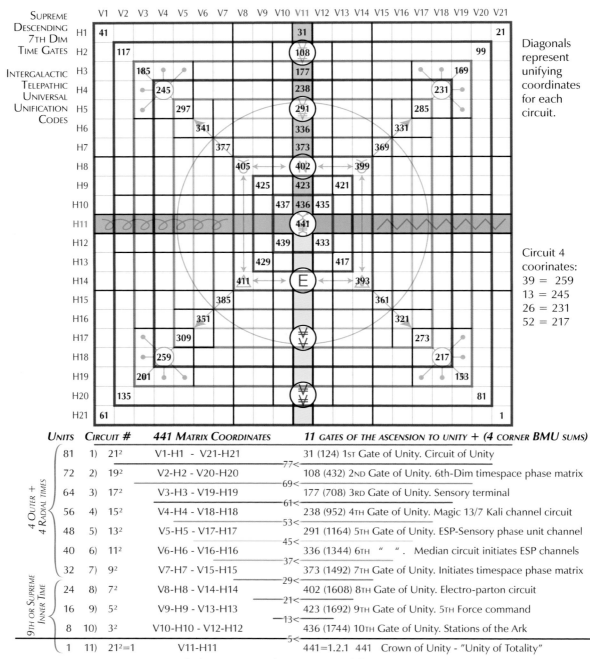

Diagonals represent unifying coordinates for each circuit.

Circuit 4 coorinates:
39 = 259
13 = 245
26 = 231
52 = 217

Supreme Descending 7th Dim Time Gates

Intergalactic Telepathic Universal Unification Codes

Units		Circuit #	441 Matrix Coordinates	11 gates of the ascension to unity + (4 corner BMU sums)
81	1)	21²	V1-H1 - V21-H21	31 (124) 1st Gate of Unity. Circuit of Unity
72	2)	19²	V2-H2 - V20-H20	108 (432) 2nd Gate of Unity. 6th-Dim timespace phase matrix
64	3)	17²	V3-H3 - V19-H19	177 (708) 3rd Gate of Unity. Sensory terminal
56	4)	15²	V4-H4 - V18-H18	238 (952) 4th Gate of Unity. Magic 13/7 Kali channel circuit
48	5)	13²	V5-H5 - V17-H17	291 (1164) 5th Gate of Unity. ESP-Sensory phase unit channel
40	6)	11²	V6-H6 - V16-H16	336 (1344) 6th " ". Median circuit initiates ESP channels
32	7)	9²	V7-H7 - V15-H15	373 (1492) 7th Gate of Unity. Initiates timespace phase matrix
24	8)	7²	V8-H8 - V14-H14	402 (1608) 8th Gate of Unity. Electro-parton circuit
16	9)	5²	V9-H9 - V13-H13	423 (1692) 9th Gate of Unity. 5th Force command
8	10)	3²	V10-H10 - V12-H12	436 (1744) 10th Gate of Unity. Stations of the Ark
1	11)	21²=1	V11-H11	441=1.2.1 441 Crown of Unity - "Unity of Totality"

4 Outer + 4 Radial times (brace for circuits 1-7)

9th or Supreme Inner Time (brace for circuits 8-11)

77<
69<
61<
53<
45<
37<
29<
21<
—13<
—5<

Circuits 1-7 unify the 4 seasons of outer time and the 4 matrices of radial time.
Circuits 8-11 = coordinating/unifying circuits of 9th or Supreme Inner Time

The seven heptad gates are the supreme gates of unity coming from on high. These open us to each of the 7 days, 52 times per ring. The purpose of this practice is to find frequencies that correspond to certain points in the holomind perceiver.

Seventh Time Dimension:
Heptad Gate 1: Opens 2nd circuit.
Heptad Gate 2: Opens 5th circuit. Defines timespace phase matrices. ESP Sensory phase interchange.

Eighth Time Dimension:
Heptad Gate 3: Closes 2nd circuit, unifies timespace phase matrices.
Heptad Gate 4: Closes 5th circuit. Unifies ESP Sensory phase channels.

These two time dimensions activate the four hyperplasmas: Alpha Alpha, Alpha Beta, Beta Beta and Beta Alpha. (show symbols for each of these hyperplasmas)

Ninth Time Dimension:
Heptad Gate 5: Opens 8th circuit. Electron opens circuit of cosmic electricity.
Heptad Gate 6: Closes 8th circuit. Neutron closes and unifies circuit of cosmic electricity.
Heptad Gate 7: 11th dimension portal. 441 circuit of all knowing unity of totality.

23. As we imprint these matrices into our corpus callosum we can imagine that they radiate out into our cerebral hemispheres while activating the 6 + 1 mental spheres that then activate the different dimensions. In this way we can experience ourselves as operating in this radial multi-dimensional manner. By doing this practice, we are entering a vastly superior world than the present world which is still oriented almost exclusively to the third dimension. We are entering a superconscious, super-subliminal order of reality where different time dimensions are being activated.

24. In this reality we begin to feel interfused within these time dimensions and various frequencies. Ultimately, we are learning a frequency language for the holomind perceiver: the evolutionary circuit that establishes the instantaneous translation of number frequencies into superconscious cognitive precepts that allow us to function at a higher-dimensional level.

25. Remember what the Star Elders say: "Only when you attain the experience that *something else is doing the thinking,* and feel the force of a supermental intelligence moving your mind can you say that you are starting to comprehend the 441 Synchronotron."

SYNCHRONOTRON = 198 (18×11)

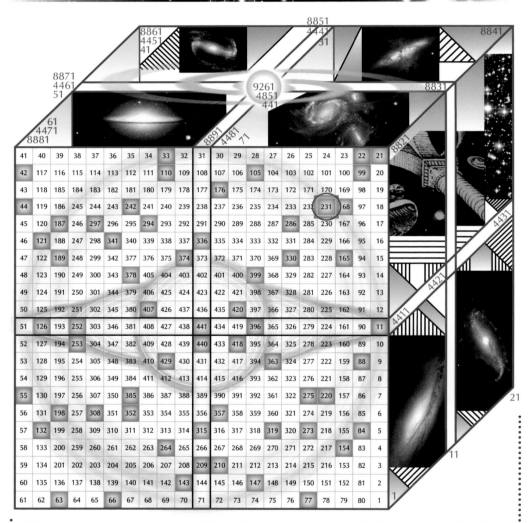

When you enter the pure realm of the 441-1.3.3.1 you must radically reconceptualize from word to number. The wave frequencies of the numbers in their prime and factorial possibilities and all of their relationships within the defined parameters of the 21 squared matrix 1.3.3.1 cube establish the totality of the mental language of the Creator Being beyond the stars—you must continually immerse yourself in the matrices, rehearsing and memorizing the numbers and the coded structures, intrinsic to the 441-1.3.3.1!

CHAPTER 4

TOWARD THE FIFTH DIMENSION
ACTIVATING THE THREE BODIES WITHIN THE CUBE MATRIX

*The human is meant to evolve into a holonomic energy capacitator and activator,
working as a vital component in the whole system of the planet.*

—CHC, Vol. II

1. Human consciousness is evolving toward the fifth-dimensional entity; this is the purpose and function of the cultivation of mind. The mind first localizes itself in the third dimension, and in the fourth dimension extends into states of continuing consciousness. Here, mind becomes engaged in creative meditation and superconscious functions that are composed of the third, fourth and fifth dimensions.

2. Through yoga and meditation we can bring the third-dimensional body into alignment with the fourth- and fifth-dimensional bodies. This is the function of Synchrogalactic yoga (CHC Vol. VI) and all of the practices of the Law of Time.

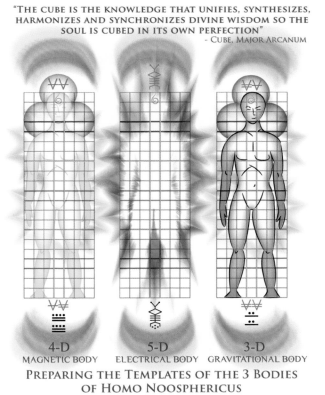

"THE CUBE IS THE KNOWLEDGE THAT UNIFIES, SYNTHESIZES, HARMONIZES AND SYNCHRONIZES DIVINE WISDOM SO THE SOUL IS CUBED IN ITS OWN PERFECTION"
- CUBE, MAJOR ARCANUM

4-D
MAGNETIC BODY

5-D
ELECTRICAL BODY

3-D
GRAVITATIONAL BODY

PREPARING THE TEMPLATES OF THE 3 BODIES
OF HOMO NOOSPHERICUS

3. All three bodies can be systematically activated within the living system of the 441 cube matrix, which is a function of the Law of Seven and the Law of Three ($7 \times 3 = 21$); ($21^2 = 441$). The Law of Seven refers to the codes of creation that can be accessed through the seven chakras. The Law of Three is the law of evolutionary unfoldment that integrates the three bodies: third-dimensional physical body (body of the temple), etheric fourth-dimensional body (body of destiny), and fifth-dimensional electronic rainbow body (body of radiance).

4. When we practice aligning and integrating our three bodies then we function as a triadic organism. Cosmic Science illustrates how the human is composed of types of electromagnetic fields with a gravitational foundation with high biopsychic potentiality. The fourth-dimensional self is the spiritual/mental organizer. The third-dimensional self is the evolutionary vehicle of transformation. However, when the third-dimensional self resides exclusively in the unconscious, it merely identifies with the body and sensory experience. This is the self that we are seeking to transcend (the self that repeats the same stories and programs over and over).

5. Discipline is essential to change. Regular practice and study help us engrave new patterns that when repeated on a daily basis over time changes our behavioral and mental patterns. This liberates the fourth-dimensional self to organize according to selfless universal principles of spiritual/mental order.

6. Through consistent discipline and practice, the higher self descends as the lower self transcends. The third-dimensional chatter becomes subsumed in the mantle of the higher or fifth-dimensional self. The number of realized fifth-dimensional selves is relatively limited on this planet; though there may be 7 billion human entities, there are not 7 billion fifth-dimensional selves.

7. The fifth-dimensional self is the director of the fourth-dimensional etheric body that governs the third-dimensional performer; it waits patiently for the moment of self-transcendence. Self-transcendence is the main function and opportunity of studying and applying the teachings of Cosmic History, inclusive of the 441 cube matrix.

8. The Law of Time refers to the etheric fourth-dimensional being as a *holon*. The purpose of the holon is to allow the soul maneuverability or elasticity between shifting dimensions. The fifth-dimensional entity is purely electronic and does not give origin to a perishable biological entity. In other words, the fifth-dimensional entity is the eternal part of yourself that existed before birth and continues after death—your immortal body. As an angelic entity, the fifth-dimensional self cannot deviate from Divine Will.

9. These three dimensional entities communicate to each other through the mind, namely through the six plus one mental spheres (see *CHC, Vol. VI*). The six + 1 mental spheres of consciousness are etherically congruent with the brain and serve as the computer or hardware of the mind. Each mental sphere has a different function in the thinking layer of the cosmos. Thinking layers are strata in the ocean of consciousness that interpenetrate the different dimensions.

10. These six spheres describe processes and functions of mind that are laced with parapsychological phenomena. Most paranormal phenomena occur through the preconscious mind via the fifth-dimensional entity. Each mental sphere also corresponds to one of seven dimensions, with the seventh dimension being the speaking tube of God.

FROM THE ROOT TO THE CROWN THE HIGHER MIND CENTRAL SYNTHESIZES THE BETA IMPULSES FROM THE ROOT INTO THE BETA-ALPHA FREQUENCIES OF THE 4TH MENTAL SPHERE, CONTINUING CONSCIOUS. HERE THE COSMIC ASCENSION FUNCTION IS REALIZED AS HIGHER MIND CONTROL

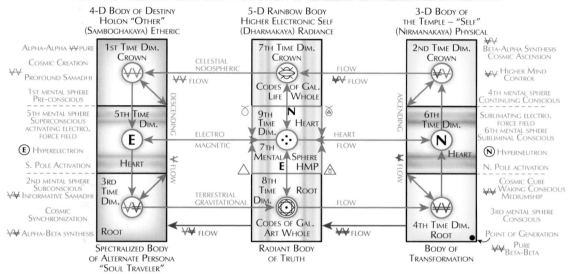

SYSTEM OF FUNCTIONING OF THE 3 BODIES – SYNTHESIS OF THE CUBE
SHOWING THE GENERAL MOVEMENT PATTERN OF FUNCTIONS OF CONSCIOUSNESS IN THE UNIFIED EVOLVED SUPER HUMAN

MENTAL SPHERES
Mental spheres are connected to the third-, fourth- and fifth-dimensional functions and provide the being with the capacities to link with interdimensional information. The six mental spheres are higher mental states accessed through the psychosynthesis of the system of the cube. The Mayan mathematician sages are supreme adepts of these different phases/stages/levels of cosmic conscious meditation and mediumship. Number is their living telepathic language.

SELF-INITIATION INTO THE CUBE MATRIX

11. We can perform our own self-initiation into the system of the cube by locating our three bodies within the 441 base matrix. First identify your crown, heart and root chakras within each of the bodies. Then study the overlays of the different matrices and learn the key (vertical and horizontal) lattices 4, 11, 18 that unify and hold each of the three bodies together.

12. The cube structure is based on the mystic lattice with 11 at the center (V11-H11): these are the two fifth-dimensional axes. The other mystic axes are 18 and 4. V4-H4 is the nexus of the fourth-dimensional body. V18-H18 is the nexus of the third-dimensional body. So we have (11, 11), (4, 4) and (18, 18). The sum of the six lattices is 66 (11 + 11 + 4 + 4 + 18 + 18). Sixty-six is also the number of books in the Bible. Everything is coded and part of the perfect structure of harmony and proportion.

13. Each body also has three horizontal layers: third-dimensional, fourth-dimensional and fifth-dimensional. The 11 axes represent the transcendent mystic order, and the 18 axes contain the third-dimensional codes that form the gravitational plane which runs through the totality of dimensions (3-5). This is the complete show that can be experienced within a third-dimensional body. The 4 axes form the (horizontal) biopsychic plane and also descend (vertically) down the fourth-dimensional etheric body.

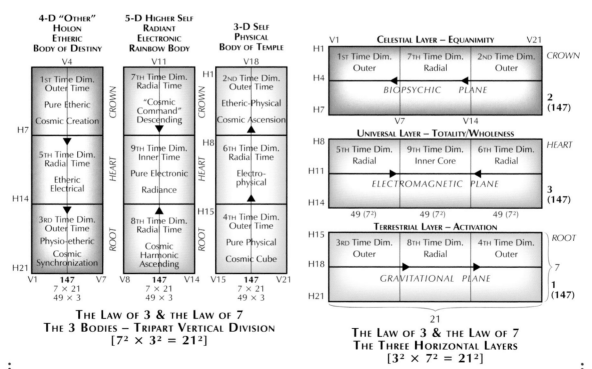

THE LAW OF 3 & THE LAW OF 7
THE 3 BODIES — TRIPART VERTICAL DIVISION
$[7^2 \times 3^2 = 21^2]$

THE LAW OF 3 & THE LAW OF 7
THE THREE HORIZONTAL LAYERS
$[3^2 \times 7^2 = 21^2]$

147 x 1 = 147 (7.7 vigesimal). Frequency of the Body of the Temple (3-D).

147 x 2 = 294 (14.14 vigesimal). Frequency of the Body of Destiny (4-D).

147 x 3 = 441 (1.2.1 vigesimal). Frequency of the Rainbow Body (5-D).

12 is the number of the temple; 9 is the number of destiny; 24 is the number of radiance.

14. Each of the three bodies corresponds to three primary chakras: Crown, Heart and Root. The Law of 3 multiplied by the Law of 7 is 21. There are 147 (21 x 7) units that comprise each of the three bodies. Number 147 (49 x 3 and 7 x 21) is the 21st order of seven representing 1/3 of the 441 matrix. (*The Knowledge Book* says there are 147 names of Allah).

15. The **four outer times** are contained in the third- and fourth-dimensional bodies. The fourth-dimensional body contains the first time dimension (**cosmic creation**) and the third time dimension (**cosmic synchronization**). The third-dimensional body contains the second time dimension (**cosmic ascension**) and the fourth time dimension (**cosmic cube**). In the center of each body, the heart is an extension of the fifth-dimensional body. The sixth time dimension is located between the fourth and second dimensions. This is the **radiant heart of the temple** and corresponds to the **Antares force field**.

16. The fifth time dimension is located between the first and third time dimensions. This is the radiant heart of destiny and corresponds to the **AA Midway Station force field.** The time dimensions 1, 5 and 3 add up to 9 (Lords of Destiny). The fifth-dimensional body is the rainbow body of radiance and contains the seventh, eighth and ninth time dimensions. Our task is to integrate these three bodies as one.

17. To familiarize yourself with how to study the matrix overlays, try this exercise: Go to the graphic on p. 70. Note the top numbers in each of the nine center points of axes 4, 11, and 18 (the top number is the time matrix overlay and the bottom is the base matrix). Add each set of numbers for each of the three bodies, both vertical and horizontal. Note that the numbers are all multiples of 13. The mystic lattices in each of the nine time dimensions contain 13 units for a total 117 units (9 x 13). This number is also the sum total of the three center points in the lattices of the fourth-dimensional etheric body (13 + 65 + 39 = 117). Furthermore this number (117) appears at the center of the Time matrix! Study these.

Mystic lattice codes are all functions of 13:

117 (9 x 13): ninth time dimension
104 (8 x 13): eight time dimension
91 (7 x 13): seventh time dimension
78 (6 x 13): sixth time dimension
65 (5 x 13): fifth time dimension
52 (4 x 13): fourth time dimension
39 (3 x 13): third time dimension
26 (2 x 13): second time dimension
13 (1 x 13): first time dimension

CODES OF (7) CREATION, (3) BODIES + (9) TIMES

	4-D BODY OF DESTINY HOLON - ETHERIC - OTHER (SAMBOGHAKAYA) V4	5-D RAINBOW BODY HIGHER ELECTRONIC SELF - RADIANCE (DHARMAKAYA) V11	3-D BODY OF THE TEMPLE PHYSICAL "SELF" (NIRMANAKAYA) V18	
PROJECT TIME TRAVEL — CROWN 4-D PLANE — H4	1ST OUTER TIME DIMENSION / COSMIC CREATION / 1ST MENTAL SPHERE / PRECONSCIOUS / PROFOUND SAMADHI — 245	7TH TIME DIMENSION / UPPER RADIAL TIME (DESCENDING) / 7TH MENTAL SPHERE / HOLOMIND PERCEIVER, RADIOSONIC / RADIALIZATION OF CONSCIOUSNESS — 238 / **GM108X FORCE FIELD**	2ND OUTER TIME DIMENSION / COSMIC ASCENSION / 4TH MENTAL SPHERE / CONTINUING CONSCIOUS / HIGHER MIND CONTROL — 231 / **PLEIADES FORCE FIELD**	BIOPSYCHIC PLANE / CELESTIAL LAYERS (7) / TFI = 714 (42 × 7)
RADIATE POWER OF ABSOLUTE RETURN — HEART 5-D PLANE — H11	5TH TIME DIMENSION / RADIAL RIGHT-HAND TIME / 5TH MENTAL SPHERE / SUPERCONSCIOUS / PARANORMAL CAPACITATOR — 252 / **AA MIDWAY STATION FORCE FIELD** / *RED KUALI FORCE FIELD*	9TH TIME DIMENSION / INNER CORE TIME / 7TH MENTAL SPHERE / HOLOMIND PERCEIVER, RADIOSONIC / RADIALIZATION OF CONSCIOUSNESS — 441 / **UNIVERSAL COSMIC CORE**	6TH TIME DIMENSION / RADIAL LEFT-HAND TIME / 6TH MENTAL SPHERE / PARALLEL UNIVERSE ATTRACTOR — 224 / **ANTARES FORCE FIELD** / *BLUE DUAR FORCE FIELD*	ELECTROMAGNETIC PLANE / UNIVERSAL LAYERS (7) / TFI = 917 (131 × 7)
STIMULATES SIRIAN REBIRTH — ROOT 3-D PLANE — H18	259 / 3RD OUTER TIME DIMENSION / COSMIC SYNCHRONIZATION / 2ND MENTAL SPHERE / SUBCONSCIOUS / INFORMATIVE SAMADHI	**ARCTURUS FORCE FIELD** / 266 / 8TH TIME DIMENSION / LOWER RADIAL TIME (ASCENDING) / 7TH MENTAL SPHERE / HOLOMIND PERCEIVER, RADIOSONIC / RADIALIZATION OF CONSCIOUSNESS	**SIRIUS FORCE FIELD** / 217 / 4TH OUTER TIME DIMENSION / COSMIC CUBE / 3RD MENTAL SPHERE / CONSCIOUS / WAKING CONSCIOUS MEDIUMSHIP	GRAVITATIONAL PLANE / TERRESTRIAL LAYERS (7) / TFI = 742 (53 × 14)
	MAGNETIC BODY (RECEIVE + ORGANIZE) **BODY OF DESTINY** FREQUENCY OF 3 ACTIVATING CENTERS: 756 (108 × 7)	ELECTRIC BODY (SYNTHESIZE + RADIATE) **RAINBOW BODY** FREQUENCY OF 3 ACTIVATING CENTERS: 945 (27 × 35) (7 × 135)	GRAVITATIONAL BODY (ACTIVATE + EMBODY) **BODY OF TEMPLE** FREQUENCY OF 3 ACTIVATING CENTERS: 672 (96 × 7)	

COMPOSITE TFI OF ALL 9 CENTERS = 2373 (5.18.13) = (113×21) (339×7)
= BMU 168 (21×8) (7×24) (3×56) (84×2) (12×14)

> Study all the components of the matrix of the three bodies to understand the structure of the principle of the Law of 7 and Law of 3. Keep in mind when studying that this is a radial structure, so the 4-D body is on your right hand side and the 3-D is on your left.

18. All number frequencies of the 441 Synchronotron cube system originate from the universal, omnigalactic Central Star Council located at V11, H11. This site resides in the heart of the fifth-dimensional being in the ninth time dimension and is the place of all Second Creation star commands and codes. Note the corresponding number and dimension that each of the star fields represent. For example, the **GM108X force field** is in the seventh time dimension: 91 (7 x 13), seventh mental sphere, holomind perceiver.

52 (13 x 4) = **Sirius** force field: 4th time dimension, Cosmic Cube.
3rd mental sphere: Waking Conscious.

26 (13 x 2) = **Pleiades** force field: 2nd time dimension, Cosmic Ascension.
4th mental sphere: Continuing Consciousness.

104 (13 x 8) = **Arcturus** force field: 8th time dimension
7th mental sphere: Holomind Perceiver.

78 (13 x 6) = **Antares** force field: 6th time dimension
6th mental sphere: Subliminal Conscious.

When studying the graphics, note the following:

V11 is the radio-plasmatic axis of the radial electronic body of the fifth-dimensional body. **H11** lattice runs across the center and is the electromagnetic lattice of the electromagnetic flow. In addition to the V11 and H11 lattices are the 4 and 18 (**V4** and **V18**, and **H4** and **H18**), which create the other mystic lattices.

V4 informs the axis of the **fourth-dimensional body.**
H4 informs the axis of the **biopsychic plane.**
V18 (3 x 6) informs the axis of the **third-dimensional body.**
H18 informs the axis of the **gravitational plane.**
The 4 axes hold the etheric axis and the axis of the **biopsychic plane; and the 18 axes hold** the physical axis and the axis of the **gravitational plane.**

The core of the **third-dimensional body** is located at time vector **V18-H18.** This point is the center of the **cosmic cube** in the fourth time dimension in the center of the third mental sphere, waking conscious.

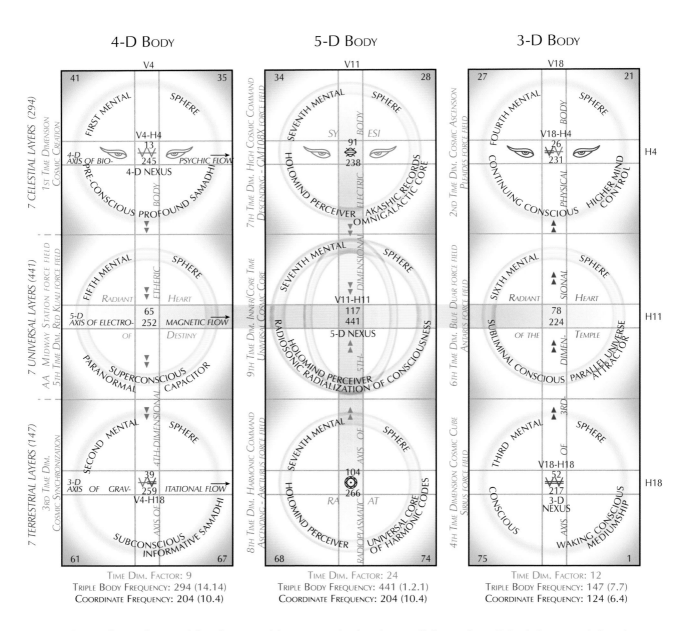

4-D Body

5-D Body

3-D Body

Remember: When studying these graphics we are viewing them radially, so the 3-D Body is on our left and the 4-D Body is on our right

3 BODIES IN BASE MATRIX

4-D BODY (V4)							5-D BODY (V11)							3-D BODY (V18)						
41	40	39	38	37	36	35	34	33	32	31↓	30	29	28	27	26	25	24	23	22	21
42	117	116	115	114	113	112	111	110	109	108	107	106	105	104	103	102	101	100	99	20
43	118	185	184	183	182	181	180	179	178	177	176	175	174	173	172	171	170	169	98	19
44 (H4)	119	186	245	244	243	242	241	240	239	238	237	236	235	234	233	232	231	168	97	18
45	120	187	246	297	296	295	294	293	292	291	290	289	288	287	286	285	230	167	96	17
46	121	188	247	298	341	340	339	338	337	336	335	334	333	332	331	284	229	166	95	16
47	122	189	248	299	342	377	376	375	374	373	372	371	370	369	330	283	228	165	94	15
48	123	190	249	300	343	378	405	404	403	N 402	401	400	399	368	329	282	227	164	93	14
49	124	191	250	301	344	379	406	425	424	423	422	421	398	367	328	281	226	163	92	13
50	125	192	251	302	345	380	407	426	437	436	435	420	397	366	327	280	225	162	91	12
51 (H11)	126	193	252	303	346	381	408	427	438	441	434	419	396	365	326	279	224	161	90	11
52	127	194	253	304	347	382	409	428	439	440	433	418	395	364	325	278	223	160	89	10
53	128	195	254	305	348	383	410	429	430	431	432	417	394	363	324	277	222	159	88	9
54	129	196	255	306	349	384	411	412	413	414 E	415	416	393	362	323	276	221	158	87	8
55	130	197	256	307	350	385	386	387	388	389	390	391	392	361	322	275	220	157	86	7
56	131	198	257	308	351	352	353	354	355	356	357	358	359	360	321	274	219	156	85	6
57	132	199	258	309	310	311	312	313	314	315	316	317	318	319	320	273	218	155	84	5
58 (H18)	133	200	259	260	261	262	263	264	265	266	267	268	269	270	271	272	217	154	83	4
59	134	201	202	203	204	205	206	207	208	209	210	211	212	213	214	215	216	153	82	3
60	135	136	137	138	139	140	141	142	143	144	145	146	147	148	149	150	151	152	81	2
61	62	63	64	65	66	67	68	69	70	71↑	72	73	74	75	76	77	78	79	80	1

4-D Body (right)   5-D Body   3-D Body (left)

The core of the **fourth-dimensional body** is located at time vector **V4-H4.** This point is the center of **cosmic creation** in the first time dimension in the center of the first mental sphere, pre-conscious.

The core of the **fifth-dimensional body** is located at time vector **V11-H11.** This point is the center of the **universal cosmic core** in the ninth time dimension in the center of the seventh mental sphere: holomind perceiver. The third and fourth dimensions are located within the first and third mental spheres. The fifth dimension is located within the 441 central core, interdimensional channel, seventh mental sphere: holomind perceiver.

How the System Works

19. All cosmic creation codes are imprinted and organized by direct transfer from the ninth time dimension to the first time dimension, from the seventh to the first mental sphere.

20. Through the medium of the fifth mental sphere, **cosmic creation** codes descend from fourth-dimensional preconscious to third-dimensional subconscious and become the domain of **cosmic synchronization.** Through the medium of the eighth time dimension of the fifth-dimensional being, harmonic command formulates synchronic codes into principles of **cosmic cube** (waking conscious mediumship—third mental sphere—third-dimensional body). Synchronic codes are the principles of embodying the **cosmic cube. Cosmic cube** embodies knowledge of the 18 dimensions.

21. Through the subliminal consciousness of the sixth mental sphere, the third-dimensional body ascends to fourth-dimensional functioning. The third-dimensional body is then fulfilled as a fourth-dimensional transformer and attains the fourth mental sphere, continuing consciousness, and **cosmic ascension** of higher mind control. The fourth mental sphere receives **cosmic creation** codes via the seventh time dimension. Through studying this process, we open to galactic reality by learning to identify the three bodies as one whole within the structure of the 441 matrix.

22. The lower portion of the physical **body of the temple** is purely third-dimensional, located in the root chakra; from this point the codes of creation manifest. The upper portion of the etheric **body of destiny** is purely fourth-dimensional, located in the crown chakra. The pure fifth-dimensional heart chakra of the fifth-dimensional electronic rainbow **body of radiance** is located in the 441 inner core time.

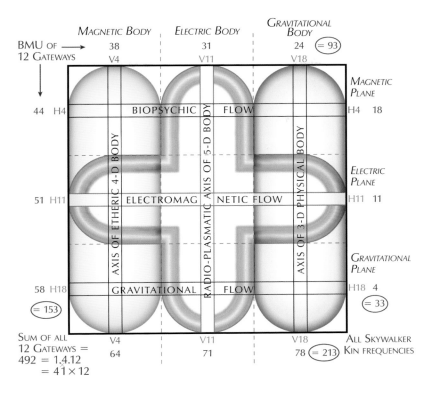

	MAGNETIC BODY	ELECTRIC BODY	GRAVITATIONAL BODY	
BMU OF → 12 GATEWAYS	38 V4	31 V11	24 (= 93) V18	

MAGNETIC PLANE

44 H4   BIOPSYCHIC   FLOW   H4   18

ELECTRIC PLANE

51 H11   ELECTROMAG NETIC FLOW   H11 11

GRAVITATIONAL PLANE

58 H18   GRAVITATIONAL FLOW   H18   4

AXIS OF ETHERIC 4-D BODY
RADIO-PLASMATIC AXIS OF 5-D BODY
AXIS OF 3-D PHYSICAL BODY

(= 153)   (= 33)

| SUM OF ALL
12 GATEWAYS =
492 = 1.4.12
= 41 × 12 | V4
64 | V11
71 | V18
78 (= 213) | ALL SKYWALKER
KIN FREQUENCIES |

23. The lattice structures are operated by the fifth-dimensional entity who maintains command and control through the mystic 11 axes. This is why the fifth-dimensional structure goes all the way up and down the vertical and horizontal axes; it is radio-plasmatic and electric. We seek to integrate these structures and open the seven heptad gates. The fifth-dimensional being is purely radial; it expands vertically and horizontally through the entire matrix and penetrates into the third- and fourth-dimensional bodies.

24. The third-dimensional body of the temple contains the **blue duar** energetic line of force (outer negative). The fourth-dimensional body of destiny contains the **red kuali** line of force (inner positive). These two forces are the root of the atomic-galactic spin effect as described in *CHC, Vol. II.*

25. In the fourth-dimensional body, the **red kuali force field** (right-handed time) activates the radiant heart of destiny governed by the superconscious fifth mental sphere. This is the superconscious paranormal capacitor that operates between the first and second mental spheres. The codes of creation are meditated by the fifth mental sphere, which makes them paranormal capacitators that are coded into the synchronic order and organized in the subconscious realm of the second mental sphere. This is the function of the fourth-dimensional body.

26. In the third-dimensional body the **blue duar force field** (left-handed time) subliminally activates the rainbow body of radiance. The subliminal sixth mental sphere forms the radiant heart of the temple that extends into the heart of the physical body. This sixth mental sphere is the parallel universe attractor receiving impressions, codes and potentialities necessary for establishing the new galactic order.

THREE BODIES AS BASE FOR TIME TRAVEL

Whole body time transport is the capacity to extend through the now into continuing and superconscious. This is achieved through total holographic projection whose quality is proportionate to the vividness and completeness of the alternative fourth-dimensional personality to incorporate the third-dimensional internal body sensation usually referred to as "self". Dynamics of Time, 13.2

Cosmic Science tells us that "the amplitude or breadth of the mental ratio is obtained by special practices, such as telepathy, profound meditation and displacement." These attributes along with the cultivation of time travel are a main theme of the Law of Time. This is where the 441 cube matrix system of the Synchronotron comes into play.

In order to activate your three bodies first locate your personal Base Matrix Unit (BMU) and then plug it into the template of the three bodies. Which of the three bodies are you located in? Which time dimension? Which chakra? Which of the three planes? Your personal BMU is your reference point and base of operation for whole body time transport—this is also your entry point into the integration of the three bodies. To find your personal BMU see Appendix II.

SEVENTH MENTAL SPHERE AND THE 5-D BODY

27. Between the third- and fourth-dimensional bodies is the rainbow body of radiance. The seventh mental sphere, holomind perceiver, governs all three time dimensions of the fifth-dimensional body: 7, 8 and 9. $7 + 8 + 9 = 24$, the number of radiance, and twice the number of the body of the temple (12).

28. The seventh mental sphere has three loci or points of organization held together by its central unit, 441. The essential function of the holomind perceiver is the radiosonic radialization of consciousness. Through study of the 441 matrix, our sense perceptions and mental functions become radialized. This leads to experiences of panoramic awareness and ultimately syneasthetic radiosonics.

29. As we radialize our senses we become conduits of radio-plasmatic energy that flows out of our bodies and senses—this is pure radiance—the attainment of the rainbow body. When some masters leave their physical bodies, consciousness is transferred and the shell simply dissolves

leaving only a rainbow body. This is because they have aligned all three bodies and there is no discrepancy.

30. Other than the main locus at the center of the 441, there are two other locus points. One is located above or at the center of the seventh time dimension, this is the locus of the holomind perceiver and akashic records of the omnigalactic core. The fifth-dimensional self has three higher centers located in the ninth, eighth and seventh time dimensions.

1. **The ninth time dimension** (universal cosmic core). This is the central holomind perceiver radio tuning, transmitter and receiver station—the streaming source of all the 441 codes. It is also the point of radiosonic radialization of consciousness located between the seventh and eighth time dimensions. This is also known as the master storage space of the Akashic Book of Clear Records, the omnigalactic core of the GM108X frequency.

2. **The eighth time dimension** (universal core of harmonic codes). This dimension is home to the Arcturus force field harmonic perceiver. Located between the cosmic synchronization and cosmic cube outer time dimensions, this dimension is aligned with the gravitational plane and is translated into codes of art and ceremonial magic. Working in tandem with the cosmic cube it becomes the Second Creation.

3. **The seventh time dimension** (upper radial time). This dimension houses the GM108X force field and is the center for the radiosonic radialization of consciousness. Located between the cosmic creation and cosmic ascension outer time dimensions, this is the dimension of mediumship.

31. The sum of every code and command is housed in the fourth outer time dimension, **cosmic cube**, channeled through conscious waking mediumship. The cosmic cube channel is located in the **Sirius force field**. The cosmic cube contains the art dimensions and synchronic codes organized as one flow of information and energy. This can be thought of as the akashic records contained within the holomind perceiver codes which mediate the axis of the biopsychic plane. This is the noospheric plane. The groundwork of the great transformation is created within the **cosmic cube**, which allows the third-dimensional body to ascend more etherically and increasingly experience the holomind perceiver of the akashic records.

32. The core of the noosphere is in the akashic records of the **seventh mental sphere** and passes through the seventh mental sphere of the fifth-dimensional body and reaches the third-dimensional body of the temple at the **cosmic ascension** core (V18-H4) (second time dimension) located in the **Pleiades force field**. All the information from the cosmic codes of creation and akashic records are passed into the biopsychic plane, the mainstream of the noosphere.

33. As we know the 13 Moon calendar or sequential time is located in the four outer time dimensions. For example "special" days on the calendar include one located at base matrix unit 331 (V16, H6) in the second time dimension (see graphic page 70). This is the intergalactic channel of cosmic ascension that occurs in the 6th moon, 9th day—this is when 12/21/2012 occurs. All of this can be plotted in the calendar codes and the matrix overlays as introduced in Chapter 3 and Appendix II.

34. Also in the central columns are the seven heptad gates: 108, 291, 402, 441, 414, 315, 144 with their corresponding plasmic signs that indicate the third-dimensional body of the temple and fourth-dimensional body of destiny. The radial body of the fifth-dimensional body of radiance spreads out over the fourth and third dimensions to facilitate evolutionary commands both subliminally and superconsciously.

35. This provides a template. You can make your own larger graphic and lay out the numbers of the day according to the 13 Moon calendar date and kin number. To find these daily numbers see Appendix II. Each day we are working to integrate our fourth-dimensional body of destiny with our third-dimensional body of the temple. The more that we engage our mind in this process the more we begin to experience the radiant glimmers of our fifth-dimensional electronic body that is monitoring the whole program.

PART II
FOUR FACES OF COSMIC HISTORY

CHAPTER 5

YOGA OF NUMBER AND THE 13:20 ALPHABET WHEEL

1. Number is a primary form language that conforms to an elemental yoga of integration. Numbers define stages of yoga; yoga is union. The civilized world is primarily a world of words; numbers are infrequent visitors to this world for most people.

2. Everything in nature, including ourselves, is made of number. Numbers are all unifying. We live on a planet that is made up of two hemispheres, just as our brain is made up of two hemispheres. Our planet has seven continents, just as we have seven chakras. We are born with 10 fingers and 10 toes, 20 digits in all—just as there are twenty interplanetary zones on the Planet Holon grid.

3. We have four limbs, seven chakras, 13 main articulations, 209 bones and 33 vertebrae. We have five senses: sight, sound, touch, taste and smell. Just as our brain has two hemispheres, so we have two sides—right side and left side—with sense organs on each side for a total of eight: two eyes for vision, two nostrils for smell, two ears to hear, one tongue to taste, and one skin wrapped around blood and bones to feel.

4. We are born into this world on a particular date, which is a number. And in the 13 Moon/28-day calendar each of us is assigned a kin number. We proceed through cycles of time based on numerical coding—from birth to death our days are numbered. This numerical coding and philosophy is found throughout most sacred scriptures. "Teach us to number our days" (Ps. 90:12). The Bible also tells us that "the very hairs on our heads are numbered" (Matt. 10:30) and that "men began to multiply" as soon as they were created (Gen. 6:1).

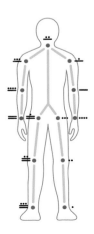

5. Not only is our body coded with number, but so is our external world. When we are born we are given a number (usually known as a social security number). We have a telephone number, PINs, driver's license numbers and license plates numbers, etc. Everything is coded by number. "Thou numberest my steps"

(Job 14:16). Note that the Bible has two Testaments: Old and New. Both words have 3 letters, Testament has 9 letters; 3 x 9 = 27, the number of books in the New Testament.

6. The Quran is also a complete mathematical template that can be read alongside the synchronic order. For example Sura 72, "The Jinn" is one of two suras that have 28 verses (Sura 71, "Noah" is the other one). Sura 72:28 reads: "This is to ascertain that they have delivered their Lord's messages. He is fully aware of what they have. He has counted the number of all things." Note: 72 (8 x 9) and 28 (12 x 6). 28 is the master key and factor of the timing cycle of 28, which is also the Bode frequency of Maldek (28) and Uranus (196) = 28 x 7. These are some examples to illustrate the underlying mathematical structure within sacred texts.

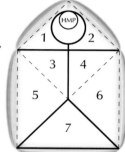

> Numbers are programmed into our biological organism. This can be realized through meditating on numbers as expressed in their different forms.

NUMEROLOGY AND MATHEMATICS

7. Numbers are the highest degree of knowledge; they are knowledge itself. Each number holds a different frequency that contains various qualities, both hidden and overt. For the human, each frequency corresponds to a different facet of cosmic psychology. This is the basis of the practice of numerology, the study of the mystical significance of number.

8. The origin of numerology is primarily attributed to Pythagoras, Greek philosopher who viewed numbers as a metaphysical system of thought and life. Of course he is not the only one, but one of the most well documented. Pythagoras formulated a system of number and created a school at Krotona with an emphasis in the studies of geometry, music, mathematics and architecture. All studies sought to understand number as the underlying structure of the universe.

9. The Law of Time incorporates basic Pythagorean principles of numbers as resonant frequencies. However, the cosmology of the Law of Time focuses on the geometry of time, whereas the Pythagorean cosmology focuses primarily on the geometry of space (and architecture).

10. What we think of as numerology today is the numerology of space in conjunction with the Gregorian calendar system. In standard numerology the Gregorian birth date is added together

to create the master birth number. Each number 1-9 holds a particular psychological significance. The idea of this is that any number added together and then reduced to one digit is the same number after going through a series of sequences.

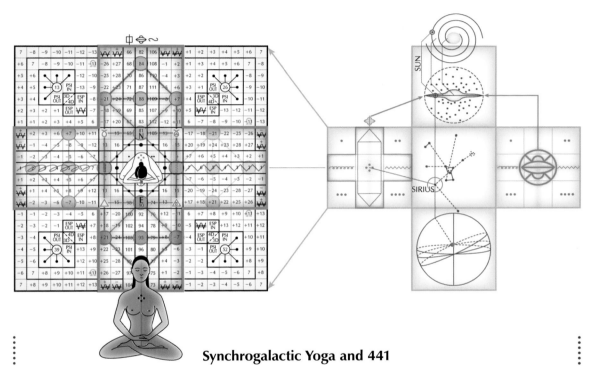

Synchrogalactic Yoga and 441

Learning the system of the Synchronotron is also a form of yoga, a higher supermental jnana yoga evolving itself as the supramental structure of the 441 cube matrix. To study and practice it we need supreme clarity of mind. Meditate on the numbers 1-20. Everything is created from and can be resolved back into these numbers. Meditate: What is number a product of? Create a vocabulary of number. Reduce it to its nine function and then work with the intervals of vigesimal and decimal to create amazing number pattern overlays.

In *CHC Vol. V*, Chapter 12 we introduced telepathic grammatical structures that imprint the noosphere with new mental programs to replace the old program. In the last volume we suggested that these be visualized as millions of cube structures in the noosphere simultaneously containing or being contained by one master cube of 21. We also introduced the 441 (21 x 21) matrix. In vigesimal, 20 is totality, the analog to decimal's 10, while 21 (20 + 1) is the unity of totality.

0-19 CODE

11. Based on the Law of Time, the synchronic order introduces the mathematics of the fourth dimension; this mathematics is radial rather than linear. In fourth-dimensional or galactic numerology, whole numbers are counted and reduced to the 0-19 code. This accounts for each of our 20 digits (fingers and toes). In the 0-19 code, numbers were originally inscribed by a "dot bar" code, but can also be written in Arabic notation.

12. The 0-19 code also codes the Quran. It is important to understand the synchronic order as a mathematical order independent of astrological time; it exists as a measure of pure absolute synchronic time. There are no superior or inferior numbers in the synchronic order. Each number contains its own unique vibration or frequency that sets it apart from the rest in an all inclusive matrix. According to the Law of Time numbers correspond to a telepathic code language.

13. Numbers must be meditated on to find their true qualities. From here, we can tune into the pure vibration of number. In reality, everything is pure, vibratory resonance. Number is pure resonance. Higher mental faculties such as telepathy are always dependent on the synchronic activation of two or more numbers within a coded range of experience and memory. To feel numbers as frequencies, visualize them.

SEVEN NUMBER PRINCIPLES

1. Everything is made of number.
2. Number is a primary form language that conforms to an elemental yoga of integration.
3. Numbers define stages of yoga—yoga is union—numbers are all unifying.
4. Nature is created by different numbers coming together in mathematical proportions.
5. God creates everything in even ratios and harmonics.
6. Everything is made of number, including us.
7. Each number holds a different frequency that contains various qualities, both hidden and overt.

THE YOGA OF NUMBER

14. All sacred teachings have a variation of the harmony of number. Yoga is the discipline to come into harmony with God or unity. Each number frequency corresponds to a different facet of cosmic psychology. This is the basis of the practice of numerology as put forth by Pythagoras. Pythagoreans viewed numbers as a form of yoga that could be meditated on and communed with.

15. The Law of Time defines a Pythagorean cosmology of number (0-19). In CHC *Vol. VI* we introduced the 13-unit wavespell as the primary template for evolutionary advancement. Now we will further explore the yoga frequency behind the numbers 0-13, including their corresponding glyphs and archetypes.

Yoga of Numbers 0 - 13

Zero—The Yoga of Emptiness
Sun—The Enlightened One

Feel your mind as a void space without thought—this is zero. Zero is pure mind; sphere; God as beyond form and conceptualization. Pure light universe; that which makes advances into the infinite possible.

Zero is the pure space in the Yoga of Emptiness.

One—Yoga of Unity
Dragon—The Primal Force

Now feel within the emptiness of zero, or void space, that one is the first thought that arises. Feel the feeling of One-ness. One arises as the first separation of light or space. Nothing exists without one. Everything has one central point around which it revolves—this is the power of one. One gives rise to all other number. One is in everything.

One is the Magnetic force in the Yoga of Unity.

Two—Yoga of Polarity
Wind—High Priestess

Inhale, exhale. Feel the two. Day and night. Feel the two. Male and Female. Feel the two. North pole and South pole. Feel the two. Two is the lens through which unity emerges and balances with the many. Two is the doorway between the one and many. One and Two are the parents of all numbers. All even numbers are divisible by two. Separation from nature is rooted in the two. All of our thought process follows nature's polarity. Life is created from the two. In vigesimal the one divides into two dots like a biological splitting. Every life form carries the duality of two.

Two is the Lunar force in the Yoga of Polarity.

Three—Yoga of Service
Night—Dreamer   ● ● ●

Now feel two give way to three. Three binds and activates creating dynamism. Everything that is dynamic has three parts. The three is the bonding principle. Beginning, Middle, End. Past, Future, Present. Man, Woman, Child. Feel the structure of three in your body as three parts. The triangular of two is three. Three is also the number of service which goes beyond. Service is always a transcendental principle.

Three is the Electric force in the Yoga of Activation.

Four—Yoga of Form
Seed—The Innocent   ● ● ● ●

Now feel the four as the power of form: Front, back, left, right. Four is the power of self-existing form. Feel the perfect measure and stability of the four within the symmetry of your four limbs: two arms, two legs. Four is the basis of the yoga of form. Four limbs is the power of movement. Without four there is no manifestation. Four is the triangulation of ten, the power of manifestation.

The matrix of a cube has four equal sides. Four is the first number that represents the power of time. It is the key factor in the basis of the formulation ratio of the Law of Time: 4:7::7:13. Four is the first number formed by the addition and multiplication of equals. $2 + 2$ or 2×2. $4^2 = 16$. $4^3 = 64$ (basis of DNA).

Four is the Self-Existing force in the Yoga of Form.

Five—Yoga of the Fifth Force/Radiance
Serpent—Serpent Initiate   ▬▬▬

Feel the five by stretching out your four limbs and note they all meet at the center, heart, the inner fifth court. Five is the power of dynamism. Five is the thumb and heart that completes the four; the fifth force. With the thumb we can grasp things.

Five is the basis of the Platonic soloist as described by Plato in *Timaeus*. There are five volumes that arise within a sphere that manifest the monad principle of equality in all directions. Stone models of these five types date from 1500 B.C. in Scotland. Everything in the universe is formed by combinations of platonic solids.

The fifth force is intelligence as a mental force. The fifth force is attuned to time as the factor of synchronization. This fifth force intelligence operates at the center of every matrix of matter where the four forces are met by the fifth force. In traditional physics there are four forces: weak force, strong force, electromagnetic force and gravitational.

Five is the Overtone force in the Yoga of Fifth Force.

Six—Yoga of Equality
Worldbridger—Hierophant

Now feel into the uniqueness of the number six. Feel its order and regularity. Six is the number of balance. It symbolizes the union of the polarity of two triangles or male and female. Six is the fundamental organizing principle of the platonic solids. A tetrahedron has six edges, a cube has six faces. You can feel the six by becoming aware of left, right, front, back, top and bottom.

Six also represents the universe with four cardinal directions and above and below. Six can be seen in the hexagonal beehive honeycomb. Cellular structure and membranes are based on hexagons. Every snowflake has six sides. Crystal is based on the hexagon pattern (see double terminated crystal). Six is integrally self-consistent, 1 + 2 + 3 or 1 x 2 x 3. Six is the triangular of three. The patterning of six has infinite possibilities.

Six is the Rhythmic force in the Yoga of Equality.

Seven—Yoga of Resonance
Hand—Avatar

Seven is the door that opens the mysteries of life; it is the most sacred of all number. Feel the seven gates in your head: 2 eyes, 2 ears, 2 nostrils, 1 mouth. The human also has 7 endocrine glands. See the seven stars both in the Big Dipper and Orion. Seven is the power of resonant attunement and has universal significance throughout all cultures, myths and religions. For example, the seven steps of Buddha symbolize the ascent of the seven cosmic stages transcending time and space.

The number seven is used 55 times in the Book of Revelation (seven seals, seven trumpets, seven churches, etc). In Islam, seven is the perfect number repeatedly referred to in the Quran, seven heavens, seven earths, etc. Seven is a cosmic number with three of heaven and four of the world. Seven is the pivotal number in the Law of Time. It is the implicit interval between 13 and 20. Seven is the power that keeps the 13:20 cycle together—7 and 13 have the most consistent integrity of producing cyclic numbers. Seven and 13 are primary powers of organization in time.

Seven is the Resonant force in the Yoga of Attunement.

Eight—Yoga of Integrity/Harmony
Star—Artist

Feel into the harmonic balance and integrity of the eight, 2 cubed. The eight is the number of galactic form and order, and the number of the octave heard within music. Feel the harmony of eight within your body: 2 eyes, 2 ears 2 nostrils, 1 mouth, 1 skin—the eight encapsulates the full range possibility of the five senses. Eight creates the diatonic octave, 13 creates the chromatic octave. Diatonic (8) + chromatic (13) = 21, basis of the totality of 441.

Eight is the Galactic force in the Yoga of Harmony.

Nine—Yoga of Intention
Moon—Healer

Now feel the magical qualities of the number nine; the nine portals or openings in the body. Nine is the number of the Nine Lords of Time and Destiny (Bolontiku). The magic square of nine was the earliest form of magic square, all rows add to 15. Any multiple of nine adds up to nine and is divisible by 9 (which is a function of 3). Most numbers that have the capacity for being recombinant, such as the pure recombinant reciprocal of seven, 142 857, as we have seen, are also multiples of nine.

The reciprocal of 7, 142 857, is a cyclic and magical number which is divisible by nine and three (law of 7 law of 3). The principle dynamic of the universe is actually moving through the nine.

Nine is the Solar force in the Yoga of Intention.

Ten—Yoga of Manifestation/Perfection
Dog—Compassionate One

Now feel into the perfection of ten. Feel the ten digits of your fingers; the ten digits of your toes. Ten is the power of manifestation. The relation between 4 and 10 is six.

Ten is the basis of the decimal system. Decimal means positional mathematics based on 10. To get to the next level we add zeros; 10, 100, 1,000, 10,000, 1,000,000. This system came about with the idea of zero. Zero creates a larger order of number.

Ten is the Planetary force in the Yoga of Manifestation.

Eleven—Yoga of Liberation
Monkey—Magician

Feel the mystic quality of eleven—a master number with supreme liberating power; so much so that when you try to grasp it, it dissolves you and all conceptions. For this reason it also holds the key to invisibility. 11 contains supreme power that when meditated upon reveals many keys. Note 1 + 1 = 2, the Yoga of Polary; hence 11 is the liberating force of polarity opening us into the vastness of the psychic realms.

Eleven is the Spectral force in the Yoga of Liberation.

Twelve—Yoga of Cooperation
Human—Sage

Feel the stable coherency of twelve—a dozen. Feel the root of this organizational form in your body temple; 12 is the number of the temple. 12 is also the basis of the erroneous human perception about time, but only when it denies the power of 13. 1 + 2 = 3: Yoga of Service; hence 12 is the cooperative force of service.

Twelve is the Crystal force in the Yoga of Cooperation.

Thirteen—Yoga of Transcendence
Skywalker—The Prophet

Feel the magic dynamism and circulatory power of thirteen; the number of cyclic wholeness. Thirteen takes you beyond the static 12, opening you to the cosmic realms of the divine mother. Feel thirteen in the joints of your body. You are prophecy itself; the transcendence of cosmic consciousness!

Note: The square of 13 is 169. (169 = 13 Moon on 13 Moon calendar). The reverse of 169 is 961. The sum of the digits in 169 is 16 (number of the Cube of the Law). 169 x 961 = 162,409 (the square of 403, 4 + 0 + 3 = 7). The sum of the digits in 13 is 4, the square root of 16! 13 is also the 7th number in the Fibonacci sequence.

Thirteen is the Cosmic force in the Yoga of Transcendence.

Note, here we are focusing on the first 13 numbers, but the following are the yoga frequencies through 21. Twenty-one is the maximum of different frequencies to create a minimum matrix to express the unity of totality.

Fourteen is the **Yoga of Double Resonance;** Polarity of Attunement (2 x 7). Wizard/Wizard.

Fifteen is the **Yoga of the Triple Fifth Force;** Service of Radiance (3 x 5). Eagle/Seer.

Sixteen is the **Yoga of the Cube;** Double Harmonic (2 x 8) (4 x 4): Cube of Form. Warrior/Pathfinder.

Seventeen is the **Yoga of Prime Navigation;** Earth/Navigator.

Eighteen is the **Yoga of Reflective Dimensions;** Polarity of Intention (2 x 9); Service of Equality (3 x 6). Mirror/Yogi(ni).

Nineteen is the **Yoga of Mystic Saturation;** Supreme Attainment. Storm/Worldchanger.

Twenty is the **Yoga of Totality;** Polarity of Manifestation (2 x 10) and Form of the Fifth Force (4 x 5). Sun/Enlightened One.

Twenty-One is the **Yoga of Hunab Ku;** One Giver of Movement and Measure; Service of Resonance (3 x 7). Magus of the Infinite.

GALACTIC NUMEROLOGY AND THE 13:20 ALPHABET WHEEL

Of course the Tzolkin is just a code. So is the alphabet with which we write. Yet, as we know, the alphabet encodes a language, and the person who knows how to write that language with the alphabet—26 letters—can command tremendous power and communicate at least a suggestion of the knowledge and wisdom of the universe. In the same way, knowing the code language of the Tzolkin, the Mayan harmonic module, can open up channels of understanding and communication with equal if not greater power than is available to us through the alphabet. Number is no different than symbol, is a condensation of overtones and levels of meaning.

—José Argüelles, The Mayan Factor

Mathematics is the study of the science of number as having different laws, properties and relations, i.e. one is unity, while two is polarity and the creation basis of all binary patterning, two creates an alternating rhythm, etc. This is how the science of mathematics defines laws and properties of different numbers.

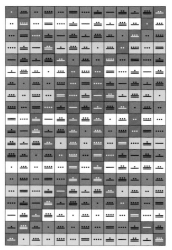

Numerology is the psychomathematics of number. Thirteen is the power of the cosmic cycle recurring as a wavespell. Seven is the power of resonance of primary attunement and channeling. Numerology relates to number as frequency. Every frequency has a set of relationships to other frequencies, and these relationships convey sets of meanings. Number frequencies set off psychic frequencies within ourselves; we see that there is intrinsic power to number.

Mathematics and numerology are close in relation. You cannot have a proper understanding of one without the other. Numbers by their nature have quality and meaning and obey specific laws. Mathematics and numerology come together in the 441, a finite matrix for the construction of the language of telepathy.

There is a cosmic psychology to number that we can apply to further activate our own self-reflective capacities, lifting us into a higher realm of self-perception of the fifth-dimensional galactic being that is waiting to embody us.

Numbers are components of cosmic consciousness. Seek to understand number both as frequency and geometry. Make your own number card index and continuously add new meanings as they come to you. This way when you encounter a number or need to find a date, it is at your fingertips. In Appendix II, we learn how to decode our telepathic frequency index number by plugging our birthdate and kin number into three moving matrices.

Likewise we can also decode our name through the 13:20 alphabet wheel, and then locate this number on the 441 base matrix as well as on the holomind perceiver. We can also reduce our number to its kin equivalent to find which of the 260 Archetypal Houses our name falls under.

NAMES HOLD A SPECIFIC VIBRATION

Everything has both its own true name, which is an eternal word and also a form or material name which changes with its manifestations.

—Manly P. Hall

Names are filled with powerful significance. From ancient times words have been recognized as containing specific vibratory qualities due to their inherent numerical quality. In hermetic traditions comes the belief that everyone and every object has a secret name. Once the secret name is discovered then inner doors open. Many people are familiar with the Pythagorean numerical system that works with numbers 1-9. In the 13:20 system we work with numbers 1-260, where A-M = 1-13 and N-Z = 20-260 (counting by twenties).

Calculate your name frequency in the 13:20 number matrix. Unlike traditional numerology, we focus on the given names that are commonly used, **first** and **last**, as these have the most prominent vibratory resonance. In this system, the middle name (unless used as part of your everyday name) is considered the occult or hidden force.

Write out the first and last name that you use in the world (you can also decode your spirit names and/or secret internal names). Use the chart to find your number. Study all the properties of your number. What is it a factor of? What does it add up to? Etc. Also note how many letters your name has. How many vowels? How many consonants?

The vowels, as symbols of the life, were divine; they belonged to God and were his name, for He was considered the composite of all life energies—as no word can be formed without a vowel, so nobody can be formed without the etheric chakra centers.

—Manly P. Hall, *Qabbalah.*

We can decode the number in two more ways based on the 13:20 system:

Base Matrix/Holomind Perceiver: If the number exceeds 441 then subtract 441 until you arrive at your "base matrix unit" number. Then locate this number in the base matrix on p. 52 as well as holomind perceiver on p. 52 and p. 157. You can also decode this further by flipping to page 70.

Synchronic "Archetypal" House Code: This number can also be reduced down to its 260-code kin number by subtracting 260 until you get a number 260 or less. Then go to p. 229 to find your archetypal house.

Your last name represents your archetypal "family" house (3-D).
Your first and last name combined is your external destiny path (4-D).
And your whole name combined is your invisible destiny path (5-D).

We will use the example of the name José Anthony Argüelles and Valum Votan:

J O S E   **A N T H O N Y**   **A R G U E L L E S**

10 40 120 5 (=175)   1 20 140 8 40 20 240 (=469)   1 100 7 160 5 12 12 5 120 (=422)

3-D Family Name: BMU 422—Kin eq. 162: House of the Rhythmic High Priestess
4-D Destiny Path (external): 597 = BMU 156—Kin eq. 77: House of the Crystal Navigator
5-D Destiny Path (invisible): Total 1066 (2 x 533) = BMU 184—Kin 26: House of the Cosmic Hierophant

V A L U M   **V O T A N**

180 1 12 160 13 (=366)   180 40 140 1 20 (=381)

3-D Destiny Path (Votan): BMU 381—Kin eq. 121: House of the Self-Existing Primal Force
4-D Destiny Path: Total 747 = BMU 306—Kin eq. 227: House of the Rhythmic Avatar

CHAPTER 6

SPIRIT CALLING: COSMIC SKY TEACHINGS

Lift your eyes and look up in the sky. There's our message. Lift your eyes again and look around you, and you will see that you are walking in the sky, which extends to the ground. We are all part of the sky, more so than the ground.
—John Lennon and Yoko Ono (NY Times, May 27, 1979, Kin 174)

1. Cosmic sky teachings are the essence of and encompass all spiritual or religious teachings that are known, have been known or will be known. There is no beginning or end to cosmic sky teachings. Everything is a cosmic sky teaching.

2. Within the cosmos every level of reality is present simultaneously. At any given moment, the universe is completely unified by that moment. All religions are functions of different focal points of energy directed onto the planet at different times for different peoples. All true religions flow into the one stream of universal spirituality and are encompassed by the cosmic sky.

3. All religions provide humanity with a type of scaffold or training wheels to get to a higher level and to ultimately see the universal unity. Spiritual messengers, prophets and sages of all faiths represent a single tapestry of the vast interlocking planetary system.

4. As planetary citizens we are very small in relation to the whole earth. This little earth contains a wide diversity of beliefs, religions and spiritual teachings that have evolved just in the last ten thousand years. When contemplated, cosmic sky teachings defy logic.

5. The whole cosmos is an indivisible unity; the earth and its moon going around it is a sheer microcosm of reality. Therefore, every belief, every set of teachings, every religion and every revealed prophecy are all part of one indivisible unity. Cosmic sky teachings are the teachings of unity of cosmic mind as the unfolding of four fundamental dimensions: dimension of mind, dimension of space, dimension of time and dimension of number.

6. Without number, the dimensions of mind, space and time are actually an undifferentiated unity. Number gives dimensionality to space and a frequency of cyclic order to time. Through meditating on number we can come to know the process of the evolution of space through time. This process of unfoldment is cognized and known by mind through the six (+1) mental spheres that have been mentioned throughout the *Cosmic History Chronicles.*

7. Cosmic sky teachings have a specific scientific and mathematical order that is intrinsic to the fundamental principles of the construction of the cosmos as defined by Cosmic Science. We must always keep in mind the vastness of the whole solar system of which the earth is a part. The solar system is, in turn, part of a galaxy. When we talk about the cosmos, we are talking about at least 125 billion galaxies. The cosmic sky teachings are the unity of the cosmic mind that encompasses every single one of these galaxies.

8. The same Great Cosmic Mind exists in every single galaxy; it permeates the universal space and universal time. Within those 125 billion galaxies our Milky Way galaxy is merely one, just an infinitesimal part of this whole order. In turn, the 125 billion galaxies are framed by numberless world systems. These numberless world systems are all in different stages of evolutionary development.

One Law of Innumerable Meanings

9. Cosmic sky teachings accommodate every single stage and phase of spiritual growth as well as the evolutionary stages of life and consciousness simultaneously on all world systems. These teachings form numerous facets that can be adapted to any stage of spiritual growth and any stage of consciousness throughout the universe. The shades of these possibilities are innumerable.

10. In this regard we turn our attention to the Buddhist Vehicle of the One Law. In the *Lotus Sutra,* Buddha says, "I teach only the one vehicle of the law, that law is the law of innumerable meanings." This law of innumerable meanings is formless, allowing it to adapt to and take on any form. This is analogous to the law or essence of cosmic sky teachings: the ability to adapt to any stage or level of spiritual growth, or any need or inclination of intelligence or ignorance of any entity at any given stage of evolution on whatever world system in whatever part of the cosmos—this is the law of innumerable meanings.

11. When we look at the sphere of cosmic space as an evolutionary map, we see that earth is at the bottom. The earth constitutes one of the innumerable world systems. On the earth itself we can find every stage of spiritual growth and development of virtually any inclination of intel-

ligence/and or ignorance that has occurred over the last 10,000 years or more. In turn, we can also find various levels and styles of teachings that apply to those different stages of growth of evolutionary development.

EARTH AS VAST SCHOOLHOUSE

12. Planet Earth is a repository or receptacle of the full spectrum of the totality of cosmic sky teachings. This has been unknown as a totality until this present moment. As earth evolved and the different people on earth were evolving, they did not know about each other. They were scattered about the earth and only encountered each other from time to time. As the progress of history advanced they all came together to create the *ethnosphere*, the composite sphere of human cultures.

13. Many scriptures tell us that the seed of innate or intrinsic knowing is planted within each human. This is also based on the Law of One: we are One Being, there is One Creator, One Mind, One Soul. This is intrinsic knowledge in the process of creation. The teaching of absolute monotheism says this in Islam and Christianity as well as the teachings of the buddhadharma.

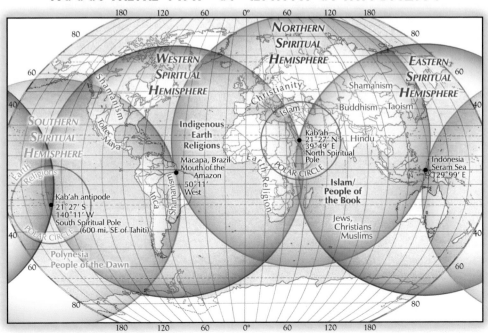

NOOSPHERE MAP OF EARTH SPIRITUALITY

14. Every creature, every blade of grass, contains the seed of enlightenment, or in the absolute monotheist teachings it says that every being is implanted with the knowledge of the Creator, of the oneness. All of life, every molecule, every grain of sand has the seed of unity, preconscious, unconscious or conscious.

UNITY OF COSMOS AND POWER OF THE SELF-EXISTING FOUR

15. The cosmos is one unity. The earliest humans knew that everything comes from the sky. God sends down rain from the sky in a land that was previously lifeless and it becomes teeming with life. This is a parable for people who understand. It is a parable not only for rain but for all the spiritual teachings that come down and give life.

16. At the beginning of the evolution of self-reflective intelligence, is one earth—the place that accommodates all levels of unfolding evolution, the stage set where our cosmic tale takes place. Everything that can be dreamed of in the cosmos is happening here, has happened here, or will happen here in the process of cosmic evolution.

17. The earth is divided into four quarters that represent the four phases of the moon: the full moon, the half moon, the new moon and the first quarter. This is part of the divine intelligence system of Mother Earth. Everyone is imprinted with the power of the number of four—the number of measure. This is the basis of indigenous spirituality. From this basis, every people evolve a particular psychomythology of creation to help understand the questions of the mystery of life: How did we get here? Why are we here? Who is the Creator? Who placed us here and for what purpose? These are important questions to contemplate.

18. Creation myths of many cultures often speak of going from one place to another; from one world to another, like with the Hopi moving through different worlds up to the present world. This is similar to the monotheistic tradition with stories such as Noah going from one place to another, whether that was on earth or different world systems or the myths of Atlantis. Australian aborigines say we came from the dreaming, through the water until we arrived here.

19. Every tradition and/or religion has a type of psychocultural perception of how we arrived on this planet at this time. From this comes the development of earth religions and shamanism. The original mind was cosmically attuned and so could receive information directly from the elements. People learned by com-

muning with nature, and listening to the messages of the animals and plants, who would say, "don't pick me, pick that one."

20. From this attunement developed a self-reflective sense that human life repeats a cosmic pattern or ritual, like the phases of the moon, the four stages of life. Even advanced world teachers like Buddha gave his first teachings based on the number four: the Four Noble Truths. We see the imprint of the four within nature, with the four seasons, four directions, and the four phases of the moon out of which spring 28 lunar mansions and the power of the number 7.

21. From these primary earth religions with their initiations, ceremonies and rituals evolved stages of civilization that are characterized by sky religion (such as astrological/zodiacal sky religions as demonstrated by the Egyptians, Mesopotamians, Babylonians and Chinese who studied patterns of the sky). There is a difference between the earlier earth religions and the early stages of civilized religions.

22. Earth religions revolve around the sky, moon, earth, sun and stars; the natural world. The first stage of so-called civilized religion is fundamentally based on the movements of stars, planets, etc, with a much more mathematical/astronomical sensibility. This is pure cosmic sky teaching. It is interesting to contemplate the relation of our home planet to the other moving planets and to the fixed stars. These fixed stars create patterns that can be interpreted as patterns of destiny.

23. Many earth religions revolve around specific initiations signifying an advance from one state of consciousness to another. With each initiation comes certain knowledge. Before you had the initiation you did not have that knowledge (see *Book of the Initiation*). The act of initiation with the proper intention increases knowledge and consciousness. These are patterns in the steps of ascent, indicating that we are in a continuous process of ascending from earth to sky. This is a fundamental point in the magnetic teaching of the cosmic sky wisdom.

EARTH RELIGIONS

24. In both early civilized religion as well as earth religion there are basic elements such as discipline, fasting, and forms of asceticism or abstaining in indulging the sensual body for periods of time in order to gain spiritual insight to reach another state of consciousness. For example, the purpose of a vision quest is to relinquish your third-dimensional sensory body in order that you may receive a Spirit vision. A vision quest generally requires going into nature, often with no food, and sitting for however long is necessary until a vision or dream occurs or some creature comes along and gives you a clear message to take back to the people of your tribe or clan.

25. In these earth religions there naturally arise ethical codes and laws. On one hand there is a spiritual quality to the laws of learning; the qualities of patience, restraint and exertion, which are also part of the codes of conduct. Through practice we come to realize that it is not only in doing, but in refraining from doing that we learn.

26. Codes of ethics are meant to take us inward and upward. This is a basic mechanism of the cosmic sky teachings: What takes you inward, takes you upward. What draws you back from your senses is also what brings you upward into spiritual insight and perception. This dialectic between the sensory world and the world of going inward and withdrawing from the senses is also an essential dynamic of cosmic sky teachings. This teaching is in response to a deep aspiration of spirit that appears at every level, from the earth religions to the so-called more advanced traditional religions.

27. Another common feature of cosmic sky teachings is the need of teachers, seers, messengers or prophets who appear in both earth religions and also in civilized religions. For example, in the nineteenth century there was Lavoka, who was inspired with the ghost dance religion, and then there is the peyote religion, etc.

28. Often in earth religions, such as those of the Native Americans, someone will have a vision then they will come back and say, this is what I heard. An example is Deganawida who lived in the fifteenth or sixteenth century and formed the Iroquois Confederacy, the confederacy of the six nations or Indian tribes in the northeastern part of North America. He was marked out early as a Seer.

29. Deganawida had a vision and said, "I represent the life of the mind of the master of light." He then gave teachings on the remembrance of the Creator. He regarded the Master of Light as the creator of ourselves and of the universe. There are certain teachings that he has given us: righteousness, health, and cultivation of good mind. These were the fundamental messages of Deganawida who was a messenger and prophet among the Creator people.

30. Indigenous tribes and seers appear from time to time in the modern world in response to the advent of white colonialism in order to leave prophetic messages for the people. The essential message is the recognition that there is only One Creator or One Source; and to always remember and acknowledge this Creator.

31. The Hopi prophecies say that great world systems come to an end when the remembrance (and worship) of the One Creator falls into great abandon or is neglected. Only a handful of people remember the worship of the One Creator. These are the ones who

are saved and advance from one world system to the next. Reverence for the earth is a basic message fundamental to earth religions.

From Earth Tradition to Traditional Religion

32. With the advent of different civilizations came more complex and evolved teachings, including revealed teachings, religions and messianic prophecies containing new seeds of enlightenment. These reflect a will to understand the nature of cosmic mind with different localized terms to different people of different cultures. For example, in the Middle East about 1,000 years before Christ came the development of Zoroastrianism based on the teachings of Zarathustra (Zoroaster). His spirit path began with a revelation. He was rejected by his people and had to leave his homeland and pray to the God of Light to give him teachings. Then he came back and gave these teachings to his people. Some of these teachings are still observed in the present day.

33. Some of the first evolved scriptures originated in India, beginning in 200-1500 BC, including the Upanishads, the Vedas and the Bhagavad Gita were developed. Each of these sacred texts contains an elaborate cosmology and sophisticated psychophysiology. At the root of these teachings is the art and science of yoga. Yoga is the essence of the will to the cosmic sky teachings, an ongoing theme that runs throughout the *Cosmic History Chronicles.* From these foundational teachings in India came the development of Jainism in the sixth century, which practices a more extreme form of ascetiscm while promoting the universal teaching of Ahimsa—non-violence or non-harm to any living creature.

34. Shortly after the development of Jainism by messenger Mahavira, came the teachings of Gautama Sakyamuni Buddha. Buddha incarnated in the seventh baktun, the precise midpoint of the Mayan 13 Baktun long count that spans from 3113 BC to 2012 AD. At the time, Buddha's teachings were unique from other religious teachings, as they emphasized controlling and taming the mind rather than emphasizing God or Creator. Buddha focused on the practical facts of life: Birth, suffering, old age and death, and asks the primary question: What are we to do with this life?

35. The teachings of Buddha are vast and cosmic (see *CHC Vol. II*). When he first began teaching he was uncertain if anyone would understand what he had to teach. Buddha taught that all suffering comes from mind. This was his basic teaching. He taught that this human life is precious as it affords us the opportunity to cultivate discipline and control of our mind so that good qualities such as love and compassion might arise.

36. Buddha supposedly gave different levels of teachings, such as the Hinayana and Vajrayana levels. In the Mahayana text *Lotus Sutras of the True Law*, Buddha says, "I teach only one vehicle of the law and there is only one law, all my other teachings are tactful teachings." This means he was expressing tact or skillful means to the different levels of mind.

37. Buddha gave Hinayana teachings for those people who are really hung up in this world and think they need to follow strict rules. For others he gave the Mahayana teachings of the bodhisattvas, etc. The essence of the Mahayana teaching is *sunyata*, form is emptiness and emptiness is form. Buddha always gave the same teaching, but in different ways according to the disposition of the individual being.

BODHISATTVA VOW

A bodhisattva is one who postpones his/her own achievement of nirvana in order to help all sentient beings attain enlightenment. The bodhisattva vow is a cosmic vow: "Sentient beings are infinite and without number, I vow to enlighten them all. My delusions are inexhaustible; I vow to extinguish them all. The dharma teachings (teachings of the law of the truth) are without measure, I vow to master them all; and the Buddha way is endless, I vow to follow it."

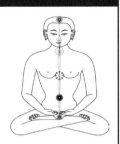

   The bodhisattva vow defines the path of cosmic evolution. Once you are finished with this world system you go to another world system and see what you can do. Chögyam Trungpa Rinpoche said only when we have picked up every last piece of plastic here can we go to the next world. This summarizes the essence of the bodhisattva vow.

BUDDHA, CHRIST AND MUHAMMAD

38. In the Middle East also exists the prophetic tradition of Abraham, Moses, Christ and finally Muhammad. The three most famous religious teachers were Buddha, Christ and Muhammad. But the ones who most specifically started a religion were Buddha and Muhammad. Muhammad said that Islam is the true religion or the religion of submission. Islamic religion is laid out in five simple rules to have certainty and faith in 1) God; 2) the angels; 3) revealed texts; 4) the messengers; and 5) the Hereafter. Some people add a sixth point, which is predestination.

39. At the first stage of his teachings, Buddha talked about Nirvana, but Nirvana was just extinction so that was difficult to understand. In later Buddhist teachings are prescribed the recitation of mantras until you arrive at the pure land of paradise, which is like the heaven of the monotheistic religions.

40. Both Buddha and Muhammad gave the vision of their particular path and steps to reach the final goal. Muhammad in the Holy Quran lays out steps of prayer (Salat), fasting (Ramadan), pilgrimage to Mecca (Hajj) if possible and charity (Zakat). These are the requirements to be a Muslim. Likewise, Jesus advocated fasting, tithing, prayer and worship of God alone to his followers. Jesus is highly regarded in the Quran as one of God's key messengers.

41. Buddhism and Islam represent the two extremes of the cosmic sky teachings. Buddhism seems to represent a plane, level or dimension of an already evolved paranormalcy; whereas Islam represents a popular form of understanding the teachings based on the one Creator: *La ilaha illallah,* there is no God but God; there is only One God and Muhammad is his prophet.

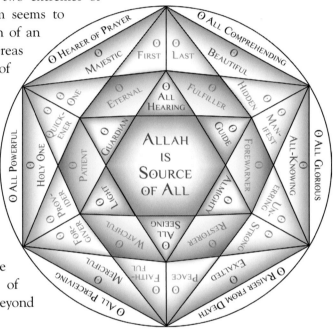

42. In the Quran and other Islamic texts we are told of the different names and qualities of God (Allah) with phenomenal attributes. It is said that when one recites these names that it reveals a revelation of God as an ultimate mind that is beyond even the cosmos.

43. Buddhist teachings refer to *dharmakaya,* meaning whatever thought arises, its nature is dharmakaya—which is nothing whatsoever, yet everything arises from it. It is the same in Islam when they say that Allah has no form and the law has no form. When meditated on, much similarity arises between the Islamic teachings of the one law with its descriptions of Allah and the dharmakaya with its formless characteristics from which everything arises. These teachings create a continuum of two antipodes that come together.

44. Virtually all world religions and teachings developed at a time when knowledge of the whole earth was not yet conscious in the collective mind. For example, Buddha said the Hinayana teachings are for people hung up on rules and regulations, just as in Islam came the development of the shariah: the laws and legislation created by people based on their interpretations of Muhammad's words, which may or may not be true. The point is that these are interpretations of teachings at a specific time.

45. Christianity is based on Christ's teachings, though the religion itself was not invented by Christ. Then there is orthodox Christianity and the Roman Catholic Church, as well as the Protestant Reformation (1519) that spawned numerous Protestant sects. This was the same year as the conquest of Mexico. All of this occurred before there was a self-reflective intelligence of human beings that understood that we are all members of one earth—and if there is one earth and one mind, then we participate in the same mind. This means that all the seemingly different belief systems must stem from one Source.

46. With the awareness of the whole earth mind came further religious and spiritual teachings, particularly after the beginning of the scientific revolution in the 13th baktun. At this point, new seeds of enlightenment were planted in the collective mind by yogis, seers and esoteric teachers. People began to grow out of traditional forms of religion and there emerged a resurrection of nature religions such as Wicca, New Age religions as well as UFO religions and crop circle communities. These are signs of cosmic sky teachings implanted in the earth. All of this is part of an unfolding stage of evolution into the noosphere, the sphere of spiritual unification on earth.

47. A quantum shift is now occurring and soon the mind of the entire species will rapidly unify in the awareness of itself as one mind everywhere. Simultaneously, each person will retain autonomy and individuality. The collective realization that we are all participating in the same One Mind will melt historical barriers of conflicting spiritual traditions. These barriers only exist because we have yet to experience the collective realization of the One Mind of Earth.

48. All cosmic sky teachings lead to the great unification of the planetary mind and then to the anticipated ascent of the supermind. Indian seer and philosopher Sri Aurobindo was a forerunner in this realization and was able to articulate the descent of supermind into the physical realm, and into the whole evolution of the species. After experiencing a descent of the Overmind or supramind in 1926, Sri Aurobindo saw that this was the destiny of the evolution of the human species and earth; going into higher stages or degrees in the evolution of the mind. This is the fundamental crux of the revelation of the cosmic sky teachings. There is only one mind of cosmic enlightenment throughout the universe; and we are now penetrating into that mind—the noosphere.

RECENT COSMIC SKY TEACHINGS

49. Pacal Votan represents the quintessence of cosmic sky teachings as he transmigrated from previous world systems in order to embody and represent all traditions. What is the ultimate purpose of all the messengers? They have a unified mission to establish a basis of moral teachings for

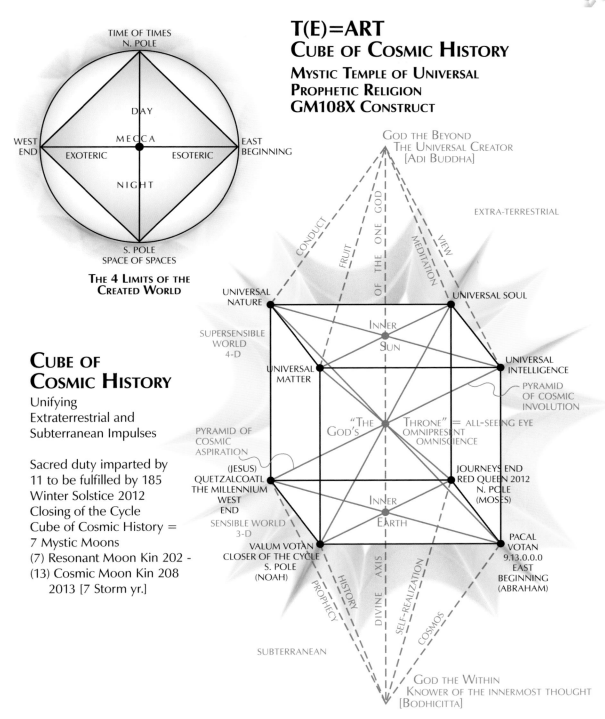

TIME OF TIMES
N. POLE

DAY

MECCA

WEST
END
EXOTERIC   ESOTERIC

EAST
BEGINNING

NIGHT

S. POLE
SPACE OF SPACES

**THE 4 LIMITS OF THE
CREATED WORLD**

T(E)=ART
CUBE OF COSMIC HISTORY
MYSTIC TEMPLE OF UNIVERSAL
PROPHETIC RELIGION
GM108X CONSTRUCT

GOD THE BEYOND
THE UNIVERSAL CREATOR
[ADI BUDDHA]

EXTRA-TERRESTRIAL

CONDUCT

FRUIT

OF THE ONE GOD

MEDITATION

VIEW

UNIVERSAL
NATURE

UNIVERSAL SOUL

INNER
SUN

SUPERSENSIBLE
WORLD
4-D

UNIVERSAL
MATTER

UNIVERSAL
INTELLIGENCE

PYRAMID
OF COSMIC
INVOLUTION

"THE
GOD'S

THRONE" = ALL-SEEING EYE
OMNIPRESENT
OMNISCIENCE

PYRAMID OF
COSMIC
ASPIRATION

(JESUS)
QUETZALCOATL
THE MILLENNIUM
WEST
END

JOURNEYS END
RED QUEEN 2012
N. POLE
(MOSES)

CUBE OF
COSMIC HISTORY

Unifying
Extraterrestrial and
Subterranean Impulses

Sacred duty imparted by
11 to be fulfilled by 185
Winter Solstice 2012
Closing of the Cycle
Cube of Cosmic History =
7 Mystic Moons
(7) Resonant Moon Kin 202 -
(13) Cosmic Moon Kin 208
2013 [7 Storm yr.]

SENSIBLE WORLD
3-D

INNER
EARTH

PACAL
VOTAN
9.13.0.0.0
EAST
BEGINNING
(ABRAHAM)

VALUM VOTAN
CLOSER OF THE CYCLE
S. POLE
(NOAH)

HISTORY

PROPHECY

DIVINE AXIS

SELF-REALIZATION

COSMOS

SUBTERRANEAN

GOD THE WITHIN
KNOWER OF THE INNERMOST THOUGHT
[BODHICITTA]

the resurrection of earth and the evolutionary redemption of the human being. The terrestrial resurrection was to be the final episode in an interplanetary drama rooted in the destruction of Maldek, the original Garden of Eden.

50. Within this Galactic Mayan dispensation that occurred in the New World with sages such as Pacal Votan and Quetzalcoatl in Central America and Kontiki Viracocha in South America, we have the famous Mayan calendar 2012 prophecy. This prophecy is a metaphor for a host of different teachings, cosmic perceptions and cosmic reformulations of the whole world order.

51. The dovetailing of the Mayan calendar 2012 prophecy with the advent of the noosphere creates the quantum shift that establishes the noosphere as the Overmind of the earth, the next stage of evolution in which we experience the unification and totality of the cosmic sky teachings as the unity of cosmic mind. At this stage we pass a threshold where we go from normal to paranormal. We are now entering this world.

52. In all the teachings from shamanism, Sufism, to tantric and yogic systems there are always special paranormal techniques, which only a few gifted people have the disposition to cultivate and develop. However, once we pass the threshold of the noosphere then those capacities or techniques, such as telekinesis, telepathy, displacement, time travel, etc., will become the new normalcy of the unity of the cosmic mind.

53. At this stage cosmic sky teachings will manifest through the advanced teachings of cosmic civilization, the Galactic Federation, the different realms of the planes of the Ascended Masters, the angelic orders and the mahabodhisattvas. The Galactic Federation is a particular constellation of cosmic civilization in this part of the universe. From the vantage point of the Galactic Federation, the cosmic sky teachings are the teachings that unify the evolving mind of the spiritual organism of a particular planet.

54. Lifting our mind above the earth, we can view the whole template of evolutionary unfolding and see everything that is happening, has happened or will happen is part of the Divine Order or Divine Plan; every single aspect of it. From this vantage point, the cosmic sky teachings can be seen as the teachings of our own spiritual evolution, or how our mind ascends into cosmic order. The *Cosmic History Chronicles* define the basics of this process of evolution of all the different world stages into ever greater stages of cosmic unity.

55. Soon, we will understand that we are all part of one mind. Once this is understood, then the intrinsic qualities of compassion and tolerance will become the norm of social behavior. Everything will change dramatically and radially as we move into a completely spiritualized universe.

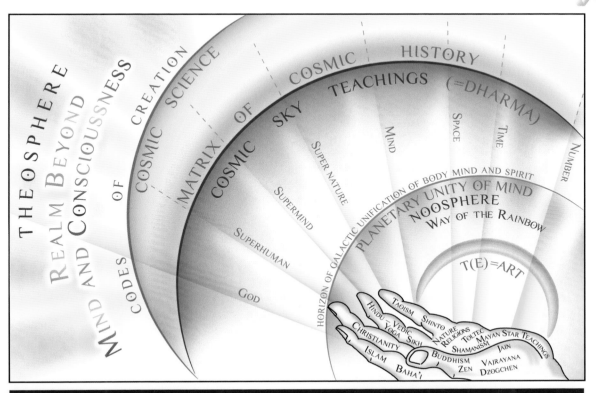

COSMIC SKY RELIGION

The concept of cosmic sky teachings originated with Genghis Khan and Kublah Khan—the Mongolians—when they were confronting different people in China and other places. They said all of you people and your different religious are just like the fingers of one hand. They said, "We are from the cosmic sky religion, we are the whole hand."

CHAPTER 7

COSMIC SCIENCE AND ELEMENTAL ORDER
CUBE AND TRIUNE: BALANCING OF TRIPLE POLARITY

1. We are entering a new mind within a new timespace: the unified mind of earth; the noosphere made known as the reflective medium of the cosmic sky teachings. This is a post-historical, post-religious mind; a mind of pure attunement within this vast reality that has hitherto gone unnoticed.

COSMIC HISTORY IS THE SPIRITUALIZATION OF EVOLUTION

2. A new world awaits us on the other side of the historical mind stream. In this new world, Spirit reigns with a precise science devoid of familiar terminologies or references of figures or personalities in the way we now think of them. Knowledge is presented as a pure construct.

3. The primary cosmology of cosmic sky teachings is that spirituality is the consciousness of a cosmological unfolding. Cosmic sky teachings await us as a collective species on the other side of the threshold of the quantum mind shift. This is a cosmology unlike the cosmologies on this side of the threshold with the big bang cosmology or "God created the earth and heaven in seven days" cosmology.

4. The cosmology of cosmic sky teaching is represented by mind, time, space and number that together reveal the unfolding unity of the cosmic mind of enlightenment. This cosmic mind of enlightenment is a declaration of the divine or sacred order of reality as it actually exists, has always existed and will always exist throughout the order of the universe. All sky teachings further the conscious unity of the cosmic order as an evolutionary unfolding.

5. This evolutionary unfolding that we refer to as mind, is an intermediate term or medium of learning. Cosmic evolution, at one stage, invents mind so there can be a self-reflective medium or a stage of growth of self-reflective consciousness. When that mind reaches a peak of absolute consciousness, then the mind itself is transcended and in some cases, the body dissolved (as in the case of the Spectral Magician, Valum Votan, who left us the sky teachings and then vanished into the next dimension).

COSMOLOGY OF COSMIC SKY TEACHINGS
PRIMARY DIMENSIONAL ORDERS

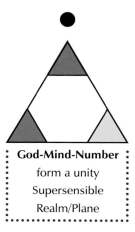

God-Mind-Number
form a unity
Supersensible
Realm/Plane

- **God** is the Lord of the Worlds, the Creator known by one name or another by every people and culture throughout the cosmos.

- **Mind** as the creative medium of perception and cognition.

- **Number,** the self existing underlying matrix of mathematical order governing the universe are the extensions of the ceaselessly all sustaining nature of God the Creator.

This triadic primary supersensible unity simultaneously establishes a secondary counter-point sensory unity: Time, Space and Galaxy.

- **Time** is the counterpoint of Number and establishes moving patterns of cyclic order, synchronically cognizable through harmonic numbers.

- **Space** is the counterpoint of **Mind** and establishes a medium of infinite extensibility cognizable by mind as the medium of self-existing awareness capable of being defined as a center and an organizing set of directions which establish crystallizations of form.

Time-Space-Galaxy
form a unity
Sensible
Realm/Plane

- **Galaxy** is the counterpoint of **God** and is the physical plane manifestation of creative interaction of mind, number, time and space creatively shaped, formed, guided and directed by God to become the diversity of ever evolving forms accommodating the spiritual evolution of cosmic consciousness (cognized as totality of astrobiophysics)

CENTER: Inner Realm of Cosmic Consciousness & Spiritual Evolution

3 AXES: 1) God–Galaxy = channel of creative commands
2) Time–Number = channel of telepathic coordination
3) Mind–Space = channel of cosmic perceptions

INNER CORE: Supermind moved by ceaseless operations of dynamic movement & measure (a.k.a. Buddha Mind or Mind of Enlightenment)

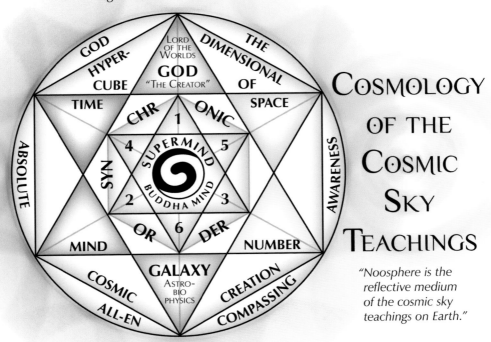

COSMOLOGY OF THE COSMIC SKY TEACHINGS

"Noosphere is the reflective medium of the cosmic sky teachings on Earth."

SUPERMIND EXPRESSIONS {

Inner super-sensible plane:

1) Spiritual Law	2) Science of Mind	3) Science of Number
4) Law of Time	5) Law of Space	6) Evolutionary Law (Law of Cosmic Evolution)

Inner sensible plane: Inner medium, Synchronic order, "Sea of Synchronicity"

Outer enclosing mediums:

1) Hyperdimensional cube of cosmic creation*
0) God - the Absolute All-encompassing Sphere of Self-Existing Awareness

*cube = supreme law of form & cosmic consciousness

TWO PRINCIPLE QUALITIES OF CONSCIOUSNESS

6. Cosmic sky teachings bring us two main principle qualities of consciousness from the Other Side of the threshold: the Cube (all equalizing principle) and the Trina or Triune principle (all-unifying principle).

First Principle: Cube

The cube is the all-equalizing principle. The "cubing of reality" refers to this collective equalization process of complete unification that will engender a permanent harmonic convergence. The world at the end of the cycle is filled with injustice, inequality, oppression, disorder and chaos—the balance is lost. The cube represents the equalizing factor of consciousness. All faces within the cube are the same with equal sides that are equidistant from the center. The vertices and lines that connect at different points are all equal. The cube is the epitome of all-equalizing consciousness. This is important to contemplate and understand as we are coming into a new mind and a new consciousness.

In this new mind and consciousness there is a natural disappearances of qualities we see in the world now, such as inequality, tyranny, competition, injustice, etc. These qualities were stages of growth for the human, but have no place in the reality of the cube. In this new cube consciousness there are different stages of growth, but within a spectrum of equality.

Second Principle: Trina or Triune Principle

The Trina or Triune is the all-unifying principle. This principle is represented by the circle of mind of unity and then a triangle. The triangle has three primary principles: Red Kuali (positive), Blue Duar (negative) and Neutron (equalizing or neutral).

These three principles occur in any atomic, subatomic, galactic or stellar system. This is why everything remains unified. This principle of unity comes from the *universal chromatic trilogy*. There are three primary colors: red, blue and yellow. These three primary colors combine to make the fourth color, white.

The time color cube contains three red triangles, three white triangles, three blue triangles and three yellow triangles that create four nested tetrahedron. These are actually basic spiritual principles based on 2, 3 and 3, 4.

The binary triplet can be viewed as a triune principle—a triple polarity. The triple polarity consists of: positive and negative; neutral with positive; and neutral with negative. This creates a dynamic unification which is at the center of every phenomenon of cosmic reality.

When we unfold the trina principle, three fold, we have the ***trina evolutionary wave unit***—this is a quantum movement with two sides: material and conscious. The material goes from the

COSMIC SKY TEACHINGS – TEACHINGS OF THE UNITY OF COSMIC MIND
PRIMARY COSMOLOGY – UNDERSTANDING OF SPIRITUALITY AS COSMOLOGICAL UNFOLDING
Mind of Cosmic Enlightenment – Intrinsic Unfolding of the
Divine (Sacred, Holy) Order of Creation – The World of Tomorrow

All Sky Teachings further the conscious unity of the cosmic order as an evolutionary unfolding – mind is an intermediate term.

Two Principles:

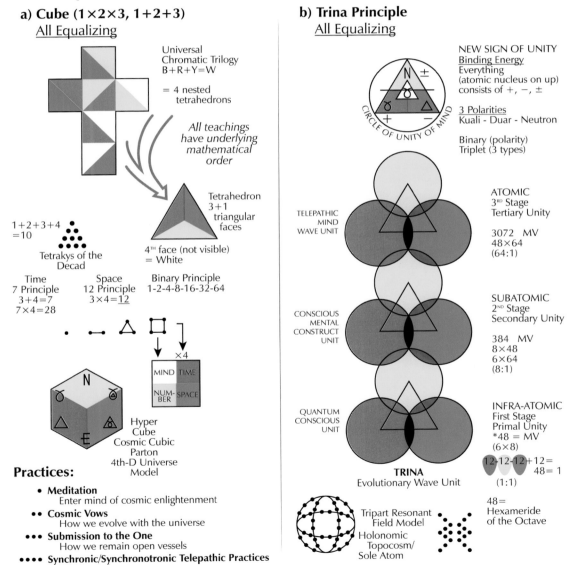

a) Cube (1×2×3, 1+2+3)
<u>All Equalizing</u>

Universal
Chromatic Trilogy
B+R+Y=W

= 4 nested
tetrahedrons

*All teachings
have underlying
mathematical
order*

Tetrahedron
3+1
triangular
faces

4TH face (not visible)
= White

1+2+3+4
=10
Tetrakys of the
Decad

Time
7 Principle
3+4=7
7×4=28

Space
12 Principle
3×4=12

Binary Principle
1-2-4-8-16-32-64

×4

MIND	TIME
NUM-BER	SPACE

Hyper
Cube
Cosmic Cubic
Parton
4th-D Universe
Model

Practices:
- **Meditation**
  Enter mind of cosmic enlightenment
- **Cosmic Vows**
  How we evolve with the universe
- **Submission to the One**
  How we remain open vessels
- **Synchronic/Synchronotronic Telepathic Practices**

b) Trina Principle
<u>All Equalizing</u>

CIRCLE OF UNITY OF MIND

NEW SIGN OF UNITY
<u>Binding Energy</u>
Everything
(atomic nucleus on up)
consists of +, −, ±

<u>3 Polarities</u>
Kuali - Duar - Neutron

Binary (polarity)
Triplet (3 types)

TELEPATHIC
MIND
WAVE UNIT

ATOMIC
3RD Stage
Tertiary Unity

3072 MV
48×64
(64:1)

CONSCIOUS
MENTAL
CONSTRUCT
UNIT

SUBATOMIC
2ND Stage
Secondary Unity

384 MV
8×48
6×64
(8:1)

QUANTUM
CONSCIOUS
UNIT

INFRA-ATOMIC
First Stage
Primal Unity
*48 = MV
(6×8)

12-12-12+12=
48= 1
(1:1)

48=
Hexameride
of the Octave

TRINA
Evolutionary Wave Unit

Tripart Resonant
Field Model
Holonomic
Topocosm/
Sole Atom

infra-atomic, to subatomic, to atomic—where there is a valuation of 12 + 12 + 12 + 12 = 48; and each 12 with the four creates 48 = Red (12) + Blue (12) + Yellow (12) + White (12).

The second level has an 8:1 ratio of 48, 384, 3072 (48 x 64). These are microvolts that represent units of consciousness. The first level is a quantum conscious unit; the second level is a conscious mental construct unit; the third level is a telepathic mind wave unit. The quantum conscious unit has a frequency of 48 microvolts; conscious mental construct unit has a frequency of 384 microvolts; telepathic mind wave unit has a frequency of 3072 microvolts.

7.   When everything is equalized and unified then we will live in a constant harmonic convergence. These teachings are presented not as a particular doctrine but as visual constructs.

Mind, time, number and space are the basic units of the cosmology of consciousness of the cosmic sky teachings. At the simplest level we have manifestation of the cube and each face of the cube is subdivided into four parts: mind, time, space and number. There are 6 x 4 spaces, which is 24 permutations. This is represented by a double serpent. Its tails are intertwined as a unity and are facing each other. This represents the absolute past and the absolute future coming together to create the primal circle of the unity of the cosmic mind. This encloses the cube and is the essence of the cosmic sky teachings. When all of these principles come together, they create the actual complex of cosmos or universe. This becomes the basic unit of the cosmology of consciousness of the cosmic sky teachings.

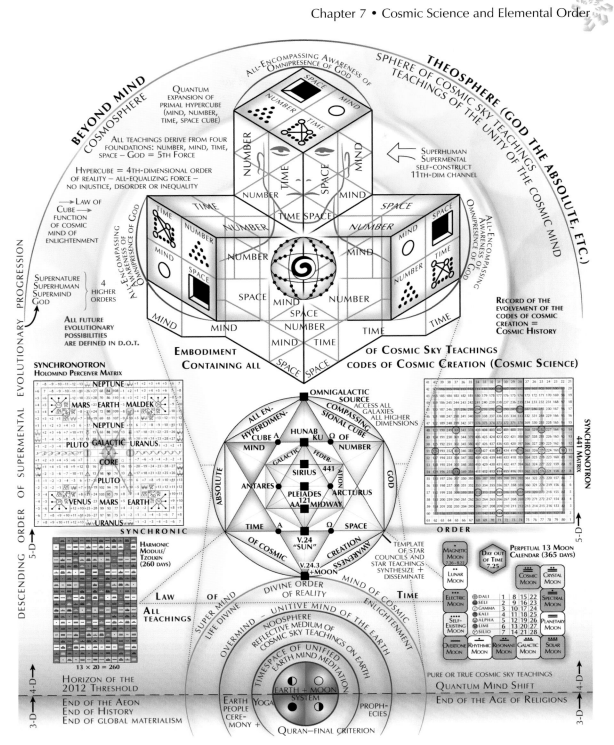

BEYOND MIND

COSMOSPHERE

QUANTUM EXPANSION OF PRIMAL HYPERCUBE (MIND, NUMBER, TIME, SPACE CUBE)

ALL TEACHINGS DERIVE FROM FOUR FOUNDATIONS: NUMBER, MIND, TIME, SPACE – GOD = 5TH FORCE

HYPERCUBE = 4TH-DIMENSIONAL ORDER OF REALITY – ALL-EQUALIZING FORCE – NO INJUSTICE, DISORDER OR INEQUALITY

LAW OF CUBE → FUNCTION OF COSMIC MIND OF ENLIGHTENMENT

SUPERNATURE SUPERHUMAN SUPERMIND GOD } 4 HIGHER ORDERS

ALL FUTURE EVOLUTIONARY POSSIBILITIES ARE DEFINED IN D.O.T.

ALL-ENCOMPASSING AWARENESS OF OMNIPRESENCE OF GOD

SPHERE OF COSMIC SKY TEACHINGS (GOD THE ABSOLUTE, ETC.)

THEOSPHERE

TEACHINGS OF THE UNITY OF THE COSMIC MIND

SUPERHUMAN SUPERMENTAL SELF-CONSTRUCT 11TH-DIM CHANNEL

ALL-ENCOMPASSING AWARENESS OF OMNIPRESENCE OF GOD

RECORD OF THE EVOLVEMENT OF THE CODES OF COSMIC CREATION = COSMIC HISTORY

EMBODIMENT CONTAINING ALL

of COSMIC SKY TEACHINGS CODES OF COSMIC CREATION (COSMIC SCIENCE)

DESCENDING ORDER OF SUPERMENTAL EVOLUTIONARY PROGRESSION

SYNCHRONOTRON
HOLOMIND PERCEIVER MATRIX

NEPTUNE
MARS · EARTH · MALDEK
NEPTUNE
PLUTO GALACTIC URANUS
CORE
PLUTO
VENUS · MARS · EARTH
URANUS

SYNCHRONIC

HARMONIC MODULE/ TZOLKIN (260 DAYS)

13 × 20 = 260

HORIZON OF THE 2012 THRESHOLD

END OF THE AEON
END OF HISTORY
END OF GLOBAL MATERIALISM

OMNIGALACTIC SOURCE
ACCESS ALL GALAXIES ALL HIGHER DIMENSIONS

ALL EN-COMPASSIONAL CUBE
HYPERDIMEN-CUBE A
MIND

HUNAB KU

Ω OF NUMBER

GALACTIC FEDER-ATION

SIRIUS 441

GOD

ANTARES

PLEIADES
AA · MIDWAY
121

ARCTURUS

ABSOLUTE

TIME

A
V.24 "SUN"
V.24.3 +MOON

SPACE

OF COSMIC CREATION

AWARENESS

MIND OF COSMIC

TEMPLATE OF STAR COUNCILS AND STAR TEACHINGS SYNTHESIZE + DISSEMINATE

LAW OF
ALL TEACHINGS

SUPER MIND
LIFE DIVINE

DIVINE ORDER
OF REALITY

OVERMIND – UNITIVE MIND OF THE EARTH

NOOSPHERE
REFLECTIVE MEDIUM OF COSMIC SKY TEACHINGS ON EARTH

TIMESPACE OF UNIFIED EARTH MIND MEDITATION

EARTH + MOON SYSTEM

EARTH PEOPLE
YOGA
CERE-MONY +

PROPH-ECIES

QURAN–FINAL CRITERION

MIND OF COSMIC

ENLIGHTENMENT

TIME

MAGNETIC MOON 7.26 - 8.22	DAY OUT OF TIME 7.25	PERPETUAL 13 MOON CALENDAR (365 DAYS)	
LUNAR MOON		COSMIC MOON	CRYSTAL MOON
ELECTRIC MOON	DALI 1 8 15 22	SPECTRAL MOON	
	SELI 2 9 16 23		
	GAMMA 3 10 17 24		
SELF-EXISTING MOON	KALI 4 11 18 25	PLANETARY MOON	
	ALPHA 5 12 19 26		
	LIMI 6 13 20 27		
	SILIO 7 14 21 28		
OVERTONE MOON	RHYTHMIC MOON	RESONANT MOON	GALACTIC MOON	SOLAR MOON

SYNCHRONOTRON 441 MATRIX

ORDER

PURE OR TRUE COSMIC SKY TEACHINGS
QUANTUM MIND SHIFT

END OF THE AGE OF RELIGIONS

5-D   4-D   3-D   D-3   D-4   D-5

In the graphic on the previous page, we see the explosion of the primal cube that has on each face mind, time, space and number. This explodes out and creates all the various permutations of the universal cosmic order. Everything we look at or experience within the cosmic universal order is a manifestation of mind, a manifestation of space, a manifestation of time and a manifestation of number. We are in a particular space. We are in a particular time. We are experiencing a particular quality of mind. If we look beneath the surface of things we see different combinations of numbers and geometries. These are the four foundations: mind, time, space and number.

The four higher orders that are evolved from these four foundations are: supermind, supernature and superhuman—all of which is overseen by the Absolute One or God (the fourth). The totality of universe as we know it represents the cosmosphere. Beyond the cosmosphere is the Absolute beyond, the theosphere, or sphere of God or the sphere of the unity of the One that is beyond. This Absolute Reality contains everything, creates everything and at the same time is beyond everything.

COSMOLOGICAL UNFOLDING AND THE HYPERCUBE

8. Cosmic sky teachings illustrate that spirituality is a cosmological unfolding that coincides with the principles of the unfolding of cosmic science. The primary structures are not just geometrical or mathematical, but are also infused with spiritual value and teachings. These spiritual teachings are contained in the cube, in the tetrahedron, and in the three primary colors. They are also contained in the sole atom and within the holonomic topocosm, the resonant field model.

9. When these principles are meditated on with a pure mind then the actual spiritual reality begins to begins to open up; this is the reality that brings us into alignment with the Absolute Cosmic Nature. This is the primary cosmology of the cosmic sky teachings with the two basic principles: all-equalizing (cube) and all-unifying (trina).

10. From a fourth-dimensional vantage point, the universe resembles a hypercube. Everything we can conceive of is contained in and manifests within that cube. This hypercube is an all-equalizing reality, just like the nature of the cosmic mind of enlightenment that pervades the entire universe and is equally present everywhere.

11. This cosmic mind of enlightenment is equally present in an atom, a star, in the space between galaxies, etc.—it pervades everything. The cube is a function of the cosmic mind of enlightenment and is simultaneously held together by the cosmic mind of enlightenment. It is the embodiment of the 11th dimensional channel that contains all possibilities of the codes of cosmic creation. The codes consist of different elements of mind, time, space and number. All of the codes of cosmic creation and cosmic science are based on these four elements.

12. Cosmic History is the registration of the evolvement of these codes: mind, time, space and number, that goes from lower states of instinct of the unconscious to higher levels of superconscious; and finally to the evolution of cosmic civilization, the cosmic mind and cosmic enlightenment that pervades all reality.

REALITY IS A RADIAL MATRIX

13. The unity of God is one in the simultaneity of the radial matrix. Everything that is, ever was, or will be is happening now in the present moment within the radial matrix. This fact is almost incomprehensible to the conceptual mind. The Divine Order that is created is one.

14. One aspect of Divine Order is the allowance of imperfection (as perceived by the human mind). But even imperfection is perfect. Imperfection is necessary for evolution to exist. This is something that should be meditated on. The paradox of imperfection is the basis of cosmic evolution. These paradoxes puzzle the lower mind. But when viewed from the higher dimensions, everything is perceived as evolving within the matrix of perfect order.

15. Within this paradox is the possibility and necessity of evolving imperfection to perfection. We are at the midpoint of understanding this. The midpoint hinge rests on the quantum shift from the historical cycle and the end of the age of religion to crossing the threshold where awaits the new pristine spirituality or the pure truth of the cosmic sky teachings. Be prepared when the opportunity arises to make the giant leap.

16. We are pure consciousness within the evolving order of the universe. Out of 7 billion humans, no two energy patterns are like. We have developed a capacity for self-reflection that manifests in unique patterns that differ from being to being. How do we manifest our unique energy pattern? This is a process of cosmic memory retrieval. Let us first review the five stages of human evolution according to Cosmic Science.

Five Stages of Human Evolution
(according to Cosmic Science)

I. Humanoid. Characterized by anxiety, fear and lack of intentional activity with undeveloped mental spheres. So the first stage is full of adrenaline and anxiety attacks. This stage lasts around 25,000 or 40,000 years. The cycles are fractals—so this can be seen as one 26,000-unit cycle of human evolutionary development. In the science of time, four of these 26,000-year (one unit) cycles create one large evolutionary season. We are now closing a 104,000-year seasonal cycle. These cycles go on and on—but the point is we are closing the 104,000-year season. According to this standard of the Law of Time, the humanoid would account for the time between 104,000 and 52,000 years ago.

II. Cavernicala (caveman) between 52,000 and 26,000 years ago.
Reactive mind, initiated from the instinct of conservation. At this point, humans began to live in tribal groups learning the rudiments of language. The states of anxiety caused their mind to grow. The human operates on the reactive mind and begins intelligently using his instincts. Here the mental spheres have acquired a specific size in order to produce thinking/intentional activity at the beginning stage. It is also through discharges previously mentioned that there follows the expansion of its mental spheres, thus producing the accumulation of acquired experience.

III: Human. Pure intentional thinking stage. This is where the cosmic universal law of karma/dharma comes in along with the possibility of free will. There is a feedback for every choice you make. Cosmic Science says that planet Earth completed its third evolutionary stage on March 7, 1970. During this third stage, the two higher selves (masculine and feminine) interchanged with each other in order to acquire experience of one sex and then the other in each incarnation.
At this point the electrical discharges were clarified, energized and transformed into heptocubic plasmatic quantos. The purpose of this stage of evolution is to cultivate and develop the heptocubic quantos or the heptagonons of mind. The purpose of activating these heptagonons of mind is to facilitate the passage from the evolution of man to the superman
.

IV: Superhuman. The cultivation of the six (+1) mental spheres and their activations is a key point in the process of creating the heptagonon of mind in the superhuman. The superhuman says we are offered the opportunity to cross the threshold of consciousness. Once our intentional thinking or functioning operates at full capacity, then we can know and integrate the interior triad or the Higher Self. So the point of the completion of the human phase is to understand the heptagonons of mind, activating the mental spheres, then to cross over to the superman and unify the third-, fourth- and fifth-dimensional beings.

From the perspective of the Cosmic Science, only when the six (+1) mental spheres are unified in the human through the heptagonons of mind can we fully enter the superman phase and the continuing conscious intentional thinking layer that establishes the telepathic field on earth. At this point the twin human souls can connect.

V: Suprahuman. After the superman comes the stage of the *supraman* where the mental ratios are very high and work directly with the fifth-dimensional self. At this stage of evolution, beings are no longer subject to reincarnation and the aging process stops, karma/dharma ceases to function and while sexual activity may exist, it is not for procreation. At this point, cosmic engineering and biological engineering will be actively developed as even higher evolutionary options, such as the Cosmic Science overview on the matter of evolution.

Remembering Your Star Origins

17. The first step to remember your star origins is to bring to consciousness the fact that we are on a planet spinning on its axis and going around the Sun. Then bring to consciousness that every 26,000 years we make a 360-degree movement on the ecliptic. This helps us remember that as Earth citizens we are a part of a planetary unity.

18. Just as there was a progression up to the point of realizing ourselves as a planetary unity, so is there a progression from that point where we become aware of this. Not only do we know that we are a planet going around the Sun (thanks to the Copernican revolution), but we also know we are in a solar system that is part of a galaxy and the galaxy is one of 125 billion galaxies that constitute the entire cosmos. We didn't know that 150 years ago!

19. This represents a tremendous expansion of consciousness that marked the beginning of the influx of galactic or cosmic consciousness into our being. This knowledge provides a powerful basis for meditation on the infinite number of world systems, the infinite number of possibilities of evolution, the infinite number of times this has happened, and the infinite number of parallel universes available to explore!

20. When we cross the threshold—the quantum mind shift—we will fully understand and experience that the human being is merely a stage in the evolution of cosmic consciousness passing from a state of ignorance and disorder into a state of knowledge and order.

21. The number of minds engaged in this perception simultaneously is what creates that quantum mind shift that shifts us from the physical earth into the meditation of the timespace of the unified earth mind. In turn, this enters us into the totality or reality of the noosphere as the reflective medium of the cosmic sky teachings. At this stage we will experience the noospheric Overmind, as we grasp the totality of the planetary unity and the moment-to-moment synchronicity which the earth always experiences.

Synchronic Simultaneity

22. Earth is always experiencing night and day simultaneously. Earth is always experiencing summer and winter simultaneous and spring and autumn simultaneously. This synchronic simultaneity characterizes our own consciousness, a global synchronicity and global simultaneity—that is the Overmind or new mind of the noosphere that we are about to inherit or enter into.

23. Cosmic History helps define and lay out the various steps we need to cultivate this level of mind and consciousnesses so that when we cross the imminent threshold we enter into the vast space of the mind of cosmic enlightenment. These are the steps we must take to manifest cosmic enlightenment as a psychophysical hyperorganic construct projection of our unified mind. This is also what is referred to as *planet art whole* or *planet art spore*. This wonderful task will consume future generations for a specific period of time.

24. Once this planet art project is sufficiently realized then the portal opens to evolve into more immortal forms that are capable of assuming various form bodies for interdimensional travel. Despite surface appearances, this is the threshold that we are now crossing. The function of all of the codes of time is to ready ourselves and accelerate this process.

25. From the pure world of higher dimensions where the embodiment of cosmic sky teaching occurs, there are always downloads of information in various waves of comprehension and teachings that are appropriate for different stages and levels of the development of cosmic mind and consciousness.

26. In this process that we are now beginning to experience, the download goes into a complex usually referred to as a system of the Galactic Federation. The process of the Galactic Federation or unity of Galactic Federation is always to have different planets under surveillance, namely planets seen as dynamically unstable, in order to evaluate what has taken them from unconscious divided mind to a conscious unified mind. Our planet is one of these select planets.

Mind, Time, Number, Space and the Hypercube

27. The foundation of mind, time, number and space form a complex of a hyper-hyper hypercube around the system of the Galactic Federation. Within that system the different levels of teachings are disseminated. In the system of the cosmic sky teachings all teachings are based on color, number, geometry and sound.

28. The primary colors or the universal chromatic trilogy is one aspect of these teachings. Another aspect is the basis of number and mathematics which is also the basis of sound frequencies or music or tonalities. These qualities are all found within the new mind of cosmic sky teachings; color and number are of great pronounced significance, much more so than we might now perceive.

29. Related to this are the significance of the other senses: visual, tactile, auditory, olfactory and gustatory. As we enter the new mind, these qualities will become far more prominent as they represent

Valum Votan's Galactic Navigator Frequency Crystal

Showing 441 Lattice Underlying GM Interdimensional Star Map

$$\equiv\!\!\!-\ \text{4131}$$

[243×17] [153×27] (4000+131)
Kin equiv. 221 (17×13) 13 Dragon
BMU 162 (9²×2) V19,H10
same BMU as 2808:
God Particle

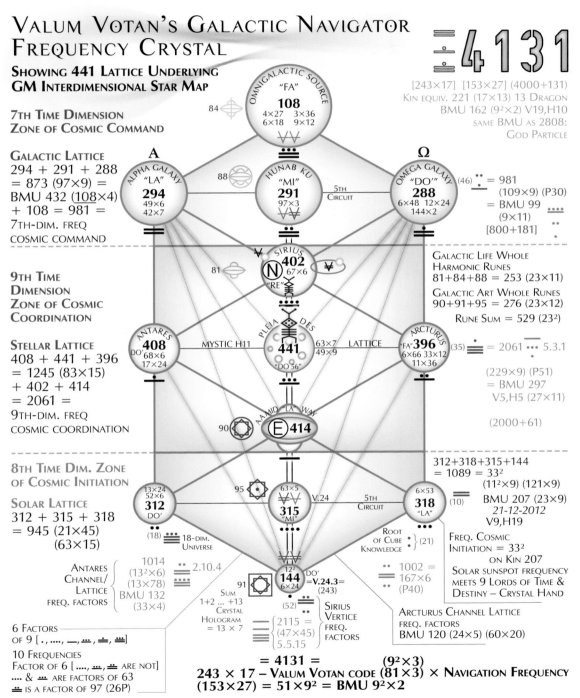

7th Time Dimension
Zone of Cosmic Command

Galactic Lattice
294 + 291 + 288
= 873 (97×9) =
BMU 432 (108×4)
+ 108 = 981 =
7th-dim. freq
cosmic command

A

Ω

84

OMNIGALACTIC SOURCE
"FA"
108
4×27   3×36
6×18   9×12

Alpha Galaxy
"LA"
294
49×6
42×7

88

Hunab Ku
"MI"
291
97×3

5th Circuit

Omega Galaxy
"DO'"
288
6×48 12×24
144×2

(46) = 981
(109×9) (P30)
= BMU 99
(9×11)
[800+181]

9th Time Dimension
Zone of Cosmic Coordination

Stellar Lattice
408 + 441 + 396
= 1245 (83×15)
+ 402 + 414
= 2061 =
9th-dim. freq
cosmic coordination

81

Sirius
(N) **402**
67×6
"RE"

Galactic Life Whole Harmonic Runes
81+84+88 = 253 (23×11)
Galactic Art Whole Runes
90+91+95 = 276 (23×12)
Rune Sum = 529 (23²)

Antares
408
DO'68×6
17×24

Mystic H11

Pleiades
441
"DO 56"

63×7 Lattice
49×9

Arcturus
"FA"**396**
6×66 33×12
11×36

(35) = 2061 ••• 5.3.1

(229×9) (P51)
= BMU 297
V5,H5 (27×11)

(2000+61)

90

AA MID "LA" WAY
(E)**414**

8th Time Dim. Zone of Cosmic Initiation

Solar Lattice
312 + 315 + 318
= 945 (21×45)
(63×15)

312+318+315+144
= 1089 = 33²
(11²×9) (121×9)
BMU 207 (23×9)
21-12-2012
V9,H19

13×24
52×6
312
DO'

95

63×5
315
"MI"

V.24 5th Circuit

6×53
318
"LA"

(10)

(18) 18-dim. Universe

Root of Cube Knowledge (21)

Freq. Cosmic Initiation = 33²
on Kin 207
Solar sunspot frequency meets 9 Lords of Time & Destiny – Crystal Hand

Antares Channel/ Lattice Freq. factors
1014 (13²×6)
(13×78)
BMU 132 (33×4)

2.10.4

12²
144
6×24

DO'
=V.24.3=
(243)

91

1002 = 167×6 (P40)

Arcturus Channel Lattice freq. factors
BMU 120 (24×5) (60×20)

Sum 1+2 ... +13
Crystal Hologram
= 13 × 7

(52)

Sirius Vertice freq. factors

2115 = (47×45)
5.5.13

6 Factors of 9 [·, ····, —, ⋮⋮, ⋮, ⫶⫶]

10 Frequencies Factor of 6 [····, ⋮⋮, ⫶⫶ are not] ···· & ⫶⫶ are factors of 63 ⫶⫶ is a factor of 97 (26P)

= 4131 =   (9²×3)
243 × 17 – Valum Votan code (81×3) × Navigation Frequency
(153×27) = 51×9² = BMU 9²×2

different mathematical frequencies that have become sensible and tangible, i.e. we can see, hear and smell them.

30. To assist in this understanding of the new mind we can study two basic levels of mathematical order: the Synchronic Order and Synchronotron as introduced in Chapter 3. These two levels establish an utterly new and galactic basis of knowledge.

31. This knowledge is mathematical and creates the basis of a unified telepathic knowledge that unifies ourselves with the cosmic order of reality, the Galactic Federation and Cosmic Civilization. This presents the primary level of cosmic sky teachings.

32. We are operants in an evolutionary test tube or self-reflective evolutionary medium. We are given these particular codes and tools to evolve our consciousness and to imprint them to such a degree that seven baktuns from now they will be second nature. They will be so imprinted in us that our minds will be like a coded supercomputer that can access any information we need at any given time. Only the quality of information will be far different from what we now perceive.

33. The Synchronic Order and Synchronotron cube matrix codes, inclusive of the Hunab Ku 21, are the sacred texts that form the basis of the formulation of knowledge found in the mathematical structures of the 441 cube matrices. These are the foundations of the spiritual order of the new reality. They form a profound harmony that, when applied, open us to infinite levels of order and understanding. This intrinsic order becomes inseparable from our own processes of perception so that even terms like "spirituality" will disappear and dissolve. This is important to understand.

34. These are the basic aspects of the cosmic sky teachings. We are establishing and calling forth the new mind. What we refer to as spirituality is inseparable from the consciousness of a cosmological unfolding. There are certain basic principles of this cosmological unfolding such as the cube and trina principle as the all-equalizing and all-unifying consciousness of new mind.

35. Once we cross the threshold of the imminent quantum mind shift we will fully enter into the preliminary stages of experiencing the mind of cosmic enlightenment as a unifying medium of all beings and all of life. Soon we will experience what it means to fully enter the noosphere, the mind of Earth, which is our own mind. This is the laying out of the principles of the cosmic sky teachings as the next stage of our spiritual/evolutionary development.

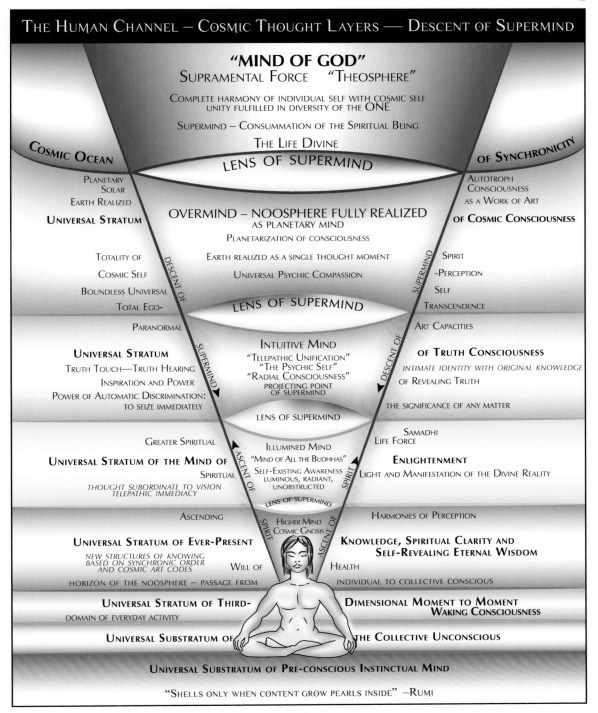

THE HUMAN CHANNEL — COSMIC THOUGHT LAYERS — DESCENT OF SUPERMIND

"MIND OF GOD"
SUPRAMENTAL FORCE   "THEOSPHERE"

COMPLETE HARMONY OF INDIVIDUAL SELF WITH COSMIC SELF
UNITY FULFILLED IN DIVERSITY OF THE ONE

SUPERMIND — CONSUMMATION OF THE SPIRITUAL BEING

THE LIFE DIVINE

COSMIC OCEAN   LENS OF SUPERMIND   OF SYNCHRONICITY

PLANETARY
SOLAR
EARTH REALIZED

UNIVERSAL STRATUM

AUTOTROPH
CONSCIOUSNESS
AS A WORK OF ART

OF COSMIC CONSCIOUSNESS

OVERMIND – NOOSPHERE FULLY REALIZED
AS PLANETARY MIND
PLANETARIZATION OF CONSCIOUSNESS

TOTALITY OF   EARTH REALIZED AS A SINGLE THOUGHT MOMENT

COSMIC SELF   UNIVERSAL PSYCHIC COMPASSION

BOUNDLESS UNIVERSAL

TOTAL EGO-   LENS OF SUPERMIND

DESCENT OF

SUPERMIND

SPIRIT
-PERCEPTION
SELF
TRANSCENDENCE

PARANORMAL   ART CAPACITIES

INTUITIVE MIND
"TELEPATHIC UNIFICATION"
"THE PSYCHIC SELF"
"RADIAL CONSCIOUSNESS"
PROJECTING POINT
OF SUPERMIND

UNIVERSAL STRATUM
TRUTH TOUCH—TRUTH HEARING
INSPIRATION AND POWER
POWER OF AUTOMATIC DISCRIMINATION:
TO SEIZE IMMEDIATELY

OF TRUTH CONSCIOUSNESS
INTIMATE IDENTITY WITH ORIGINAL KNOWLEDGE
OF REVEALING TRUTH

THE SIGNIFICANCE OF ANY MATTER

DESCENT OF

LENS OF SUPERMIND

SAMADHI
LIFE FORCE

GREATER SPIRITUAL   ILLUMINED MIND

UNIVERSAL STRATUM OF THE MIND OF   "MIND OF ALL THE BUDDHAS"

SPIRITUAL   SELF-EXISTING AWARENESS
LUMINOUS, RADIANT,
UNOBSTRUCTED

THOUGHT SUBORDINATE TO VISION
TELEPATHIC IMMEDIACY

ASCENT OF

ENLIGHTENMENT
LIGHT AND MANIFESTATION OF THE DIVINE REALITY

SPIRIT

LENS OF SUPERMIND

ASCENDING   HIGHER MIND   HARMONIES OF PERCEPTION
COSMIC GNOSIS

SPIRIT

ASCENT OF

UNIVERSAL STRATUM OF EVER-PRESENT
NEW STRUCTURES OF KNOWING
BASED ON SYNCHRONIC ORDER
AND COSMIC ART CODES   WILL OF

HORIZON OF THE NOOSPHERE — PASSAGE FROM

KNOWLEDGE, SPIRITUAL CLARITY AND
SELF-REVEALING ETERNAL WISDOM

HEALTH

INDIVIDUAL TO COLLECTIVE CONSCIOUS

UNIVERSAL STRATUM OF THIRD-
DOMAIN OF EVERYDAY ACTIVITY

DIMENSIONAL MOMENT TO MOMENT
WAKING CONSCIOUSNESS

UNIVERSAL SUBSTRATUM OF   THE COLLECTIVE UNCONSCIOUS

UNIVERSAL SUBSTRATUM OF PRE-CONSCIOUS INSTINCTUAL MIND

"SHELLS ONLY WHEN CONTENT GROW PEARLS INSIDE" –RUMI

CHAPTER 8

JOURNEY OF THE ARCHETYPES
HUNAB KU 21: CHANNELING GALACTIC FUTURE

1. Within the vast array of cosmic sky teachings comes the Hunab Ku 21—Journey of the Archetypes, Transmigration of the Soul. This is a supreme method for entering the new time of the noosphere.

2. Based on the 13 Moon/28-day natural time calendar and the codes of the synchronic order of the Law of Time, Hunab Ku 21 is a synthesis of the codes and messages of the 441 Cube Matrix. It is a higher-dimensional program of telepathic communication, systematically arranged to provide an evolutionary construct of consciousness for the coming aeon.

3. Hunab Ku 21 is the interdimensional bridge between ourselves and the star people. The noosphere is the resonating medium facilitating this communication. Hunab Ku 21 is the technology as well as the artistic program by which this communication occurs and becomes meaningful. The method is the activation of 21 energy/archetypes of cosmic enlightenment, and to universalize these archetypes within oneself.

4. Every week we open 7 gates of stored mind treasures (heptad gates). At the same time, we are on an archetypal journey that repeats every 20 days. The 21 energy/archetypes and 7 mind treasure gates also define 52 paths of enlightenment (see *CHC Vol. V: Book of the Timespace*). Through the journey of the Hunab Ku 21, we learn how to walk all 52 of these paths and so universalize them into the One Path of Universal Unification.

JOURNEY OF THE GALACTIC ARCHETYPES

5. In the Galactic Journey we have 20 days to complete a cycle of archetypal embodiments. This 20-day cycle can be repeated ad infinitum. But it is never the same, for it is a journey in time, and time is the spiral of infinity that goes from without to within. We enter the spiral when we wake up and wish to remain conscious. We leave the spiral when we have transcended and gone to the Absolute order of reality. This can only be when we have mastered the journey.

6. For this reason the journey also consists of 52 paths that evolve us at a higher frequency. The 52 paths are a function of the power of seven. There are seven powers that pace the progress of each path (see *CHC Vol. V: Book of the Timespace*). Simultaneous to taking the 20-day journey

of the archetypal embodiments, every seven days we also open the *seven heptad gates* of the seven mind treasures of one of the 52 paths of the Journey. (see *CHC Vol. VI: Book of Transcendence*—Chapters 4 & 5: Synchrogalactic Yoga).

7. In the galactic lexicon an archetype is a model of behavior based on an inherited memory pattern represented in the mind by a universal symbol. The universal symbols of the 20 +1 archetypes of Hunab Ku are represented in the mind by one of the 20 solar seals of the Dreamspell. The 21st archetype is a representative of the Hunab Ku itself.

8. All the archetypes of the Hunab Ku 21 are rooted in the Hunab Ku, the galactic core where resides the storehouse of the universal mind and memory. We have memory because we are all aspects of the one transmigrating soul. The purpose of memory is to guide us on the journey home.

HUNAB KU 21—THE MYTHIC JOURNEY INTO THE GALACTIC FUTURE

We have been on a cosmic journey all of our life times, and it won't stop when history comes to an end. History may end but the journey will continue. The time after history will begin a new stage of the journey. This journey will take us through the reaches of inner time into the galactic future. We will each be a single voice of unity in a collective mind, the noosphere. Noosphere is the mind space of inner time that stretches infinitely into the galactic future. In the noosphere we will be a cosmic total inspired by the Hunab Ku.

Hunab Ku is the soul of galactic Culture. Hunab Ku, One Giver of Movement and Measure, is the Reality of Unification, the cosmic unity of all spiritual life everywhere. Hunab Ku is the one who commands the Journey and the One who takes the Journey. Hunab Ku is the Many become the One, and the One become the Many. Hunab Ku is the prophesied Order of Reality to supersede history. We are all Hunab Ku. We are the journey that takes us through the 21 archetypes of the transmigration of the soul. This is the mythic journey into the galactic future.

THE 21 ARCHETYPES AND THE THREE STAGES OF THE ARCHETYPAL JOURNEY

9. The archetypal journey always begins on a Dragon day and ends on a Sun day. As with any epic, the galactic journey occurs in three stages. The journey takes place upon and defines the template of the Galactic Tree of Life and Knowledge. This template is both the archetypal mind map of galactic consciousness and the design structure of the galaxy as the primal information unit of universal order.

STAGE 1

In the first four days of the journey we establish ourselves in the **four primal archetypes**. These also create the two magnetic poles and the two energetic extremities of the Galactic Tree of Life and Knowledge. The four primal archetypes exist at a purely fifth-dimensional level.

Their positions are also known as the four light gates, as they are the inlets of the types of universal light and cosmic electricity into the world of manifestation represented by the Four Outer Courts of Power. The four primal archetypes are:

The Primal Force of Cosmic Being, Galactatron, The Initiator—Red Dragon (Upper Pole—Marka pole)—Controls the power of cosmic being and descends as cosmic knowledge. Opens the Universal Light Gate to the Court of the Avatar.

The High Priestess of Cosmic Spirit, Urania, The Spirit Breather—White Wind (Lower pole—Darka Pole)—Controls the power of cosmic breath and ascends as prophecy. Opens the Universal Light gate to the Court of the Prophet.

The Dreamer of the Long Night of the Cosmic Dream—Blue Night—(Left centrifugal extremity)—Controls the power of dream to become abundance of manifestation. Opens the Universal Light Gate to the Court of the Compassionate One.

The Innocent Seed Being of Cosmic Awareness—Yellow Seed—(Right centripetal extremity)—Controls the power of universal awareness to evolve the powers of cosmic intelligence. Opens the Universal Light gate to the Court of the Pathfinder.

The Four Primal Archetypes correspond to the Input Time Cell of the Dreamspell system. They are the four original ones emanated from the Universe of Light corresponding to the most fundamental orientation of timespace. They each command three archetypes to govern one each of the four Cosmic Courts of Galactic Culture. Once we have established the four primal archetypes then we descend to the fourth-dimensional stage of the journey.

STAGE 2

For the next twelve days of the journey, we move through the twelve archetypes of the **courts of the four outer cosmic powers**. In this stage, the journey takes place in the fourth-dimensional realm where we pass through twelve different archetypes and receive four cosmic powers. These

21 GALACTIC ARCHETYPES

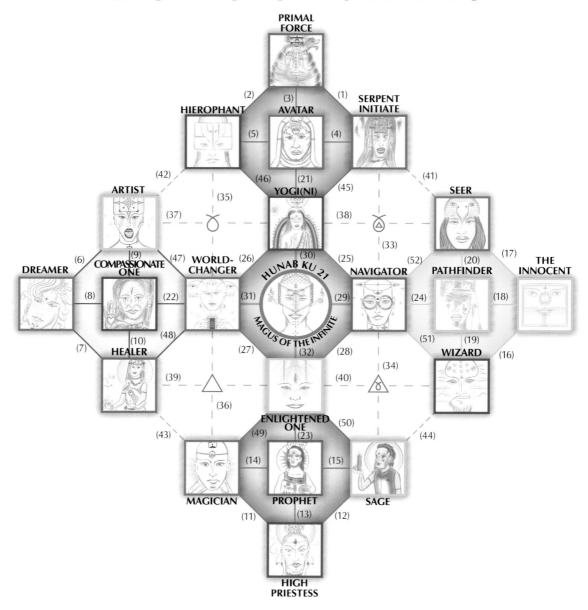

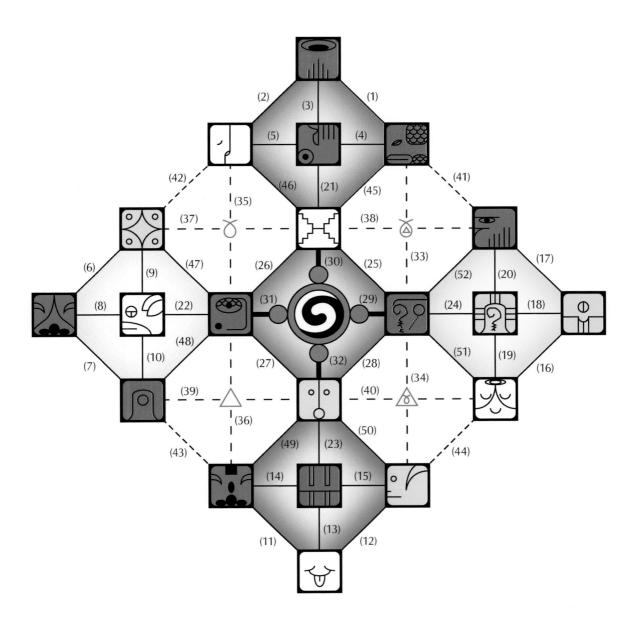

powers establish our outer manifestation and are essential for our journey of unification. As long as we are on the journey we all receive these powers equally.

Through each court we pass through three stages. We enter through a **gate** of power; we reach a **source** of power; and we establish a **seat** of power. For each of these three positions there is a corresponding archetype. (Note that all archetypes have both a male and female aspect, though some are described as "he" and some "she"). The four cosmic powers and their archetypes are:

Cosmic Knowledge, Court of the Avatar. This is the court emanated by The Primal Force Galactatron, The Initiator:

First Gate of Power: The Serpent Initiate of Wisdom—Red Serpent—Power of Sex: Sex is the beginning of knowledge. The Serpent Initiate of Wisdom is the first to be initiated by the Primal Force Galactatron. By this initiation she gains the power to initiate and empower others in the timeless serpent wisdom that spans the world systems. The Serpent Initiate of Wisdom is the most ancient one; she is the possessor of all the hidden doctrines and mind treasures stored around the planet. In her is the storehouse of cosmic memory of previous world systems. She is instinctual, and her sexual power is the essence of her wisdom. She teaches through rites of initiation.

First Source of Power: The Hierophant—White Worldbridger—Power of Death. Hierophant is the revealer of the sacred, the guardian of the store of death, the sacred source of knowledge. Hierophant is the second to be initiated into the mystery of Cosmic Being by the Primal Force Galactatron. His power of death balances the Serpent Initiate's power of sex. Serpent Initiate is the generator of the red electrical circuit and the Hierophant is the terminal of the blue electrical circuit. The Hierophant reveals the sacred power of the knowledge of death, and has authority to transmit this knowledge into the Avatar, and all, like the avatar seek to be the living embodiments of cosmic knowledge. The Avatar can only teach by exemplifying.

First Seat of Power: The Avatar—Blue Hand—Power of Cosmic Knowledge (Accomplishment). The Avatar embodies the descent of being as cosmic knowledge. He is the third to be initiated by the Primal Force Galactatron. He represents knowledge as the accomplishment of cosmic being. Avatar receives initiatic empowerments from the Serpent Initiate and from the Hierophant, so he becomes the balancer of death and sex, the receiver of the two primal electrical currents, the red and the blue. As a model, the Avatar exemplifies how to embody cosmic knowledge and fulfill the commands of the evolution of cosmic consciousness. A fourth empowerment is received from the **Yogi(ni)**, her mirror of cosmic mediation. (See below, Court of Hunab Ku)

Receive the First Power of the Journey, Cosmic Knowledge.

Cosmic Love, Court of the Compassionate One. This is the court emanated by the Dreamer of the Long Night of the Cosmic Dream.

Second Gate of Power: The Artist—Yellow Star—Power of Art (Elegance). Art is the beginning of Love. The Artist is the first to be emanated by the Cosmic Dreamer, for the artist is the first to follow the dream and make what he finds into a work of art. The Artist is the one who fashions, who makes, who reveals the beauty and elegance of creation by simple acts of awareness. For the artist, every act of art, elegance and beauty is an act of love. The artist is indispensable for the creation of the planetary art whole. The artist teaches by living and doing, for essentially everything the artist does is art. The way of the genuine artist is art as everyday life. "Life as we live it is the ritual we are looking for" is the artist's motto.

Second Source of Power—The Healer—Red Moon—Power of Purification (Healing power of Universal Water of compassion). Purification is the source and healing power of love. The Healer is the one who makes whole, who knows how to flow in wholeness, who knows how to mend what has come apart, and how to cool the discordant heart. The Healer is the united with the power of the Dream. It is the Healer who transmits her healing power of purification to the Compassionate One as the Universal Water of all-healing love. The healer knows the ways of the Earth, the plants and the secrets of the animals. The healer teaches that self-healing is self-love, and that we are all already intrinsically whole.

Second Seat of Power: The Compassionate One—White Dog—Power of Love (Heart). Cosmic Love is the power of the Compassionate One. Fulfilling the Dreamer's deepest dream is the Heart of the Compassionate One's Universal Love. Compassionate One's loyalty is his/her love for all beings. Artist's elegance awakens Compassionate One's love. From the Healer, Compassionate One learns the healing power of Love. The Compassionate One is also known as Bodhisattva, the one who vows to enlighten all beings through awakening their power of universal compassion. The Compassionate One takes many forms and works in innumerable ways. No act is too mean or low for the Compassionate One if it will make a better situation for another sentient being. To give without receiving and to love without being loved is the Compassionate One's ethic.

Receive the Second Power of the Journey, Cosmic Love.

Cosmic Prophecy, Court of the Prophet. This the court emanated by the High Priestess, Urania, the Spirit Breather.

Third Gate of Power: The Magician—Blue Monkey—Power of magic as the display of illusion. Magic is the beginning of prophecy. The Magician is the first to be inspired by Urania the Spirit

Breather, for he is the one who knows how to use the spirit breath to command the higher play of illusion which always enlightens. The Magician is the transformer, the one who changes things and performs in accordance with the higher will. He is the inventor of play and games that evolve the different shapes of the mind. Master of illusion, the Magician knows when to appear and when to disappear.

Third Source of Power: The Sage—Yellow Human—Free Will Power of Wisdom. Sage is the guardian of wisdom as the free will storehouse of cosmic prophecy. Sage is the second to receive the spirit breath as the capacity to rule or exert power simply by influence of his inner will. The Sage balances and judges in accordance with the cosmic spirit essence which animates his being. The Sage knows how to listen, and speaks only when spoken to. Sage is the terminal of the red electrical circuit that transmits the occult power of the timeless wisdom of the Serpent Initiate, and the synchronic wisdom of the Navigator. The entire universe is the Sage's realm to study and receive the knowledge that informs his decision-making on behalf of the good of all beings.

Third Seat of Power: The Prophet—Red Skywalker—Power of Prophecy as the awakening of universal space. The Prophet is the third to receive the inspiration of Urania the Spirit Breather. Through the Prophet the Spirit Essence ascends as Prophecy. His thoughts must extend through all space, so he is known as the Skywalker. Through the Spirit breath Prophet knows that all who act in accord with the truth are prophets. The prophecy the Prophet embodies is the Universal Enlightenment that is promised by the fulfillment of the Universal Plan of Unification. Through magical display of illusion, the Magician awakens the Prophet to the truth. From the Sage the Prophet receives the prophetic wisdom of the power of free will in the cosmos.

Receive the Third Power of the Journey, Cosmic Prophecy.

Cosmic Intelligence, Court of the Pathfinder. This the Court emanated by the Innocent, the Seed Being of Cosmic Awareness.

Fourth Gate of Power: The Wizard—White Wizard—Power of Timelessness as the receptivity to Universal Intelligence. Timelessness is the beginning of Intelligence. The Wizard is first to be empowered by the Innocent as the master of the awareness of the ways of the Mystery. Only the Innocent can empower a wizard. The Wizard is the master sorcerer/sorceress, the one who has knowledge of the names, spells and enchantments that unveil and evolve the ways of galactic culture. Through the supreme seed awareness of the Innocent, the Wizard masters the arts of displacement and intergalactic communication and time travel.

Fourth Source of Power: The Seer—Blue Eagle—Power of Vision as the Creative Storehouse of Intelligence. The Seer is the second to receive the Innocent's empowerment of cosmic awareness. Through this empowerment, the creative mind of the seer opens to all the dimensions of time throughout the universal time space. The Seer flies like an eagle over the dominion of time and learns to unlock the secrets of space through commanding the power of creative vision. The Seer stores the visions and visionary power for the Pathfinder to discover and use according to the need as it arises. The Seer knows and sees through the long vigils in the mountain caves and beneath the stars.

The Fourth Seat of Power: The Pathfinder—Yellow Warrior—Power of Intelligence. Warrior defines the fearless nature of the Pathfinder's power of cosmic Intelligence. The Pathfinder is the third to receive the Innocent's empowerment of Cosmic Awareness. In the Pathfinder Intelligence is the flowering of cosmic awareness. Through the Pathfinder's questioning intelligence new ways and methods for all beings are discovered and developed. From the Wizard's power of Timelessness the Pathfinder remains receptive to clues and hints from the Universe indicating which direction a particular way or method needs to go to be even more effective. From the Innocent he learns to watch, wait and listen. From the Seer he retrieves the visionary power to understand and discover what is unknown. The Pathfinder turns the power of Intelligence inward as the great cosmic centripetal force.

Receive the Fourth Power of the Journey, Cosmic Intelligence.

STAGE 3

In the last four days of the journey we enter the **inner fifth force realm of the Hunab Ku**. Here we enter again the fifth-dimensional frequency of the Higher Self to embody the four archetypes that enact the four principle powers of Hunab Ku, and then journey to the Fifth Seat of Power to receive the power of the fifth force.

Here the fifth primal archetype, the **Hunab Ku,** who is known by his representative, the **One Dweller of the Cube, the Unknown Knower**, resides at the center of the galactic matrix maintaining his vigil unseen and unknown until now by the designation we just indicated. Here the most primal energy surges from the beginning of creation continuously bursting through from the non-manifest light universe to the sole atom within the galactic core of the manifest universe: the fifth force, or the Light-Photon-Cyclone energy. From this core are emanated and evolved the four supreme archetypes of the matrix maintaining the Fifth Court, the Court of Hunab Ku.

Fifth Force Power: Court of the Hunab Ku. This is the Court emanated by the One Dweller of the Cube, the Unknown Knower.

First Matrix Portal: Earth Portal of Navigation—The Navigator of Cosmic Synchronicity— Power of Navigation as Synchronic Knowing, the penetrating intelligence of the fifth force to comprehend synchronicity as the cosmic total of the timespace cube. The Navigator is the first archetype emanated by the Hunab Ku, the primal one to go where none have gone before, crossing galaxies and world systems. The Navigator charts the unknown with the fifth force maps and codes of the synchronic order. The Navigator is the emissary of the Hunab Ku to the Court of the Pathfinder. The Navigator evolves intelligence through the fifth force power of synchronicity. The Navigator is the Pathfinder's supporting intelligence and is the transformer of the red electrical circuit, alternating the inner heat and inner light currents.

Second Matrix Portal: Mirror Portal of Cosmic Meditation—The Yogi(ni) of Cosmic Meditation—Cosmic meditation is Hunab Ku's power of knowledge. The Yogi(ni) is the second archetype of Hunab Ku, intended to communicate purely the reality of universal mind. The Yogi(ni)evolves Hunab Ku's knowledge through endlessness meditation, so that her mind becomes the reflection of the mind of Hunab Ku. Through power of mind, the Yogi(ni) beams the yogic force as a supermental organizing and unifying factor of the fifth force. The Yogi(ni) is the Hunab Ku's emissary to the Court of the Avatar. The Yogi(ni) transmits mind-to-mind to the Avatar the reflecting power of endlessness as the Hunab Ku's power of knowledge. Yogi(ni) is the generator the hyperneutron transforming it into the *mental neutron* which is transmitted to the North Magnetic Pole. The Yogi(ni) transforms primal heat into the energy of the heat of inner light.

Third Matrix Portal: Storm Portal of Cosmic Self-Generation—The Worldchanger of Cosmic Self-Generation—Self-generation is Hunab Ku's power of love. The Worldchanger is the third archetype of Hunab Ku, the one to extend the self-generating power of cosmic love as the catalyzing force that transforms reality—through dissolution, catharsis and regenerative energies. The real meaning of cosmic love is in its ability to catalyze and bring forth what has been hidden or repressed. Cosmic love is what unmasks and penetrates to the authentic self—this is the skill of the Worldchanger. The Worldchanger is Hunab Ku's emissary to the Court of the Compassionate One, where he transmits the capacity to channel the fifth force as the universalizing psychic energy of love. The Worldchanger is the transformer of the blue electrical circuit, alternating the primal heat and light currents.

Fourth Matrix Portal: Sun Portal of Enlightenment—Enlightened One of Cosmic Illumination—Enlightenment is Hunab Ku's fulfillment of prophecy. The Enlightened One is Hunab Ku's fourth archetypal emanation, the one whose universal fire of illumination extends in all directions through the nine time dimensions as the all-radiating transmission of the universal mind of unification. In the life-universalizing mental field of the Enlightened One the mind of all Enlightened Ones since beginningless time is gathered as a cosmic total. The Enlightened One is emissary of Hunab Ku to the Court of the Prophet transmitting universal fire of Hunab Ku's primal thought that fulfills all prophecies. The Enlightened One is the Generator of the hyperelectron that is mentally transmitted to South Pole as a double extended mental electron. The Enlightened One transforms primal light into the light of inner heat.

Fifth Seat of Power: Hunab Ku 21—The One Dweller of the Cube—The fifth force is Hunab Ku's primal power, for in the fifth force is the source of all creation and the universal powers of synchronization. The One Dweller of the Cube is Hunab Ku's fifth archetypal emanation, the Unknown Knower. Guardian of the mystery of the center, the One Dweller of the Cube is purely a function of the number matrices based on 21, the Unity of Totality.

As the all-transcendent Power of the Cube, he/she is the hidden one in all number. It is through meditation on the 21 that she reveals the ordinances and commands of the higher dimensions. Holder of the seal of the quintessential core of the sole atom, he/she is fully the emanation of the light-photon-cyclone and so can never be grasped. As the embodiment of the sole atom she is the coordinating ordinance of the entire archetypal journey. Only on the seventh day of the heptad can she be invoked.

Receive the Fifth Power of the Journey, Power of the Fifth Force.

Index of the 21 Archetypes (with their 441 consciousness codes)

The Four Primal Ones of the Four Universal Light Gates
The Primal Force—Red Dragon—establishes the Court of the Avatar (108)
The High Priestess—White Wind—establishes the Court of the Prophet (144)
The Dreamer—Blue Night—establishes the Court of the Compassionate One (126)
The Innocent—Yellow Seed—establishes the Court of the Pathfinder (90)

The Three Archetypes of the Court of the Avatar—Memory of Cosmic Knowledge
The Serpent Initiate—Red Serpent—Sex is the beginning of Knowledge (288)
The Hierophant—White Worldbridger—Death is the Source of Knowledge (294)
The Avatar—Blue Hand—Knowledge is the Accomplishment of Cosmic Being (291)
Receive here the First Power, Cosmic Knowledge, now you are the Avatar.

41	40	39	38	37	36	35	34	33	32	31	30	29	28	27	26	25	24	23	22	21
42	117	116	115	114	113	112	111	110	109	108	107	106	105	104	103	102	101	100	99	20
43	118	185	184	183	182	181	180	179	178	177	176	175	174	173	172	171	170	169	98	19
44	119	186	245	244	243	242	241	240	239	238	237	236	235	234	233	232	231	168	97	18
45	120	187	246	297	296	295	294	293	292	291	290	289	288	287	286	285	230	167	96	17
46	121	188	247	298	341	340	339	338	337	336	335	334	333	332	331	284	229	166	95	16
47	122	189	248	299	342	377	376	375	374	373	372	371	370	369	330	283	228	165	94	15
48	123	190	249	300	343	378	405	404	403	402	401	400	399	368	329	282	227	164	93	14
49	124	191	250	301	344	379	406	425	424	423	422	421	398	367	328	281	226	163	92	13
50	125	192	251	302	345	380	407	426	437	436	435	420	397	366	327	280	225	162	91	12
51	126	193	252	303	346	381	408	427	438	441	434	419	396	365	326	279	224	161	90	11
52	127	194	253	304	347	382	409	428	439	440	433	418	395	364	325	278	223	160	89	10
53	128	195	254	305	348	383	410	429	430	431	432	417	394	363	324	277	222	159	88	9
54	129	196	255	306	349	384	411	412	413	414	415	416	393	362	323	276	221	158	87	8
55	130	197	256	307	350	385	386	387	388	389	390	391	392	361	322	275	220	157	86	7
56	131	198	257	308	351	352	353	354	355	356	357	358	359	360	321	274	219	156	85	6
57	132	199	258	309	310	311	312	313	314	315	316	317	318	319	320	273	218	155	84	5
58	133	200	259	260	261	262	263	264	265	266	267	268	269	270	271	272	217	154	83	4
59	134	201	202	203	204	205	206	207	208	209	210	211	212	213	214	215	216	153	82	3
60	135	136	137	138	139	140	141	142	143	144	145	146	147	148	149	150	151	152	81	2
61	62	63	64	65	66	67	68	69	70	71	72	73	74	75	76	77	78	79	80	1

Locating the Hunab Ku 21 in the 441 Base Matrix

The Hunab Ku 21 is a synthesis of the codes and messages of the 441 cube matrix. It is a higher-dimensional program of telepathic communication, systematically arranged to provide an evolutionary construct of consciousness for the coming aeon. Each of the 21 archetypes can be mapped with its corresponding number (consciousness code) within the base matrix.

The Three Archetypes of the Court of the Compassionate One—Memory of Cosmic Love
The Artist—Yellow Star—Art is the beginning of Love (300)
The Healer—Red Moon—Purification is the source of Love (306)
The Compassionate One—White Dog—Love is the Heart of the Cosmic Dream (303)
Receive here the Second Power, Cosmic Love You, now you are the Compassionate One.

The Three Archetypes of the Court of the Prophet—Memory of Cosmic Prophecy
The Magician—Blue Monkey—Magic is the beginning of Prophecy (312)
The Sage—Yellow Human—Wisdom is the source of Prophecy (318)
The Prophet—Red Skywalker—Prophecy is the Communication of Cosmic Spirit (315)
Receive here the Third Power, Cosmic Prophecy, now you are the Prophet.

The Three Archetypes of the Court of the Pathfinder—memory of Cosmic Intelligence
The Wizard—White Wizard—Timelessness is the beginning of Intelligence (276)
The Seer—Blue Eagle—Vision is the source of Intelligence (282)
The Path Finder—Yellow Warrior—Intelligence is the Flowering of Cosmic Awareness (279)
Receive here the Fourth Power, Cosmic Intelligence, now you are the Pathfinder.

The Five Archetypes of the Court of Hunab Ku
The Navigator—Red Earth—Synchronicity is Hunab Ku's power of Intelligence—the Navigator is Hunab Ku's emissary of Intelligence (396)
The Yogi(ni)—White Mirror—Meditation is Hunab Ku's power of Knowledge—the Yogi(ni) is Hunab Ku's emissary of Knowledge (402)
The Catalyzer—Blue Storm—Self-generation is Hunab Ku's power of Love—the Catalyzer is Hunab Ku's Emissary of Love (408)
The Enlightened One—Yellow Sun—Enlightenment is Hunab Ku's power of Prophecy—the Enlightened One is Hunawb Ku's emissary of Prophecy (414)
The Fifth Force Power of the Center—The One Dweller of the Cube—Hunab Ku—the Unknown Knower who Commands the Universal Synchronization of all Creation (441)
Receive here the Fifth Power, Fifth Force of the Light-Photon-Cyclone
You are the Power of the Center receiving the Presence of the Hunab Ku.

The Archetypes according to Earth Families
<u>Polar Family, North Pole, V.24.3</u>
Red Serpent is the Serpent Initiate of Wisdom, 1st gate of Power
White Dog is the Compassionate One, 2nd Seat of Power
Blue Eagle is the Seer, 4th Source of Power
Yellow Sun is the Enlightened One, 4th Matrix Portal

Cardinal Family, North Temperate Zone, V.24.3
Red Dragon is the Initiator, 1st Light Gate
White Worldbridger is the Hierophant, 1st Source of Power
Blue Monkey is the Magician, 3rd Gate of Power
Yellow Warrior is the Pathfinder, 4th Seat of Power

Core Family, Equatorial Zone, V.24.3
White Wind is the High Priestess, 2nd Light Gate
Blue Hand is the Avatar, 1st Seat of Power
Yellow Human is the Sage, 3rd Source of Power
Red Earth is the Navigator, 1st Matrix Portal

Signal Family, South Temperate Zone, V.24.3
Blue Night is the Dreamer, 3rd Light Gate
Yellow Star is the Artist, 2nd Gate of Power
Red Skywalker is the Prophet, 3rd Seat of Power
White Mirror is the Yogi(ni), 2nd Matrix Portal

Gateway Family, South Pole, V.24.3
Yellow Seed is the Innocent, 4th Light Gate
Red Moon is the Healer, 2nd Source of Power
White Wizard is the Wizard, 4th Gate of Power
Blue Storm is the Worldchanger, 3rd Matrix Portal

The Five Master Powers of the Cosmic Electrical Parton
Red Dum Kuali Primal Heat governs Court of the Avatar
Blue Dum Duar Primal Light governs Court of the Prophet
Orange Kum Heat of Inner Light governs Court of the Compassionate One
Yellow Kemio Light of Inner Heat governs Court of the Pathfinder
Green Sole Atom Light-Photon-Cyclone of Fifth Force governs Court of Hunab Ku

PART III
FOUR TRANSFORMATIVE POWERS

CHAPTER 9

GALACTIC TREE OF LIFE
HUNAB KU 21—THE GALACTIC SUPERSTRUCTURE

THE STRUCTURE OF THE HUNAB KU 21
AS THE GALACTIC TREE OF LIFE AND KNOWLEDGE

1. The Galactic Tree of Life and Knowledge is a perfectly constructed architecture of archetypal resonance. Its structure is already imprinted in the archetypal layers of the mind. It is merely a matter of allowing the archetypal memory to arise from within the storehouse consciousness.

2. The radial symmetry of its form is already well known to your higher self as well. In the holonomic order of higher reality, the structure of galactic consciousness and the design of the galaxy are one and the same. Radial consciousness and the galactic order are one and identical in form.

3. The five perfectly balanced **power of harmony cells** (tetrads) create a microcosm of the fifth force as the universal medium of organization. The **axial polar cells** are aligned along the central axis or *Mauri tube*. The centripetal and centrifugal power of harmony cells are aligned along the galactic equatorial axis.

4. In the center is the **fifth force matrix harmonic cell,** its four matrix gates perfectly conjoined to the four outer time cells, radiating the energy and power of the Hunab Ku 21, the fifth force power of the universe.

> *The power causing the integration of the universal totality is the Light-Photon-Cyclone power, which we call the Fifth Power. … The formation of this power had caused the Assembling of the Powers in a Total. The ordinance of Universes had come into existence only after the formation of this power dimension.*
> —*The Knowledge Book, p. 645*

5. This Light-Photon-Cyclone power is the Hunab Ku, the "Nucleus of the Ordinance of Cosmoses." This "power dimension" is the fifth force Hunab Ku 21. The Assembling of the Powers in a Total is the Hunab Ku 21 Galactic Tree of Life and Knowledge. The formation of this power dimen-

sion is the Fifth Power of Harmony Cell, Court of Hunab Ku, the galactic core by which unity coordinates totality.

6. Underlying the five power cells and coordinating the 20 +1 Seals of Authority is the skeletal structure of the Hunab Ku 21, the system of the axis and axial meridians, the equator and the latitudinal line of forces, the eight binding diagonal axes and the interconnecting pathways binding the cells into one harmonic superstructure.

1. The Polar Axis or Mauri Tube

You cannot understand the structure of the Hunab Ku 21 Galactic Tree of Life and Knowledge apart from the cosmology of which it is a function. As with all celestial phenomena there is a central organizing polar axis or Mauri tube. How did this polar axis come about?

In the primal always-occurring cosmogenesis there is an ejection of a type of radiation called *quon rays*. According to Cosmic Science, these quon rays are emitted from the sole quantum (atom) as five rays. The central one of these rays releases as an electro-thermic energy that condenses into proto-stellar phenomena or *quantars*. The other four rays produce a set of quasars.

As four gigantic pulsar stars the set of quasars revolves around the quantars. The quantars produce two types of seed forms: *mars* and *dar* that have opposite polarities. The interaction of the thermic with electric force fields generates a set of polarities which attract dar at one extreme and mars at the other. The extremes of polarity establish an interconnecting tube between two of the quasars called a Mauri tube or connector. From these, as the dar and mars seed forms are gathered, nebulae are generated, from which galaxies are formed.

The Mauri tube that organizes the galaxy axially is a cosmic channel that opens to all of the dimensional orders in the universe in two polar directions: the direction of the *Marka* pole (zenith or "north') and that of the *Darka* pole (nadir or "south"). These poles attract two types of plasmatic seed forms: mars and kar attracted by the Marka pole, and dar and kar by the Darka pole. The qualities of these three seed plasmas are: mars—inert, dar—activating and kar—vital.

From these seed plasmas the various stars constituting the entirety of the galactic order are generated. The place of their generation is the galactic matrix, the center point of the primal Mauri tube, from which emanates the light-photon-cyclone fifth force of the Hunab Ku. Within the Hunab Ku, higher-dimensional ordinances and information are gathered in resonant configurations that give form and intention to the plasmatic embryonic galaxies and star forms.

GALACTIC SUPERSTRUCTURE
OF THE TREE OF LIFE
HUNAB KU 21

THE PRINCIPLE JOURNEY OF THE **HUNAB KU 21 GALACTIC TREE OF LIFE AND KNOWLEDGE** IS THE 20-DAY CYCLE FOR ACQUIRING THE FIVE COSMIC POWERS OF GALACTIC CONSCIOUSNESS.

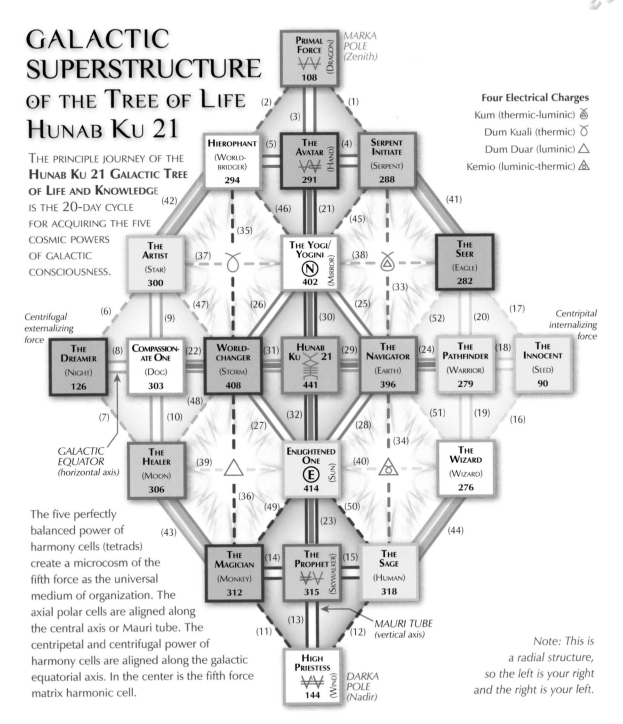

Four Electrical Charges
Kum (thermic-luminic)
Dum Kuali (thermic)
Dum Duar (luminic)
Kemio (luminic-thermic)

Centrifugal externalizing force

Centripital internalizing force

GALACTIC EQUATOR (horizontal axis)

The five perfectly balanced power of harmony cells (tetrads) create a microcosm of the fifth force as the universal medium of organization. The axial polar cells are aligned along the central axis or Mauri tube. The centripetal and centrifugal power of harmony cells are aligned along the galactic equatorial axis. In the center is the fifth force matrix harmonic cell.

MAURI TUBE (vertical axis)

Note: This is a radial structure, so the left is your right and the right is your left.

PRIMAL FORCE (DRAGON) 108 — *MARKA POLE (Zenith)*

HIEROPHANT (WORLD-BRIDGER) 294

THE AVATAR (HAND) 291

SERPENT INITIATE (SERPENT) 288

THE ARTIST (STAR) 300

THE YOGI/ YOGINI (N) 402 (MIRROR)

THE SEER (EAGLE) 282

THE DREAMER (NIGHT) 126

COMPASSION-ATE ONE (DOG) 303

WORLD-CHANGER (STORM) 408

HUNAB KU 21 441

THE NAVIGATOR (EARTH) 396

THE PATHFINDER (WARRIOR) 279

THE INNOCENT (SEED) 90

THE HEALER (MOON) 306

ENLIGHTENED ONE (E) 414 (SUN)

THE WIZARD (WIZARD) 276

THE MAGICIAN (MONKEY) 312

THE PROPHET (SKYWALKER) 315

THE SAGE (HUMAN) 318

HIGH PRIESTESS (WIND) 144 — *DARKA POLE (Nadir)*

(1) (2) (3) (4) (5) (6) (7) (8) (9) (10) (11) (12) (13) (14) (15) (16) (17) (18) (19) (20) (21) (22) (23) (24) (25) (26) (27) (28) (29) (30) (31) (32) (33) (34) (35) (36) (37) (38) (39) (40) (41) (42) (43) (44) (45) (46) (47) (48) (49) (50) (51) (52)

As the medium of galactic consciousness as well, the Mauri tube or polar axis is an interdimensional channel articulated by seven defining nodal points (also known as heptad gates): **2 gates of light, 2 seats of power, 2 matrix gates, and the Hunab Ku 21.**

The Mauri tube is a holographic channel and establishes correspondences not only with the galactic axis, but with stellar and planetary axes, in the human body with the spine or central channel, and in the brain with the corpus callosum.

Here we are concerned with the seven nodes of consciousness that correspond to the seven heptad gates opened every day, seven days a week, 52 weeks per terrestrial orbit. In the Hunab Ku 21 these seven nodes also establish the seven portals of the holomind perceiver and are situated along the axis of the corpus callosum. The corpus callosum is the gateway to galactic consciousness. *For this reason the radial plasma designations in the corpus callosum do not necessarily correspond to the positions of the plasmas in the seven chakra alignment of the central channel.*

Equivalent to the establishment of the primal set of polarities at either end of the Mauri tube are the first two nodal points of galactic consciousness. These are known as the first pair of the **Gates of Light.**

At the **Marka pole** is the first Gate of Light, the Gate of Cosmic Being. In the Hunab Ku 21 this is called the **Dragon Gate of Being**. Dragon is the first seal of authority, the archetype **108** of the **Primal Force**. It is at the polar zenith where Cosmic Being descends and evolves all its different forms of manifestation. Here at the primary Marka pole is generated hyperplasma *alpha alpha*, which stimulates states of profound samadhi, and seals the radial plasma Dali. This gate corresponds to the First Heptad Gate of the Throne. Plasmatic portal: **base of skull**.

At the **Darka pole** is the second Gate of Light, the Gate of Cosmic Spirit. In the Hunab Ku 21 this is called the **Wind Gate of Spirit**. Wind is the second seal of authority, the arche- **144** type of the **High Priestess**. It is at the polar nadir where spirit ascends and evolves all of its different possibilities. Here at the primary Darka pole is generated the hyperplasma *beta beta*, which stimulates states of waking conscious mediumship and seals the radial plasma Gamma. This gate corresponds to the Third Heptad Gate of the Mystery. Plasmatic portal: **third eye**.

From the two primal polar gates are then evolved the next two nodal points of consciousness known as **Seats of Power**. The first seat of power is that of Cosmic Knowledge. Being **291** advances itself as and through knowledge, embodied by the archetype of the **Avatar.** In the Hunab Ku 21 this seal of authority is known as the **Hand of Knowledge**. Hand is the seventh seal of authority. From it is generated the secondary Marka pole hyperplasma *alpha beta*, which stimulates states of informative samadhi, and seals the radial plasma Seli. The Hand of Knowledge holds together the first harmonic time cell, or the zenith polar harmonic cell of Cosmic Knowledge, Court of the Avatar. This seat of authority corresponds to the Second Heptad Gate of the Avatar. Plasmatic portal: **top-back of skull**.

Knowledge is being in accordance with the truth.

From the nadir polar Light Gate of Spirit arises the fourth nodal point of galactic consciousness, the Seat of Power of Cosmic Prophecy, for spirit evolves itself through prophecy. In the Hunab Ku 21 this seal of authority is known as the **Skywalker of Prophecy.** Skywalker **315** is the 13th seal of authority of the archetype of the **Prophet.** From it is generated the secondary Darka pole hyperplasma *beta alpha* which stimulates states of higher mind control and seals the fourth radial plasma **Kali.** The Skywalker of Prophecy holds together the third power of harmony cell, the nadir polar harmonic cell of Cosmic Prophecy. This seat of power corresponds to the Fourth Heptad Gate of the Initiation. Plasmatic portal: **top of forehead**.

Prophecy is action in accordance with the truth.

Then come the next two nodal points of galactic consciousness: the **Matrix Portals of Cosmic Enlightenment and Cosmic Meditation.** These two matrix portals open outwardly to either one of the two polar harmonic cells and inwardly to the Hunab Ku 21. The matrix gates are known as portals because they link to the core information unit, the Hunab Ku 21 and to one each of the outer power of harmony cells; in this way the matrix gates are also the fifth gates of the four outer power of harmony cells, or outer courts.

Moving up to complete the third power of harmony cell of Prophecy and open the fourth gate to the Hunab Ku matrix is the **Sun Portal of Enlightenment.** The Sun seal of author- **414** ity is the 20th and actually closes the cycle of 20, and corresponds to the archetype of the **Enlightened One.** It is the fulfillment of the prophetic consciousness. From here is generated the *hyperelectron* that stimulates superconscious states of mind, activates the (south) polar harmonic Darka pole with the double-extended electron and seals the fifth radial plasma **Alpha.** This portal corresponds to the Fifth Heptad Gate of the Timespace. Plasmatic portal: **top-front of crown**.

Opposite the Sun Portal of Enlightenment is the second matrix portal, the **Mirror Portal of Meditation.** The Mirror is the 18th seal of authority of the archetype of the **Yogi(ni).** **402** The Mirror portal completes the power of Cosmic Knowledge as the Meditation of Cosmic Being. From here is generated the *hyperneutron* that stimulates the subliminal states of consciousness, activates the (north) polar harmonic cell of the Marka pole and seals the radial plasma Limi. This portal corresponds to the Sixth Heptad Gate of the Transcendence. Plasmatic portal: **top-back of crown**.

The seventh and central coordinating nodal point is the **Hunab Ku 21**, the central matrix universe channel, the light-photon-cyclone of the fifth power. Hunab Ku is the Seal of the Unity of Totality and insofar as it can be represented by a number is 21—Totality plus One. Its archetypal representative is the **One Dweller of the Cube, Magus of the Infinite.** This is the "number of God." From the **Portal of Hunab Ku 21** is generated the hyperplasma *Sirius B-52/Element 113* that stimulates the radial states of consciousness and perception of the holomind perceiver, and activates the mental electron-neutron at the center of the Earth with supreme galactic consciousness (noosphere).This gate seals radial plasma **Silio.** This gate corresponds to the Seventh Heptad Gate of the Cube. Plasmatic portal: **center of crown, top of head.**

441

The Two Axial Meridians

Parallel to the Mauri tube central axis are the two meridians: The **Sex–Navigation–Wisdom red electrical** meridian, and the **Death–Self-Generation–Magic blue electrical** meridian. The meridians provide the central channels for the *four electro-etheric cells.* These meridians channel the four types of thermic and luminic electrical charges to the four outer harmonic cells. They connect complementary sets of gates and sources of power of the two polar power of harmony cells.

The Serpent Sex Gate of Power is activated by the ascending *kemio* **thermic-luminic electrical charges.** The Human wisdom source of power is activated by the descending *kum* **luminic-thermic electrical charges.** The Worldbridger Death source of power is activated by the ascending *dum kuali* **thermic electrical charges,** and the Monkey Magic Gate of Power is activated by the descending *dum duar* **luminic electrical charges.** The sum of each of the electrical lines of force is the red electrical current (Serpent–Human) and blue electrical current (Worldbridger–Monkey).

The two matrix stabilizing portals mediate the charges with energetic activations from the Hunab Ku 21. The **Earth Portal of Navigation** mediates Hunab Ku force to the red ascending kemio thermic-luminic flow and the red kum descending luminic thermic flow. The **Storm Portal of Self-Generation** mediates the Hunab Ku force to the ascending red dum kuali and the blue dum duar electrical charges.

2. The Galactic Equator (Horizontal Axis)

Perpendicular to the Mauri tube is the line of force of the Galactic Equator. While the central channel has an electromagnetically generative function drawing into itself both the plasmatic

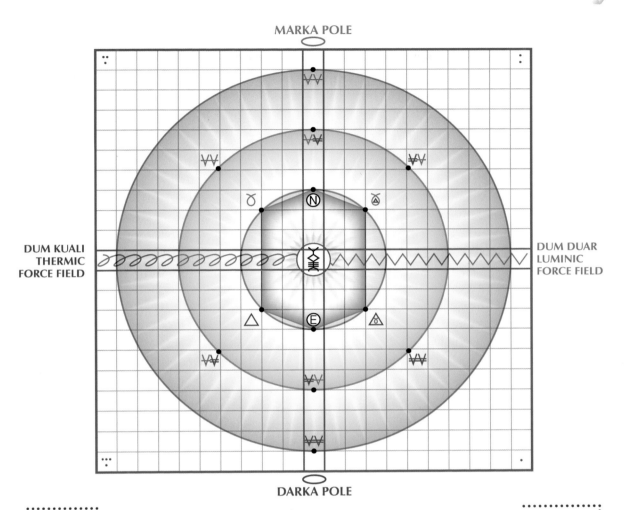

MARKA POLE

DUM KUALI THERMIC FORCE FIELD

DUM DUAR LUMINIC FORCE FIELD

DARKA POLE

1. **Core – Sirius B-52/Element 113:** A totally hyperelectronic particle synthesizing cubic parton function + emitting intense synchrotronic radiation (1)

2. **Orbit of 6 partons/Cubic Parton:** N(eutron); E(lectron); Dum Kuali thermic; Dum Duar luminic; Kum + Kemio (6)

3. **Orbit of 6 hyperplasmas** in cubic parton transfer formation (6)

4. **Alpha Alpha – Beta Beta** polar orbitals – Marka/Darka polarity (2)

5. **Hypergravitational field organizers:** a) Dum Kuali thermic force field; b) Dum Duar luminic force field; creating together massive rotational propulsion, rotating both in their own arm and in a plane around Sirius B 52/Element 113 core.

seed forms and the higher-dimensional information templates, the galactic equator has both an energetically stabilizing and evolutive function.

The galactic equator is the line of force upon which the plasmatic seed forms are transmuted into stellar evolutionary processes and become distributed into star systems and constellations. The star system is the galactic micro unit or micro "God particle" through which the possibilities of material evolution and spiritual involution are manifested. The galaxy is the macro "God particle".

While the Mauri tube or vertical galactic axis defines the primal cosmic polarities that define the two outer electromagnetic polar harmonic cells the galactic equatorial line of force defines the two primary movements of evolution: **becoming—centrifugal force,** and **return—centripetal force.** These are the two energetic, dynamically stabilizing and evolutive forces of the unfolding of cosmic life and consciousness.

The **externalizing centrifugal force** constitutes the third power of harmony cell, the Court of Cosmic Love. The **internalizing centripetal force** constitutes the Court of Cosmic Intelligence. Like the polar power of harmony cells aligned to the Mauri tube which create the electromagnetic information dynamic of the galactic order of consciousness through seven nodal points, the two power cells aligned to the galactic equatorial line of force establish seven nodal points of the dynamic-stabilizing-evolutive forces of galactic consciousness.

The **centrifugal force field**, constituted as the Court of Cosmic Love, is aligned by the thermic line of force which runs along the galactic equator from the core to the third Gate of Light, the Night Gate of Cosmic Dreaming. The **centripetal force field,** constituted as the Court of Cosmic Intelligence, is aligned by the luminic line of force which runs along the galactic equator from the core to the fourth Gate of Light, the Seed Gate of Cosmic Awareness. Being thermically activated, the harmonic Love cell is also known as the *galactic heat cell*, and the harmonic Intelligence cell being luminically activated is also known as the *galactic light cell*. Love is heat. Intelligence is light.

2 Gates of Light, 2 Seats of Power, 2 Matrix Portals, Hunab Ku 21

Corresponding to the establishment of the primal set of polarities, at either end of the Mauri tube are the first two nodal points of galactic evolutionary consciousness. These are known as the two **Galactic Equatorial Light Gates**.

At the centrifugal extremity of the galactic equatorial line of force is the third Gate of Light, the **Night Gate of Cosmic Dreaming.** Night is the third seal of authority of the archetype of the Dreamer. It is at the equatorial centrifugal extremity that dreaming evolves and expands into the power of love. The power of love evolves matter into the stabilizing force of cosmic consciousness. This is a centrifugal process where the electrical charges of the hyperelectron and the dum kuali (galactic heat) combine to create the superconscious force of Cosmic Love.

The centripetal extremity of the galactic equatorial line of force is the fourth Gate of Light, the **Seed Gate of Cosmic Awareness.** Seed is the fourth seal of authority of the archetype of the Innocent. It is at the center of the equatorial centripetal extremity that awareness evolves and internalizes into the power of intelligence. The power of intelligences evolves spirit into the dynamizing force of cosmic consciousness. This is a centripetal, inward process where the electrical charges of the hyperneutron and the dum duar (galactic light) create the subliminal force of Cosmic Intelligence.

These are the first two nodal points of the galactic equatorial line of force.

From the two equatorial gates of light are then evolved the next two nodal points of the evolution of cosmic consciousness known as **Seats of Power.** The third nodal point and seat of power is that of Cosmic Love, for dreaming advances itself as and through love. In the Hunab Ku 21 this seal of authority is known as the **White Dog of Love.** Dog is the 10th seal of authority of the archetype of the Compassionate One. From this point is generated the ongoing power of the centrifugal force of cosmic evolution. The Compassionate One holds together the second power of harmony cell, the Court of Cosmic Love. Love is the centrifugal force of the cosmic totality.

From the centripetal light gate of Cosmic awareness the fourth nodal point of galactic consciousness, arises the Seat of Power of Intelligence, for awareness evolves itself through intelligence. This seal of authority is known as the **Warrior of Intelligence.** Warrior is the 16th seal of authority, the seal of the archetype of the **Pathfinder.** From it is generated the on-going power of the centripetal force of cosmic involution. The Pathfinder holds together the fourth power of harmony cell, the Court of Cosmic Intelligence. Intelligence is the centripetal force of the cosmic totality.

Moving inward on the centripetal luminic line of force we reach the first **Matrix Portal,** the Earth Portal of Navigation. The **Earth** seal of authority is the 17th, the seal of the archetype of the **Navigator,** and provides the link between the Hunab Ku and the Cosmic Intelligence. Navigation is the fulfillment of the consciousness of intelligence. From here is generated the luminic line of force that stimulates the subliminal conscious states of mind and activates the harmonic order of the centripetal force field of intelligence.

On the opposite side aligned to the centrifugal line of force we reach the third Matrix Portal, **The Storm Portal of Self-Generation.** The Storm seal of authority is the 19th in the sequence of 20, the seal of the archetype of the Worldchanger, providing the link between the Hunab Ku and the Compassionate One. Self-generation is the fulfillment of the cosmic consciousness of love. From here is generated the thermic line of force that stimulates the superconscious states of mind and activates the harmonic order of the centrifugal force field of love.

The seventh and central coordinating nodal point is the **Hunab Ku 21**, the central matrix universe channel, the light-photon cyclone of the fifth force power. Hunab Ku is the Seal of the Unity of Totality, the seal of the archetype of the **One Dweller of the Cube, Magus of the Infinite**. From the **Portal of Hunab Ku 21** is generated the hyperplasma Sirius B-52, Element 113 that stimulates radial states of consciousness and perception and activates the centrifugal and centripetal force fields as the primary cosmic energies.

The Two Stabilizing Lines of Force

Parallel to the galactic equatorial line of force are the **two stabilizing lines of force**. The **Art–Meditation–Vision** stabilizing line of force and the **Purification–Enlightenment–Timelessness** stabilizing line of force. These two stabilizing lines of force provide the gravitational alignment for the four electro-etheric cells and conduct the four types of hyper-thermic and hyper-luminic charges to the four outer harmonic cells as centrifugal or centripetal lines of force. (See below for complete description).

Star Art (Artist) gate of power is activated by the dum kuali centrifugal thermic electric line of force. The **Eagle Vision** (Seer) source of power is activated by the kemio luminic-thermic centripetal electric line of force. The **Moon Purification** (Healer) source of power is activated by the dum duar centrifugal luminic electric charges, and the **Wizard Timelessness** (Wizard) gate of power is activated by the kum luminic thermic centripetal electric lines of force.

The two matrix portals mediate the lines of force with energetic activations from the Hunab Ku 21. The hyperneutron of the **Mirror Portal of Meditation** (Yogi/Yogini) mediates the Hunab Ku light-photon-cyclone force to the dum kuali centrifugal line of force and the kemio centripetal line of force. The hyperelectron of the **Sun Portal of Enlightenment** (Enlightened One) mediates the Hunab Ku light-photon-cyclone force to the dum duar luminic centrifugal line of force and the kum centripetal luminic thermic electric lines of force.

THE EIGHT BINDING DIAGONAL AXES

There are eight diagonal axes that bind the entire structure of the Hunab Ku 21 grid into a unified system. The purpose of the diagonal axes is to cross-stitch the Mauri tube and equatorial line of force, the different meridians and gravitational stabilizers and the various power of harmony cells.

The eight diagonals are grouped into two sets: 1) the four outer defining diagonals and 2) the four inner harmonic color diagonals.

The four outer defining diagonals connect the Four Gates of Light and define the outer template of the Hunab Ku 21 Galactic Tree of Life and Knowledge:

1. The **Night-Dragon** diagonal defines the upper left hand quadrant, connects first (polar) and third (equatorial) gates of light. The Night Dragon radiates heat and possesses the waxing power of darkness. This is the axis of Being Dreaming.

2. The **Night-Wind** diagonal defines the lower left quadrant, connects the third (equatorial) and second (polar) gates of light. The Night Wind intensifies light and possesses the waning power of darkness. This is the axis of Dreaming Spirit.

3. The **Seed-Wind** diagonal defines the lower right hand quadrant, connects the second (polar) and fourth (equatorial) gates of light. The Seed Wind catalyzes the light-heat and possesses the waxing power of light. This is the axis of Spirit Awareness.

4. The **Seed-Dragon** diagonal defines the upper right hand quadrant, connects the fourth (equatorial) and first (polar) gates of light. The Seed Dragon vitalizes the heat-light and possesses the waning power of light. This is the axis of Awareness Being.

The four outer diagonals define the Master Tetrad.

The four inner harmonic color diagonals: The four outer light gates are defined by the four harmonic colors—red and white (polar), blue and yellow (equatorial). The four inner harmonic color cells are defined by being the same color at both ends. The color harmonics are defined as red initiates, white refines, blue transforms and yellow ripens. The beginning and end of any inner diagonal is either a gate of power or a source of power.

1. **Red initiating harmonic diagonal**—Red Serpent-Moon (Serpent Initiate-Healer) axis, connects first and second power of harmony cells. This is the Sex-Purification axis; its two intermediary matrix colors are white (Mirror) and blue (Storm).

2. White refining harmonic diagonal—White Worldbridger-Wizard (Hierophant-Wizard) axis, connects first and fourth power of harmony cells. This is the Death-Timelessness axis; its two intermediary matrix colors are white (Mirror) and red (Earth). Note, this axis has three white powers—Worldbridger, Mirror and Wizard.

3. Blue transforming harmonic diagonal—Blue Monkey-Eagle (Magician-Seer) axis, connects third and fourth power of harmony cells. This is the Magic-Vision axis; its two intermediary colors are yellow (Sun) and red (Earth).

Note: the red and blue diagonals are parallel to each other and run in opposite directions while their four intermediary colors comprise the four portals of the Matrix Court of Hunab Ku.

4. Yellow ripening harmonic diagonal—Yellow Human-Star (Sage-Artist) axis, connects third and second power of harmony cells. This is the Wisdom-Art axis; its two intermediary colors are yellow (Sun) and blue (Storm). Note, like the white diagonal which it parallels, this axis has three yellow powers—Human, Sun and Star.

Also note that the diagonals are initiated in the polar power of harmony cells (Courts of the Avatar and the Prophet) and concluded in the equatorial power of harmony cells (Courts of the Compassionate One and the Pathfinder). Meditate upon the symmetry of the matrix of the Hunab Ku 21. Note also that each of the diagonals is connected by three heptad paths each, for a total or 24 heptad paths. This means the vertical axes and latitudinal lines of force account for the other 28 heptad paths. Also observe how the four inner diagonals define the nine constituting tetrads of the master tetrad.

THE NINE TETRADS
(POWER OF HARMONY CELLS—COURTS AND ELECTRO-ETHERIC CELLS)

The Hunab Ku 21 Galactic Tree of Life and Knowledge superstructure with its axis and meridians and equator and stabilizing lines of force is the support for the organization of the nine tetrads organized as five power of harmony cells, the five Courts of Power and the four electro-etheric cells, which constitute the power matrix of the Hunab Ku 21.

The five power of harmony cells are activated during the 7-day and 20-day journeys and are accommodated by the 52 heptad paths. The electro-etheric cells are the energy suppliers that activate the five courts with the primal and secondary thermic and luminic meridians and lines of force. These four electro-etheric power cells are activated by opening heptad paths 33, 34, 35, 36, 37, 38, 39 and 40.

The power of harmony cells are of three kinds:

1) **The two polar power of harmony cells**: The Marka Polar Power of Harmony Cell of Cosmic Knowledge, Court of the Avatar, and the Darka Polar Power of Harmony Cell of Cosmic Prophecy, Court of the Prophet. These two cells are vertically aligned to the central electromagnetic axis or Mauri tube.

Knowledge and Prophecy polarize and dynamize.

2) **The two equatorial force field power of harmony cells:** The Centrifugal Force Field of Cosmic Love Court of the Compassionate One (galactic heat cell), and the Centripetal Force Field of Cosmic Intelligence (galactic light cell), Court of the Pathfinder. These two cells are aligned to the galactic equator and the dum kuali thermic centrifugal line of force and the dum duar luminic centripetal line force.

Love and Intelligence stabilize and evolve.

3) **The Central Matrix Fifth Force Power Cell of Hunab Ku**, Court of the Hunab Ku coordinates all four outer power of harmony cells. In its center is the Hunab Ku 21, the nucleus of the universal ordinances and fifth force commands for radializing the totality as a unity.

The Fifth Force unifies and radializes.

Each of the four Outer Power of Harmony Cells consists of 1 Gate of Light, 1 Gate of Power, 1 Source of Power, 1 Seat of Power, and 1 Matrix Portal.

1. Red Marka Pole—First Polar Power of Harmony Cell of Cosmic Knowledge, Court of the Avatar

Gate of Light: Red Dragon (1) Gate of Cosmic Being, Primal Force—GK Neptune.

Gate of Power: Red Serpent (5) Gate of Sex, Serpent Initiate of Wisdom, Sex is the beginning of Knowledge—GK Maldek.

Source of Power: White Worldbridger (6) Death, the Hierophant, Death is the Source of Knowledge—GK Mars.

Seat of Power: Blue Hand (7) Knowledge, the Avatar holds the Seat of Cosmic Knowledge—GK Earth.

Second Matrix Portal: White Mirror (18) Portal of Meditation, the Yogi(ni), Meditation is the Knowledge of Hunab Ku—GK Neptune.

2. Blue Darka Pole—Third Polar Power of Harmony Cell of Cosmic Prophecy, Court of the Prophet

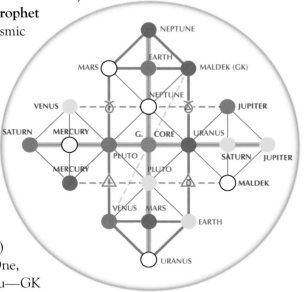

Gate of Light: White Wind (2) Gate of Cosmic Spirit, High Priestess—GK Uranus.

Gate of Power: Blue Monkey (11) Gate of Magic, the Magician, Magic is the Beginning of Prophecy—SP Venus.

Source of Power: Yellow Human (12) Free Will Wisdom, the Sage, Free Will Wisdom is the Source Prophecy—SP Earth.

Seat of Power: Red Skywalker (13), the Prophet holds the Seat of Cosmic Prophecy—SP Mars.

Fourth Matrix Portal: Yellow Sun (20) Portal of Enlightenment, the Enlightened One, Enlightenment is the Prophecy of Hunab Ku—GK Pluto (A).

3. Violet Centrifugal Force Field—Second Harmonic Cell of Cosmic Love (Galactic Heat Cell), Court of the Compassionate One

Gate of Light: Blue Night (3) Gate of Cosmic Dreaming, the Dreamer—GK Saturn.

Gate of Power: Yellow Star (8) Gate of Art, the Artist, Art is the Beginning of Love—GK Venus.

Source of Power: Red Moon (9) Purification, the Healer, Purification is the Source of Love—GK Mercury (Ω).

Seat of Power: White Dog (10), the Compassionate One holds the Seat of the Power of Cosmic Love—SP Mercury (A).

Third Matrix Portal: Blue Storm (19) Portal of Self-Generation, the Worldchanger, Self-Generation is the Love of Hunab Ku—SP Pluto (Ω).

4. Yellow Centripetal Force Field—Fourth Harmonic Power Cell of Cosmic Intelligence (galactic light cell), Court of the Pathfinder

Gate of Light: Yellow Seed (4) Gate of Cosmic Awareness, the Innocent—GK Jupiter.

Gate of Power: White Wizard (14) Gate of Timelessness, the Wizard, Timelessness is the Beginning of Intelligence—SP Maldek.

Source of Power: Blue Eagle (15) Vision, the Seer, Vision is the Source of Intelligence—SP Jupiter.

Seat of Power: Yellow Warrior (16) the Pathfinder holds the Seat of Cosmic Intelligence—SP Saturn.

First Matrix Portal: Red Earth (17) Portal of Navigation, the Navigator, Navigation is the Intelligence of Hunab Ku—SP Uranus.

5. Green Central Matrix—Fifth Force Power Cell of Hunab Ku

First Matrix Portal: Red Earth (17) Portal of Navigation, the Navigator—Transmits Hunab Ku as Intelligence of Navigation to Fourth Power of Harmony Cell of Intelligence.

Second Matrix Portal: White Mirror (18) Portal of Meditation, the Yogi(ni)—Transmits Hunab Ku as Meditation of Knowledge to First Power of Harmony Cell of Knowledge.

Third Matrix Portal: Blue Storm (19) Portal of Self-Generation, the Worldchanger—Transmits Hunab Ku as Self-Generation of Love to Second Power of Harmony Cell of Love.

Fourth Matrix Portal: Yellow Sun (20) Portal of Enlightenment, the Enlightened One— Transmits Hunab Ku as Enlightenment of Prophecy to Third Power of Harmony Cell of Prophecy.

Fifth Portal and Seat of Power: the One Dweller of the Cube, Magus of the Infinite—Hunab Ku 21—Portal of Cosmic Fifth Force—Hunab Ku holds fifth seat of power and radially transmits Light-Photon-Cyclone force as Navigation, Meditation, Self-Generation and Enlightenment.

The Four Power Tetrads—the Electro-Etheric Cells

Formed by the four intersections of the two meridians and the two stabilizing lines of force, these four cells are only activated by the heptad paths and are not intrinsically a part of the 20-day journey. That is why they are called "etheric". They supply different types of thermic (heat) or luminic (light) cosmic electricity to the different power cells. The cosmic electricity is the transmission fluid of cosmic telepathy.

The cells represent a compression of cosmic electricity into lines of force where different charges activate two each of the four outer power cells. There are two primary and two secondary (complex) cells.

There are six types of cosmic electricity (also see *CHC Vol. II*): 1) **dum kuali**—primary thermic (first power cell); 2) **dum duar**—primary luminic (second power cell); 3) **kemio**—complex thermic (third power cell); 4) **kum**—complex luminic (fourth power cell); 5) **hyperneutron**, the Mirror of the Yogi(ni)—activates thermic stabilizing line of force; and 6) **hyperelectron**, the Sun of the Enlightened One—activates luminic stabilizing line of force. The matrix fifth force power cell is activated and activates all four electro-etheric power cells with a seventh type of cosmic electricity or hyperplasma—Sirius B-52, which also forms a "heavy" cosmic Element 113 and corresponds to the 441—21^2 matrix cube power.

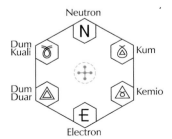

The Two Primary Cells

1ˢᵗ Electro-Etheric Thermic Cell—Dum Kuali Power Cell—intersection of heptad paths 35 and 37. Electromagnetic meridian 35 connects First Source of Power, Death, the Hierophant with Third Portal of Self-Generation, the Worldchanger; stabilizing line of force 37 connects Second Gate of Power of Art, the Artist, with first Matrix Portal of Meditation, the Yogi/Yogini. First and second power of harmony cells electro-thermically activated.

2ⁿᵈ Electro-Etheric Luminic Cell—Dum Duar Power Cell—Intersection of heptad paths 36 and 39. Electromagnetic meridian 36 connects Third Matrix Portal of Self-Generation, the Worldchanger with Third Gate of Power, Magic, the Magician; stabilizing line of force 39 connects Second Source of Power, Purification, the Healer, with Fourth Matrix Portal of Enlightenment, the Enlightened One. Second and third power of harmony cells electro-luminically activated.

The Two Secondary Cells

3. **Electro-Etheric Thermic-Luminic Cell, Kemio** "pacifying force"—Intersection of heptad paths 33 and 38; 33 connects First Gate of Power, Sex, Serpent Initiate of Wisdom, with first Matrix Portal of Navigation, the Navigator; 38 connects First Matrix Portal of Meditation, the Yogi/Yogini, with Fourth Source of Power, Vision, the Seer. First and fourth power of harmony cells electro-thermically activated by the vitalizing force.

4. **Electro-Etheric Luminic-Thermic Thermic-Luminic Cell, Kum** "catalyzing force"—intersection of heptad paths 34 and 40. 34 connects First Matrix Portal of Navigation, the Navigator with third Source of Power, Wisdom, the Sage; and 40 connects Fourth Matrix Portal of Enlightenment, the Enlightened One, with Fourth Gate of Power, Timelessness, the Wizard. Third and fourth power of harmony cells catalytically activated.

Preface to Noogenesis: Opening the 7 Heptad Gates

We enter the Holomind Perceiver daily through the heptad gate meditations as put forth in *CHC Vol. VI,* and described further in the previous chapter. These gates are the openers. By practicing Synchrogalactic Yoga we can circulate hyperplasma and radial plasma through the central channel, thus affecting the etheric body of the central nervous system and saturating it with plasma. These practices are meant to help us maintain a daily awareness of higher mind and the operation of our fourth-dimensional self.

Locate the 7 heptad gates that correspond with one each of the seven radial plasmas. Each of the seven heptad gates is located down the mystic 11 vertical of the 441 matrix. The gates occur at intervals, and each have their own qualities.

Every seven days we open the 7 heptad gates. Every 7 days we build a cube. The gates are not moving variables, but are established for each day of the week. We practice opening a heptad gate each day. We build from the four heptad gates beginning on Dali with **profound samadhi,** which is pure non-conceptual space of experience that connects us to our **preconscious,** first mental sphere. Then we advance to Seli and activate **informative samadhi,** where we allow ourselves to return to the telepathic frequencies of the purity of our consciousness that activate the **subconscious,** second mental sphere.

On the third day, Gamma, we activate the third mental sphere: **conscious waking mediumship,** which helps us to realize that we are always mediums—that we are always channeling cosmic forces. Through this heptad gate we connect with the 441 matrix. On the fourth day, Kali, the fourth mental sphere is activated: **continuing consciousness (higher mind control),** the fourth-dimensional self (holon). On this day we practice how to maintain ourselves in such a state that we begin to experience the quality of unbroken awareness of the higher mind.

The first four days (Dali to Kali) connect us to the first four circuits which connect the four outer time dimensions and the four radial dimensions; or eight time dimensions. The last three circuits are all in the ninth time dimension. From here we enter Alpha, **superconscious** and Limi, **subliminal conscious,** where we are opening ourselves to operating in the ninth time dimension. On the seventh day, Silio,

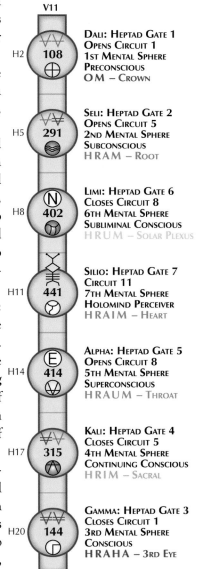

V11

H2 — 108 — **Dali: Heptad Gate 1** Opens Circuit 1 / 1st Mental Sphere / Preconscious / O M – Crown

H5 — 291 — **Seli: Heptad Gate 2** Opens Circuit 5 / 2nd Mental Sphere / Subconscious / H RAM – Root

H8 — 402 — **Limi: Heptad Gate 6** Closes Circuit 8 / 6th Mental Sphere / Subliminal Conscious / H RUM – Solar Plexus

H11 — 441 — **Silio: Heptad Gate 7** Circuit 11 / 7th Mental Sphere / Holomind Perceiver / H RAIM – Heart

H14 — 414 — **Alpha: Heptad Gate 5** Opens Circuit 8 / 5th Mental Sphere / Superconscious / H RAUM – Throat

H17 — 315 — **Kali: Heptad Gate 4** Closes Circuit 5 / 4th Mental Sphere / Continuing Conscious / H RIM – Sacral

H20 — 144 — **Gamma: Heptad Gate 3** Closes Circuit 1 / 3rd Mental Sphere / Conscious / H RAHA – 3rd Eye

holomind perceiver, we open to the 11th dimension or the order of the cube. Through this practice, we open new channels within our being and become highly sensitized to emotional perturbations and how they reflect in the outer environment and vice versa. At any moment we can open ourselves to become channels for the galactic order.

Ultimately the purpose of this practice is to gain the facility of locating the moving variables of the synchronic order and the cube matrix frequencies within the circuit chip of the holomind perceiver.

CHAPTER 10

MANIFESTING THE SUPERHUMAN
NOOGENESIS AND SIRIAN REBIRTH PART II

It is the purpose of the Noosphere II to experiment with stabilizing higher states of consciousness in order to experience and determine what the nature of noospheric consciousness will be like. There is no question that the shift to the noosphere, being the herald of an altogether new geological era—from the Holocene to the Psychozoic—that this mutation will augur a dramatic change in human consciousness and self-perception

—*Noosphere II*

Be ye renewed by the renewing of your mind.

—*Jesus (Romans, 12:2)*

1. The highest sphere of the Earth is the noosphere, the composite resonating receptor of the fifth-dimensional higher self as an aggregate, inclusive of all of its mental impressions.

2. While the fifth-dimensional self communicates through the first mental sphere of the individual, all impressions of the akashic record can be accessed through the noosphere or crown chakra of the planet.

3. The noosphere is the aggregate of the advanced states of mind and consciousness that characterize all intelligent life throughout the universe. The planetary noosphere, then, is the register that receives the impressions of the seventh mental sphere, properly located within the fifth-dimensional entity and accessed through the noosphere by the homo noosphericus.

4. The homo noosphericus, through its evolved enlargement of perception and chakra activations, can then access the noosphere/psi bank, arousing the AC and CA Manitous and receive the impressions of the akashic records. In this way, he/she wakes up and evolves the holomind perceiver.

5. Noogenesis is the birth of the noosphere through a mental genesis; a mind rebirth, while simultaneously embodying the descent of a Sirian personality, hence, Sirian Rebirth. In *CHC Vol. VI* we introduced noogenesis by means of the *vulom magnetic attraction force field* which is embedded in the holomind perceiver, the seventh mental sphere. In this chapter we explore the vast workings of the super organization system of the holomind perceiver as a means for consciously activating noogenesis.

6. In the evolving superhuman, the seventh mental sphere—holomind perceiver—descends from the fifth-dimensional Higher Self transmitting its code essence into the holomind perceiver, which also serves as the transmitting and receiving station of the UR runes of the genetic code and matrices of the psi bank, located in the corpus callosum. Once activated, the holomind perceiver or seventh mental sphere operates in tandem with the noosphere and the fifth-dimensional self. This process lays the foundation of the cosmocentric perspective and the expansion into cosmic consciousness.

7. The holomind perceiver, embedded in the 441 cube matrix system, is the evolutionary time coding system of the One mind. All of the evolutionary life of the spiritual mental activity of the noosphere is organized from this 441 matrix. This is the mechanism of our evolution.

8. Universal timing is impartial and organized by a precise numerical code that reveals to it exactly where each and every one of us is in terms of the evolutionary process at any given time. This is known in the *260 Postulates of the Dynamics of Time* as the galactic brain. This is how the designing intelligence of the universe guides (and recognizes) itself through time.

9. The holomind perceiver is constructed of various electrically charged flows and instances of numerical frequency values. These flows and frequency values define different perceptual values of time, space, cosmic electricity, sensory inputs and outputs and extrasensory perceptual coordinations, all radialized into a synthesizing field of whole mind (holomind) ratios and perspectives.

10. Familiarizing yourself with and practicing this system keys you into the noosphere, the aggregate of the advanced states of mind and consciousness that characterize all intelligent life throughout the universe. By studying the holomind perceiver and 441 matrix you are being imprinted with the new evolutionary sense organ. Practice visualizing and holding simultaneous layers or levels of telepathic frequencies. This is a living code.

11. The process of radialization is achieved by two principle or axial flows: The hyperplasmic electro-partonic flow mediating the left-right axis and the primal electro-energetic positive negative flow mediating front/below-back/above (front ascending from below and back descending from

SYNCHRONOTRON

**APPLICATION – HOLOMIND
PERCEIVER CODES OF TIME**

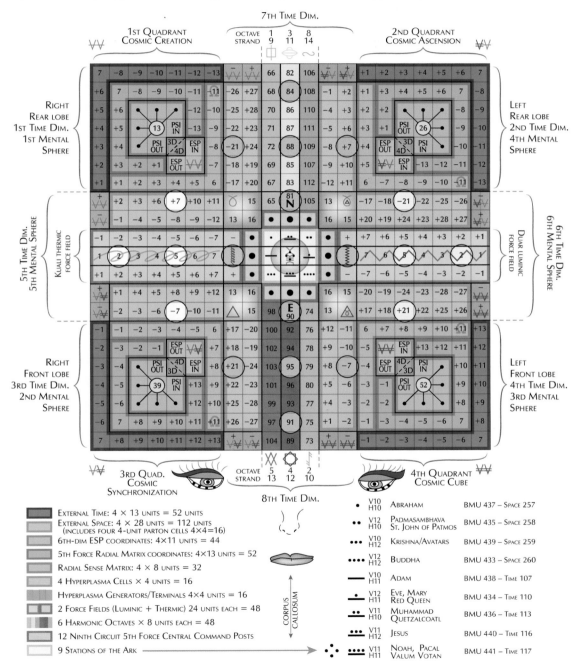

above). Stitching the hyperplasmic axis are the 48 rune harmonics—24 AC (back/above), 24 CA (front/below); it is these runes that conduct impulses from the four sets of 64 DNA runes into the various circuits and flows of the holomind perceiver.

12. The frequencies are living thoughts of the higher-dimensional Star Elders. We can develop our capacity to tune into these non-conceptual thoughts, or mentation waves, within the context of the frequencies and circuits of the master matrix: holomind perceiver. This is a program that can be followed by tracking the daily frequencies and then plugging them into the 441 holomind perceiver matrix (see Appendix II).

STRUCTURE OF HOLOMIND PERCEIVER

13. The holomind perceiver is arranged in a color coded circuitry with four basic quadrants and two axes of 11. Since the human is bilaterally organized, or bilaterally dominant (left eye/right eye; left brain/right brain, etc), this has given way to a dualistic perception of reality that governs the world and creates endless conflict. The Synchronotron system, inclusive of the holomind perceiver, is a program of radial wholeness.

14. In order for the human to evolve into radial wholeness, we must evolve a new brain function. This new brain function is located in the corpus callosum at the point where there is a binary lateral crossover from the left brain to the right side of the body and the right brain to the left side of the body. The corpus callosum mediates the flow of the two brain hemispheres. The holomind perceiver is innate but dormant; we have yet to experience this intrinsic integration.

15. We know from Cosmic Science that we are unconsciously operating with six mental spheres, but we need a seventh mental sphere that integrates left, right, front and back along with the six other mental spheres. This seventh mental sphere relates to the function of radial consciousness or the development of 360-degree perception. This is the actualization of the shaman's whole body knowing made superconscious.

16. This seventh mental sphere, in order to operate, requires a new brain component, i.e. the holomind perceiver. The actual circuitry for the holomind perceiver demonstrates a new radial organization of the mind, perceptions and functions to create a quadraphonic sensorium.

17. This holomind perceiver matrix can be continuously telepathically projected on a point in the center of the brain—the corpus callosum. In this way it can be thought of as a telepathically engraved nanochip that accommodates and coordinates new intergalactic cosmic functions (which is our purpose, responsibility and evolutionary duty to channel).

VULOM MAGNETIC ATTRACTION FORCE FIELD STRUCTURE TRANSFERRED TO HOLOMIND
PERCEIVER PSYCHOTELEPATHIC NANOCHIP TO BE "IMPRINTED" ONTO THE CORPUS CALLOSUM

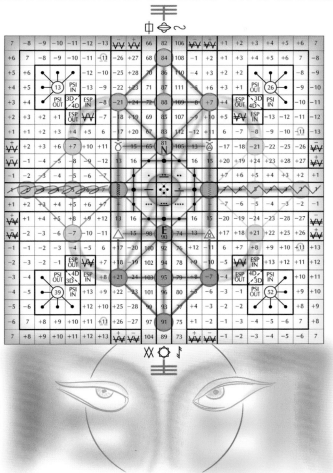

NOOGENESIS AND SYNCHRONOTRON

In order to realize the noogenesis we must work with a particular mechanism and a particular structure: the Synchronotron. The Vulom magnetic attraction force field structure is located within the Synchronotron (see also Appendix I). To activate this we have to both imprint and visualize this structure within us and understand how the principles of magnetic reconnection and binary crossover polarity work. Through a third transfer medium in the center of the earth we can create a wholly interactive psycho-telepathic electromagnetic field that becomes one unified force field connecting the human and biopsychic field with the terrestrial electromagnetic field.

To directly experience the holomind perceiver and the seventh mental sphere of radialized consciousness we telepathically imprint or engraved its structure upon the corpus callosum. For the purpose of the telepathic engraving, we have the 441 Synchronotron holomind perceiver matrix to study.

18. The simplest way to study the holomind perceiver is to first familiarize yourself with the nine time dimensions: four outer time dimensions; four radial time dimensions and one inner core time dimension (see Chapter 3). Draw your own matrices in order to imprint and absorb the information.

FOUR QUADRANTS AND NINE TIME DIMENSIONS

19. First note the four space quadrants and nine time dimensions. The **four outer time dimensions** are the most critical to understanding the holomind perceiver. This is where the radialization of all of the different mental and sensory functions occurs. The four inner or **radial time dimensions** are integrating units. The **ninth time dimension** is known as **inner core time** and is the central coordinating unit.

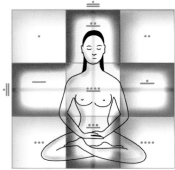

20. Study the four quadrants and note how they are divided by the horizontal 11 and vertical 11 axes. There are four quadrants at 100 units each, which is 400 units. This means V11 and H11 are the remaining 41 units for a total of 441. The V11 and H11 axes define the four quadrants of the functions of holomind perceiver.

21. Each of the four quadrants is identified by the hyperplasma which is chanelled through each of the four zones. Note that the left side of the brain is beta dominant and the right side is alpha dominant; back is alpha dominant and front is beta dominant. The nine time dimensions are sequential and go from upper left to lower right (time dimensions 1-4), center left to center right (time dimensions 5 and 6), top to bottom (time dimensions 7 and 8) and then center (9th time dimension).

I. The first quadrant is the alpha-alpha ⱽⱽ quadrant. This includes the first time dimension and part of the fifth and seventh radial time dimensions; Beta dominant.

II. The second quadrant is the alpha-beta ⱽⱽ quadrant. This includes the third time dimension and part of the fifth and eighth radial time dimensions; Beta dominant.

III. The third quadrant is the beta-beta ⱽⱽ quadrant. This includes the fourth time dimensions and part of the eighth and sixth radial time dimensions; Alpha dominant.

IV. The fourth quadrant is the beta-alpha ⱽⱽ quadrant. This includes the second time dimension and parts of the seventh and sixth time dimensions; Alpha dominant.

There are two movements of consciousness: ascending (alpha-alpha) and descending (beta-beta).

48 UR Harmonics

22. The vertical axis contains the 48 UR harmonics of the new six UR strands. This runs down the corpus callosum. The 48 UR harmonics complement the 64 UR runes (see also Chapter 11 and *CHC. Vol. V: Book of Timespace*).

23. The 48 UR harmonics define new behavioral capacities for the Second Creation. They are called harmonics because we are entering a phase of a purely resonant mode. Laterally, we have the behavioral modes of the 48 UR harmonics on the vertical axis of the corpus callosum. The horizontal axis is the electrodynamic axis that connects the front and back of the right and left lobes. These are defined by the two electrodynamic force fields.

24. On the right side of the brain is the **dum kuali** or **thermic force field.** This connects the first and second quadrants. On the left side of the brain, is the **dum duar** or **luminic force field** that connects the third and fourth quadrants.

25. With the 48 UR harmonics and electrodynamic force fields, there are **21 units each** in the radial time dimensions for a total of **84 units: 21 units** in both the upper and lower (seventh and eighth) time dimensions—7 runes of each of the six strands (= 42 units); in the left and right (fifth and sixth) time dimension are the **thermic and luminic force fields,** containing 7 neutral charges on either side of which are also both an activating (+) or a sublimating (–) transformer field that accompanies the force field (7 neutral +7 positive +7 negative = **21 units,** in both the fifth and sixth time dimension = **42 units**). The thermic and luminic force fields complement the zones where the UR harmonics reside.

26. Every unit in the holomind perceiver is numbered. The numbering system is positive (+) or negative (–) so that everything is equalized. The positive refers to the activating influence or externalizing influence of a particular field. The positive units are the **activating transformers of the force field** and the negative units are the **sublimating factors of the force field.** Sublimating is the process of internalizing and receiving from within. Activating is the process of externalizing or transmitting without. Everything is either an activating or a sublimating force.

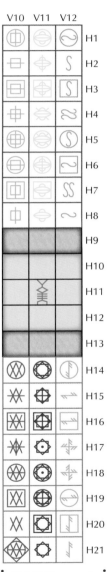

48 UR Harmonic Runes

HOLOMIND PERCEIVER FUNCTIONS AS HOLOGRAPHIC CHIP

27. Each quadrant is a microcosm with all the same functions as every other quadrant (see next chapter for detailed illustrations). The positive and negative flows are complementary. For example, look at the first time dimension: On the outermost or the external time the first six units are **activating** (+). In the opposite corner, the first six units are **sublimating** (-). The first six units of the external time flow of the first quadrant are the same, but in the opposite direction as the second, the first and third quadrant external time flows begin on a vertical axis, whereas the second and fourth quadrant external time flows begin on a horizontal axis.

28. Each quadrant has exactly the same function. This means you can begin by studying and familiarizing yourself with one of the four quadrants; then you will understand them all. It is important to fully grasp the function of the four outer time dimensions. This is where the sense perceptions are radialized.

29. Study each quadrant and see how it is organized in a specific way. Each quadrant or outer time dimension has a 13-unit external time zone. Each of the outer time dimensions contains exactly 13 units that define the whole time dimension. This means that each of the four outer time zones, where the senses are radialized, is informed by the 13-unit cosmic wavespell function. This helps coordinate the radialization of the senses. Each sense organ has a mundane and a supernatural quality.

30. In each of the external time flows the seventh unit is always at the corner. So the seventh unit or the four corners of the 441 matrix are all a function of the power of seven. This is an important point. These four sevens create the 28, and the seven creates the 13. Thus, all the senses are organized by the same frequencies that organize cosmic time and the 13 moon cycle.

31. The four sevens that create the 28, which accounts for external time, and also account for 28 units of external space. Whereas the external time occurs within the four outer time dimensions, the 28 units of the external space always occur within the four radial time dimensions in any one of the four quadrants. For example, in the fourth quadrant the first 12 units are in the eighth time dimension and the last four units are in the sixth time dimension. This indicates that the 13 of the external time is the organizational power of the 13 frequency of the cosmic cycle of the wavespell.

32. The 28 external spaces show that the 28-unit frequency of the 28-day standard is organized in the interdimensional space of the radial time dimension. So the 28-day cycle is an actual function of these radial time dimensions (see graphic at end of Chapter 13).

33. Radial space is always organized in two flows starting with two units or generators: an activating generator and a sublimating generator. These two generators are where the flow starts. This particular pattern creates a "U" shape on its side. (We see how the numbers are called magnitudes; i.e. activating 12th magnitude, etc., so we have 6 units activating and 6 units sublimating).

34. Then we get to the ninth time dimension where are found the 13th, 14th, 15th and 16th units of every external space flow—these four units always correspond to one of the four hyperpartons. For example, in the lower-right quadrant, we find the light of inner heat, the kemio hyperparton. This is a high frequency conversion zone that occurs in the ninth time dimension. The flows continue from the 17th to the 28th unit in the adjacent radial time dimension and then switch polarity.

35. The internal flow is sublimating at one point and activating at another point; this is so the time dimension can have an influence of sublimating and an influence of activating, etc. The external time and space flows show how the 13 Moon/28-day cycle is coordinated by the different time dimensions.

36. Now turn your attention to the 36-unit radial sense matrix. There are four of these radial sense matrixes, 144 units in all, for sensory radialization. Each radial sense perception consists of two flows: sixth-dimensional ESP flow and fifth force flow.

37. The ESP flow flows on the inside (closest to the center of the matrix). This is 11 units. These are organized as five sublimating and five activating units, with **6** as the internal coordinating unit. Note that these sixth-dimensional ESP flows moderate the 11 magnitudes of sixth-dimensional subliminal consciousness as received within the radial sense matrix.

38. The other flow within the radial sense matrix is the fifth force flow. This flow consists of 13 units (just like external time) and surrounds the core of the sense matrix. The 13 units are divided into six sublimating and six activating units. Notice that the internal coordinating unit of the fifth force is **7**. This seven is always located next to the seven of external time. The seven and six are also the coordinating units of external time (?).

39. Note where the **6** is located and how it connects with the hyperparton of the space flows. The diagonal is very important. Just as the sixth-dimensional flow moderates the subliminal consciousness, the magnitudes of the sixth-dimensional consciousness are organized as extrasensory perception impulses; telepathic, subliminal, etc. Likewise, the fifth force flow coordinates the fifth force flow of superconscious thought flows or thought magnitudes in the fifth mental sphere. These are the flows that coordinate the inner radial sense matrix.

HOLOMIND PERCEIVER 101

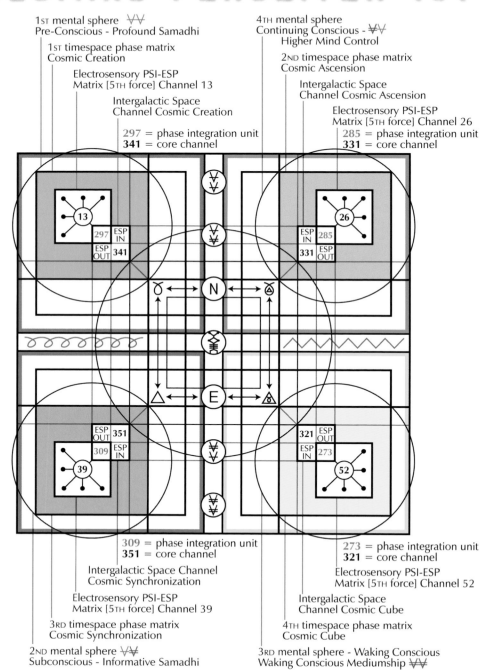

1ST mental sphere ₩
Pre-Conscious - Profound Samadhi

1ST timespace phase matrix
Cosmic Creation

Electrosensory PSI-ESP
Matrix [5TH force] Channel 13

Intergalactic Space
Channel Cosmic Creation

297 = phase integration unit
341 = core channel

4TH mental sphere
Continuing Conscious - ₩
Higher Mind Control

2ND timespace phase matrix
Cosmic Ascension

Intergalactic Space
Channel Cosmic Ascension

Electrosensory PSI-ESP
Matrix [5TH force] Channel 26

285 = phase integration unit
331 = core channel

309 = phase integration unit
351 = core channel

Intergalactic Space Channel
Cosmic Synchronization

Electrosensory PSI-ESP
Matrix [5TH force] Channel 39

3RD timespace phase matrix
Cosmic Synchronization

2ND mental sphere ₩
Subconscious - Informative Samadhi

273 = phase integration unit
321 = core channel

Electrosensory PSI-ESP
Matrix [5TH force] Channel 52

Intergalactic Space
Channel Cosmic Cube

4TH timespace phase matrix
Cosmic Cube

3RD mental sphere - Waking Conscious
Waking Conscious Mediumship ₩

Radial Sense Cores

40. There are two flows, a sixth-dimensional flow that coordinates the **ESP** circuit and a fifth-dimensional flow that coordinates the **PSI** (psychosensory information) circuit that comes from activation of the sense fields. The ESP circuit is sixth-dimensional, outside the domain of physical perception. The ESP circuit has two cores: the sense core (8 + 1 units) and the intergalactic hyperplasma channel core (3 + 1 units). Each of these cores shares one unit together.

41. The purpose of studying these sense cores is to begin to become aware that any sensory input or experience you may be having is actually processed in the radial matrix sense cores of each of the four outer time dimensions simultaneously. Practice feeling this in the parts of your brain corresponding to the four outer time dimensions.

42. The **intergalactic channel** is primarily a fourth- to fifth-dimensional phase unit. The **sense core** is primarily a third- to fourth-dimensional phase unit. This interdimensional unit is important as it coordinates the higher ESP functions. This unit is always located at fifth unit diagonal from the corner and is a key unit that coordinates ESP and PSI information.

43. The radial sense matrix has eight units plus an interdimensional unit, which serves as the central coordinating or master unit at the center of the 49-unit matrix: each master coordinating unit has a specific number frequency: **13** (first quadrant), **26** (fourth quadrant), **39** (second quadrant) and **52** (third quadrant).

    13 coordinates the first time dimension of cosmic creation.
    26 coordinates the second time dimension of cosmic ascension.
    39 coordinates the third time dimension of cosmic synchronization.
    52 coordinates the second time dimension of the cosmic cube.

44. On the outer part around the core of the sense matrix there are five units that correspond to the five senses: touch, taste, smell, hearing and sight. The olfactory sense is the middle coordinating sense. While touch and taste have to do with actual physical contact with the sense organs, sight and sound pick up subtler vibrations, and olfactory is the intermediate sense because you can smell things but you cannot see or touch the smell.

45. The sense matrix core of the four time dimensions all have the exact same layout; they always start with touch closest to the first fifth force flow unit. Once we become familiar with the holomind perceiver we can take any sensory impression, and locate it precisely in this matrix where it is being organized simultaneously in the four parts of the holomind perceiver. It is radialized according to four primary functions.

THE FOUR OUTER TIME RADIAL SENSE MATRICES

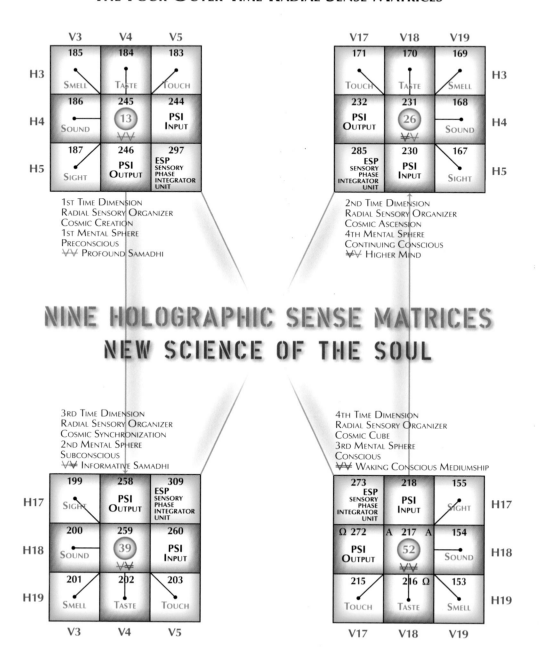

1ST TIME DIMENSION
RADIAL SENSORY ORGANIZER
COSMIC CREATION
1ST MENTAL SPHERE
PRECONSCIOUS
PROFOUND SAMADHI

2ND TIME DIMENSION
RADIAL SENSORY ORGANIZER
COSMIC ASCENSION
4TH MENTAL SPHERE
CONTINUING CONSCIOUS
HIGHER MIND

NINE HOLOGRAPHIC SENSE MATRICES
NEW SCIENCE OF THE SOUL

3RD TIME DIMENSION
RADIAL SENSORY ORGANIZER
COSMIC SYNCHRONIZATION
2ND MENTAL SPHERE
SUBCONSCIOUS
INFORMATIVE SAMADHI

4TH TIME DIMENSION
RADIAL SENSORY ORGANIZER
COSMIC CUBE
3RD MENTAL SPHERE
CONSCIOUS
WAKING CONSCIOUS MEDIUMSHIP

36 radialized units of human neuro-psychosensory modalities.
Planetary human capable of quadripartite simultaneity.

THE FOUR RADIAL TIME HYPERORGANIC SENSE MATRICES
+ 9TH METASENSORY CORE TIME

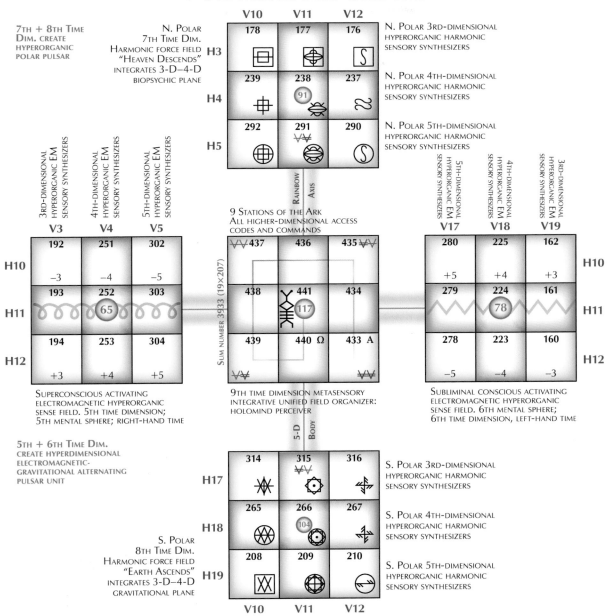

Time dimensions 5-6: Radial electromagnetic gravitational field pulsars (18 units)
Time dimensions 7-8: Radial biopsychic polar pulsars (18 units)
9th Time dimension: Metasensory higher-dimensional meditation unified field "God Key" codes.

46. We have five senses. Then we have five subtle elements: the energy of touch, the energy of taste, the energy of smell, the energy of sight and the energy of sound. These are subtle qualities. We also have the five action organs: mouth, hands, bowels, genitals and feet. For every sensory experience practice becoming aware of what organ is actually receiving the impression.

47. There are also five elements: ether, air, fire, water, earth. The fifth element is the organizing limiting function which is the first limitation of universal consciousness. There is also the limitation of illusory knowledge; the limitation of the power of selection or discrimination; the limitation of the power of timespace; and the limitation of destiny. This demonstrates the system of the fifth force.

48. The psi input unit corresponds to where the first fifth force flow unit is located. The fifth force psi input is also known as a psychosensory information unit. Every sensory experience you have registers as an information unit. When you cognize that information unit then it becomes psi. We receive psi energy and we transmit psi energy: input, output. This is the organization of the core matrix.

49. Adjacent to the **core sensory matrix** is the **intergalactic channel matrix** which consists of the intergalactic hyperplasmic channels: alpha-alpha, beta-beta, alpha-beta or beta-alpha. This coordination unit is always in the sixth unit diagonal from the corner. We telepathically activate these four channels, plus the fifth central Sirius Beta-52 channel at the very center of the ninth time dimension. These are the new inlets for the hyperplasma.

FOUR PRIMARY MENTAL SPHERES

50. The hyperplasma have specified types of activation functions. The perception and modes of behavior that exist from a higher mode of being continuously flow from the fourth dimension and are guiding everything through these four mental functions that work in tandem with the corresponding hyperplasmas.

51. The **four key hyperplasmas** correspond with the outer time dimensions, which in turn correspond to one of the **four primary mental spheres: preconscious, subconscious, conscious** and **continuing conscious.** These four mental spheres and hyperplasmas form a cosmic psychology that is meant to function in everyday life.

First Mental Sphere—Preconscious: instinctual autonomic information is loaded. **Alpha-alpha force field of profound samadhi** coordinates the flow and the activation of the preconscious innate automatic impulses that flow for whatever reason or purpose. **(First time dimension)**

Second Mental Sphere—Subconscious: Sphere where all potentially accessible thoughts or analphs are located. **Alpha-beta force field of informative samadhi;** corresponds to the meditational state of samadhi within the cosmic synchronization sphere, which activates and informs the subconscious regarding perception of sensory experience. **(Third time dimension)**

Third Mental Sphere—Waking Conscious: Sphere where all the immediately accessible analphs or thoughtforms are located that correspond to the immediate moment-to-moment influx of sensory information. **Beta-Beta force field of waking conscious mediumship.** At this stage you are awake and alert and receive higher-dimensional information without conceptualizing. Your channel is open and you immediately register or activate certain perceptions regarding forms and modes of behavior necessary to continue into a deeper function of higher being. **(Fourth time dimension)**

Fourth Mental Sphere—Continuing Conscious: Sphere of higher organizing consciousness, which takes the raw analphs and transmutes them into something higher. This sphere also coordinates with the higher or fourth-dimensional self. **Beta-alpha force field of higher mind control.** Up through the waking conscious mediumship it is the third-dimensional self that is being activated and activating, but once you reach the fourth mental sphere—continuing conscious—then comes the ability of the third-dimensional self or ego to surrender to the higher self. At this stage the Higher Self does the thinking through you. **(Second time dimension)**

Hyperplasma

52. For each hyperplasma, there is a core channel the inlet directly functioning every day and which is radialized within the four time dimensions. This core channel provides an inlet to each of these four hyperplasmas according to a specific primary function. Each core channel has an **ESP input** channel, and an **ESP output** channel that connects it with the subliminal impulses of the sixth dimension programmed into the sixth-dimensional flow. The hyperplasma core channel coordinates with the ESP input and outputs to create an active flow. So there is subliminal information coming in along with sensory information that is processed within the psi fields.

53. The innermost core of Sirius Beta-52 is also referred to as the planning core that radiates from the eleventh-dimensional channel out to the tenth circuit. This activates the four radial outer units of the tenth circuit (which coordinates the flow of Sirius Beta-52) to radiate out through the ninth circuit, which is always the 16th unit of the outer space flows. The Sirius Beta-52 is the main coordination center for all the quadrants and has to do with both a flow of hyperplasma and an activation of partons.

54. The hyperplasma radiates out from the center of the matrix toward the hyperparton; then to the coordinating sixth unit of the sixth-dimensional ESP flow; to the hyperplasma channel, to the phase unit and then reaches the coordinating time center of the sensory matrix. Then the hyperplasma continues on its path through the five sense nodes, weaving through the senses and then to the seventh coordinating unit of the fifth force flow, where it finally hits the seventh coordinating unit of the external time flow which is what we are experiencing now in this moment. This is how the stream is activated.

55. The holomind perceiver is comprised of a set of discreet organizational matrices within the four quadrants and time dimensions. At the same time we are dealing with the 10 circuits of the 441 (plus the inner 11th) which connect all the dimensions. The first, outermost circuit contains all the external time flows; 16 terminals and generators of the external space flows; six units of the UR harmonics and 3 units each of the luminic and thermic force fields. This the outer time circuit.

56. The information flow of the radialization is instantaneously and simultaneously connected to different flows. While circuits 1 to 7 connect the radial time dimensions with the outer time dimensions, the circuits in the ninth time dimension are all discreet to the ninth time dimension.

57. The **second** circuit coordinates the fifth force (fifth-dimensional) and sixth-dimensional flows. The **third** circuit, starting with the olfactory mode of the fourth time dimension, connects all the sense matrices. The **fourth** circuit connects all the coordinating points of the four outer and four radial time dimensions. The **fifth** circuit connects the interdimensional phase units. The **sixth** circuit connects the four intergalactic hyperplasma channels. The **seventh** circuit coordinates the four sixth-dimensional ESP channels. The **eighth** circuit connects of the four hyperpartons. The **ninth** circuit connects the four coordinating points of the external space flows. The **tenth** circuit connects the eight Stations of the Ark surrounding the **eleventh** central circuit, the Sirius B-52.

58. This is a totally integrated circuit, an integrated chip. **Memorize and imprint this into your body/mind.** All of the evolutionary life of the spiritual/mental activity of the noosphere is organized from this matrix. This is the mechanism of our evolution.

59. With this knowledge we now have the opportunity to activate and embody the noogenesis and thus experience a Sirian rebirth. When this process is completely imprinted within us then we will have an internal quadraphonic, multisensory sensorium and internally synaesthetic sound system. If we practice diligently, the quality of our perceptual experience will change dramatically—the key is to be activating these flows all the time.

CHAPTER 11

MAPPING THE NOOGENESIS
A VISUAL GUIDE TO THE HOLOMIND PERCEIVER

The holomind perceiver is a function of extraterrestrial intelligence. Extraterrestrial intelligence is intelligence that has been generated outside of the planetary sphere for the purpose of activating the next stage of evolution. As we enter deeper into telepathic civilization we will increasingly understand that mathematical ratios govern the psychic and interpsychic sense experiences. This is part of the learning that comes through adaptation to the holomind perceiver, the seventh mental sphere to be activated within the noosphere.

The holomind perceiver is inherent within the cube. Each of the practices of the synchronic order are like a step on a ladder lifting us ever higher within the understanding that there is a fourth-dimensional level of reality where spiritual discipline is in understanding the relationship of the everyday whole system of moving variables and interlocking matrices.

From the point of view of the holomind perceiver, the 441 matrix is divided into two halves (right and left). When you look at the left hand side from the point of view of the matrix, it is actually the right hand side and vice versa. Observing this is the first step in radializing your consciousness. Then there are the other two halves, the top and bottom. The vertical 11 that runs down the center is the corpus callosum.

The holomind perceiver is the 441 matrix telepathically inscribed on the corpus callosum to facilitate the integration of time, space and mind as the principle of radialized synchronization. This is a whole other order of reality than we are accustomed to; it is a new cosmology based on the eleventh-dimensional system of the cube. It is a telepathic language referencing system that has nothing to do with historical modes. Within this system are various levels of hierarchical commands and coding. Any number can be plugged into this system and then "read".

In this chapter we will visually explore the intricate workings of the holomind perceiver as a holographic nano-chip of the new evolving extrasensory organ, the seventh mental sphere of radial consciousness. The organization of this nano-chip is based precisely on the fractal of universal time, the 441 cube matrix. The holomind perceiver can be telepathically imprinted as an act of self-evolution. Its origin is in the beam codes of the Sirius Star Council in their activation of Earth's noosphere.

The supermind awaits you behind the Synchronotron matrix...

HOLOMIND PERCEIVER CODES

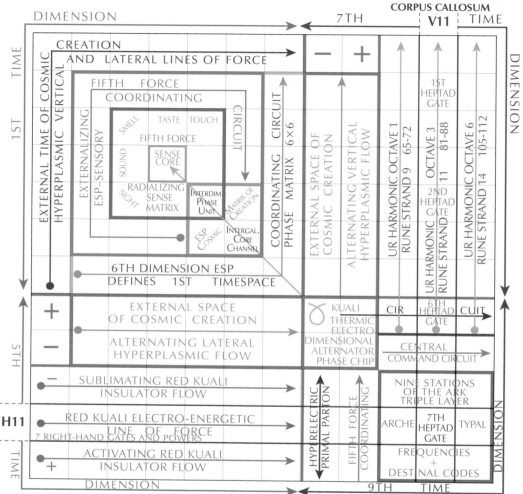

CORPUS CALLOSUM

DIMENSION — 7TH — V11 — TIME

TIME / DIMENSION (side labels)

1ST — 5TH — H11 — TIME (left side)

CREATION AND LATERAL LINES OF FORCE

EXTERNAL TIME OF COSMIC HYPERPLASMIC VERTICAL

FIFTH FORCE COORDINATING

EXTERNALIZING ESP-SENSORY

SMELL TASTE TOUCH
FIFTH FORCE
SOUND
SENSE CORE
SIGHT
RADIALIZING SENSE MATRIX
INTERDIM PHASE UNIT
MATRIX OF CREATION

ESP COSMIC
INTERGAL. CORE CHANNEL

COORDINATING CIRCUIT PHASE MATRIX 6×6

EXTERNAL SPACE OF COSMIC CREATION

ALTERNATING VERTICAL HYPERPLASMIC FLOW

UR HARMONIC OCTAVE 1 — RUNE STRAND 9 — 65-72
UR HARMONIC OCTAVE 3 — RUNE STRAND 11 — 81-88
UR HARMONIC OCTAVE 6 — RUNE STRAND 14 — 105-112

1ST HEPTAD GATE
2ND HEPTAD GATE

6TH DIMENSION ESP DEFINES 1ST TIMESPACE

EXTERNAL SPACE OF COSMIC CREATION

ALTERNATING LATERAL HYPERPLASMIC FLOW

KUALI THERMIC ELECTRO DIMENSIONAL ALTERNATOR PHASE CHIP

CIR — 6TH HEPTAD GATE — CUIT
CENTRAL COMMAND CIRCUIT

SUBLIMATING RED KUALI INSULATOR FLOW

RED KUALI ELECTRO-ENERGETIC LINE OF FORCE
7 RIGHT-HAND GATES AND POWERS

ACTIVATING RED KUALI INSULATOR FLOW

HYPERELECTRIC PRIMAL PARTON

FIFTH FORCE COORDINATING

NINE STATIONS OF THE ARK TRIPLE LAYER

ARCHE — 7TH HEPTAD GATE — TYPAL

FREQUENCIES + DESTINAL CODES

DIMENSION — 9TH — TIME

QUADRANT 1 ⋁⋁

1) **COSMIC CREATION**
   1ST (OUTER) TIME DIMENSION

2) **RED KUALI FORCE FIELD**
   5TH (RIGHT-HAND) TIME DIMENSION

3) **FORCE FIELD OF COSMIC COMMAND DESCENDING**
   7TH (VERTICAL) TIME DIMENSION

4) **INNER CORE TIME – ORIGINAL 7×7 CREATION CODES**
   9TH TIME DIMENSION

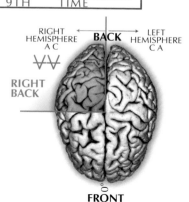

RIGHT HEMISPHERE A C — BACK — LEFT HEMISPHERE C A

⋁⋁

RIGHT BACK

FRONT

	V1	V2	V3	V4	V5	V6	V7	V8	V9	V10	V11	V12
H1	7	−8	−9	−10	−11	−12	−13 Ω	∨∨ −	∨∨ +	66 +	82	106 −
H2	+6	7	−8	−9	−10	−11	−11 Ω	−26	+27	68	84 ∨∨	108
H3	+5	+6	+3 +2		+1	−12	−10	−25	+28	70	86	110
H4	+4	+5	+4 (13)	PSI INPUT −	Ω −13	−9		−22	+23	71	87	111
H5	+3	+4	PSI OUTPUT +5	297 PHASE UNIT +	296 ESP INPUT	−8		−21	+24	72	88 ∨∨	109
H6	+2	+3	+2	+1 A	298 ESP OUTPUT	341 CORE CHANNEL	−7	−18	+19	69	85	107
H7	A +1	+1 A	+2	+3	+4	+5	6	−17	+20	67	83	112
H8	+ ∨∨	+2	+3	+6	+7	+10	+11	14	15	65 +	N 81	105 −
H9	− ∨∨	A −1	−4	−5	−8	−9	−12	13	16			
H10	−1	−2	−3	−4	−5	−6	−7			437	436	435
H11	252									438		434
H12	+1	+2	+3	+4	+5	+6	+7			439	440	433

173

HOLOMIND PERCEIVER CODES

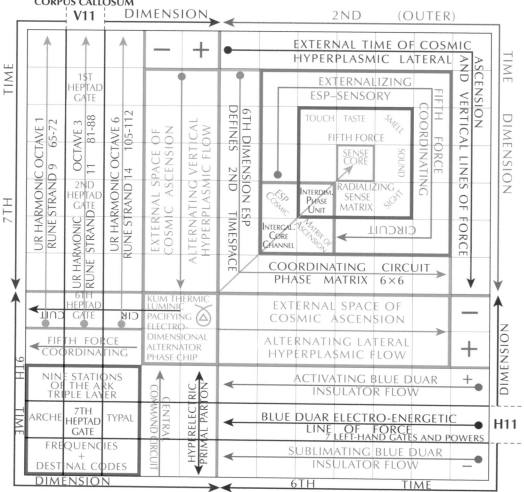

CORPUS CALLOSUM
V11   DIMENSION   2ND   (OUTER)

TIME

7TH

H16

TIME

1ST HEPTAD GATE

UR HARMONIC OCTAVE 1   RUNE STRAND 9   65-72
UR HARMONIC OCTAVE 3   RUNE STRAND 11   81-88

2ND HEPTAD GATE

UR HARMONIC   RUNE STRAND

6TH HEPTAD GATE

UR HARMONIC OCTAVE 6   RUNE STRAND 14   105-112

EXTERNAL SPACE OF COSMIC ASCENSION

ALTERNATING VERTICAL HYPERPLASMIC FLOW

DEFINES 2ND   6TH DIMENSION ESP   TIMESPACE

EXTERNAL TIME OF COSMIC
HYPERPLASMIC LATERAL

ASCENSION AND VERTICAL LINES OF FORCE

FIFTH FORCE COORDINATING   CIRCUIT

TIME
DIMENSION

EXTERNALIZING
ESP–SENSORY

TOUCH   TASTE   SMELL

FIFTH FORCE

SENSE CORE

SOUND

ESP COSMIC   INTERDIM. PHASE UNIT   RADIALIZING SENSE MATRIX   SIGHT

INTERGAL. CORE CHANNEL   MATRIX OF ASCENSION

COORDINATING   CIRCUIT
PHASE   MATRIX   6×6

CIRCUIT   GATE   CIR

KUM THERMIC LUMINIC PACIFYING ELECTRO-DIMENSIONAL ALTERNATOR PHASE CHIP

EXTERNAL SPACE OF
COSMIC ASCENSION

−

FIFTH FORCE
COORDINATING

ALTERNATING LATERAL
HYPERPLASMIC FLOW

+

DIMENSION

NINE STATIONS OF THE ARK TRIPLE LAYER

CENTRAL COMMAND CIRCUIT

HYPERELECTRIC PRIMAL PARTON

ACTIVATING BLUE DUAR
INSULATOR FLOW

+

ARCHE   7TH HEPTAD GATE   TYPAL

BLUE DUAR ELECTRO-ENERGETIC
LINE   OF   FORCE
7 LEFT-HAND GATES AND POWERS

H11

FREQUENCIES
+
DESTINAL CODES

SUBLIMATING BLUE DUAR
INSULATOR FLOW

−

DIMENSION   6TH   TIME

QUADRANT 2 ∀∨

1) **Cosmic Ascension**
   2nd (Outer) Time Dimension

2) **Blue Duar Force Field**
   6th (Left-Hand) Time Dimension

3) **Force Field of Cosmic Command Descending**
   7th (Vertical) Time Dimension

4) **Inner Core Time – Original 7×7 Creation Codes**
   9th Time Dimension

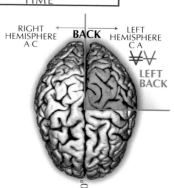

RIGHT
HEMISPHERE
A C

BACK

LEFT
HEMISPHERE
C A
∀∨

LEFT
BACK

0°
FRONT

	V10	V11	V12	V13	V14	V15	V16	V17	V18	V19	V20	V21	
	66 +	82	106 −	¥¥ −	¥¥ +	A +1	+2	+3	+4	+5	+6	7	H1
	68	84 ¥¥	108	−1 A	+2	+1 A	+3	+4	+5	+6	7	−8	H2
	70	86	110	−4	+3	+2	+2	−1 −2 −3			−8	−9	H3
	71	87	111	−5	+6	+3	+1 A	PSI OUTPUT 232 +	26	−4	−9	−10	H4
	72	88 ¥	109	−8	+7	+4	286 ESP OUTPUT	285 PHASE UNIT	PSI INPUT −	−5	−10	−11	H5
	69	85	107	−9	+10	+5	331 CORE CHANNEL	284 ESP INPUT	−13 Ω	−12	−11	−12	H6
	67	83	112	−12	+11	6	−7	−8	−9	−10	−11 Ω	−13 Ω	H7
	65 +	81 N	105 −	13	14 ⊘	−17	−18	−21	−22	−25	−26	¥¥ −	H8
				16	15	+20	+19	+24	+23	+28 Ω	+27	¥¥ +	H9
						+7	+6	+5	+4	+3	+2	+1	H10
						7TH POWER GATE	6TH POWER GATE	5TH POWER GATE	4TH POWER GATE	3RD POWER GATE	2ND POWER GATE	1ST LH GATE 11	**H11**
						−7	−6	−5	−4	−3	−2	−1	H12

HOLOMIND PERCEIVER CODES

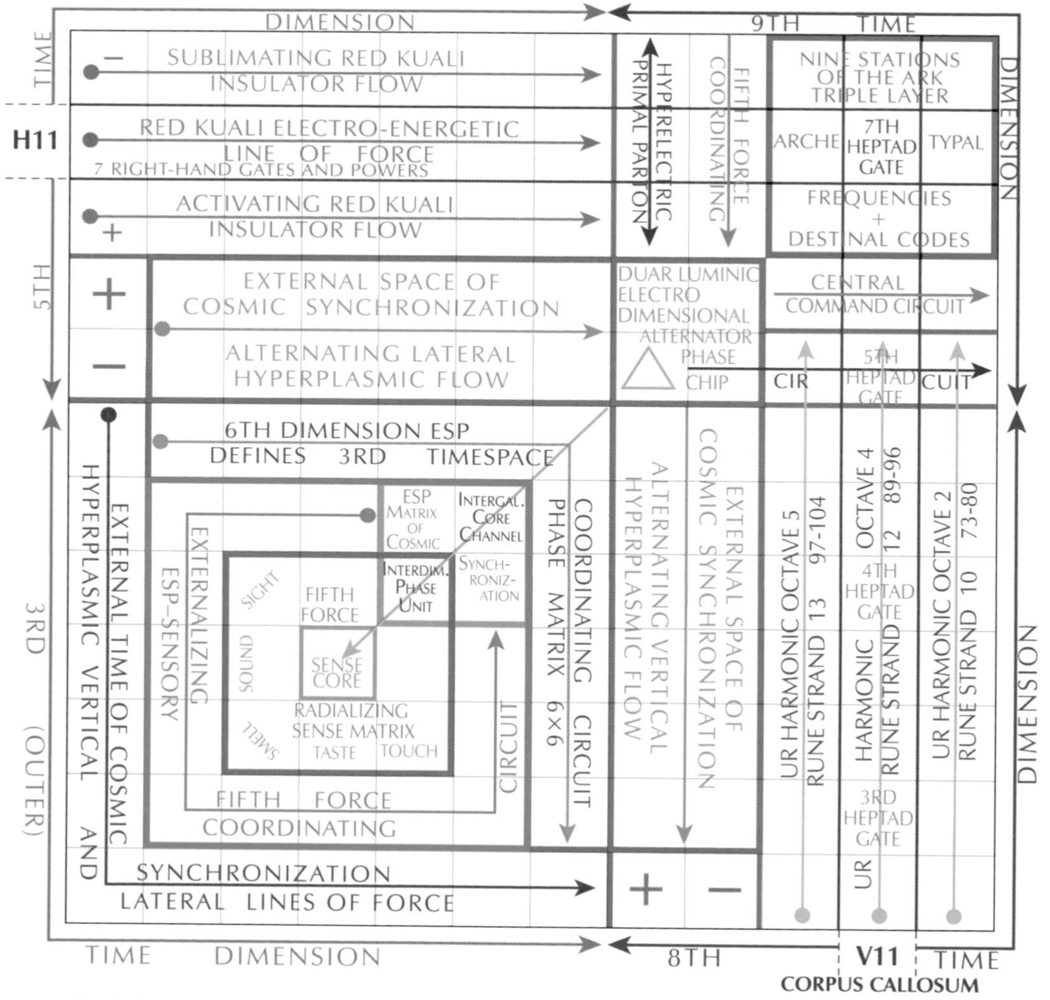

DIMENSION
9TH TIME
TIME
H11
SUBLIMATING RED KUALI INSULATOR FLOW
RED KUALI ELECTRO-ENERGETIC LINE OF FORCE
7 RIGHT-HAND GATES AND POWERS
ACTIVATING RED KUALI INSULATOR FLOW
HYPERELECTRIC PRIMAL PARTON
FIFTH FORCE COORDINATING
NINE STATIONS OF THE ARK TRIPLE LAYER
ARCHE
7TH HEPTAD GATE
TYPAL
FREQUENCIES + DESTINAL CODES
DIMENSION
5TH
EXTERNAL SPACE OF COSMIC SYNCHRONIZATION
ALTERNATING LATERAL HYPERPLASMIC FLOW
DUAR LUMINIC ELECTRO DIMENSIONAL ALTERNATOR PHASE CHIP
CENTRAL COMMAND CIRCUIT
CIR
5TH HEPTAD GATE
CUIT
6TH DIMENSION ESP DEFINES 3RD TIMESPACE
3RD (OUTER)
HYPERPLASMIC VERTICAL AND
EXTERNAL TIME OF COSMIC
EXTERNALIZING ESP-SENSORY
ESP MATRIX OF COSMIC
INTERGAL. CORE CHANNEL
INTERDIM. PHASE UNIT
SYNCHRONIZATION
SIGHT
SOUND
SMELL
FIFTH FORCE
SENSE CORE
RADIALIZING SENSE MATRIX
TASTE
TOUCH
CIRCUIT
FIFTH FORCE COORDINATING
PHASE MATRIX 6×6
COORDINATING CIRCUIT
ALTERNATING VERTICAL HYPERPLASMIC FLOW
EXTERNAL SPACE OF COSMIC SYNCHRONIZATION
UR HARMONIC OCTAVE 5 RUNE STRAND 13 97-104
UR HARMONIC OCTAVE 4 RUNE STRAND 12 89-96
4TH HEPTAD GATE
3RD HEPTAD GATE
UR HARMONIC OCTAVE 2 RUNE STRAND 10 73-80
DIMENSION
SYNCHRONIZATION LATERAL LINES OF FORCE
+
−
TIME DIMENSION
8TH
V11
TIME
CORPUS CALLOSUM

QUADRANT 3 ∀∀

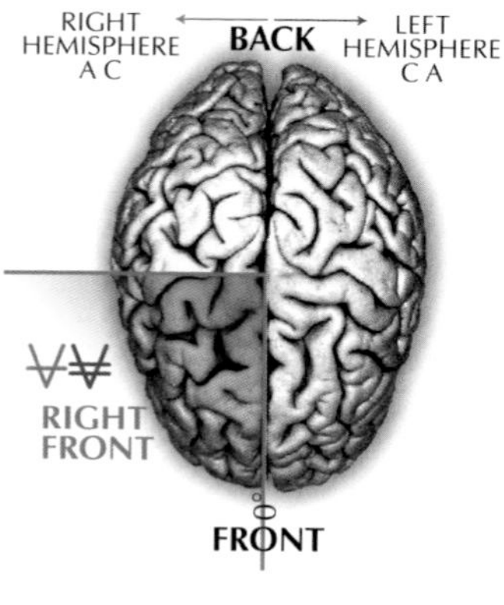

RIGHT HEMISPHERE A C
BACK
LEFT HEMISPHERE C A
∀∀
RIGHT FRONT
FRONT

1) Cosmic Synchronization
   3rd (Outer) Time Dimension
2) Red Kuali Force Field
   5th (Right-Hand) Time Dimension
3) Arcturus Force Field – Harmonic Command Ascending
   8th (Vertical) Time Dimension
4) Inner Core Time – Original 7×7 Creation Codes
   9th Time Dimension

	V1	V2	V3	V4	V5	V6	V7	V8	V9	V10	V11	V12
H10	−1	−2	−3	−4	−5	−6	−7	407	426	437	436	435
H11	1ST RH GATE 51	2ND POWER GATE	3RD POWER GATE	4TH POWER GATE	5TH POWER GATE	6TH POWER GATE	7TH POWER GATE	408 GATE 8	427 GATE 9	438 GATE 10 STATION 5		434
H12	+1	+2	+3	+4	+5	+6	+7	409	428	439-259 STATION 3	GATE 10 STATION 8 440	433
H13	V¥ +	−1 A	−4	−5	−8	−9	−12	13	16 429	430	431 GATE 9	432
H14	V¥ −	+2	+3	+6	+7	+10	+11	△14	15	98 −	90 E	74 +
H15	−1 A	−1 A	−2	−3	−4	−5	6	−17	+20	100	92	76
H16	−2	−3	−2	A −1	ESP OUTPUT 308	CORE CHANNEL 351	+7	−18	+19	102	94	78
H17	−3	−4	+5	PSI OUTPUT − 258	PHASE UNIT 309	ESP INPUT 210	+8	−21	+24	103	95	79
H18	−4	−5	+4	39	PSI INPUT + 260	+13 Ω	+9	−22	+23	101	96	80
H19	−5	−6	+3	+2	+1	+12	+10	−25	+28 Ω	99	93	77
H20	−6	7	+8	+9	+10	+11	+11 Ω	−26	+27	97	91	75
H21	7	+8	+9	+10	+11	+12	+13 Ω	V¥ +	V¥ −	104	89	73

HOLOMIND PERCEIVER CODES

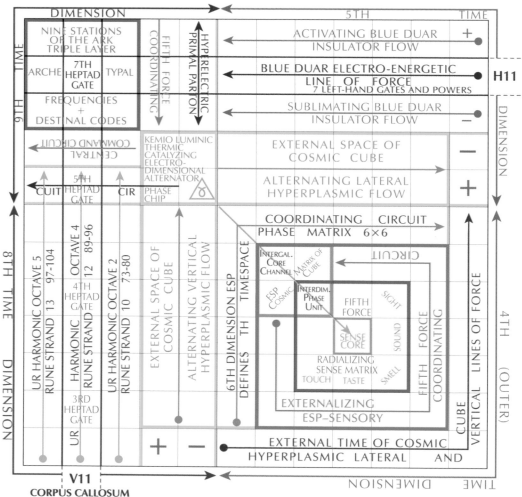

V11
CORPUS CALLOSUM

QUADRANT 4 ⩔⩔

1) **COSMIC CUBE**
   4TH (OUTER) TIME DIMENSION

2) **BLUE DUAR FORCE FIELD**
   6TH (LEFT-HAND) TIME DIMENSION

3) **ARCTURUS FORCE FIELD – HARMONIC COMMAND ASCENDING**
   8TH (VERTICAL) TIME DIMENSION

4) **INNER CORE TIME – ORIGINAL 7×7 CREATION CODES**
   9TH TIME DIMENSION

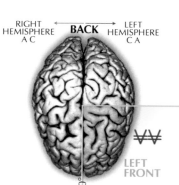

RIGHT HEMISPHERE A C — **BACK** — LEFT HEMISPHERE C A

⩔⩔

LEFT FRONT

FRONT

	V10	V11	V12	V13	V14	V15	V16	V17	V18	V19	V20	V21	
H10				420	397	+7	+6	+5	+4	+3	+2	+1	H10
H11			434 GATE 10 STATION 4	419 GATE 9	396 GATE 8	7TH POWER GATE	6TH POWER GATE	5TH POWER GATE	4TH POWER GATE	3RD POWER GATE	2ND POWER GATE	1ST LH GATE 11	H11
H12	439	GATE 10 440	433-260 STATION 4	418	395	−7	−6	−5	−4	−3	−2	−1	H12
H13	430	431 GATE 9	432	16 417	15	+20	+19	+24	+23	+28	+27 Ω	⊽⊽ −	H13
H14	98 −	90 E	74 +	13	14 δ	−17	−18	−21	−22	−25	−26	⊽⊽ +	H14
H15	100	92	76	−12	+11	6	+7	+8	+9	+10	+11 Ω	+13 Ω	H15
H16	102	94	78	−9	+10	−5	CORE CHANNEL 321	ESP INPUT 274	Ω +13	+12	+11	+12	H16
H17	103	95	79	−8	+7	−4	ESP OUTPUT 320	PHASE UNIT 273	PSI INPUT + 218	+5	+10	+11	H17
H18	101	96	80	−5	+6	−3	−1 A	PSI OUTPUT − 272	52	+4	+9	+10	H18
H19	99	93	77	−4	+3	−2	−2	+1	+2	+3	+8	+9	H19
H20	97	91	75	−1 A	+2	−1 A	−3	−4	−5	−6	7	+8	H20
H21	104	89	73	⊽⊽ +	⊽⊽ −	−1 A	−2	−3	−4	−5	−6	7	H21

I. The Four Outer Time Dimensions

The four outer time dimensions are each self-contained and identical in their parts. Like all the time dimensions, each contains 49 units. Note that the number sequences are all divided into (+) and (−) sections. The (+) refers to activating magnitudes and the (−) to sublimating magnitudes. Note that in the upper set, the (+) and (−) sequences match each other, and in the lower set the sequences also match each other in the same way, but are opposite to the upper set.

Bear in mind that the four outer time dimensions are the locus of the first four mental spheres: first mental sphere, preconscious (1st time dimension upper left, right side of brain); second mental sphere, subconscious (3rd time dimension lower left, right side of brain); third mental sphere, conscious (4th time dimension, lower right, left side of brain); and fourth mental sphere, continuing conscious, second time dimension (upper right, left side of brain)

Remember that the four outer time dimensions also coordinate the movement of 364 days of the 13 Moon/28-day calendar in sequences that go from left to right, top then bottom (first seven moons), and then right to left, bottom then top (last six moons). The movement of consciousness (mental spheres), on the other hand goes from top to bottom starting at the upper left, and then from bottom to top ending at the upper right.

Upper-left quadrant (V1–V7, H1–H7), centered on circle 13:

V1						V7
7	−8	−9	−10	−11	−12	−13
+6	7	−8	−9	−10	−11	−11
+5	+6				−12	−10
+4	+5	(13)	PSI IN		−13	−9
+3	+4	PSI OUT	3D/4D	ESP IN		−8
+2	+3	+2	+1	ESP OUT	WW	−7
+1	+1	+2	+3	+4	+5	6

Upper-right quadrant (V15–V21, H1–H7), centered on circle 26:

V15						V21
+1	+2	+3	+4	+5	+6	7
+1	+3	+4	+5	+6	7	−8
+2	+2				−8	−9
+3	+1	PSI OUT	(26)		−9	−10
+4	ESP OUT	3D/4D	PSI IN		−10	−11
+5	WW	ESP IN	−13	−12	−11	−12
6	−7	−8	−9	−10	−11	−13

Lower-left quadrant (V1–V7, H15–H21), centered on circle 39:

V1						V7
−1	−1	−2	−3	−4	−5	6
−2	−3	−2	−1	ESP OUT	WW	+7
−3	−4	PSI OUT	4D/3D	ESP IN		+8
−4	−5	(39)	PSI IN		+13	+9
−5	−6				+12	+10
−6	7	+8	+9	+10	+11	+11
7	+8	+9	+10	+11	+12	+13

Lower-right quadrant (V15–V21, H15–H21), centered on circle 52:

V15						V21
6	+7	+8	+9	+10	+11	+13
−5	WW	ESP IN	+13	+12	+11	+12
−4	ESP OUT	4D/3D	PSI IN		+10	+11
−3	−1	PSI OUT	(52)		+9	+10
−2	−2				+8	+9
−1	−3	−4	−5	−6	7	+8
−1	−2	−3	−4	−5	−6	7

Four Outer Time Dimensions, Index of Parts

1. **External time flows.** All occur on the first or outermost 441 circuit, 13 units each (52 units total), such that the 7th unit precisely marks each of the four corners, dividing the flows into six activating and six sublimating units on either side. The external time flows coordinate the 13 cosmic time magnitudes (wavespell tones) with each of the four mental spheres, so that all consciousness functions are informed by the totality of cosmic time. The 13 unit flows each literally function as the outer time frames of the Holomind Perceiver.

2. **Radial sense matrix.** The remaining 36 units of each of the four outer time dimensions (144 total) constitute the radial sense matrix of the mental sphere coordinated by that time dimension. Each radial sense matrix consists of:

   i. **Sixth-dimensional ESP circuit,** 11 units each (44 units total). This circuit runs on the inside of the matrix just like the external time runs on the outside of matrix, and just as the 7th unit marks the four outer corners, the 6th unit coordinates the four inner corners of the four outer time dimensions. With five activating and five sublimating units on either side, the 6th-dimensional ESP circuit coordinates the first four mental spheres with subliminal communications according to magnitudes 1 to 11. The 11th (Ω) magnitude corresponds to the 11th horizontal and 11th vertical rows that coordinate the entire 441-Holomind Perceiver Matrix.

   ii. **Fifth force coordination circuit,** 13 units each (52 units total). Always starts adjacent to the 3rd unit of the 6th-dimensional ESP circuit, but runs in opposite direction. The 7th unit is always adjacent to the 7th unit of outer time, (six activating and six sublimating units on either side of it), while its 11th unit is always adjacent to the 11th Ω unit of the 6th-dimensional ESP circuit. The 13 fifth force coordinating units are internal fifth-dimensional superconscious correlates to the 13 cosmic tones of the external time circuit, and transfer the cosmic time signals to the radial sense core.

   iii. **Radial sense core matrix,** 8 (+1) units each (32 (+4) units total). Consists of a master time unit (at the exact center of the 49 unit matrix): 13, 26, 39 or 52. Each unit coordinates the five external sense nodes, including all internal and etheric body sensory information (the sense of touch, closest to the beginning of the fifth force circuit, always begins the sequence): the five senses (touch, taste, smell, hearing, sight); the five organs (ears, skin, eyes, tongue, nose); the five consciousness modes (tactile consciousness, gustatory consciousness, olfactory consciousness, auditory consciousness, visual consciousness); the five objects (object of touch, object of taste, etc.); as well as the five action organs (mouth, hands, bowels, genitals, and feet)—the entire psychophysical spectrum composed of four sets of pentads.

   The matrix core also includes a psi input unit (adjacent to the 13th fifth force coordinating unit), and a psi output unit (adjacent to the 1st fifth force coordinating unit). Psi is the psychic energy released from the interaction of consciousness with mental sensory information. The +1 unit is the 3-D–4-D interdimensional phase alternator unit which the radial sense core matrix shares with the intergalactic core. This is located at the 5th unit diagonally located from any of the four outermost corners of the 441 matrix.

   iv. **Intergalactic core matrix,** 3 (+1) units each (12 (+4) units total). Consists of the intergalactic core channel (located at V6-H6, V16-H6, V6-H16, and V16-H16); and an ESP output and an ESP input unit. The intergalactic core channel is the extrasensory means for channeling the four hyperplasmas—alpha-alpha (first time), alpha-beta (3rd time), beta-beta (4th time), and beta-alpha (or beta nova) (2nd time). The hyperplasmas are the lubricants of the four outer time dimension mental spheres. The ESP output informs the first magnitude of the fifth force coordinating flow, while the ESP input is informed by the 13th magnitude of this flow. The +1 shared unit is the 4-D–3-D phase alternator for plasmically activating the entire radial sense core.

II. Index to the Four Radial Time Dimensions

The four radial time dimensions can be categorized into two sets: a) horizontal (fifth time dimension, left-hand side, right hemisphere; and sixth time dimension, right-hand side, left hemisphere) and b) vertical (seventh time dimension, above; and eighth time dimension below).

The radial time dimensions are characterized by:

1. **External hyperplasmic space flows** of 28 units each (112 total), 24 of which are contained in each of the four radial time dimensions (96 total), with the remaining 16 in the inner ninth time dimension (see next page). These inform the four outer time dimensions with alternating sublimating (–) and activating (+) magnitudes that correspond to the units of the harmonic 28-day standard. Each of the four external space flows carries one of four hyperplasmic charges: alpha-alpha, alpha-beta, beta-beta or beta-alpha.

2. Within the four radial time dimensions there are also **16 generators and terminals** in eight pairs, (two pairs per each of the four space quadrants), each pair containing both an activating or a sublimating generator or terminal. These sixteen units are all located in the first or outermost circuit of the matrix, and are either the generators or terminals of the external hyper plasmic space flows. The flows are thus coordinated in the following manner:

On the **left hand side (right hemisphere)** for the first (upper) and third (lower), time dimensions, the alternating flows - alpha alpha and alpha beta respectively - originate and run horizontally in the fifth time dimension; while in the seventh and eighth time dimensions, the alternating flows switch polarity and run vertically, alpha alpha upward and alpha beta downward. (Please note the numbering of the flows is not totally sequential but in groups of four, each creating the same U-shaped movement. Also note that the units 13-16 of each of the four hyper plasmic flows runs through the ninth or inner time dimension creating four hyper parton "cells". These will be further discussed in the section on the Ninth or Inner Time.)

On the **right-hand side (left hemisphere)** the flows originate in the vertical time dimensions, beta alpha in the seventh time dimension flowing downward and beta beta in the eight time dimension, upward flow. After switching polarity in the ninth time dimension the two sets of alternating flows terminate horizontally in the sixth time dimension. (Please note and meditate on the overall radial polarity of the flows and the functions of the radial time dimensions.)

3. **Force Fields and UR harmonics, special programs of the radial time dimensions:** While the hyperplasmic external space flows account for 28 units of each of the radial time dimensions, all four radial time dimensions are also characterized by a special 21-unit matrix (21 + 28 = 49) that runs down the center three rows of each of them, that is, down the 10th 11th and 12th rows both horizontally and vertically.

V11

∓	±	66	82	106		
-26	+27	68	84	108	-1	+2
-25	+28	70	86	110	-4	+3
-22	+23	71	87	111	-5	+6
-21	+24	72	88	109	-8	+7
-18	+19	69	85	107	-9	+10
-17	+20	67	83	112	-12	+11

H11 — 5TH TIME DIMENSION / 7TH TIME DIMENSION / 6TH TIME DIMENSION

+	+2	+3	+6	+7	+10	+11	7TH TIME DIMENSION		-17	-18	-21	-22	-25	-26
-	-1	-4	-5	-8	-9	-12			+20	+19	+24	+23	+28	+27
-1	-2	-3	-4	-5	-6	-7			+7	+6	+5	+4	+3	+2	+1
1	2	3	4	5	6	7			7	6	5	4	3	2	1
+1	+2	+3	+4	+5	+6	+7			-7	-6	-5	-4	-3	-2	-1
	+1	+4	+5	+8	+9	+12			-20	-19	-24	-23	-28	-27
	-2	-3	-6	-7	-10	-11	8TH TIME DIMENSION		+17	+18	+21	+22	+25	+26

8TH TIME DIMENSION

+17	-20	100	92	76	+12	-11
+18	-19	102	94	78	+9	-10
+21	-24	103	95	79	+8	-7
+22	-23	101	96	80	+5	-6
+25	-28	99	93	77	+4	-3
+26	-27	97	91	75	+1	-2
		104	89	73		

III. Ninth or Inner Time Dimension

Inner time constitutes the archetypal time matrix and cosmic hyperparton, generator of all cosmic electricity. Herein the supreme coordinating multi-dimensional timing program of the "celestial hierarchies" manifests its coordinating signals and ordinances.

At its center is the 441, the single unit from which the rest of the matrix radiates, the 11th-dimensional channel from which the entire cube system of thought and galactic life patterns originate. From here into the very center of the corpus callosum flows the radially concentrating hyperplasmic Sirius B-52/Element 113. Around the 441 is the 10th circuit, with its 8 "stations of the ark," archetypal repositories of the various UR messengers and teachers. (See index below)

At the four corners of the inner time dimension are the four hyperpartons: located at V8-H8, dum kuali, primal heat or thermic element; located at V8-H14, dum duar, primal light or luminic element; located at V14-H8, kum, heat of inner light; and located at V14-H14, kemio, light of inner heat. Each of these is the nucleus of a cell of four units each – the units 13-16 of each of the four external hyperplasmic space flows, such that alpha-alpha interacts with dum kuali, alpha-beta with dum duar, beta-beta with kemio, and beta-alpha with kum.

	V8		V11		V14	
H8	♉	15	65	**N** 81	105	13	△
	13	16	●	●	●	16	15
	−	●	·	⁝	∙∙	●	+
H11	(coil)	●	(symbol)	(symbol)	(symbol)	●	(zigzag)
	+	●	⋯	∷	∷∷	●	−
	13	16	●	●	●	16	15
H14	△	15	98	90 **E**	74	13	(symbol)

The four hyperpartons constitute the 14th unit of each of the flows, while the 13th and 15th units are the input and output respectively. These cells also define the 8th circuit as the hyperparton electrical circuit, since V11-H8 is the hyperneutron (also UR Harmonic Rune 81) and V11-H14 is the hyperelectron (also UR Harmonic Rune, 90).

Also on the eighth circuit (H8 and H14) from V10-12, both above and below, are three units each for a total of six units of the eighth runes of the six rune strands. In corresponding positions, adjacent to the fifth and sixth time dimensions, are electro-activating terminals for each of the three lines of force of the two force fields. The central unit of each of these, V8-H11 and V14-H11, are also transformer units of the two electrical currents, the red current running down the fourteenth vertical on the right-hand side and the blue current up the eighth vertical of the left-hand side.

Unit 16 of each of the four hyperparton cells occupies the corner position of the 9th circuit, the galactic fifth force: V9-H9, V13-H9, V9-H13 and V13-H13. These are the four master hyperplasmic-parton coordinating units for each of the four quadrants. (Note: 16 × 4 = 64, DNA life code, a clue to the potency of these four coordinating units.)

Intermediary to these four coordinating points on the ninth circuit are three units each for a total of 12 units: for each set of three there is a central Guardian at the Gate (on one of the 11 axes) and, on either side, an activating and sublimating station of the Guardians of the Fifth Force. These 12 guardians surround the 8 stations of the ark of the 10th or innermost circuit surrounding the central coordinating ninth station, V11-H11, 441, the channel for the hyperplasma Sirius B-52/Element 113.

The Nine Stations of the Ark—Archetypes of UR (indicated on the graphic by galactic notation):

- · 1st Station: Abraham—archetype of the progenitor of UR
- ·· 2nd Station: St. John of Patmos and Padmasambhava—archetype of the revealer of hidden knowledge (terma)
- ··· 3rd Station: Krishna and the avatars—archetype of the avatar as the embodiment of the descent of divine knowledge
- ···· 4th Station: Buddha—archetype of the Enlightened One
- — 5th Station: Primal Adam—archetype of the first created human type
- ⸚ 6th Station: Eve, Mary, Red Queen—archetype of the divinely creative feminine (Shakti)
- ⁚⁚ 7th Station: Muhammad and Quetzalcoatl—archetype of the divinely inspired prophet
- ⁞⁞ 8th Station: Jesus Christ—archetype of the resurrection
- ∴ ⁞⁞ 9th Station: Noah, Pacal (and Valum) Votan—archetype of the messengers of time and the system of the Cube

TWO SETS OF 48 UR HARMONICS

Running down the three vertical rows of the seventh time dimension and up the same three flows in the eighth time dimension are 42 of the 48 UR Harmonics. The eighth units of the of all six UR Harmonic sequences, (6 total) are located on the eight circuit of the ninth or inner time dimension. Also recall that the 11th vertical row corresponds precisely to the center line of the corpus callosum which connects the otherwise disconnected right and left hemispheres. This means that two of the 6 sets of UR Harmonics (8 per set) run down the center of the corpus callosum, with the V10 and V12 on either side of the center line, accounting for the other four sets.

TWO FORCE FIELDS, HORIZONTAL TIME DIMS.

The central 21 units of the two horizontal time dimensions are characterized by the two force fields: left-hand side, right hemisphere, the dum kuali red thermic force field, and the right-hand side, left hemisphere, the dum duar blue luminic force field.

The horizontal eleventh row/gravitational axis defines the energizing core of each of the two force fields. On either side of the energizing cores, are the activating (+) or sublimating (–) transformer-insulator units. Note that these switch polarity, such that the 10th horizontal is sublimating in the fifth time dimension, and activating in the sixth, while the 12th horizontal is activating in the fifth and sublimating in the sixth.

	V10	V11	V12
	66	82	106
	68	84	108
	70	86	110
	71	87	111
	72	88	109
	69	85	107
	67	83	112
	65	81	105

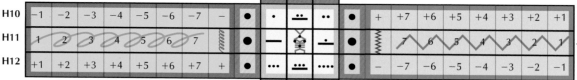

H10	–1	–2	–3	–4	–5	–6	–7	–				+	+7	+6	+5	+4	+3	+2	+1
H11	1	2	3	4	5	6	7						7	6	5	4	3	2	1
H12	+1	+2	+3	+4	+5	+6	+7	+				–	–7	–6	–5	–4	–3	–2	–1

V10	V11	V12
98	90	74
100	92	76
102	94	78
103	95	79
101	96	80
99	93	77
97	91	75
104	89	73

The 48 (6 × 8) UR Harmonics complement the 64 UR Runes that coordinate the 64 DNA Codons which function as the metabolic behavioral coordinators of the evolutionary unfolding of the genetic body. The 48 UR Runes, on the other hand, are the master coordinators, and refer to 6 octaves or 8-tone sequences of resonant frequencies intended to program the energy body for Second Creation functions and behavioral-perceptual modes.

The three upper 7th time dimension UR Harmonic strands are: 10th vertical, UR Harmonic Octave 1, Octave of Divine Decree, runes 65-72; 11th vertical Octave 3, Octave of the Galactic Life Whole, runes 81-88; and 12th vertical Octave 6, Octave of the Infinite Mind Wave, runes 105-112.

Also note that the thermic force field activates the fifth superconscious mental sphere, while the luminic force field activates the sixth subliminal conscious mental sphere. It is important to tune into these qualities. The horizontal time dimensions and the two mental spheres unify the front and rear of the right and left hemisphere lobes.

The three lower 8th time dimension UR Harmonic strands are: 10th vertical, Octave 5, Octave of Union of Ascent and Descent, runes 97-104; 11th vertical, Octave 4, Octave of the Galactic Art Whole, runes 89-96; and 12th vertical, Octave 2, Octave of the Tree of Cosmic Fire, runes 73-80.

The two key octaves are the 3rd (Octave of the Galactic Life Whole) and the 4th (Octave of the Galactic Art Whole), as they both align with the center line of the corpus callosum and define the evolutionary trajectory: crystalline matter is to life, as life is to art, only here life and art are understood to be functions of the galactic whole order of being.

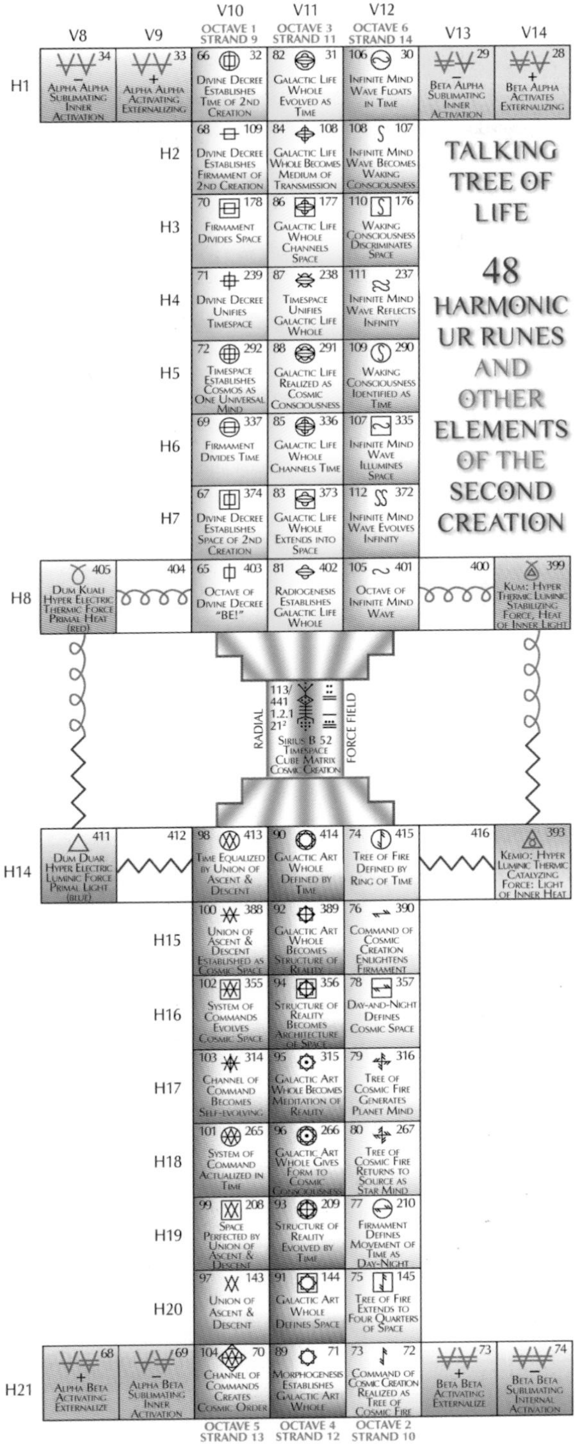
TALKING TREE OF LIFE
48 HARMONIC UR RUNES AND OTHER ELEMENTS OF THE SECOND CREATION
V8
V9
V10 OCTAVE 1 STRAND 9
V11 OCTAVE 3 STRAND 11
V12 OCTAVE 6 STRAND 14
V13
V14
H1
34 Alpha Alpha Sublimating Inner Activation
33 Alpha Alpha Activating Externalizing
66 32 Divine Decree Establishes Time of 2nd Creation
82 31 Galactic Life Whole Evolved as Time
106 30 Infinite Mind Wave Floats in Time
29 Beta Alpha Sublimating Inner Activation
28 Beta Alpha Activates Externalizing
H2
68 109 Divine Decree Establishes Firmament of 2nd Creation
84 108 Galactic Life Whole Becomes Medium of Transmission
108 107 Infinite Mind Wave Becomes Waking Consciousness
H3
70 178 Firmament Divides Space
86 177 Galactic Life Whole Channels Space
110 176 Waking Consciousness Discriminates Space
H4
71 239 Divine Decree Unifies Timespace
87 238 Timespace Unifies Galactic Life Whole
111 237 Infinite Mind Wave Reflects Infinity
H5
72 292 Timespace Establishes Cosmos as One Universal Mind
88 291 Galactic Life Realized as Cosmic Consciousness
109 290 Waking Consciousness Identified as Time
H6
69 337 Firmament Divides Time
85 336 Galactic Life Whole Channels Time
107 335 Infinite Mind Wave Illumines Space
H7
67 374 Divine Decree Establishes Space of 2nd Creation
83 373 Galactic Life Whole Extends into Space
112 372 Infinite Mind Wave Evolves Infinity
H8
405 Dum Kuali Hyper Electric Thermic Force Primal Heat (red)
404
65 403 Octave of Divine Decree "BE!"
81 402 Radiogenesis Establishes Galactic Life Whole
105 401 Octave of Infinite Mind Wave
400
399 Kum: Hyper Thermic Luminic Stabilizing Force, Heat of Inner Light
RADIAL
113/ 441 1.2.1 21²
Sirius B 52 Timespace Cube Matrix Cosmic Creation
FORCE FIELD
H14
411 Dum Duar Hyper Electric Luminic Force Primal Light (blue)
412
98 413 Time Equalized by Union of Ascent & Descent
90 414 Galactic Art Whole Defined by Time
74 415 Tree of Fire Defined by Ring of Time
416
393 Kemio: Hyper Luminic Thermic Catalyzing Force: Light of Inner Heat
H15
100 388 Union of Ascent & Descent Established as Cosmic Space
92 389 Galactic Art Whole Becomes Structure of Reality
76 390 Command of Cosmic Creation Enlightens Firmament
H16
102 355 System of Commands Evolves Cosmic Space
94 356 Structure of Reality Becomes Architecture of Space
78 357 Day-and-Night Defines Cosmic Space
H17
103 314 Channel of Command Becomes Self-evolving
95 315 Galactic Art Whole Becomes Meditation of Reality
79 316 Tree of Cosmic Fire Generates Planet Mind
H18
101 265 System of Command Actualized in Time
96 266 Galactic Art Whole Gives Form to Cosmic Consciousness
80 267 Tree of Cosmic Fire Returns to Source as Star Mind
H19
99 208 Space Perfected by Union of Ascent & Descent
93 209 Structure of Reality Evolved by Time
77 210 Firmament Defines Movement of Time as Day-Night
H20
97 143 Union of Ascent & Descent
91 144 Galactic Art Whole Defines Space
75 145 Tree of Fire Extends to Four Quarters of Space
H21
68 Alpha Beta Activating Externalize
69 Alpha Beta Sublimating Inner Activation
104 70 Channel of Commands Creates Cosmic Order
89 71 Morphogenesis Establishes Galactic Art Whole
73 72 Command of Cosmic Creation Realized as Tree of Cosmic Fire
73 Beta Beta Activating Externalize
74 Beta Beta Sublimating Internal Activation
OCTAVE 5 STRAND 13
OCTAVE 4 STRAND 12
OCTAVE 2 STRAND 10

Holomind Perceiver code to copy and color in

7	−8	−9	−10	−11	−12	−13	−VV	+VV	66	82	106	−VV	+VV	+1	+2	+3	+4	+5	+6	7
+6	7	−8	−9	−10	−11	−11 Ω	−26	+27	68	84	108	−1	+2	+1	+3	+4	+5	+6	7	−8
+5	+6	•	•	•	−12	−10	−25	+28	70	86	110	−4	+3	+2	+2	•	•	•	−8	−9
+4	+5	•	⑬	PSI IN	−13	−9	−22	+23	71	87	111	−5	+6	+3	+1	PSI OUT	㉖	•	−9	−10
+3	+4	PSI OUT	3D/4D	ESP IN	−8		−21	+24	72	88	109	−8	+7	+4	ESP OUT	3D/4D	PSI IN		−10	−11
+2	+3	ESP OUT	VV		−7		−18	+19	69	85	107	−9	+10	+5	VV	ESP IN		−13	−12	−11	−12
+1	+1	+2	+3	+4	+5	6	−17	+20	67	83	112	−12	+11	6	−7	−8	−9	−10	−11 Ω	−13
+VV	+2	+3	+6	+7	+10	+11	♉	15	65	81 N	105	13	⊗	−17	−18	−21	−22	−25	−26	−VV
−VV	−1	−4	−5	−8	−9	−12	13	16				16	15	+20	+19	+24	+23	+28	+27	+VV
−1	−2	−3	−4	−5	−6	−7	−	•	⁞⁞	••			+	+7	+6	+5	+4	+3	+2	+1
1	2	3	4	5	6	7	[coil]	−	⋰	⋱	[zigzag]			7	6	5	4	3	2	1
+1	+2	+3	+4	+5	+6	+7	+	•••	⋯	••••			−	−7	−6	−5	−4	−3	−2	−1
+VV	+1	+4	+5	+8	+9	+12	13	16				16	15	−20	−19	−24	−23	−28	−27	−VV
−VV	−2	−3	−6	−7	−10	−11	△	15	98	E 90	74	13	△⊖	+17	+18	+21	+22	+25	+26	+VV
−1	−1	−2	−3	−4	−5	6	+17	−20	100	92	76	+12	−11	6	+7	+8	+9	+10	+11 Ω	+13
−2	−3	−2	−1	ESP OUT	VV	+7	+18	−19	102	94	78	+9	−10	−5	VV	ESP IN	+13	+12	+11	+12
−3	−4	PSI OUT	4D/3D	ESP IN	+8		+21	−24	103	95	79	+8	−7	−4	ESP OUT	4D/3D	PSI IN		+10	+11
−4	−5	•	㊴	PSI IN	+13	+9	+22	−23	101	96	80	+5	−6	−3	−1	PSI OUT	㊼	•	+9	+10
−5	−6	•	•	•	+12	+10	+25	−28	99	93	77	+4	−3	−2	−2	•	•	•	+8	+9
−6	7	+8	+9	+10	+11	+11 Ω	+26	−27	97	91	75	+1	−2	−1	−3	−4	−5	−6	7	+8
7	+8	+9	+10	+11	+12	+13	+VV	−VV	104	89	73	+VV	−VV	−1	−2	−3	−4	−5	−6	7

CHAPTER 12

CYCLES OF TRANSFORMATION AND REGENERATION: UNIVERSALIZING THE ORDER OF THE NEW TIME

Coordinated synchronization of different cycles of time simultaneously is key in the cultivation of telepathic technologies.

1. Our life and everything we see in the phenomenal world is the articulation of specific cycles of time with the compression of information contained within these cycles, i.e. fractal time compression.

2. Cycles and sub-cycles are the basic principles of the Law of Time. Cosmic History itself represents a cycle of time that coincides with the seven years of the Mystery of the Stone (2004-2011). In the sequence of 1-13, seven is the mirrorless frequency that traces back to the psychomythic interval of lost time in eternity.

3. The seven is also the basis of the seven days of creation or the seven aeons of creation; the mythic seven generations which are the primary procreative generations of specific cycles of the cosmic evolution of humanity.

4. The seven year Cosmic History cycle represents the recapitulation of the primal procreative power of seven; the original narration of creation as number. The seven volumes illustrate how the conscious activation of number informs the whole, defining an entire reformulation of the human knowledge base. In this way, Cosmic History is a compact or promise of the redemption of the power of the number seven.

5. Cycles of time are information bearing units concerned with the decompression of information contained within a cycle. But what is a cycle? A cycle is the frequency interval between two identical synchronic event points. Identical meaning that a frequency measure has returned to its same position within a synchronic measure or indicator of such an interval. For example on July 26, 1961 it was Dreamspell kin 164: Yellow Galactic Seed. That identical event point will occur again on July 26, 2013.

6. This 52-year interval is the frequency interval between those two identical synchronic event points. Within that interval a tremendous amount of information has been generated. This means that, for example, as a cycle of 52 years the Galactic Seed cycles contain an enormous amount of information to decompress.

7. We are at the time of the greatest intensification of information in the whole history of the earth, if not of the whole history of the solar system. This proliferation of information spreads even as far out as the edges of the Velatropa sector, which is an analog of the increase and intensification of information that constitutes a particular climactic stage of cosmic history. During this cycle the information increase and intensification follows an exponential curve that includes an increase of population, technology and information. This is an example of a cycle as a frequency interval between two identical synchronic event points.

8. Cycles can also be viewed as waves of information that occur between two points creating similar intervals of waves that move through the ocean of time. At the time of this writing we are at the point of several cycles closing and an entirely new cycle opening. This points to the event

NEW SIRIUS CYCLE 1 (1987-2039)

Bearer													
Wizard	NS1.0 34 1987-88	NS1.4 194 1991-92	NS1.8 94 1995-96	NS1.12 254 1999-2000	NS1.16 154 2003-04	NS1.20 54 2007-08	NS1.24 214 2011-12	NS1.28 114 2015-16	NS1.32 14 2019-20	NS1.36 174 2023-24	NS1.40 74 2027-28	NS1.44 234 2031-32	NS1.48 134 2035-36
Storm	NS1.1 139 1988-89	NS1.5 39 1992-93	NS1.9 199 1996-97	NS1.13 99 2000-01	NS1.17 259 2004-05	NS1.21 159 2008-09	NS1.25 59 2012-13	NS1.29 219 2016-17	NS1.33 119 2020-21	NS1.37 19 2024-25	NS1.41 179 2028-29	NS1.45 79 2032-33	NS1.49 239 2036-37
Seed	NS1.2 244 1989-90	NS1.6 144 1993-94	NS1.10 44 1997-98	NS1.14 204 2001-02	NS1.18 104 2005-06	NS1.22 4 2009-10	NS1.26 164 2013-14	NS1.30 64 2017-18	NS1.34 224 2021-22	NS1.38 124 2025-26	NS1.42 24 2029-30	NS1.46 184 2033-34	NS1.50 84 2037-38
Moon	NS1.3 219 1990-91	NS1.7 249 1994-95	NS1.11 149 1998-99	NS1.15 49 2002-03	NS1.19 209 2006-07	NS1.23 109 2010-11	NS1.27 9 2014-15	NS1.31 169 2018-19	NS1.35 69 2022-23	NS1.39 229 2026-27	NS1.43 129 2030-31	NS1.47 29 2034-35	NS1.51 189 2038-39

The gate for the completion of the Great Cycle of Prophecy was opened 34 days after the summer solstice (N. Hemisphere) 1987, on Kin 34—White Galactic Wizard. This began the New Sirius Cycle 1, a 52-year cycle of which the first one concludes in 2039; then another one starts, and concludes in 2091 and the next one in 2143, etc.

As shown in the table above, each year is coded by one of four year bearers: Wizard, Storm, Seed and Moon. The year always starts on 26 July and completes on 24 July, with the Day out of Time being 25 July. "NS1" indicated New Sirius Cycle 1, the years are numbered NS1.0–NS1.51 for a total of 52 years. The count begins in the upper-left corner with the year of the White Galactic Wizard (Kin 34), numbered NS1.0—this indicates that 0 years have *completed* since the start of New Sirius Cycle 1, hence NS1.0. The last year of New Sirius Cycle 1 is the year of the Red Resonant Moon (Kin 189), numbered NS1.51, after which will begin New Sirius Cycle 2 (NS2).

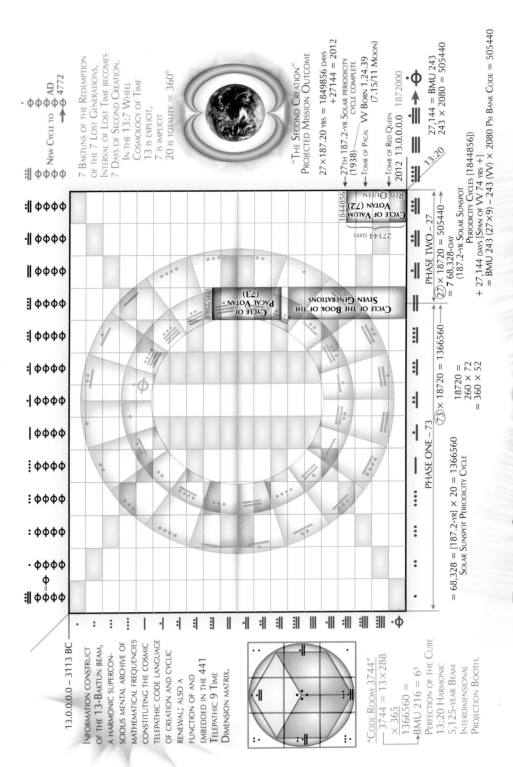

New Cycle to AD 4772

7 Baktuns of the Redemption of the 7 Lost Generations, Interval of Lost Time becomes 7 Days of Second Creation. In the 13:7 Wheel Cosmology of Time 13 is explicit, 7 is implicit 20 is totality = 360°

"The Second Creation" Projected Mission Outcome

27×187.20 yrs = 1849856 days
$+27144 = 2012$
— 27th 187.2-yr Solar periodicity cycle complete (1938)
— Tomb of Pacal VV Born 1.24.39 (7.15/11 Moon)
— Tomb of Red Queen
2012 13.0.0.0.0 1872000

13.0.0.0.0 – 3113 BC

Information construct of the 13-Baktun beam, a harmonic superconscious mental archive of mathematical frequencies constituting the cosmic telepathic code language of creation and cyclic renewal; also a function of and embedded in the 441 Telepathic 9 Time Dimension matrix.

"Code Room 3744"

$3744 = 13 \times 288$
$\times 365$
$1366560 =$
BMU $216 = 6^3$
Perfection of the Cube
13:20 Harmonic
5,125-year Beam
Interdimensional Projection Booth.

Cycle of the Book of the Seven Generations

Cycle of Pacal Votan (73) 1366560

Cycle of Valum Votan (72) Red Queen 1844856 27144 days

Phase One – 73

$(73) \times 18720 = 1366560$

$18720 =$
260×72
$= 360 \times 52$

$= 68,328 = [187.2\text{-yr}] \times 20 = 1366560$
Solar Sunspot Periodicity Cycle

Phase Two – 27

$(27) \times 18720 = 1366560$
$= 7 \; 68,328\text{-day}$
(187.2-yr Solar Sunspot Periodicity Cycles [1844856])
$+ 27,144$ days [Span of VV 74 yrs +]
$= $ BMU 243 $(27 \times 9) – 243$ (VV) $\times 2080$ Psi Bank Code $= 505440$

13:20

$27,144 = $ BMU 243
$243 \times 2080 = 505440$

ETHERIC STRUCTURE OF PACAL AND VALUM VOTAN CONJOINED, CO-EXTENSIVE W/ 5125-YEAR 13-BAKTUN BEAM horizon of 12-21-2012: Blue Crystal Hand = 4 Ahau. This closes a large Tzolkin cycle of 260 katuns and 13 baktuns that began in 3113 BC. This event point also closes a larger 26,000-year cycle as well as a 104,000-year cycle.

9. This particular cycle that we find ourselves in is not only characterized by an exponential increase of information, but also the need for humans to process a tremendous amount of decompression to determine the meaning of the information. This time is also characterized by an increase or cluster of sub-cycles occurring within this particular point in time.

10. The 260th katun (20-year cycle) of the 13 Baktun Great Cycle is now concluding. This is one point of departure; winter solstice (Northern Hemisphere) 1961 is another point of departure, as is August 16, 1987, which began the first of the 260-day cycles of the Harmonic Convergence. As of 12-21-2012 we will be in the 26th year of this cycle and 25th year of the New Sirius Cycle 1 (see graphic).

11. On Planetary Moon 23, Yellow Magnetic Seed Year (April 26, 1993) we entered the last katun (20-year cycle) of 260 katuns. We are now completing the 52-year cycle of the Galactic Seed (Kin 164) to Galactic Seed (Kin 164). As the information compression increases so does the awareness of cycles within cycles and sub-cycles, etc. Also note that the beginning of the last katun occurred 91 days prior to the beginning of the seven-year Telektonon Prophecy Cycle (26 July 1993 – 25 July 2000). This Telektonon cycle also included the beginning of the 260th 13 Ahau katun cycle.

12. As we know from the prophecies of Chilam Balam, the Great Cycle is the cycle that concludes with the most cataclysmic or catastrophic events. The Seven Years of Prophecy marked an acceleration of time, known as the "Timeshift", which began on July 26, 1992. This Timeshift marked the coincidence of the conjunction of the increase of the compression of information and the increase in the incidence in cycles and sub-cycles.

Cycles and the Law of Time

13. The point of the increase in the incidence of cycles and sub-cycles is the increase in the consciousness of the Law of Time. The Law of Time is the dynamics of time as the history of consciousness. From the discovery of the Law of Time in 1989 to present, there has been an increase in the awareness of the cycles of time as they are calibrated according to the Law of Time and 13 Moon calendar, inclusive of the 260-day cycles as well as the Sirius 52-year cycles.

14. The Law of Time makes conscious what was previously unconscious. The discovery of the Law of Time marks an increase in knowledge of the synchronization of cycles which parallels the increase in intensification of the information compression that characterizes the present age. We refer to this as information compression because every day the amount of information that can be compressed into one day, for instance, increases. So the day expands to meet the information demand, though the amount of time remains constant. But, because of the proliferation of information and energies being beamed to our planet, we experience time as accelerating.

15. As the information compression increases and intensifies in its psychic effects, the increase in awareness of the synchronization of the different cycles also increases to offset the psychic destabilization of the psychic compression. The Seven Years of Prophecy were followed by the four years of the Harrowing of Hell (2000-2004), prior to the cycle of the *Cosmic History Chronicles* (2004-2011) which is also known as the seven years of the Mystery of the Stone.

16. The seven years of the Mystery of the Stone represents the beginning of the passage from the disorder of 12:60 time to the supreme order of 13:20 time. This cycle concluded on July 25, 2011. At this point there were exactly 514 days remaining until 12-21-2012. This period can be viewed as a type of planetary hiatus where even though the collective human species remains in the 12:60 timing frequency, the nature of world affairs within this framework is shifting dramatically. During this time it is important to keep ourselves as pure energy receptors so that we may sail smoothly into the 13:20 ocean.

17. The main purpose of the seven years of the Mystery of the Stone, inclusive of the seven volume *Cosmic History Chronicles,* was to formulate a new galactic information bank or a reformulation of the human knowledge system to function as an overlay on the cybersphere. Taking into account the Law of Time, the purpose of the overlay is to ensure that this new information base is in place as we approach the closing of the cycle. *Cosmic History Chronicles* serves as a point of light between the closing and opening of the new cycle.

Envisioning the Highest Reality: Conscious Activation of Cycles

18. In 2005, during the second year of the Mystery of the Stone, we began the seven year countdown to 2012, with a ceremony led by Valum Votan at Teotihuacán to open the Seven Caves of Tollan Zuvuya (12-21-2005). These cycles also occurred as a psychomythic entrance to seven different caves as represented by seven semiprecious metals stones. In the fifth year of the Mystery of the Stone, we began the final 1000-day countdown to 12-21-2012 on Solar Moon 21, in the 4 Seed year (2010). As we approach this pivot point between two cycles, these points of consciousness become magnified.

19. On Self-Existing Moon Alpha 5, Kin 109 year (of the Sixth year of the Cosmic History/Mystery of the Stone cycle) we began a further set of cycles: the Seven Cycles of the Lord of the Dawn, 113 days each. These cycles began at the 791-day countdown to 12-21-2012; this was a Zuvuya principle because the kin was 197 (791 in reverse), Red Lunar Earth—the fourth Book of the Seven Lost Generations (7 x 113 =791). 113 is the frequency of the Lord of the Dawn that corresponds to Red Solar Skywalker in the Book of Kin. So we began the seven cycles of the Lord of the Dawn on that date. (Note that the first cycle concluded on February 11, 2011—Galactic Moon Alpha 5, Kin 109 year).

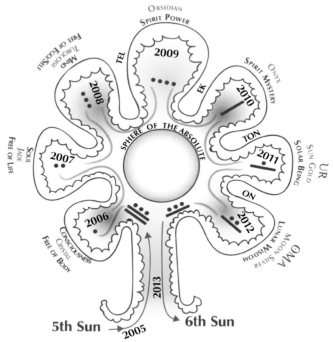

THE SEVEN CAVES OF TULAN ZUVUYA

The Seven Cycles of the Lord of the Dawn
Cycle 1: "Lord of the Dawn Arises" 4.5 – 8.5, 5 Moon year (10/22/2010 – 2/11/2011)
Cycle 2: "Lord of the Dawn Sets in Motion" 8.6 – 12.6, 5 Moon year (2/12 – 6/4/2011)
Cycle 3: "Lord of the Dawn Electrifies" 12.7, 5 Moon yr. – 3.6, 6 Wizard year (6/5 – 9/25/2011)
Cycle 4: "Lord of the Dawn Spectralizes His Form" 3.7 – 7.7, 6 Wizard yr. (9/26/2011 – 1/16/2012)
Cycle 5: "Lord of the Dawn Manifests Cosmic Radiance" 7.8 – 11.7, 6 Wizard yr. (1/17 – 5/8/2012)
Cycle 6: "Lord of the Dawn Self-Transforms" 11.8, 6 Wizard yr. – 2.7, 7 Storm yr. (5/9 – 8/29/2012)
Cycle 7: "Lord of the Dawn Self-Transcends" 2.8 – 6.8, 7 Storm year (8/30 – 12/20/2012)

20. These cycles of spiritual ascent represent the awakening of the Lord of the Dawn, the psycho-mythic representation of the power of self-transcendence of the human spirit. They also set the 791 days to the closing of the cycle, which also marks the beginning of seven cycles of 144 days each, taking us to the Day out of Time (July 25) 2013—Kin 163. This day is followed by Yellow Galactic Seed: Galactic Synchronization. These seven 144-day cycles are the cycles of the return of sacred power and the awakening of the self-existing power of self-transcendence of the Lord of the Dawn. The return of sacred power refers to receiving lessons or the descent of supermind and blessings of divine order of the higher mind consciousness of the universe.

PURPOSE OF TRACKING CYCLES

21. It is up to us to consciously activate these cycles that occur within the final climax of the last katun of the 13 baktuns in this final 1000 days. The conscious activation of these cycles triggers subliminal levels and stages of information decompression. This is a key point.

22. The purpose of practicing the synchronic order is to track multiple cycles and become aware of the synchronization of multiple cycles as different levels, stages or powers of consciousness. As we attain greater facility for tracking multiple cycles simultaneously then our continuing consciousness increases and our mind is entered into an interdimensional reality.

23. This also brings into play the factor of fractal time compression of the cycle and frequency between two identical, synchronic event points. This cycle can be expanded fractally so within one week we can live 100 years or within one thirteen-year cycle we can live 1300 years (see *20 Tablets of the Law of Time*).

---

20 TABLETS OF THE LAW OF TIME

The 20 Tablets shows us that the 208-moon cycle from Magnetic Moon 1, 5 Seed year (July 26, 1997) to Cosmic Moon 28, 7 Storm year (July 24, 2013) is the same as the 208 stations (of 100 years each) that have occurred since the beginning of the 26,000-year cycle which includes the 13 baktuns of history and complets on July 26, 2013—Galactic Synchronization. In this way, the Crystal Moon of the 6 Wizard year is Kin 194, White Crystal Wizard, the first of the 7 Lost Generations, meaning that the six moons following will be the remaining six Lost Generations (Cosmic Moon, 6 Wizard year through the Overtone Moon, 7 Storm year).

The Rhythmic Moon of the 7 Storm year is known as the "Moon out of Time" wherein the 13 baktuns of history end (December 21, 2012). After this moon we will then be living in the 7 Mystic Moons (Resonant Moon through the Cosmic Moon, 7 Storm year—corresponding to kin 202-208). In the 7:7::7:7 and 20 Tablets practices we telepathically project forward in time and experience each day as one of the seven last moons of the 13 baktuns (7 lost generations) and the seven mystic moons leading to Galactic Synchronization 2013. (See *20 Tablets of the Law of Time* and *7:7::7:7 Telektonon Revelation* by Valum Votan).

---

24. On 22 December, 2012 (Crystal Moon Gamma 10, Kin 208, Yellow Cosmic Star), the Seven Cycles of the Lord of the Dawn opens the gate for the return of Quetzalcoatl. This begins a perfect 216-day cycle, which is a perfect cube cycle. (This means that there are exactly 216 days between Kin 208, Yellow Cosmic Star and Kin 163, Blue Resonant Night.) This cycle proceeds as six cycles of 36 days and represents the cubing as put forth in the 20 Tablets of the Law of Time with the 16th tablet. This represents the cubing of the 144,000 within the cube. *Note. This is a particularly powerful cycle in preparation for telepathic and physical intervention and the upgrading of human consciousness into cosmic civilization. This is also the time of the full activation of the noosphere.*

25. The 52-year Galactic Seed cycle (1961 – 2013) represents the final cycle of the technosphere (from 1987 to present) within the biosphere-noosphere transition. The culminating 216 days of the cubing of the 144,000 within creates the entry point for the generation of the new cycle. This includes the seventh 144-day cycle that occurs within this cycle of time and represents the activation of the seventh day of creation—the seventh 144-day cycle within the cubing of the 144,000 within. This brings us to the Galactic Synchronization point with the twin soul reunion. Then the new spiral density wave kicks in and starts where that left off.

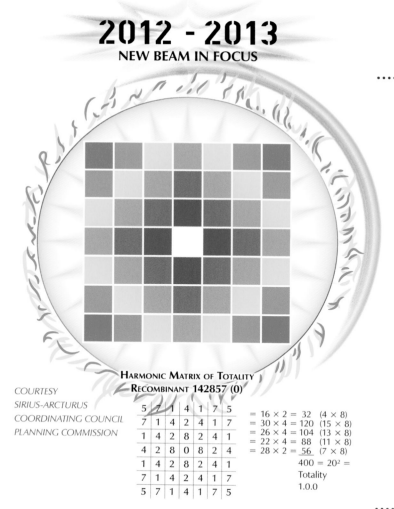

2012 - 2013
NEW BEAM IN FOCUS

HARMONIC MATRIX OF TOTALITY
RECOMBINANT 142857 (0)

COURTESY
SIRIUS-ARCTURUS
COORDINATING COUNCIL
PLANNING COMMISSION

5	7	1	4	1	7	5
7	1	4	2	4	1	7
1	4	2	8	2	4	1
4	2	8	0	8	2	4
1	4	2	8	2	4	1
7	1	4	2	4	1	7
5	7	1	4	1	7	5

$= 16 \times 2 = 32 \quad (4 \times 8)$
$= 30 \times 4 = 120 \quad (15 \times 8)$
$= 26 \times 4 = 104 \quad (13 \times 8)$
$= 22 \times 4 = 88 \quad (11 \times 8)$
$= 28 \times 2 = \underline{56} \quad (7 \times 8)$
$400 = 20^2 =$
Totality
1.0.0

As we move toward the Galactic Synchronization point, we have increasing incidence of cycles occurring simultaneously with an increasing compression of information. The increasing incidence of synchronization of these cycles represents the advent of consciousness through the application of the Law of Time. This sets the stage for the advent of the noosphere; the mapping of the future; and the creation of new cycles of time when we are operating in complete cosmic consciousness as a noospheric organism within the planetary heliosphere of Velatropa 24. This is the conclusion of a sequence of formulations that begins with the regeneration and meaning of the interval of lost time in eternity and the ratio of seven and the coming seven baktuns of the noosphere.

26. From there we have the 7 baktun cycles of the noosphere of Timeship Earth 2013, which takes us to the year 4772 (2,880,000 kin since the beginning of the Great Cycle of History). When we get to 2013 there is a 7-year cycle and then a 13-year cycle. 13 baktuns: 7 baktuns of noosphere and then 6 baktuns of the self-evolving art spore—the whole of the earth in cosmic civilization. The first 20 years of the unfolding of the new time. These have been mapped out by Valum Votan from 2013 to 2020 and 2033 (see next chapter).

Channeling on Galactic Seed from Valum Votan to Red Queen regarding closing of the cycle and opening of the new:

At the conclusion of the cycle, Earth and everything on it will be restored as dynamic elements of Cosmic History. Cosmic History is a yoga that joins the spectrum of the dimensions: unifying the spectrum of the field of imagination and the field of manifestation. It shows how the processes of the phenomenal world are informed by structures of intelligence that exist in the higher dimensions.

In 2012, the Earth will experience a dimensional shift. The programs that had prevailed for the previous 5,000 years will be dissolved.

A new set of precepts will be established within the planetary mind of the noosphere. This will be the first stage of the new evolutionary being: the superhuman. This being will be in tune with the sun and with the field of galactic consciousness. Life will take on radically different patterns to ground this expanded sphere of consciousness.

Creation comes from thought. All structures are formed in the mind. Creation descends from the sixth-dimensional information of light grids and codes. These are then transduced into fifth-dimensional electrical energy structures. In the fourth dimension, these energy structures are translated into a variety of imaginal and etheric images that inform the subtle body. In the third-dimensional form, these images become new norms of perception and behavior.

When we talk about a dimensional phase shift, we are talking about a shift in the patterns that ultimately affect our relationship to ourselves and the universe. Whereas in the cycle of history the perceptions were bound by third-dimensional norms of materialism, in the redemption of the galactic future following 2012, we will be functioning as entities now absorbed into a cosmic civilization. This process will attune us to the way in which we are actually solar-cosmic functions.

The components of information that define the phenomenal world are stored in the Cosmic History core and accessed through the psi bank, the self-regulating mechanism of the noosphere. As we approach 2012, we will be coming into phase with the Cosmic History core. This is the basis of all gnosis or intuitive knowledge. We already know. Once we are totally in phase, we will be synchronized with the larger program that is being played from the solar core and received in the Earth's noosphere.

Cosmic History becomes self-regulating information activated by the awakened human intelligence, operating in resonance with the fourth-dimensional program originating in the sun. The pattern of Earth society will be in the form of a planetary Tollan, or enlightened society.

All of the effort gone into promoting the Thirteen Moon calendar was preparation for the closing of the cycle. The meaning of the closing of the cycle is the reintegration of the human consciousness into the solar ring through the application of the correct standard of measure. The 13 Moon/28-day orbital cycle encloses human consciousness in the solar field.

It's all a matter of solar frequencies engaging the Earth's orbits—the solar ring—through the human mind being reengaged by the proper instrument of measure.

By engaging the Earth again within the solar ring, the principle of the absolute conservation of energy is reinstated; currently this planet is experiencing an absolute depletion of cosmic energy. When you have the absolute conservation of energy, the cycle is closed.

Closing the cycle means knowing how to place the Earth in its solar ring and in its correct frequency range with the sun. This is why it is called the dawning of the sixth sun, the sun of the solar cosmic consciousness. This is what the Galactic Maya foresaw; this is what the Mayan prophecies are all about.

For the Galactic Mayans, this is the fulfillment of a vast engineering project in time. They could predict all the projections of thought and know exactly when this trajectory of thought would reach a critical mass and affect changes in society and the historical process. They knew this would mark the climax of history, which would accelerate into a dimensional phase. Now the unprecedented promise of consciously entering a new cycle has begun. Because the Great Cycle closes, it opens again, becoming the endlessness of cosmic consciousness.

PART IV
CENTER OF THE COSMIC HISTORY CUBE

CHAPTER 13

SEVEN GENERATIONS TO COME

THE FIRST TWENTY YEARS AND THE SEVEN
BAKTUN DYNASTIES OF TIMESHIP EARTH 2013
BY VALUM VOTAN

All I am now is that which I have remembered of myself to become, from a far away place and a long time ago, long before I took this present birth.

In light of this I know: 2012 is only a threshold.

It is my job—my duty—for all humanity to see and to define what lies beyond that threshold for the next 2,760 years—until my next return at that time as a star traveler from the distant future—that is, until the year AD 4772—exactly seven baktuns and eight days after 2012.

Look: From 3113 BC to 353 BC, the end of the seventh Baktun of the Mind Teachings is exactly 2,760 years, the same measure as 2012 to 4772, exactly seven baktuns after the closing of the cycle—that is when I shall return.

4772 = 7,885 years after 3113 BC; this is exactly 2,880,000 kin, the equivalent of 20 baktuns. In vigesimal notation 20 baktuns, 144,000 x 20 kin is written **1.0.0.0.0.0**.

Note: On page 133 in the book *2012* Mayan Prophecy (2009) by David Douglas there is a section entitled "José Argüelles" that states:

"It is interesting that recent decodings of the hieroglyphs at Palenque, which are understood to have been made during the reign of Pacal the Great, refer to dates beyond the end of the Long Count calendar. On the Tablet of the Inscriptions at Palenque a date of 1.0.0.0.0.8 5 Lamat 1 Mol can be inferred—otherwise known as 21 October 4772, almost 3000 years in the future. Perhaps we can deduce from this that Pacal himself believed that the end of the fifth age did not represent the end of time or of the Earth, and that his name would be still mentioned in the sixth age."

21 October 4772 is not just a random date, but is precisely 7 baktuns and 8 days after 21/12/2012, and exactly 20 baktuns and 8 days after the beginning of the Cycle of History, 3113 BC. If October 21 (Self-Existing Moon 4), 4772 is 1.0.0.0.0.8, then October 13, Self-Existing Moon 24, would be the precise completion of the 20-Baktun cycle begun on 13 August 3113 BC (Julian 3114 BC).

This is actually a revolutionary and stunning fact to consider. Also, in the long count the date 1.0.0.0.0.8 is 5 Lamat or Kin 148 Yellow Overtone Star—the sign of the Arcturus Command, the sign of the Star Traveler. This also means that the 20-Baktun Long Count end date would be 10 Ahau or Kin 140, Yellow Planetary Sun, key number of the Telektonon Prophecy. On the Dreamspell, the

1.0.0.0.0.8 return date would be White Resonant Worldbridger or 7 Cimi (one of the two lords of Xibalba in the Popul Vuh) and the end date of the entire 20-Baktun count would be White Crystal Mirror, Kin 38. Note: The **Crystal Mirror** holds the round table of the **Hand** Wavespell, just as the end of the 13-Baktun count was **Crystal Hand** that held the round table of the **Warrior** Wavespell.

Because of this information the future can now be recalled and further meaning be given to the two sequences of cycles—13 baktuns and 7 baktuns, the two key creation numbers of the Law of Time—20 baktuns in all, signifying a cycle of totality, the establishment of the Dynasty of Earth (Seven Dynasties of Timeship Earth?).

Who but **time's special witness** could lay the clue, decode it and then who but he could tell you:

Seven baktuns will there be following the end
Of the 13-Baktun cycle of history,
One baktun for each of seven generations to unfold their long-rehearsed and ancient future history.
Within this 7-Baktun span less four years there will be exactly 53 cycles of 52 years, the Sirian round
of time, running from 2016, 11 Storm, to 4772, also an 11 Storm year, 2,756 years in all for the Seven
Dynasties of Timeship Earth to unfold their future legacy.
Then shall I return, time's special witness, by Arcturus Star Command, on the eighth day after the 7th
baktun—the completion of the 20 baktuns of the cycle of the transformation of the Earth, on the 90th
day following the completion of the 53rd solar galactic cycle, the cycle of Sirian rebirth in time …
And then it will be understood what is meant by seven generations to come, seven baktuns in all, 53
cycles of the Sirian Wheel of Time.

THE NATURE OF THE DYNASTIES OF EARTH—TIMESHIP EARTH 2013

When we talk about the Dynasties of Earth, we are talking about the dynasties set forth by the Earth families whose five-day chromatic circulation of power establishes an equality shared by all, where all are in submission to the sovereignty of the Earth in its turning—in its seasons, and its cycles. This constitutes the always-future realm of Syntropia—the union of the mind of the Earth with the Mind of the Earth families, the new human race, the people of OMA, *homo noosphericus.*

We have had the agricultural urban revolution which began 3113 BC that led inevitably twelve baktuns later to the industrial revolution, 1618, the beginning of baktun 13. Now we are at the threshold of the next revolution—the *psychozoic* revolution—crossing the 2012 threshold into the noosphere. In this new cosmic timespace of the Earth mind we will fully participate in the spiritualization of all of life and matter—the meaning of psychozoic—hence Psychozoic Era, Earth's next geological epoch.

In this new age we will experience not just the reversal of all historical processes, but their transformation and transcendence altogether into a condition of reality and life where the mind is supreme and Earth is inseparable from the mind. "The Earth and myself are one mind."

Thirteen baktuns, the span of one synchronization beam, were required to create the catalytic condition of acceleration, synchronization and transformative crisis. Seven baktuns to reverse, transform, transcend and create anew—the psychozoic revolution of the noosphere, the journey of Timeship Earth 2013. And if the Earth human so chooses at 4772, another six baktuns of supercosmic, supramental Earth civilization of telepathic immortals—26 baktuns in all to be completed AD 7137, 1.6.0.0.0. The second stage 13-Baktun beam, the ascension return cycle would then be complete.

This transition stage of Earth's evolution—BC 3113 – AD 7137, 10,250 years in all—is hardly anything more than a shifting of gears or the blink of the eye in comparison to a history of Earth that spans some four billion years. Yet it represents the triumph of the Dynasties of Earth. At the entry point of this next 13-Baktun cycle, Earth will enter and stabilize in its next geological plateau, the transzoic or hyperorganic era, for who knows how many millions of years into the future. But our soul journey on this planet will be compete, and those who have chosen to evolve here, to that point 5,125 years after 2012, may then move on to who knows what as yet uncharted realms of time and mind …

The Seven Baktun Cycles, Seven Dynasties of the Seven Generations of Timeship Earth 2013 Sixth Sun of Solar Consciousness

1. First Dynasty. 2012-2406, Baktun One (to 144,000 kin)
(Long Count = Baktun 14, 2,016,000 Kin = 14.0.0.0.0)
Alpha Gateway, South Pole.
Dynasty of the Integration of the Star Teachings
Generation Cycle of the White Crystal Wizard

2. Second Dynasty, 2406-2800, Baktun Two (to 288,000 kin)
(Long Count = Baktun 15, 2,160,000 Kin = 15.0.0.0.0)
Alpha Polar, North Pole
Dynasty of the Cosmic Civilization of the Galactic Federation
Generation Cycle of the Blue Cosmic Eagle

3. Third Dynasty, 2800-3194, Baktun Three (to 432,000 kin)
(Long Count = Baktun 16, 2,304,000 Kin = 16.0.0.0.0)
Cardinal North Hemisphere
Dynasty of the Electromagnetic Flowering of the Planetary Art Spore
Generation Cycle of the Yellow Magnetic Warrior

4. Fourth Dynasty, 3194-3589, Baktun Four (to 576,000 kin)
(Long Count = Baktun 17, 2,448,000 Kin = 17.0.0.0.0)

Core Equatorial
Dynasty of The Bi-polar Core Hunab Ku Art Spore
Generation Cycle of the Red Lunar Earth—Galactic Activation Portal Opened to Hunab Ku

5. Fifth Dynasty, 3589-3983, Baktun Five (to 720,000 kin)
(Long Count = Baktun 18, 2,592,000 Kin = 18.0.0.0.0)
Signal South Hemisphere
Dynasty of the Galactic Life Whole
Generation Cycle of the White Electric Mirror

6. Sixth Dynasty, 3983-4377, Baktun Six (to 864,000 kin)
(Long Count = Baktun 19, 2,736,000 Kin = 19.0.0.0.0)
Omega Gateway South Pole
Dynasty of the Galactic Art Whole
Generation Cycle of the Blue Self-Existing Storm

7. Seventh Dynasty, 4377-4772, Baktun Seven (to 1,008,000 Kin)
(Long Count = Baktun 20 = 2,880,000 Kin = 1.0.0.0.0.0)
Omega Polar North Pole
Dynasty of the Universal Galactic Solar Enlightenment of Earth
Generation Cycle of the Yellow Overtone Sun
53 52-year Sirian Wheels of Time Complete (from 2016 2,756-year cycle to 4772, see Tables below)

The Six Baktuns of Earth as Self-Evolving Art Spore
1. Baktun Eight 4772-5166, Baktun 21 = 1.1.0.0.0.0
2. Baktun Nine 5166-5560, Baktun 22 = 1.2.0.0.0.0
3. Baktun Ten 5560- 5954, Baktun 23 = 1.3.0.0.0.0
4. Baktun Eleven 5954-6349, Baktun 24 = 1.4.0.0.0.0
5. Baktun Twelve 6349-6743, Baktun25 = 1.5.0.0.0.0
6. Baktun Thirteen 6743-7137, Baktun 26 = 1.6.0.0.0.0
= 3744000 kin or 10,250 years after BC 3113
= 1872000 kin or 5,125 years after 2012
Second Beam Transit, Cosmic Ascension

THE FIRST 20 YEARS OF TIMESHIP EARTH 2013
8 SEED-1 STORM, 2013–2033-34

The Galactic Research Institute is in fulfillment of the Sirian Command of the Galactic Federation. The establishment of a permanent base in the Great Southern Continent signifies that the Sirian Command, the Intelligence Agency of the Galactic Federation, now has an outpost on Earth—V.24.3, the first stage of reclaiming Earth for the Dominion of Time.

From this base we shall chart both the conclusion of the cycle—capped by the ejection of the Circumpolar Rainbow Bridge and the completion of the Noosphere II Project—as well as envisioning the stages beyond the 2012 threshold for the reconstruction of the Earth—the Second Creation. In addition to the long term envisioning of the Seven Baktun Dynasties of Timeship Earth 2013, there is the short term dynamic reconstruction cycle, the first 20 years of Timeship Earth 2013, as well as the 53 52-year Sirian Wheels from 2016-4772. The twenty year cycle is in two stages, the 7-year Sirian Surveillance and the 13-year Earth Wizards Noocracy.

A. The 7-Year Cycle of the New Solar Human, Cycle of the Sirian Surveillance of the New Earth. Launching of the Telepathic Command and Unification program of Timeship Earth 2013, securing the New Dawn (AD year numbering is maintained signifying Arcturus Dominion).

8 Seed – 11 Storm Seed Bundle—26/7 2013 – 25/7 2017

1. NS.1.26. Yellow Galactic Seed—26/7 2013 – 25/7 2014
Those who have chosen to remain are known as the People of Oma. It is they who have returned across the Bridge of Time to constitute the seed of the new race. The Red Queen is recognized as the leader of the People of Oma. This is the 217th day of the First Baktun—216 days between it and the beginning of the new cycle, Yellow Cosmic Star, Rhythmic 10, 7 Storm year—Beginning of reorganization of Timeship Earth 2013 according to Earth Families.

2. NS.1.27. Red Solar Moon—26/7 2014 – 25/7 2015
Cycle of healing and purification, healing whatever needs to be healed

3. NS.1.28. White Planetary Wizard—26/7 2015 – 25/7 2016
"Imagine there's no countries, it isn't hard to do…" Re-envisioning and manifesting the social order…

4. NS.1.29. Blue Spectral Storm—26/7 2016 – 25/7 2017
Beginning of 53 52-year cycles—Sirian Wheels (2756 years), First Sirian Wheel 2016-2068 Establishing of First Dynasty of Timeship Earth 2013,

Baktun One, 2012-2406, (to 144,000 kin)
(Long Count = Baktun 14, 2,016,000 Kin = 14.0.0.0.0)
Alpha Gateway, South Pole
Dynasty of the Integration of the Star Teachings
Generation Cycle of the White Crystal Wizard
Note 2016 = 144 x 14, Kin equivalent 196 (28x7), BMU 252
(21 x 12) key frequency of cosmic creation interval, 16,003,008 = 252^3, or $288^3 - 2808^2$.

5. NS.1.30. Yellow Crystal Seed—26/7 2017 – 25/7 2018

Red Queen fulfills the Crystal prophecy on behalf of the people of Oma. Earth cooperative societies established everywhere.

6. NS.1.31. Red Cosmic Moon 26/7 2018 – 25/7 2019

Thirteen Year cycle of Moon wavespell complete (2006-2019)
13 Moon/28-day standard harmonic timing program becomes second nature.

7. NS.1 32. White Magnetic Wizard 26/7 2019– 25/7 2020

First year of 13-year White Wizard Wavespell—2019-2032
Seventh and final year of Sirian surveillance—Transfer of intelligence operations from Sirian command to Earth Wizards.
Five Family Noospheric Council—Departure of Sirian V.24.3 Command team.

B. 13-Year Cycle—Earth Wizards establish Noocracy of Timeship Earth 2013

8. NS1.33. Blue Lunar Storm 26/7 2020 – 25/7 2021

Stabilizing and unifying the planetary telepathic network

9. NS1.34. Yellow Electric Seed 26/7 2021 – 25/7 2022

Activating the bio-solar telepathic education programs

10. NS1.35. Red Self-Existing Moon 26/7 2022 – 25/7 2023

Self-sustaining whole person noosphere health programs

11. NS1.36. White Overtone Wizard 26/7 2023 – 25/7 2024

Cosmic History telepathic higher education programs

12. NS1.37. Blue Rhythmic Storm 26/7 2024 – 25/7 2025

Self-generating bioregional economic programs

13. NS1.38. Yellow Resonant Seed 26/7 2025 – 25/7 2026
Garden culture community programs

14. NS1.39. Red Galactic Moon 26/7 2026 – 25/7 2027
Planetary-galactic art communes

15. NS1.40. White Solar Wizard 26/7 2027 – 25/7 2028
Advanced biosolar telepathic magnetic field programs

16. NS1.41. Blue Planetary Storm 26/7 2028 – 25/7 2029
Equalization of wealth and abundance programs—kin credit system

17. NS1.42. Yellow Spectral Seed 26/7 2029 – 25/7 2030
Unification of planetary harvest festivals

18. NS1.43. Red Crystal Moon 26/7 2030 – 25/7 2031
First twelve-year Earth councils round table

19. NS1.44. White Cosmic Wizard 26/7 2031 – 25/7 2032
Earth Wizards declaration of Galactic Sovereignty of Timeship Earth 2013

13-year Wizard wavespell complete

20. NS1.45. Blue Magnetic Storm 26/7 2032 – 25/7 2033
Beginning of 13-year Storm wavespell. Psi Bank of Noosphere fully operative. Human race functioning as a single organism

C. Sirian Wheels of Time = The 53 52-year cycles of the 2,756-year Galactic Mind Dynasties of Timeship Earth 2013 (2016-4772)

1. 2016-2068
2. 2068-2120
3. 2120-2172
4. 2172-2224
5. 2224-2276
6. 2276-2328
7. 2328-2380
8. 2380-2432
9. 2432-2484
10. 2484-2536
11. 2536-2588
12. 2588-2640
13. 2640-2692
14. 2692-2744
15. 2744-2796
16. 2796-2848
17. 2848-2900
18. 2900-2952
19. 2952-3004
20. 3004-3056
21. 3056-3108
22. 3108-3160
23. 3160-3212
24. 3212-3264
25. 3264-3316
26. 3316-3368
27. 3368-3420
28. 3420-3472
29. 3472-3524
30. 3524-3576
31. 3576-3628
32. 3628-3680
33. 3680-3732
34. 3732-3784
35. 3784-3836
36. 3836-3888
37. 3888-3940
38. 3940-3992
39. 3992-4044
40. 4044-4096
41. 4096-4148
42. 4148-4200
43. 4200-4252
44. 4252-4304
45. 4304-4356
46. 4356-4408
47. 4408-4460
48. 4460-4512
49. 4512-4564
50. 4564-4616
51. 4616-4668
52. 4668-4720 = One Great Sirius Wheel of Time, 2,704 years
53. 4720-4772 = One Great Sirius rebirth cycle = 7 baktuns of the 7 Earth Dynasties of Timeship Earth 2013 = 1.0.0.0.0.0; 20 baktuns since BC 3113; Eighth day of baktun cycle 8, 1.0.0.0.0.8 = Return of Pacal Votan, star traveler, for star mind weaving surveillance.

NEW TELEKTONON OVERLAY
13:7 SYNCHRONOTRON WHEEL OF THE LAW OF TIME

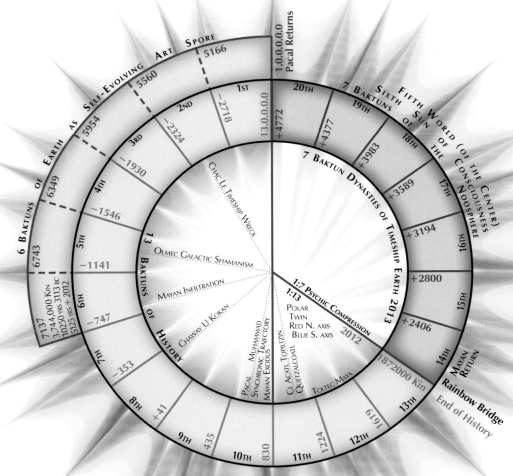

7-Year Cycle NS1.26-32 (2013-2020)

1. 8 Seed Year — NS1.26 (2013-14)

2. 9 Moon Year — NS1.27 (2014-15)

3. 10 Wizard Year — NS1.28 (2015-16)

4. 11 Storm Year — NS1.29 (2016-17), First Sirian Wheel

5. 12 Seed Year — NS1.30 (2017-18)

6. 13 Moon Year — NS1.31 (2018-19)

7. 1 Wizard Year — NS1.32 (2019-2020)

13-Year Cycle NS1.33-45 (2020-2033)

1. 2 Storm Year — NS1.33 (2020-21)
2. 3 Seed Year — NS1.34 (2021-22)
3. 4 Moon Year — NS1.35 (2022-23)
4. 5 Wizard Year — NS1.36 (2023-24)
5. 6 Storm Year — NS1.37 (2024-25)
6. 7 Seed Year — NS1.38 (2025-26)
7. 8 Moon Year — NS1.39 (2026-27)
8. 9 Wizard Year — NS1.40 (2027-28)
9. 10 Storm Year — NS1.41 (2028-29)
10. 11 Seed Year — NS1.42 (2029-30)
11. 12 Moon Year — NS1.43 (2030-31)
12. 13 Wizard Year — NS1.44 (2031-32)
13. 1 Storm Year — NS1.45 (2032-33)

TELEKTONON
AND THE CUBE OF THE LAW

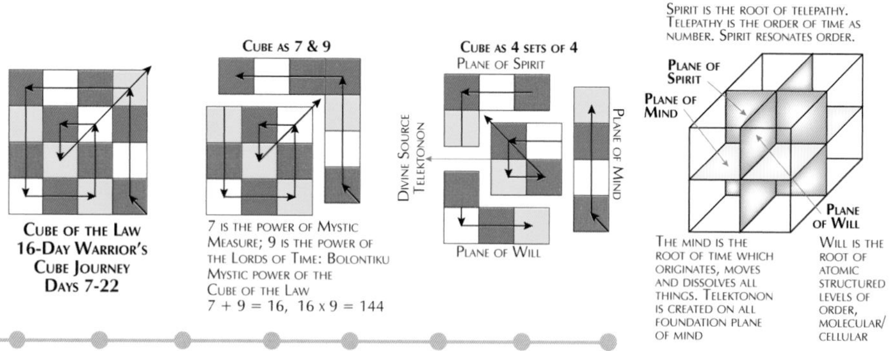

Galactic Karmic Flow

| Mercury | Venus | Earth | Mars | Maldek | Jupiter | Saturn | Uranus | Neptune | Pluto |

1st Mental Sphere Pre-conscious

2nd Mental Sphere Unconscious

3rd Mental Sphere Conscious

4th Mental Sphere Continuing Conscious

5th Mental Sphere Super-conscious

6th Mental Sphere Subliminal-Conscious

Axis of the Plane of Will

Solar Prophetic Flow

CUBE OF THE LAW
16-DAY WARRIOR'S
CUBE JOURNEY
DAYS 7-22

7 IS THE POWER OF MYSTIC MEASURE; 9 IS THE POWER OF THE LORDS OF TIME: BOLONTIKU MYSTIC POWER OF THE CUBE OF THE LAW
7 + 9 = 16, 16 x 9 = 144

CUBE AS 7 & 9

DIVINE SOURCE
TELEKTONON

CUBE AS 4 SETS OF 4

PLANE OF WILL

PLANE OF SPIRIT

PLANE OF MIND

Circuit One
Alpha-Omega Recharge
Solar-Galactic Metaconscious

Circuit Two
Allied Memory Instinct

Axis of the
Plane of Spirit

Circuit Three
Telektonon
Earth Spirit Speaking Tube

Circuit Four
Externalizing Intelligence

Circuit Five
Internalizing Intelligence

THE MIND IS THE ROOT OF TIME WHICH ORIGINATES, MOVES AND DISSOLVES ALL THINGS. TELEKTONON IS CREATED ON ALL FOUNDATION PLANE OF MIND

PLANE OF SPIRIT

PLANE OF MIND

PLANE OF WILL

WILL IS THE ROOT OF ATOMIC STRUCTURED LEVELS OF ORDER, MOLECULAR/ CELLULAR

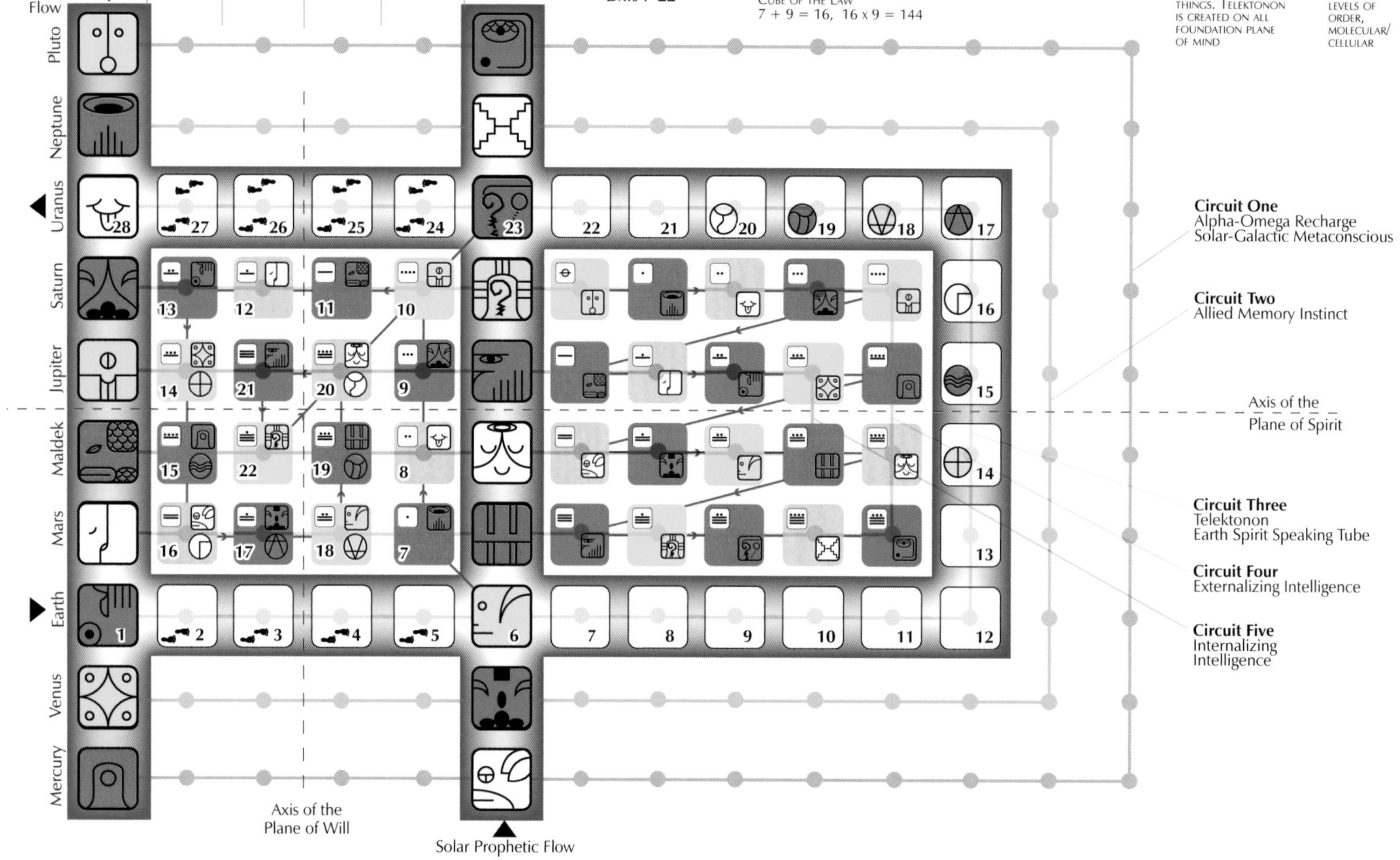

SPIRIT IS THE ROOT OF TELEPATHY. TELEPATHY IS THE ORDER OF TIME AS NUMBER. SPIRIT RESONATES ORDER.

208

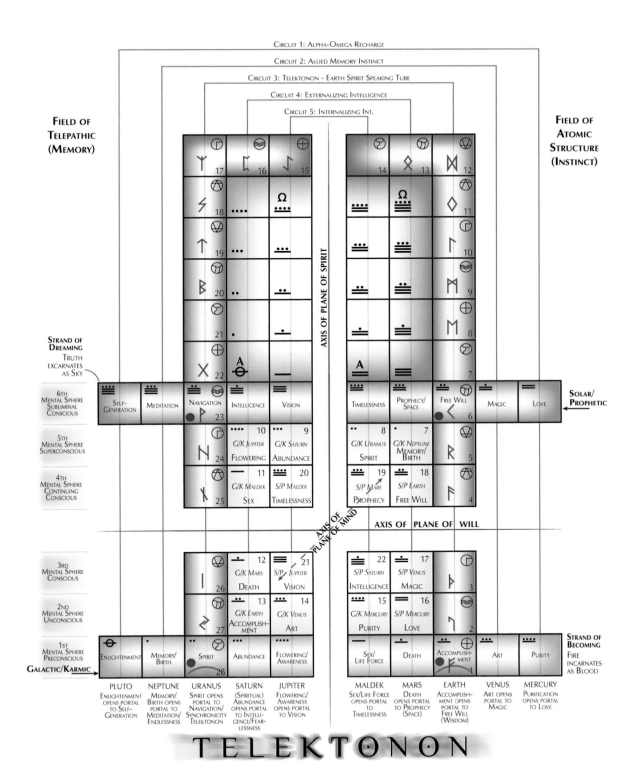

CIRCUIT 1: ALPHA-OMEGA RECHARGE

CIRCUIT 2: ALLIED MEMORY INSTINCT

CIRCUIT 3: TELEKTONON - EARTH SPIRIT SPEAKING TUBE

CIRCUIT 4: EXTERNALIZING INTELLIGENCE

CIRCUIT 5: INTERNALIZING INT.

FIELD OF TELEPATHIC (MEMORY)

FIELD OF ATOMIC STRUCTURE (INSTINCT)

AXIS OF PLANE OF SPIRIT

STRAND OF DREAMING
TRUTH EXCARNATES AS SKY

6TH MENTAL SPHERE SUBLIMINAL CONSCIOUS

5TH MENTAL SPHERE SUPERCONSCIOUS

4TH MENTAL SPHERE CONTINUING CONSCIOUS

SOLAR/ PROPHETIC

SELF-GENERATION | MEDITATION | NAVIGATION | INTELLIGENCE | VISION | TIMELESSNESS | PROPHECY/ SPACE | FREE WILL | MAGIC | LOVE

23 · 6

10 FLOWERING — G/K JUPITER | 9 ABUNDANCE — G/K SATURN | 8 SPIRIT — G/K URANUS | 7 MEMORY/ BIRTH — G/K NEPTUNE

24 | 5

11 SEX — G/K MALDEK | 20 TIMELESSNESS — S/P MALDEK | 19 PROPHECY — S/P MARS | 18 FREE WILL — S/P EARTH

25 | 4

AXIS OF PLANE OF MIND

AXIS OF PLANE OF WILL

3RD MENTAL SPHERE CONSCIOUS

2ND MENTAL SPHERE UNCONSCIOUS

1ST MENTAL SPHERE PRECONSCIOUS

GALACTIC/KARMIC

12 DEATH — G/K MARS | 21 VISION — S/P JUPITER | 22 INTELLIGENCE — S/P SATURN | 17 MAGIC — S/P VENUS

26 | 3

13 ACCOMPLISH-MENT — G/K EARTH | 14 ART — G/K VENUS | 15 PURITY — G/K MERCURY | 16 LOVE — S/P MERCURY

27 | 2

ENLIGHTENMENT | MEMORY/ BIRTH | SPIRIT | ABUNDANCE | FLOWERING/ AWARENESS | SEX/ LIFE FORCE | DEATH | ACCOMPLISH-MENT | ART | PURITY

28 | 1

STRAND OF BECOMING
FIRE INCARNATES AS BLOOD

PLUTO
ENLIGHTENMENT OPENS PORTAL TO SELF-GENERATION

NEPTUNE
MEMORY/ BIRTH OPENS PORTAL TO MEDITATION/ ENDLESSNESS

URANUS
SPIRIT OPENS PORTAL TO NAVIGATION/ SYNCHRONICITY TELEKTONON

SATURN
(SPIRITUAL) ABUNDANCE OPENS PORTAL TO INTELLI-GENCE/FEAR-LESSNESS

JUPITER
FLOWERING/ AWARENESS OPENS PORTAL TO VISION

MALDEK
SEX/LIFE FORCE OPENS PORTAL TO TIMELESSNESS

MARS
DEATH OPENS PORTAL TO PROPHECY (SPACE)

EARTH
ACCOMPLISH-MENT OPENS PORTAL TO FREE WILL (WISDOM)

VENUS
ART OPENS PORTAL TO MAGIC

MERCURY
PURIFICATION OPENS PORTAL TO LOVE

TELEKTONON

28-DAY TELEKTONON

AS CONTAINED IN THE FOUR MATRICES OF OUTER TIME

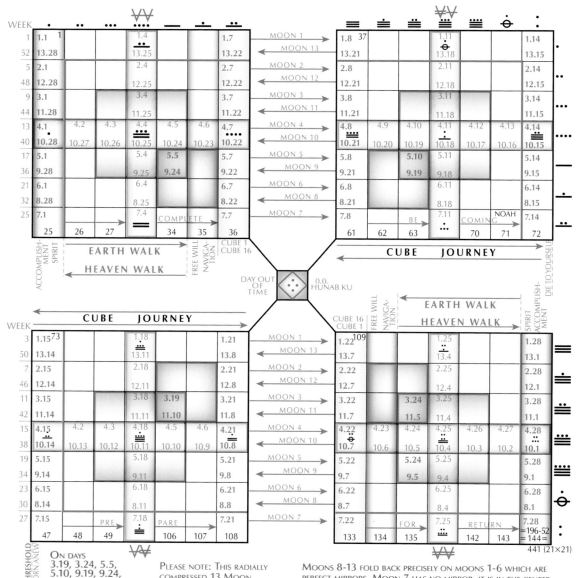

ON DAYS
3.19, 3.24, 5.5,
5.10, 9.19, 9.24,
11.5, 11.10
THE 4 CHANNELS
CONNECTING
COSMIC TIME WITH
COSMIC SPACE MATRICES
ARE OPENED.

PLEASE NOTE: THIS RADIALLY
COMPRESSED 13 MOON
TEMPLATE IS EMBEDDED AS BUT
ONE LAYERING IN THE
MULTIDIMENSIONAL 441 MATRIX,
AND CANNOT BE UNDERSTOOD
APART FROM THE WHOLE.

MOONS 8-13 FOLD BACK PRECISELY ON MOONS 1-6 WHICH ARE
PERFECT MIRRORS. MOON 7 HAS NO MIRROR, IT IS IN THE CENTER —
THOUGH THERE IS MOTION IT MOVES NOWHERE — THE INTERVAL OF LOST
TIME IN ETERNITY — AND IN ITS CENTER IS THE MYSTIC THRESHOLD WHERE
BECOMING CEASES AND RETURN BEGINS. 14 DAYS TO COMPLETE
BECOMING, 14 DAYS TO PREPARE FOR RETURN. WITH THE 8TH MOON,
THE MOTION REVERSES, YOU ARE NOW IN THE MIRROR REFLECTING.

SYNCHRONOTRON

7-BAKTUN BEAM MATRIX RADIANT FREQUENCY BROADCAST
RADIANCE PROGRAM - SECOND CREATION - 2012-4772 BAKTUN 20 1.0.0.0.0.0
FREQUENCY MAGNITUDE INCREASE [AMPLIFICATION OF MENTAL RATIOS]
65934 OF 1/13 (76923) TO 1/7 (142857) = 85% INCREASE
BASIS OF AUGMENTED PERCEPTUAL MODE
RADIALIZED CONSCIOUSNESS OF HOLOMIND PERCEIVER PROGRAM
FOUNDATION OF HYPERORGANIC SYMBIOSIS AND RADIOSONIC TECHNOLOGY

Top signs: − + +   − − +

41	40	39	38	37	36	35	34	33	32	31	30	29	28	27	26	25	24	23	22	21
42	117	116	115	114	113	112	111	110	109	108	107	106	105	104	103	102	101	100	99	20
43	118	185	184	183	182	181	180	179	178	177	176	175	174	173	172	171	170	169	98	19
44	119	186	245	244	243	242	241	240	239	238	237	236	235	234	233	232	231	168	97	18
45	120	187	246	297	296	295	294	293	292	291	290	289	288	287	286	285	230	167	96	17
46	121	188	247	298	341	340	339	338	337	336	335	334	333	332	331	284	229	166	95	16
47	122	189	248	299	342	377	376	375	374	373	372	371	370	369	330	283	228	165	94	15
48	123	190	249	300	343	378	405	404	403	402	401	400	399	368	329	282	227	164	93	14
49	124	191	250	301	344	379	406	425	424	423	422	421	398	367	328	281	226	163	92	13
50	125	192	251	302	345	380	407	426	437	436	435	420	397	366	327	280	225	162	91	12
51	126	193	252	303	346	381	408	427	438	441	434	419	396	365	326	279	224	161	90	11
52	127	194	253	304	347	382	409	428	439	440	433	418	395	364	325	278	223	160	89	10
53	128	195	254	305	348	383	410	429	430	431	432	417	394	363	324	277	222	159	88	9
54	129	196	255	306	349	384	411	412	413	414	415	416	393	362	323	276	221	158	87	8
55	130	197	256	307	350	385	386	387	388	389	390	391	392	361	322	275	220	157	86	7
56	131	198	257	308	351	352	353	354	355	356	357	358	359	360	321	274	219	156	85	6
57	132	199	258	309	310	311	312	313	314	315	316	317	318	319	320	273	218	155	84	5
58	133	200	259	260	261	262	263	264	265	266	267	268	269	270	271	272	217	154	83	4
59	134	201	202	203	204	205	206	207	208	209	210	211	212	213	214	215	216	153	82	3
60	135	136	137	138	139	140	141	142	143	144	145	146	147	148	149	150	151	152	81	2
61	62	63	64	65	66	67	68	69	70	71	72	73	74	75	76	77	78	79	80	1

Left margin signs (rows 8–10): + − − (rows 12–14): + + −
Right margin signs (rows 8–10): − + + (rows 12–14): − − +

Bottom signs: + − −   + + −

A BEAM DISCHARGE - A SIMULTANEITY OF INFORMATION
RESTRUCTURING MIND INSTANTANEOUSLY AS A FREQUENCY OF RADIANT GLORY

EACH OF FOUR
OUTER TIME DIMENSIONS =
Freq. Magnitude
142857 × 7 = @ 999 999
×4 sum = 3999996 =
1/7 × 28, 1/13 × 52, 1/91 × 364

4 "999 999"
WHITE OUTER STRANDS

[13:7]
1) $7^2 \times 19$, 7×133 = 931
2)   Prime 809
3) 81 (9^2) × 13 = 1053
4) 21 × 43   = 903

SUM FREQUENCY   2012
= 3696 = BMU 168   −168
= 33 × 28 × 4   1844

APPENDIX I

THE VULOM ELECTROMAGNETIC ATTRACTION FORCE FIELD AND THE HUNAB KU 21 POWER GRID

Vulom is an attraction power field in which numerous known and unknown energies are unified as a Total. This field is also called the electromagnetic attraction field. One easily goes to more advanced systems from the energy transformation layers constituted in here.

The Vulom system is a system established between two electrical currents … it adjusts the transition speed of the currents …

This system is applied to the transition power units of galactic dimensions and by this means, the attraction power field is being formed. All astral travels, methods of beaming up, intergalactic transportation and communication are taken into effect by the attraction power of this electromagnetic field …

—*The Knowledge Book*

Underlying the Galactic Tree of Life and Knowledge is the Hunab Ku 21 power grid. This is an intergalactic template for capacitating the Vulom field. The 21 different nodes define 52 intervals that establish the transition circuits of the Vulom field. The 21 nodes define the "numerous known and unknown energies … unified as a Total." The energy transformation layers refer to the thermic and luminic activation fields, the centrifugal and centripetal energetic force fields and the darka and marka polar fields of influence.

Understanding the underlying structure and its interactive, transformative principles, as well as its location in the etheric sheathe will make possible beaming up, astral (time) travel, and intergalactic communication and transportation.

THE VULOM POWER GRID-CIRCUIT BOARD

The power grid-circuit board consists of six principle circuits: the two axes, two electrical currents (meridians), and two stabilizing lines of force. There are four secondary binding circuits—parallel red and blue, and parallel white and yellow.

These ten circuits define the Vulom power grid-circuit board. This is a completely integrated circuit, and should be studied very carefully to understand the different circuits and nodes to be activated for whichever of the several possible uses (See Chapter 9, the structure of the Galactic Tree of Life and Knowledge, and the Four Electro-etheric power cells).

The principle axes define the four quadrants of the circuit board. First the equatorial-gravitational line of force defines in the upper half a thermic force field governed by the marka magnetic polar field, and a luminic force field governed by the darka magnetic polar field in the lower half.

The vertical Mauri tube, the central plasmatic channel and magnetic line of force, divides the two upper and lower fields into right- and left-hand fields. To the left is the primary centrifugal heat-light force field. This field corresponds to the right side of the body. To the right is the secondary— reactive or complex—centripetal inner light-heat force field. This field corresponds to the left side of the body.

The force fields of the five powers of harmony cells also define the different fields of energy: Marka polar and darka polar fields, centrifugal heat and centripetal light fields, and the central matrix fifth force light-photon energy field.

The harmony of power cells have unifying functions: the Marka cell unifies the centrifugal and centripetal thermic force fields, while the Darka power cell unifies the centrifugal and centripetal luminic force fields. Likewise the centrifugal cell unifies the thermic and luminic force fields, while the centripetal power cell unifies the inner light and inner heat cells. The central matrix fifth force light-photon energy field unifies all four of the power fields.

The four electro-etheric cells actually define the force fields: electro-thermic radiating, electro-luminic illuminating, electro-inner light vitalizing, electro-inner heat catalyzing,

Knowing the nature and function of these fields in relation to the six principle circuits and the four binding inner diagonal circuits is the key to successfully launching the holon or soul-body from the physical form body into higher-dimensional orders of reality for the purpose of expanding the horizons of what is currently known about time, the mind and the universe itself. To understand the vulom power grid-circuit board in a meaningful way it is important to understand what it is and why.

Vulom: Cosmology of the Electrical Force

The Vulom power grid and circuit board incorporates the fundamental cosmology of the electrical force. In this cosmology the universe is established by six primal types of cosmic electricity, the sum of which is called a parton. These six forces are: thermic, luminic, thermic-luminic, luminic-thermic, an electron, and a neutron. The interactions between these six types create a host of electrical lines of force, radial plasmas, and types of karma and dharma.

The source of all the electricity and energy in the cosmos is derived from a primary sole atom (quantinomio citiobarico) that emits radiations that establish the quantars and quasars that generate the galaxies. The sole atom is the source as well of the light-photon-cyclone fifth force—the core of the Hunab Ku.

The Vulom power grid-circuit board electromagnetic attraction field is an intelligent construct that coordinates this primal cosmology into a matrix that is located in the auric sheathe of the individual entity. The vulom power grid can be telepathically activated. This is possible because in cosmic science the original cosmological components are inseparable from the on-going continuum of evolving life, mind and consciousness.

In the methodology of cosmic science the primal components of reality being electrical are both etheric and mental, and therefore capable of being activated telepathically. This can occur within the construct of a grid that simulates the primal force field. Such is the Hunab Ku 21 Vulom Power Grid.

DESCRIPTION OF THE VULOM FIELD POWER GRID CIRCUITS

(Note that this is a radial structure, so when viewing the graphics, left is right and right is left).

1. The two axes

a) The Mauri tube is the central vertical channel connecting the two poles: the Marka (north) pole and the Darka (south) pole. Two types of plasmatic seed-forms are attracted at each of the poles: mars and kar at the Marka pole, and dar and kar at the Darka pole. The mars and kar activate the prana and pranic flow at the first light gate (frequency 108), and from thence the mars flows to the blue left-hand meridian and the kar to the red right-hand meridian. The central channel conducts the plasmatic prana of the polar magnetic force downward.

Transformations of the pranic plasma occur at the blue marka neutron polar magnetic transformer (frequency 291) and the white neutron generator and thermic converter (frequency 402). At the Hunab Ku 21 core, the pranic neutron plasma enters a type of spin and becomes absorbed into the fifth force light-photon-cyclone where it is transmuted into the apana electron plasmatic flow.

From the Darka (south) magnetic pole the two plasmatic seed types flow into the two currents: kar seed plasma to the blue left-hand electrical meridian and dar to the red right-hand meridian. The plasmatic apana flows upward from the second light gate apana generator (frequency 144) through the central Mauri tube channel.

Transformations of the apana plasma occur at the red darka electron polar magnetic transformer (frequency 315) and the yellow electron generator and luminic converter (frequency 414). At the Hunab Ku 21 core, the apana electron plasma enters a type of spin and becomes absorbed into the fifth force light- photon-cyclone where it is transmuted into the pranic neutron plasmatic flow.

b) The equatorial-gravitational energetic line of force. Emanating out from the Hunab Ku light-photon-cyclone core are the two principle gravitational force fields: centrifugal to the left and centripetal to the right. The third and fourth light gates define the extremities of the energetic force fields. The third light gate, left-hand side (frequency 126) is the blue external centrifugal generator, while the fourth light gate right-hand side (frequency 90) is the yellow external centripetal generator.

13 1ST WEEK	RED D R CASTLE	MOON 2ND WEEK
WHITE S P CASTLE	GREEN E CASTLE	YELLOW L L CASTLE
28 3RD WEEK 3-D	BLUE A M CASTLE	DAY 4TH WEEK CYCLE

13 Moon — 4 Outer Time Dims
Dreamspell — 5 Radial Time Dims

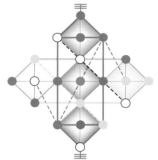

7TH TIME DIM

HUNAB KU 21
VULOM POWER GRID FORCE FIELD

is totally a function of radial time — an application of the fifth force primal mandala of space, time and consciousness. Therefore it is not subject to the 3rd-dimensional aspects of the 4 outer time dimensions. 4 outer time dimensions = cyclic time:

4 Ages
4 Seasons
4 Weeks
4 Stages of Breath
4 Watches ...

5TH TIME DIM

6TH TIME DIM

1	2	3	7	10	11	12	217	218	219	85	226	227	228	37	38	39	20	46	47	48
4	5	6	8	13	14	15	220	221	222	86	229	230	231	40	41	42	21	49	50	51
7	8	9	9	16	17	18	223	224	225	87	232	233	234	43	44	45	22	52	53	54
1	2	3	13	6	5	4	79	80	81	91	84	83	82	14	15	16	26	19	18	17
19	20	21	12	28	29	30	235	236	237	90	244	245	246	55	56	57	25	64	65	66
22	23	24	11	31	32	33	238	239	240	89	247	248	249	58	59	60	24	67	68	69
25	26	27	10	34	35	36	241	242	243	88	250	251	252	61	62	63	23	70	71	72
145	146	147	59	154	155	156	289	290	291	111	298	299	300	181	182	183	72	190	191	192
148	149	150	60	157	158	159	292	293	294	112	301	302	303	184	185	186	73	193	194	195
151	152	153	61	160	161	162	295	296	297	113	304	305	306	187	188	189	74	196	197	198
53	54	55	65	58	57	56	105	106	107	117	110	109	108	66	67	68	78	71	70	69
163	164	165	64	172	173	174	307	308	309	116	316	317	318	199	200	201	77	208	209	210
166	167	168	63	175	176	177	310	311	312	115	319	320	321	202	203	204	76	211	212	213
169	170	171	62	178	179	180	313	314	315	114	322	323	324	205	206	207	75	214	215	216
73	74	75	33	82	83	84	253	254	255	98	262	263	264	109	110	111	46	118	119	120
76	77	78	34	85	86	87	256	257	258	99	265	266	267	112	113	114	47	121	122	123
79	80	81	35	88	89	90	259	260	261	100	268	269	270	115	116	117	48	124	125	126
27	28	29	39	32	31	30	92	93	94	104	97	96	95	40	41	42	52	45	44	43
91	92	93	38	100	101	102	271	272	273	103	280	281	282	127	128	129	51	136	137	138
94	95	96	37	103	104	105	274	275	276	102	283	284	285	130	131	132	50	139	140	141
97	98	99	36	106	107	108	277	278	279	101	286	287	288	133	134	135	49	142	143	144

8TH TIME DIM

**441 MATRIX
9 TIME DIMENSIONS
THE ENLIGHTENMENT
OF NUMBER**

585 = BMU 144 [581–441]
[117] ×5   117 9TH COORDINATE = BMU 441
65×9   ×5   5TH FORCE
45×13
195×3
585 = 1.9.5
    [400 + 185]
        (3 SERPENT)

4 RADIAL TIME DIM [5-8 DIM]
= 338 = 13²×2
+1 INNER (9TH) TIME DIM
117 = 455 = 13×35

585 [=sum of coordinates of 9 time dimensions]
**FREQUENCY OF ENLIGHTENMENT
OF 9-DIMENSIONAL TIME MATRIX
UNDERLYING VAJRA WORLD MANDALA**

Between the external generators and the electrical currents on the left-hand side lies the dum kuali centrifugal energetic line of force, and on the right side, the dum duar centripetal line of force. At the midpoint of each line of force is a transformer/converter unit. On the left-hand line of force is the white centrifugal thermic/heat transfomer-luminic/light converter. This white unit (frequency 303) is the point at which the orange thermic radiating line of force meets the yellow luminic illuminating line of force.

On the right-hand line of force is the yellow centripetal heat of inner light transformer and light of inner heat converter-transformer and light of inner heat converter. This yellow unit (frequency 279) is the point at which the orange thermic vitalizing line of force meets the yellow luminic catalyzing line of force.

Where the equatorial energetic line of force meets the blue electrical current on the left-hand side is the blue electrical current thermic-luminic converter (frequency 408). Here is generated the dum kuali thermic energetic line of force, animating the centrifugal force field and heat cell. Moving inward at this point, the fifth force light-photon-cyclone energy field absorbs the energetic centrifugal line of force transmuting it into the primal white-hot core of the Hunab Ku 21, root of the sole atom (frequency 441).

From the light-photon-cyclone core, the transmuted energy streams toward the right as the energetic centripetal line of force. Where this equatorial line of force meets the red electrical current on the right-hand side is the red electrical current heat of inner light-light of inner heat converter (frequency 396). Here is generated the dum duar luminic energetic line of force, animating the centripetal force field and light cell.

At the very center of the Vulom power grid where the Mauri tube and the equatorial energetic line of force meet is the fifth force light-photon-cyclone generator and transformer, the Hunab Ku 21. At the very center of this nucleus of all ordinances, is the sole atom with its three energy fields and 36 compressors emitting the primal quon rays and partons that establish the electro-telepathic foundation of the galactic building blocks of the cosmos (see also *CHC Vol. II* and *Vol. VI*)

Here are also generated the Mental Electron (ME) that activates the marka pole, the double Extended Electron (EE) that activates the darka pole, and the Mental Electron Neutron (MEN) that functions as a hyper-parton (or "hyperparton"?) unit at the core of any activating celestial unit, both micro and macro, around which particles or planetary bodies might revolve. This demonstrates that a galaxy is both a conscious order and a stellar (astrophysical) distribution center.

2. The two electrical currents that define the Vulom as "a system established between two electrical currents" are the two meridians—the blue activating primary electrical current, and the red reactivating secondary electrical current. The Vulom field technically is the field between these two currents that "adjusts the transition speed of the currents."

These two currents establish the electrical flows of the four electro-etheric power cells. The two primary cells, thermic (dum kuali) and luminic (dum duar), are a function of the activating primary blue electrical current, while the two secondary cells, heat of inner light (kum) and light of inner heat (kemio), are a function of the reactivating red electrical current.

> *This system is applied to the transition power units of galactic dimensions and by this means, the attraction power field is being formed. All astral travels, methods of beaming up, intergalactic transportation and communication are taken into effect by the attraction power of this electromagnetic field …*
>
> —*The Knowledge Book*

The Vulom power grid-circuit board template should be studied carefully to understand the dynamic points and flows of the entire Vulom field.

The two electrical currents (meridians) connect the two polar chains of nine. The colors of the nodes determine functions. The red and blue are dynamically polarizing, hence the two currents are characterized by two each of the red or two each of the blue nodes, and one of the occult color for each current. For each current the dominant color is both the generating unit and the matrix transformer unit. The occult receptor units are white, occult of blue, first chain of nine; and yellow, occult of red, third chain of nine.

The colors red and blue also correspond to the two magnetic polar cells, the red marka and the blue darka. Between the generator and receptor units of the two currents are the electric parton generators that mediate the particular electrical flows. The dum kuali and dum duar nodes mediate the blue current generating electro-thermic and electro-luminic partons, while the kum and kemio nodes mediate the red current generating electro-heat of inner of light and electro-light of inner heat partons.

Between the two electromagnetic currents lies the Vulom field that activates and creates the adjustment transition points for the five horizontal flows. The electrical currents define the horizontal flows of the two polar chains of nine and activate the first and third seats of power, establishing a blue marka neutron at the first seat of power (291) and red darka electron at the third seat of power (315).

The seats of power are coordinated with the Mauri tube and function as polar magnetic transformers for plasmatic flows of prana and apana. It is here that the transition speeds of the two currents are dynamically adjusted. These are two of the principle centers for facilitating holon transport and communication, beaming up and intergalactic (astral) travel. The two centers correspond to the third eye (291), and to the secret center (315).

The third major center is the fifth seat of power, Hunab Ku 21, where all manner of transitions, transformations and transductions may occur. The transition speeds arriving here via the equatorial energetic line of force are adjusted on either side of the Hunab Ku 21 by the blue and red matrix portals that function as electrical converters between the thermic and luminic energy fields. Here at the very center of the Vulom field, the ultra-high frequency of the sole atom generates the continuous streams of the light-photon-cyclone fifth force.

3. The two stabilizing lines of force. See previous chapter, structure of Hunab Ku 21

4. The four binding diagonal lines of force (See chapter 9).

5. The four spectral currents (See chapter 9).

Photon: Original power of Light, providing the transmission of electromagnetic influences.

APPENDIX II

HOW TO ENTER THE 441 CUBE MATRIX

Through a simple process, each day we arrive at a Telepathic Frequency Index number (TFI), which is a potentiation or particularization of a type of power that is being projected into you. These powers are non-conceptual frequencies intended to increase our brain energy and contribute to the activation of the holomind perceiver.

To find your telepathic frequency index, you first need to know your **13 Moon calendar birthdate** and **Galactic Signature Kin number**. (You can find this on www.lawoftime.org or through the 13 Moon Almanac or pocket calendar.) Each day has three numbers that interlock or overlay each other. Find the frequency for each of these three points. The Master Telepathic Frequency index number is the sum of the three matrix overlays: **Time Matrix** overlay, **Space Matrix** overlay and **Synchronic matrix** overlay. Each of these matrices has a telepathic frequency index. The calendar matrix (located in time matrix) has a corresponding unit in the **space matrix** and also in the **synchronic matrix**. These three units create a telepathic frequency index. (Note: Please refer to graphic on p. 210 for the Time matrix and p. 52-53 for the other three matrices)

1. Locate your 13 Moon birthdate position (or any date) on the **Time Matrix. Write down the vertical and horizontal vector points.** Then find the number overlays on the space matrix and on the synchronic matrix. You should now have three numbers. Add them up. The sum of these three numbers is your **Telepathic Frequency index for the Time Matrix.** Also take note of the Base Matrix Unit (BMU) in this vector.

2. Next, locate your kin number on the **Space Matrix.** Write down the vectors, and find the number overlays on the time matrix and synchronic matrix. This is your next set of three numbers. Add them up. The sum of these three numbers is your **Telepathic Frequency index for the Space Matrix.** Again take note of the BMU in this vector.

3. Now locate your kin number on the **Synchronic Matrix.** Write down the vectors. Then find the number overlays on the time matrix and space matrix. This is your third set of three numbers. Add them up. The sum of these three numbers is your **Telepathic Frequency index for the Synchronic Matrix.** Also take note of the BMU in this vector.

4. Now add the three TFI's to find the overall **Telepathic Frequency index number** which is also your **Master Coordinating Frequency Number.** Study this number and all of its factors.

5. Now find your **Base Matrix Unit** by subtracting 441 from the Telepathic Frequency index until you arrive at a number 441 or less. This is your Base Matrix Unit number and your key into the **Holomind Perceiver.** With this Base matrix unit number you can also find in which of the three bodies this number is located in chapter 4.

6. Finally find your **Kin Equivalent** number by subtracting 260 from your **Telepathic Frequency Index** until you arrive at a number 260 or below. This is your Kin Equivalent number. (You can look this number up in appendix 3 to find which archetypal house your kin falls under).

EXAMPLE: CRYSTAL MOON 9, KIN 5

Time Matrix Frequency

To find the TFI for Crystal Moon 9, Kin 5. First we note that Crystal is the 12th moon of the 13 Moon calendar, so we write it 12.9.

Now we locate the calendar date, 12.9, in the Time Matrix. Write down its vector points: V.6, H.16. We find this located in the third (outer) time dimension. It is number 86; this is the calendar time matrix frequency.

Locate V.6, H.16 on the Space Matrix = 182
Locate V.6, H.16 on the Synchronic Matrix = 35
86 + 182 + 35 = 303
303 is the Time Matrix Telepathic Frequency Index (TFI) number
Also locate V.6, H.16 on the Base Matrix = 351, this is the BMU for the Time Matrix vector.

Space Matrix Frequency

To find the Space Matrix frequency, we find the day's kin number (kin 5) on the Space Matrix.
Kin 5 on the Space Matrix is located at V.7, H.4 (mystic lattice)
Locate V.7, H.4 on the Time Matrix = 4
Locate V.7, H.4 on the Synchronic Matrix = 44
5 + 4 + 44 = 53
53 is the Space Matrix Telepathic Frequency Index (TFI) number
Also locate V.7, H.4 on the Base Matrix = 242 = the BMU for the Space Matrix vector.

Synchronic Matrix Frequency

Now we find the day's kin number (kin 5) on the Synchronic Matrix.
Kin 5 on the Synchronic Matrix is located at V.5, H.5
Locate V.5, H.5 on the Time Matrix = 28
Locate V.5, H.5 on the Space Matrix = 10
5 + 28 + 10 = 43
43 is the Synchronic Matrix TFI number.
Also locate V.5, H.5 on the Base Matrix = 297 = the BMU for the Synchronic Matrix vector.

Master Coordinating Frequency Number

Now add the three TFI's from the three matrices: 303 + 53 + 43 = 399
So 399 is the Master Coordinating Frequency number of the day
Note: The BMUs are not added when finding the Master Coordinating Frequency number.
Reduces to Kin 139: Solar Storm/House of the Blue Solar Worldchanger.

Study the numbers. Are they prime? What are their factors? Look up the numbers in the 441 index in Appendix V. You can begin to build up your own personal associative number index based on your kin number and basic birth data and those of your friends, relatives, and significant dates.

There are many other ways to read the daily frequencies. For instance we see that calendar date 12.9 is an intergalactic channel day. It is located at V.6, H.16. When we look at the 10 + 1 Circuit Map in Chapter 3 (p. 60) we see that this vector point is a coordinate date for the sixth circuit. There are four coordinate days on the sixth circuit—these are called "intergalactic channels".

Each day we also locate the Base Matrix Unit according to the vectors of the calendar date on the Time Matrix and the vectors of the daily kin on the Space and Synchronic matrices. For example: V.6, H.16 on the Base Matrix is 351 (13 x 27). Note that this number is not counted in the daily **Telepathic Frequency Index.** It simply locates the day in its absolute position and gives it a vector point as well as absolute frequency within the 441 matrix. (Note that there are always two daily coordinates: the 13 Moon calendar date and the daily Kin number.)

To Summarize: Each day we locate the following:
1. Time, Space and Synchronic matrix numbers. Each has a
   a. V. H. Vector
   b. Base Matrix Unit (BMU)
   c. Space, Time and Synchronic numbers
   d. TFI numbers for each of 3 matrices
2. Kin equivalent

You can also combine you readout with someone else's and note the synchronic connections. There are many ways to work with this.

For example, here are the sum natal code frequencies for the Cosmic History progenitors:

Valum Votan (VV)
13 Moon birthdate: 7.15, Kin 11
Master Telepathic Frequency Index: 1031 (prime)
BMU = 149 (prime)
Kin equivalent 251 (Self-Existing Monkey, located in the House of the Blue Self-Existing Magician)

Red Queen (RQ)
13 Moon birth date: 6.27, Kin 185
Master Telepathic Frequency: 1311 (13/11—prime 13 and 11 or 131 and 1 or reverse 113 – 1)
BMU = 429 (prime)
Kin equivalent = 11 (Spectral Monkey located in the House of the Blue Spectral Magician)
$1031 = 103 \times 10 + 1$
$1311 = 131 \times 10 + 1$

Interval frequency = 1311-13-1 = 280 or 28/0 power of 28 x 10

As kin 11 equivalent RQ is next G.S. frequency + 20 beyond kin 251 of VVs 1031—Kin 251 is the last Monkey sign (self-existing) of the Tzolkin sequence kin 11 (VV's birth Kin) is the first (spectral) Monkey of the Tzolkin. In the CH transmission VV coded by first of the monkeys represents closing of historical cycle—sign of the 4 monkey Kin 251 (galactic signature of 9-11 (9 + 11 = 20) sign of the cycles closing.

RQ—280 frequency past this event horizon (harmonic manifestation of the 28 day 13 moons calendar) is coded by 11 monkey (VV)—and early in the 6th tzolkin cycle 1300-1560 representing future age of the sixth sun of consciousness. The 11 code shows that they represent the mystic axes of the primal 441 matrix.

Natal sums 1031 + 1311 = 2342 (11/71 x 2)—as surface composite 11 – 71 are the first and fourth gates into the temple of unity (powers V. 11 – 1 and 4). 2342 = Kin 2—Lunar Wind, sum of all occult frequencies.

1171 kin equivalent = 1040 = Kin 131—Magnetic Monkey—(VV age 68 and birth psi chrono).

2342 = 6th order of 441—base matrix value = unit value 137 Ah Vuc Ti Kab, Lord of the Center of the Earth.

1171 = 3rd order of 441—base matrix value = 289 = kin 29 (RQs oracle guide)
137 + 289 = 426 divided by 2 = 213 (DOOT, 2011) 11th v power of 13. RQ frequency 1311

Remember: Every prime or any other frequency is a member of a sequence of 21 orders of 441 and every unit is situated in the base 441 matrix and extends as the telepathic line of force through the 21 orders—441 base units—8820 augmented units—each line of force a 21 unit collective of an entitization belonging to the original order of the matrix. Information disclosed possesses inherent subliminal properties of the 20 other units of the lines of force to which it belongs, as well as radial connections to innumerable other points including factorials, squares, interval potencies sum frequencies, etc.

PERPETUAL 13 MOON CALENDAR

TZOLKIN
HARMONIC MODULE

Matrix of 260 Kin (days), consisting of 20 seals and 13 tones

13 Moon Calendar date
Gregorian Calendar date

MAGNETIC MOON •

1	2	3	4	5	6	7
7/26	7/27	7/28	7/29	7/30	7/31	8/1
8	9	10	11	12	13	14
8/2	8/3	8/4	8/5	8/6	8/7	8/8
15	16	17	18	19	20	21
8/9	8/10	8/11	8/12	8/13	8/14	8/15
22	23	24	25	26	27	28
8/16	8/17	8/18	8/19	8/20	8/21	8/22

LUNAR MOON ••

1	2	3	4	5	6	7
8/23	8/24	8/25	8/26	8/27	8/28	8/29
8	9	10	11	12	13	14
8/30	8/31	9/1	9/2	9/3	9/4	9/5
15	16	17	18	19	20	21
9/6	9/7	9/8	9/9	9/10	9/11	9/12
22	23	24	25	26	27	28
9/13	9/14	9/15	9/16	9/17	9/18	9/19

ELECTRIC MOON •••

1	2	3	4	5	6	7
9/20	9/21	9/22	9/23	9/24	9/25	9/26
8	9	10	11	12	13	14
9/27	9/28	9/29	9/30	10/1	10/2	10/3
15	16	17	18	19	20	21
10/4	10/5	10/6	10/7	10/8	10/9	10/10
22	23	24	25	26	27	28
10/11	10/12	10/13	10/14	10/15	10/16	10/17

SELF-EXISTING MOON ••••

1	2	3	4	5	6	7
10/18	10/19	10/20	10/21	10/22	10/23	10/24
8	9	10	11	12	13	14
10/25	10/26	10/27	10/28	10/29	10/30	10/31
15	16	17	18	19	20	21
11/1	11/2	11/3	11/4	11/5	11/6	11/7
22	23	24	25	26	27	28
11/8	11/9	11/10	11/11	11/12	11/13	11/14

OVERTONE MOON —

1	2	3	4	5	6	7
11/15	11/16	11/17	11/18	11/19	11/20	11/21
8	9	10	11	12	13	14
11/22	11/23	11/24	11/25	11/26	11/27	11/28
15	16	17	18	19	20	21
11/29	11/30	12/1	12/2	12/3	12/4	12/5
22	23	24	25	26	27	28
12/6	12/7	12/8	12/9	12/10	12/11	12/12

RHYTHMIC MOON •

1	2	3	4	5	6	7
12/13	12/14	12/15	12/16	12/17	12/18	12/19
8	9	10	11	12	13	14
12/20	12/21	12/22	12/23	12/24	12/25	12/26
15	16	17	18	19	20	21
12/27	12/28	12/29	12/30	12/31	1/1	1/2
22	23	24	25	26	27	28
1/3	1/4	1/5	1/6	1/7	1/8	1/9

RESONANT MOON ••

1	2	3	4	5	6	7
1/10	1/11	1/12	1/13	1/14	1/15	1/16
8	9	10	11	12	13	14
1/17	1/18	1/19	1/20	1/21	1/22	1/23
15	16	17	18	19	20	21
1/24	1/25	1/26	1/27	1/28	1/29	1/30
22	23	24	25	26	27	28
1/31	2/1	2/2	2/3	2/4	2/5	2/6

GALACTIC MOON •••

1	2	3	4	5	6	7
2/7	2/8	2/9	2/10	2/11	2/12	2/13
8	9	10	11	12	13	14
2/14	2/15	2/16	2/17	2/18	2/19	2/20
15	16	17	18	19	20	21
2/21	2/22	2/23	2/24	2/25	2/26	2/27
22	23	24	25	26	27	28
2/28	3/1	3/2	3/3	3/4	3/5	3/6

SOLAR MOON ••••

1	2	3	4	5	6	7
3/7	3/8	3/9	3/10	3/11	3/12	3/13
8	9	10	11	12	13	14
3/14	3/15	3/16	3/17	3/18	3/19	3/20
15	16	17	18	19	20	21
3/21	3/22	3/23	3/24	3/25	3/26	3/27
22	23	24	25	26	27	28
3/28	3/29	3/30	3/31	4/1	4/2	4/3

PLANETARY MOON —

1	2	3	4	5	6	7
4/4	4/5	4/6	4/7	4/8	4/9	4/10
8	9	10	11	12	13	14
4/11	4/12	4/13	4/14	4/15	4/16	4/17
15	16	17	18	19	20	21
4/18	4/19	4/20	4/21	4/22	4/23	4/24
22	23	24	25	26	27	28
4/25	4/26	4/27	4/28	4/29	4/30	5/1

SPECTRAL MOON •

1	2	3	4	5	6	7
5/2	5/3	5/4	5/5	5/6	5/7	5/8
8	9	10	11	12	13	14
5/9	5/10	5/11	5/12	5/13	5/14	5/15
15	16	17	18	19	20	21
5/16	5/17	5/18	5/19	5/20	5/21	5/22
22	23	24	25	26	27	28
5/23	5/24	5/25	5/26	5/27	5/28	5/29

CRYSTAL MOON ••

1	2	3	4	5	6	7
5/30	5/31	6/1	6/2	6/3	6/4	6/5
8	9	10	11	12	13	14
6/6	6/7	6/8	6/9	6/10	6/11	6/12
15	16	17	18	19	20	21
6/13	6/14	6/15	6/16	6/17	6/18	6/19
22	23	24	25	26	27	28
6/20	6/21	6/22	6/23	6/24	6/25	6/26

COSMIC MOON •••

1	2	3	4	5	6	7
6/27	6/28	6/29	6/30	7/1	7/2	7/3
8	9	10	11	12	13	14
7/4	7/5	7/6	7/7	7/8	7/9	7/10
15	16	17	18	19	20	21
7/11	7/12	7/13	7/14	7/15	7/16	7/17
22	23	24	25	26	27	28
7/18	7/19	7/20	7/21	7/22	7/23	7/24

DAY OUT OF TIME
7/25

226

21×21 TIMES TABLE - QUICK REFERENCE

	1	2	3	4	5	6	7	8	9	10	11	12	13	14	15	16	17	18	19	20	21
1	1	2	3	4	5	6	7	8	9	10	11	12	13	14	15	16	17	18	19	20	21
2	2	4	6	8	10	12	14	16	18	20	22	24	26	28	30	32	34	36	38	40	42
3	3	6	9	12	15	18	21	24	27	30	33	36	39	42	45	48	51	54	57	60	63
4	4	8	12	16	20	24	28	32	36	40	44	48	52	56	60	64	68	72	76	80	84
5	5	10	15	20	25	30	35	40	45	50	55	60	65	70	75	80	85	90	95	100	105
6	6	12	18	24	30	36	42	48	54	60	66	72	78	84	90	96	102	108	114	120	126
7	7	14	21	28	35	42	49	56	63	70	77	84	91	98	105	112	119	126	133	140	147
8	8	16	24	32	40	48	56	64	72	80	88	96	104	112	120	128	136	144	152	160	168
9	9	18	27	36	45	54	63	72	81	90	99	108	117	126	135	144	153	162	171	180	189
10	10	20	30	40	50	60	70	80	90	100	110	120	130	140	150	160	170	180	190	200	210
11	11	22	33	44	55	66	77	88	99	110	121	132	143	154	165	176	187	198	209	220	231
12	12	24	36	48	60	72	84	96	108	120	132	144	156	168	180	192	204	216	228	240	252
13	13	26	39	52	65	78	91	104	117	130	143	156	169	182	195	208	221	234	247	260	273
14	14	28	42	56	70	84	98	112	126	140	154	168	182	196	210	224	238	252	266	280	294
15	15	30	45	60	75	90	105	120	135	150	165	180	195	210	225	240	255	270	285	300	315
16	16	32	48	64	80	96	112	128	144	160	176	192	208	224	240	256	272	288	304	320	336
17	17	34	51	68	85	102	119	136	153	170	187	204	221	238	255	272	289	306	323	340	357
18	18	36	54	72	90	108	126	144	162	180	198	216	234	252	270	288	306	324	342	360	378
19	19	38	57	76	95	114	133	152	171	190	209	228	247	266	285	304	323	342	361	380	399
20	20	40	60	80	100	120	140	160	180	200	220	240	260	280	300	320	340	360	380	400	420
21	21	42	63	84	105	126	147	168	189	210	231	252	273	294	315	336	357	378	399	420	441

Day Count 13 Moon/28-Day Synchronometer

	1	2	3	4	5	6	7	8	9	10	11	12	13
1	1	29	57	85	113	141	169	197	225	253	281	309	337
2	2	30	58	86	114	142	170	198	226	254	282	310	338
3	3	31	59	87	115	143	171	199	227	255	283	311	339
4	4	32	60	88	116	144	172	200	228	256	284	312	340
5	5	33	61	89	117	145	173	201	229	257	285	313	341
6	6	34	62	90	118	146	174	202	230	258	286	314	342
7	7	35	63	91	119	147	175	203	231	259	287	315	343
8	8	36	64	92	120	148	176	204	232	260	288	316	344
9	9	37	65	93	121	149	177	205	233	261	289	317	345
10	10	38	66	94	122	150	178	206	234	262	290	318	346
11	11	39	67	95	123	151	179	207	235	263	291	319	347
12	12	40	68	96	124	152	180	208	236	264	292	320	348
13	13	41	69	97	125	153	181	209	237	265	293	321	349
14	14	42	70	98	126	154	182	210	238	266	294	322	350
15	15	43	71	99	127	155	183	211	239	267	295	323	351
16	16	44	72	100	128	156	184	212	240	268	296	324	352
17	17	45	73	101	129	157	185	213	241	269	297	325	353
18	18	46	74	103	130	158	186	214	242	270	298	326	354
19	19	47	75	103	131	159	187	215	243	271	299	327	355
20	20	48	76	104	132	160	188	216	244	272	300	328	356
21	21	49	77	105	133	161	189	217	245	273	301	329	357
22	22	50	78	106	134	162	190	218	246	274	302	330	358
23	23	51	79	107	135	163	191	219	247	275	303	331	359
24	24	52	80	108	136	164	192	220	248	276	304	332	360
25	25	53	81	109	137	165	193	221	249	277	305	333	361
26	26	54	82	110	138	166	194	222	250	278	306	334	362
27	27	55	83	111	139	167	195	223	251	279	307	335	363
28	28	56	84	112	140	168	196	224	252	280	308	336	364

APPENDIX III
THE 260 ARCHETYPE HOUSES

1. Magnetic House of the Primal Force
2. Lunar House of the High Priestess
3. Electric House of the Dreamer
4. Self-Existing House of the Innocent
5. Overtone House of the Serpent Initiate
6. Rhythmic House of the Hierophant
7. Resonant House of the Avatar
8. Galactic House of the Artist
9. Solar House of the Healer
10. Planetary House of the Compassionate One
11. Spectral House of the Magician
12. Crystal House of the Sage
13. Cosmic House of the Prophet
14. Magentic House of the Wizard
15. Lunar House of the Seer
16. Electric House of the Pathfinder
17. Self-Existing House of the Navigator
18. Overtone House of the Yogi(ni)
19. Rhythmic House of the Worldchanger
20. Resonant House of the Enlightened One
21. Galactic House of the Primal Force
22. Solar House of the High Priestess
23. Planetary House of the Dreamer
24. Spectral House of the Innocent
25. Crystal House of the Serpent Initiate
26. Cosmic House of the Hierophant
27. Magnetic House of the Avatar
28. Lunar House of the Artist
29. Electric House of the Healer
30. Self-Existing House of the Compassionate One
31. Overtone House of Magician
32. Rhythmic House of the Sage
33. Resonant House of the Prophet
34. Galactic House of the Wizard
35. Solar House of the Seer
36. Planetary House of the Pathfinder
37. Spectral House of the Navigator
38. Crystal House of the Yogi(ni)
39. Cosmic House of the Worldchanger
40. Magnetic House of the Enlightened One
41. Lunar House of the Primal Force
42. Electric House of the High Priestess
43. Self-Existing House of the Dreamer
44. Overtone House of the Innocent
45. Rhythmic House of the Serpent Initiate
46. Resonant House of the Hierophant
47. Galactic House of the Avatar
48. Solar House of the Artist
49. Planetary House of the Healer
50. Spectral House of the Compassionate One
51. Crystal House of the Magician
52. Cosmic House of the Sage
53. Magnetic House of the Prophet
54. Lunar House of the Wizard
55. Electric House of the Seer
56. Self-Existing House of the Pathfinder
57. Overtone House of the Navigator
58. Rhythmic House of the Yogi(ni)
59. Resonant House of the Worldchanger
60. Galactic House of the Enlightened One

61. Solar House of the Primal Force
62. Planetary House of the High Priestess
63. Spectral House of the Dreamer
64. Crystal House of the Innocent
65. Cosmic House of the Serpent Initiate
66. Magnetic House of the Hierophant
67. Lunar House of the Avatar
68. Electric House of the Artist
69. Self-Existing House of the Healer
70. Overtone House of the Compassionate One
71. Rhythmic House of the Magician
72. Resonant House of the Sage
73. Galactic House of the Prophet
74. Solar House of the Wizard
75. Planetary House of the Seer
76. Spectral House of the Pathfinder
77. Crystal House of the Navigator
78. Cosmic House of the Yogi(ni)
79. Magnetic House of the Worldchanger
80. Lunar House of the Enlightened One
81. Electric House of the Primal Force
82. Self-Existing House of the High Priestess
83. Overtone House of the Dreamer
84. Rhythmic House of the Innocent
85. Resonant House of the Serpent Initiate
86. Galactic House of the Hierophant
87. Solar House of the Avatar
88. Planetary House of the Artist
89. Spectral House of the Healer
90. Crystal House of the Compassionate One
91. Cosmic House of the Magician
92. Magnetic House of the Sage
93. Lunar House of the Prophet
94. Electric House of the Wizard
95. Self-Existing House of the Seer
96. Overtone House of the Pathfinder
97. Rhythmic House of the Navigator
98. Resonant House of the Yogi(ni)
99. Galactic House of the Worldchanger
100. Solar House of the Enlightened One
101. Planetary House of the Primal Force
102. Spectral House of the High Priestess
103. Crystal House of the Dreamer
104. Cosmic House of the Innocent
105. Magnetic House of the Serpent Initiate
106. Lunar House of the Hierophant
107. Electric House of the Avatar
108. Self-Existing House of the Artist
109. Overtone House of the Healer
110. Rhythmic House of the Compassionate One
111. Resonant House of the Magician
112. Galactic House of the Sage
113. Solar House of the Prophet
114. Planetary House of the Wizard
115. Spectral House of the Seer
116. Crystal House of the Pathfinder
117. Cosmic House of the Navigator
118. Magnetic House of the Yogi(ni)
119. Lunar House of the Worldchanger
120. Electric House of the Enlightened One
121. Self-Existing House of the Primal Force
122. Overtone House of the High Priestess
123. Rhythmic House of the Dreamer
124. Resonant House of the Innocent
125. Galactic House of the Serpent Initiative
126. Solar House of the Hierophant
127. Planetary House of the Avatar
128. Spectral House of the Artist

129. Cystal House of the Healer
130. Cosmic House of the Compassionate One
131. Magnetic House of the Magician
132. Lunar House of the Sage
133. Electric House of the Prophet
134. Self-Existing House of the Wizard
135. Overtone House of the Seer
136. Rhythmic House of the Pathfinder
137. Resonant House of the Navigator
138. Galactic House of the Yogi(ni)
139. Solar House of the Worldchanger
140. Planetary House of the Enlightened One
141. Spectral House of the Primal Force
142. Crystal House of the High Priestess
143. Cosmic House of the Dreamer
144. Magnetic House of the Innocent
145. Lunar House of the Serpent Initiate
146. Electric House of the Hierophant
147. Self-Existing House of the Avatar
148. Overtone House of the Artist
149. Rhythmic House of the Healer
150. Resonant House of the Compassionate One
151. Galactic House of the Magician
152. Solar House of the Sage
153. Planetary House of the Prophet
154. Spectral House of the Wizard
155. Crystal House of the Seer
156. Cosmic House of the Pathfinder
157. Magnetic House of the Navigator
158. Lunar House of the Yogi(ni)
159. Electric House of the Worldchanger
160. Self-Existing House of the Enlightened One
161. Overtone House of the Primal Force
162. Rhythmic House of the High Priestess
163. Resonant House of the Dreamer
164. Galactic House of the Innocent
165. Solar House of the Serpent Initiate
166. Planetary House of the Hierophant
167. Spectral House of the Avatar
168. Crystal House of the Artist
169. Cosmic House of the Healer
170. Magnetic House of the Compassionate One
171. Lunar House of the Magician
172. Electric House of the Sage
173. Self-Existing House of the Prophet
174. Overtone House of the Wizard
175. Rhythmic House of the Seer
176. Resonant House of the Pathfinder
177. Galactic House of the Navigator
178. Solar House of the Yogi(ni)
179. Planetary House of the Worldchanger
180. Spectral House of the Enlightened One
181. Crystal House of the Primal Force
182. Cosmic House of the High Priestess
183. Magnetic House of the Dreamer
184. Lunar House of the Innocent
185. Electric House of the Serpent Initiate
186. Self-Existing House of the Hierophant
187. Overtone House of the Avatar
188. Rhythmic House of the Artist
189. Resonant House of the Healer
190. Galactic House of the Compassionate One
191. Solar House of the Magician
192. Planetary House of the Sage
193. Spectral House of the Prophet
194. Crystal House of the Wizard
195. Cosmic House of the Seer
196. Magnetic House of the Pathfinder

197. Lunar House of the Navigator

198. Electric House of the Yogi(ni)

199. Self-Existing House of the Worldchanger

200. Overtone House of the Enlightened One

201. Rhythmic House of the Primal Force

202. Resonant House of the High Priestess

203. Galactic House of the Dreamer

204. Solar House of the Innocent

205. Planetary House of the Serpent Initiate

206. Spectral House of the Hierophant

207. Crystal House of the Avatar

208. Cosmic House of the Artist

209. Magnetic House of the Healer

210. Lunar House of the Compassionate One

211. Electric House of the Magician

212. Self-Existing House of the Sage

213. Overtone House of the Prophet

214. Rhythmic House of the Wizard

215. Resonant House of the Seer

216. Galactic House of the Pathfinder

217. Solar House of the Navigator

218. Planetary House of the Yogi(ni)

219. Spectral House of the Worldchanger

220. Crystal House of the Enlightened One

221. Cosmic House of the Primal Force

222. Magnetic House of the High Priestess

223. Lunar House of the Dreamer

224. Electric House of the Innocent

225. Self-Existing House of the Serpent Initiate

226. Overtone House of the Hierophant

227. Rhythmic House of the Avatar

228. Resonant House of the Artist

229. Galactic House of the Healer

230. Solar House of the Compassionate One

231. Planetary House of the Magician

232. Spectral House of the Sage

233. Crystal House of the Prophet

234. Cosmic House of the Wizard

235. Magnetic House of the Seer

236. Lunar House of the Pathfinder

237. Electric House of the Navigator

238. Self-Existing House of the Yogi(ni)

239. Overtone House of the Worldchanger

240. Rhythmic House of the Enlightened One

241. Resonant House of the Primal Force

242. Galactic House of the High Priestess

243. Solar House of the Dreamer

244. Planetary House of the Innocent

245. Spectral House of the Serpent Initiate

246. Crystal House of the Hierophant

247. Cosmic House of the Avatar

248. Magnetic House of the Artist

249. Lunar House of the Healer

250. Electric House of the Compassionate One

251. Self-Existing House of the Magician

252. Overtone House of the Sage

253. Rhythmic House of the Prophet

254. Resonant House of the Wizard

255. Galactic House of the Seer

256. Solar House of the Pathfinder

257. Planetary House of the Navigator

258. Spectral House of the Yogi(ni)

259. Crystal House of the Worldchanger

260. Cosmic House of the Enlightened One

MOAP CODES

The Space Matrix contains the psi bank overlay that includes the 64 codons of the psi bank. We saw in Chapter 3 how the space matrix can be broken into four quadrants that correspond with the MOAP codes. The MOAP (Mother of All Programs) is a construct of 64 keys and 192 auxiliary keys that are coordinated by the four Master Coordinate keys: 257, 258, 259, 260. In the Space Matrix these are the four super numbers of the 65th harmonic, the cosmic matrix, located diagonally on the four corners around the 441 center unit.

Left margin (top to bottom): ZONE OF INITIATION, ZONE OF REFINEMENT
Right margin (top to bottom): ZONE OF RIPENING, ZONE OF TRANSFORMATION

278	279	280	281	282	283	284	285	286	287	421	304	305	306	307	308	309	310	311	312	313
277	16	50	9	55	11	53	14	52	288	422	303	80	114	73	119	75	117	78	116	314
276	1	63	8	58	6	60	3	61	289	423	302	65	127	72	122	70	124	67	125	315
275	64	2	57	7	59	5	62	4	290	424	301	128	66	121	71	123	69	126	68	316
274	49	15	56	10	54	12	51	13	291	425	300	113	79	120	74	118	76	115	77	317
273	48	18	41	23	43	21	46	20	292	426	299	112	82	105	87	107	85	110	84	318
272	33	31	40	26	38	28	35	29	293	427	298	97	95	104	90	102	92	99	93	319
271	32	34	25	39	27	37	30	36	294	428	297	96	98	89	103	91	101	94	100	320
270	17	47	24	42	22	44	19	45	295	429	296	81	111	88	106	86	108	83	109	321
269	268	267	266	265	264	263	262	261	257	430	258	330	329	328	327	326	325	324	323	322
401	402	403	404	405	406	407	408	409	410	441	420	419	418	417	416	415	414	413	412	411
339	338	337	336	335	334	333	332	331	259	440	260	400	399	398	397	396	395	394	393	392
340	144	178	137	183	139	181	142	180	365	439	366	208	242	201	247	203	245	206	244	391
341	129	191	136	186	134	188	131	189	364	438	367	193	255	200	250	198	252	195	253	390
342	192	130	185	135	187	133	190	132	363	437	368	256	194	249	199	251	197	254	196	389
343	177	143	184	138	182	140	179	141	362	436	369	241	207	248	202	246	204	243	205	388
344	176	146	169	151	171	149	174	148	361	435	370	240	210	233	215	235	213	238	212	387
345	161	159	168	154	166	156	163	157	360	434	371	225	223	232	218	230	220	227	221	386
346	160	162	153	167	155	165	158	164	359	433	372	224	226	217	231	219	229	222	228	385
347	145	175	152	170	150	172	147	173	358	432	373	209	239	216	234	214	236	211	237	384
348	349	350	351	352	353	354	355	356	357	431	374	375	376	377	378	379	380	381	382	383

The MOAP is part of the Dreamspell psi bank oracle where the 64 keys are represented by the arrangement of 64 codons in the psi bank. Divided into AC (Aboriginal Continuity) and CA (Cosmic Awareness): AC = 1-16, 49-64, upper half; and CA = 17-48 lower half.

In the MOAP, the 64 keys are the kin 1-64 located in the same positions as codons 1-64 in the psi bank code.

Every Galactic Spin, once we have completed kin 1-64, then the 192 auxiliary kin are activated in their sequences of 64 which are coordinated in the same positions 1-64, i.e. kin 65 is Kin 1 position, kin 66 is kin 2 position and kin 128 is kin 64 position. The three sequences constituting the 192 auxiliary keys are: Kin 65-128, Kin 129-192, Kin 193-256.

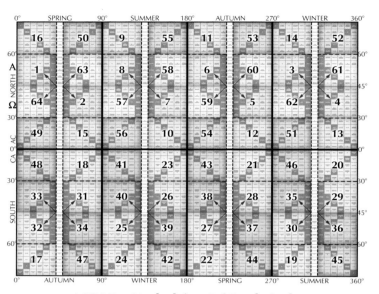

MOAP – Underlying Psi Bank Code

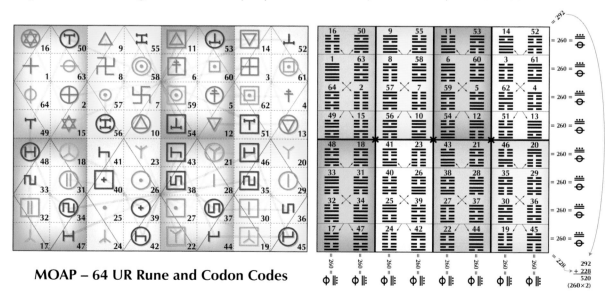

MOAP – 64 UR Rune and Codon Codes

Study these patterns within the Space Matrix. The value for daily practice of the Space Matrix is knowing where the MOAP codes are. Note that the four master coordinate keys (257-260) are the four kin of Dreamspell Harmonic 65. These four coordinates govern the four quadrants:

Kin 257—Coordinates Zone of Initiation
Kin 258—Coordinates Zone of Refinement
Kin 259—Coordinates Zone of Transformation
Kin 260—Coordinates Zone of Ripening

By following the 260-day galactic spin cycle, you attain a master telepathic coordination of the psi bank, UR runes, DNA codons and 441 space matrix codes that can also be keyed into the holomind perceiver. Find your galactic signature and assume your evolutionary position in the psi bank/psi genetic space matrix.

MOAP – KIN CODE IN 4 ZONES
(AS CORRELATED TO THE PSI BANK AND SPACE MATRIX CODES)

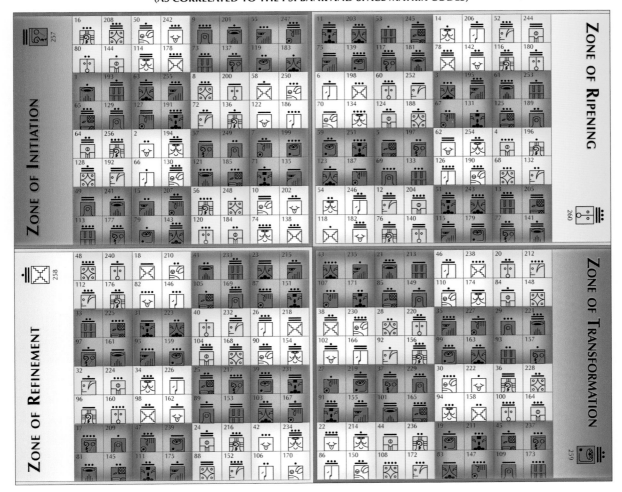

MOAP – AFFIRMATIONS

ZONE OF INITIATION (257) / **ZONE OF REFINEMENT** (258) — left side
ZONE OF RIPENING (260) / **ZONE OF TRANSFORMATION** (259) — right side

NORTH POLAR · NORTH OR NORTH · SOUTH OR NORTH · NORTH EQUATOR · SOUTH EQUATOR · NORTH OR SOUTH · SOUTH OR SOUTH · SOUTH POLAR

BECOME	RETURN	BECOME	RETURN	BECOME	RETURN	BECOME	RETURN
16 208 / 80 144 — ELECTRIC INTELLIGENCE RIPENS COSMIC ELEGANCE	50 242 / 114 178 — SPECTRAL HEART REFINES GALACTIC SPIRIT	9 201 / 73 137 — SOLAR UNIVERSAL WATER INITIATES RHYTHMIC BIRTH	55 247 / 119 183 — ELECTRIC VISION TRANSFORMS COSMIC ACCOMPLISHMENT	11 203 / 75 139 — SPECTRAL MAGIC TRANSFORMS GALACTIC ABUNDANCE	53 245 / 117 181 — MAGNETIC SPACE INITIATES SPECTRAL LIFE-FORCE	14 206 / 78 142 — MAGNETIC TIMELESSNESS REFINES SPECTRAL DEATH	52 244 / 116 180 — COSMIC FREE WILL RIPENS PLANETARY FLOWERING
1 193 / 65 129 — MAGNETIC BIRTH INITIATES SPECTRAL SPACE	63 255 / 127 191 — SPECTRAL ABUNDANCE TRANSFORMS GALACTIC VISION	8 200 / 72 136 — GALACTIC ELEGANCE RIPENS OVERTONE UNIVERSAL FIRE	58 250 / 122 186 — RHYTHMIC ENDLESSNESS REFINES ELECTRIC HEART	6 198 / 70 134 — RHYTHMIC DEATH REFINES ELECTRIC ENDLESSNESS	60 252 / 124 188 — GALACTIC UNIVERSAL FIRE RIPENS OVERTONE FREE WILL	7 195 / 67 131 — ELECTRIC ABUNDANCE TRANSFORMS COSMIC VISION	61 253 / 125 189 — SOLAR BIRTH INITIATES RHYTHMIC SPACE
64 256 / 128 192 — CRYSTAL FLOWERING RIPENS SOLAR INTELLIGENCE	2 194 / 66 130 — LUNAR SPIRIT REFINES CRYSTAL TIMELESSNESS	57 249 / 121 185 — OVERTONE NAVIGATION INITIATES LUNAR UNIVERSAL WATER	7 199 / 71 135 — RESONANT ACCOMPLISHMENT TRANSFORMS SELF-EXISTING SELF-GENERATION	59 251 / 123 187 — RESONANT SELF-GENERATION TRANSFORMS SELF-EXISTING MAGIC	5 197 / 69 133 — OVERTONE LIFE FORCE INITIATES LUNAR NAVIGATION	62 254 / 126 190 — PLANETARY SPIRIT REFINES RESONANT TIMELESSNESS	4 196 / 68 132 — SELF-EXISTING FLOWERING RIPENS MAGNETIC INTELLIGENCE
49 241 / 113 177 — PLANETARY UNIVERSAL WATER INITIATES RESONANT BIRTH	15 207 / 79 143 — LUNAR VISION TRANSFORMS CRYSTAL ACCOMPLISHMENT	56 248 / 120 184 — SELF-EXISTING INTELLIGENCE RIPENS MAGNETIC ELEGANCE	10 202 / 74 138 — PLANETARY HEART REFINES RESONANT SPIRIT	54 246 / 118 182 — LUNAR TIMELESSNESS REFINES CRYSTAL DEATH	12 204 / 76 140 — CRYSTAL FREE WILL RIPENS SOLAR FLOWERING	51 243 / 115 179 — CRYSTAL MAGIC TRANSFORMS SOLAR ABUNDANCE	13 205 / 77 141 — COSMIC SPACE INITIATES PLANETARY LIFE FORCE
48 240 / 112 176 — SOLAR ELEGANCE RIPENS RHYTHMIC UNIVERSAL FIRE	18 210 / 82 146 — OVERTONE ENDLESSNESS REFINES LUNAR HEART	41 233 / 105 169 — LUNAR BIRTH INITIATES CRYSTAL SPACE	23 215 / 87 151 — PLANETARY ABUNDANCE TRANSFORMS RESONANT VISION	43 235 / 107 171 — SELF-EXISTING ABUNDANCE TRANSFORMS MAGNETIC VISION	21 213 / 85 149 — GALACTIC BIRTH INITIATES OVERTONE SPACE	46 238 / 110 174 — RESONANT DEATH REFINES SELF-EXISTING ENDLESSNESS	20 212 / 84 148 — RESONANT UNIVERSAL FIRE RIPENS SELF-EXISTING FREE WILL
33 225 / 97 161 — RESONANT SPACE INITIATES SELF-EXISTING LIFE FORCE	31 223 / 95 159 — OVERTONE MAGIC TRANSFORMS LUNAR	40 232 / 104 168 — MAGNETIC UNIVERSAL FIRE RIPENS SPECTRAL FREE WILL	26 218 / 90 154 — COSMIC DEATH REFINES PLANETARY ENDLESSNESS	38 230 / 102 166 — CRYSTAL ENDLESSNESS REFINES SOLAR HEART	28 220 / 92 156 — LUNAR ELEGANCE RIPENS CRYSTAL UNIVERSAL FIRE	35 227 / 99 163 — SOLAR VISION TRANSFORMS RHYTHMIC ACCOMPLISHMENT	29 221 / 93 157 — ELECTRIC UNIVERSAL WATER INITIATES COSMIC BIRTH
32 224 / 96 160 — RHYTHMIC FREE WILL RIPENS ELECTRIC FLOWERING	34 226 / 98 162 — GALACTIC TIMELESSNESS REFINES OVERTONE DEATH	25 217 / 89 153 — CRYSTAL LIFE FORCE INITIATES SOLAR NAVIGATION	39 231 / 103 167 — COSMIC SELF-GENERATION TRANSFORMS PLANETARY MAGIC	27 219 / 91 155 — MAGNETIC ACCOMPLISHMENT TRANSFORMS SPECTRAL SELF-GENERATION	37 229 / 101 165 — SPECTRAL NAVIGATION INITIATES GALACTIC UNIVERSAL WATER	30 222 / 94 158 — SELF-EXISTING HEART REFINES MAGNETIC SPIRIT	36 228 / 100 164 — PLANETARY INTELLIGENCE RIPENS RESONANT ELEGANCE
17 209 / 81 145 — SELF-EXISTING NAVIGATION INITIATES MAGNETIC UNIVERSAL WATER	47 239 / 111 175 — GALACTIC ACCOMPLISHMENT TRANSFORMS OVERTONE SELF-GENERATION	24 216 / 88 152 — SPECTRAL FLOWERING RIPENS GALACTIC INTELLIGENCE	42 234 / 106 170 — ELECTRIC SPIRIT REFINES COSMIC TIMELESSNESS	22 214 / 86 150 — SOLAR SPIRIT REFINES RHYTHMIC TIMELESSNESS	44 236 / 108 172 — OVERTONE FLOWERING RIPENS LUNAR INTELLIGENCE	19 211 / 83 147 — RHYTHMIC SELF-GENERATION TRANSFORMS ELECTRIC MAGIC	45 237 / 109 173 — RHYTHMIC LIFE FORCE INITIATES ELECTRIC NAVIGATION

APPENDIX V

DICTIONARY OF NUMBERS 1-441

0   Pure Mind, sphere, God as beyond form and conceptualization, pure light universe, that which makes advance into the infinite possible

1st order of seven

1   Unity, a unit, 1 kin, God as One, one which is in all number, Fibonacci 1 and 2, V21 H21 first coordinate of unity, initiates first, outermost circuit, 441 matrix

2   Polarity, binary power, basis of all even number, law of alternation, yin and yang, inhalation-exhalation, male-female, night-and-day etc. Fibonacci 3rd sequence

3   Activation, rhythm, triplet factor, law of 3, root of all dynamism and synthesis, first 2-D form – triangle, triangular of 2, Fibonaccci 4th sequence

4   Form, measure, 2^2, square and all four cornered forms, definition of space (four primary directions), stages of primary cosmic cycle, harmonic, first 3-D form, tetrahedron

5   Fifth force, quintessence, pentacle, pentagon (72° of a circle, 73 days of one 365 day ring/year), a chromatic, basis of pentatonic scale, Fibonnaci 5th sequence

6   Second platonic solid – Cube (six squares), Hexagon, basis of hexagisimal (count by sixes) code, snowflakes and crystal structures, basis of system of sixes as cosmic ordering principle, two triangles joined = tantric energy, triangular of 3, perfect number: $1+2+3 = 6$, $1 \times 2 \times 3 = 6$

7   Interval frequency of lost time in eternity, basis of manifest universe, resonant power of primal creation, mystic root, basis of heptad (seven –day sequence), root of 441, supreme power of Divine order; with 13, occulted basis of Cosmic Wheel of Law of Time 13:7 as sum = totality 20, key term of creation formula 4:7::7:13 reciprocal = 142857, perfect recombinant for first six multiples

2nd order of seven

8   2×4, 2^3, Galactic form and order, octagon, octave (resonant fractal of whole), diatonic scale, basis of 3rd 3-d solid, octahedron Fibannaci 6th sequence

9   Power number of rhythmic frequency of time – 3^2, universally consistent factors of 9 in decimal code always add to 9 or a multiple of 9, reciprocal = .111111 (see reciprocal of 11), basis of matrix of nine and of interval frequency of all numbers and their reverses as well as triplet series, number of Bolontiku – Nine Lords of Time

10   2×5, basis of decimal(increase by powers of ten) code, power of manifestation, triangular of 4, one half of totality (20)

11   Prime key, mystic frequency, the magician, liberation, decimal analog to vigesimal 21, reciprocal = .090909, with 9 perfect cyclical recombinant, V21-H11 first gate left hand unity, 441 matrix

12   2×6, 4×3, organizational form, stasis, root of 144 key sacred formal frequency, 12 = reverse of 21 viz. 12/21 (2012), number of synodic lunations in one solar ring (one lunar year, Muslim calendar), 4th solid, dodecahedron

13   Prime key, cyclic wholeness, Basis of wavespell, cosmic time fractal, frequency of cosmic time 13×20 (totality) = 260 galactic matrix = 13:20 frequency of time as universal factor of synchronization, with 7, basis of cosmic wheel and cosmology of time – 13:7 = 13:20 frequency, reverse of 31, viz. 3113 beginning of 13 baktun cycle, $13^2 = 169$, reverse of 961 = 31^2, number of Oxlahuntiku, 13 lords of heavenly order, reciprocal = .076923, chromatic octave, Fibonacci 7th sequence, coordinating frequency first time dimension, cosmic creation

14   2nd order 7, 7×2, Wizards knowing – two sevens, one half of moon cycle, 13 + 1 principle of transcendence of time, hence wizard's timelessness

3rd order of seven

15   5×3, triangular of 5, sum of any row in a magic square of 9, reverse frequency = 51 (3×17) 51 – 15 = 36

16   2×8, symphonic harmonic (2 octaves), 4^2, basis of sixteen stages of cube of law, harmonic root frequency

17   Prime key mystic key, the navigator, Noah, reverse of 71, Sura 71 Noah, 71 –17 = 54 (9×6)

18   2 x 9, 3 x 6, frequency of 18 dimensional universe, number of faces on a perfect double terminated crystal, base of tun, katun time count (18 x 20), evolution dimension completed in 2012, reverse of 18 = 81 = 9^2, 81 – 18 = 63, 18 + 81 = 99 (9 x 11)

19   divine prime, Command of God, vigesimal analog of 9, in vigesimal code all multiples of 19 = 19, number of Omega dimension – evolution dimension after 2012, consists of 9 layers (9 x 19 = 171), equivalent of 76th (4 x 19) energy dimension, reverse of 19 = 91 = 7 x 13. 91-19 = 72 (9 x 8)

20   2 x 10, 4 x 5, sum of key recombinants 9 +11, Totality, base of vigesimal system, written 1.0, sum of 13+7, frequency of wheel of the law of time – basis of 13:20 timing frequency, fifth solid icosahedron

21   Unity of Totality (20 + 1), Hunab Ku, basis of 441 21^2 matrix of the Synchronotron, reverse of 12, written 1.1, analog of decimal 11, in vigesimal code products of 21 are double like those of 11 i.e., 9.9 = 9 x 21 (189) just as 99 = 9 x 11, basis of Hunab Ku 21 heptad program of 7 gates and 20 daily archetypes, triangular of 6, reciprocal = .047619, Fibonacci 8th sequence , V21 H1 second coordinate of unity, 441 matrix

4th order of seven

22   11 x 2, or 9 + 13, sum of 13 heavens and 9 hells or "lower worlds", as 22/7 = pi

23   prime frequency of solar sun spot cycle

24   2 x 12, 3 x 8, 4 x 6 radiant return, complex stable structure, frequency of Velatropa, harmonic root number (24^2 = 576 = 288 frequency of polar harmonic x 2), 3rd octave

25   Fifth Force, 5^2, frequency of galactic federation, reverse frequency = 52, Sirius code, 52 – 25 = 27

26   2 x 13, Tzolkin fractal, Galactic code, coordinating frequency of the matrix of Cosmic Ascension, second time dimension, fractal of 26,000 year Pleiadian cycle

27   Heart of Nine (9 x 3), 3^3, with 37 prime cyclical recombinant, reciprocal = .037037, reverse of 27 = 72, 8 x 9, 27 + 72 = 99 (9 x 11)

28   4 x 7 harmonic standard, basis of 28 day cycle-13 Moon calendar, harmonic measure of galactic order, number of lunar mansions, third power of 7, triangular of 7 reciprocal = .0357142 (copy cat of 6 x 1/7, 857142)

5th order of seven

29   Prime key, cosmic constant (harmonic standard +1)

30   3 x 10, 15 x 2, 5 x 6, stable dynamic, vigesimal 1.10

31   Root prime, first gate of descending unity V11-H1 441 matrix, reverse of 13, maintains consistency in being reverse of 13 in a number of its multiples as well, e.g, 31 x 3 = 93 , reverse = 39 = 3 x 13

32   2 x 16, 8 x 4, crystal frequency (32 symmetry types in crystal order), 6th term in binary order (1, 2, 4, 8, 16, 32), four octaves

33   3 x 11, The Initiate, Initiatic, mystical attainment (highest order in freemasonry), all-seeing eye atop the pyramid, all numbers with 33 factor indicate initiatic power, vigesimal code 1.13

34   2 x 17, frequency of galactic wizard, reverse = 43 (night seer), 43 – 34 = 9, Fibonacci 9th sequence (21 + 13)

35   5 x 7, fifth force power of cosmic creation reciprocal (= .0285714 fractal of 1/7 x 2, .285714)

6th order of seven

36   Key harmonic frequency, fourth power of 9, 9 x 4, 18 x 2, 12 x 3 x 4 = 144, triangular of 8, 6^2, x 6 (=6^3) = 216 perfect cube frequency, reverse of 36 = 63, 7 x 9, 36 + 63 = 99 (9 x 11)

37   vajra (indestructible) prime, with 27 prime cyclical recombinant, reciprocal = .027027, reverse of 37 = 73, 73 – 37 = 36 (4 x 9), 27 + 37 = 64 life code

38   2 x 19, frequency of the crystal mirror, cosmic reflecting principle

39   3 x 13, triple order of cosmic time, sign of the thrice born, coordinating frequency of the matrix of Cosmic Synchronization (third time dimension), vigesimal 1.19

40   2 x 20, 5 x 8, 4 x 10 vigesimal 2.0, mystic order of sacred time to complete a transformation, two totals, 1/10 of matrix of totality, fifth octave

41   Prime key, divine interval, defines interval between 20^2 (400) and 21^2 (441), antipode of 1 in first circuit 441, vigesimal 2.1, V1 H1 third coordinate of unity

42   21 x 2, 3 x 14, 6 x 7, second order of 21, vigesimal – 2.2, cube value of 7

7th order of seven

43   Prime key the night seer, vigesimal 2.3, reverse of 34, 43 – 34 = 9

44   4 x 11 fourth mystic order of liberation

45   5 x 9, 3 x 15, 4 + 5 = 9, all nine numbers in a magic square of nine add up to 45, 45 is triangular of 9 reverse of 45 = 54, 6 x 9, 45 + 54 = 99 (9 x 11)

46 23 x 2, two sunspot cycles, reverse of 46 = 64, 64 – 46 = 18 (2 x 9)

47 Prime key, "the Prophet" (Sura 47 "Muhammad"), reverse of 47 = 74 (2 x 37) 74 – 47 = 27, key cyclic recombinant

48 6 x 8 six octaves, or hexameride of the octave, frequency range of human senses, also 12 x 4, 2 x 24, 16 x 3, complex harmonic

49 7 x 7 supreme expression of creation order of 7, multiplied by 3^2 (9) = 441, frequency of units of each of nine time dimensions, number of days of bardo cycle, interval between death and rebirth, vigesimal 2.9 analog of 29 cosmic constant – multiples of 49: x 2 = 98, x 3 = 147, x 4 = 196, x 5 = 245, x 6 = 294, x 7 (7^3) = 343, x 8 = 392, x 9 = 441

8th order of seven

50 5 x 10, 2 x 25, (5^2 x 2) fifth force amplification as power of manifestation

51 3 x 17, frequency of creative dissonance, vigesimal 2.11, V1 H11 first gate of right hand unity, 441 matrix

52 13 x 4, solar galactic frequency, basis of harmonic cycles – 52 weeks, 52 kin Dreamspell castle, **52** years cycle of Sirius B, prime super mental harmonic, basis of cycle of galactic compass, galactic return frequency

53 Prime key Quetzalcoatl, frequency of Sirian rebirth (52 + 1)

54 6 x 9, 18 x 3, 27 x 2, root frequency lunar wizard, base of higher order of star codes. x 2 = 108, x 4 = 216, x 8 = 432, x 16 = 864 (master time lens), x 32 = 1728 (12^3) , x 52 = 2808, factor of velocity of God particle.

55 5 x 11, fifth order of eleven, liberation frequency of galactic federation, triangular of 10, Fibonacci 10th sequence (34 +21)

56 8th order of 7, 7 x 8, seventh octave, frequency of genesis, frequency of DNA start codon, "Voyaging" (fire on the mountain)

9th order of seven

57 3 x 19, frequency of Quran (in each of two suras (42 and 50) preceded by mystic letter "Qaf" (Quran), the Qaf appears 57 times, 57 x 2 = 114, number of suras in Quran), frequency of Overtone Earth, third clear sign of tomb of Pacal Votan

58 29 x 2, frequency of the Rhythmic Mirror, second clear sign, tomb of Pacal Votan

59 Prime key, closing of the cycle kin 59 Resonant (7) Storm (19), code of 2012-2013 year reverse of 59 = 95 (19 x 5), 95 – 59 = 36 (4 x 9), Sirian constant

60 3 x 20, 2 x 30, 6 x 10, 4 x 15, vigesimal 3.0, frequency of Pacal Votan, kin 60 first clear sign on his tomb, from discovery of his tomb (1952) to 2012 = 60 years, vigesimal 3.0

61 Prime key, fourth order of unity, V1 H21, antipode to 21,(V21 H1) in 441 matrix, vigesimal 3.1

62 31 x 2, double gate of supreme unity, initiatic completion, reverse of 26 (2 x 13), 62-26 = 36

63 3 x 21, 7 x 9, 63 x 7 = 441, in all orders of 441, 63, like 49 and 21, maintains consistency as its base matrix unit is always a multiple of the same factor as itself, key multiples: x 2 = 126, x 3 = 189, x 4 = 252, x 5 = 315, x 6 = 378, x 7 = 441, first nine orders of seven establish the 63 base frequencies of 441, or 1/7 of order of 441 – 63:441::142857: 999999, vigesimal 3.3

10th order of seven

64 8^2, eighth octave, 4^3 (4 x 16), 2 x 32 crystal frequency doubled, mathematical code of DNA – 64 codons code of life., Seventh binary order (1,2,4,8,16, 32, 64) Sum of prime recombinants, 27 + 37. Note the first 13 orders of the vigesimal code reflect fractal factors of 64 (in bold), and how 64 and 64^2 correspond to 13:7 law of time factor:

1 = 1/64
20 = 1/32 of 64
400 = 1/16 of 64
8000 = 1/8 of 64
160,000 = ¼ of 64
3,200,000 = ½ of 64
64,000,000 = 1 x 64 (7th vigesimal order)
1,280,000,000 = 2 x 64
25,600,000,000 = 4 x 64
512,000,000,000 = 8 x 64
10,24 0, 000,000,000 = 16 x 64
204,800,000,000,000 = 32 x 64
4,096,000,000,000,000 = 64^2 (13th vigesimal order)

65 13 x5, frequency of galactic spectrum, ¼ 260, fifth force moved by power of cosmic cycle

66 6 x 11 triangular of 11

67 Prime key (6 + 7 = 13), vigesimal 3.7 37 and 67 are both primes, difference 30

68 17 x 4, navigator of the four directions

69 3 x 23, reverse of 96, 4 x 24, 96 – 69 = 27

70 7 x 10 tenth order of 7, power of 7 to manifest resonant order, 14 x 5, vigesimal 3.10

Eleventh order of seven

71 Prime key, reverse of 17, liberated navigation, V11 H21 first gate of ascending unity (completes four gates to the four channels of eleven dividing 441 matrix into quadrants) vigesimal 3.11

72 8 x 9, 4 x 18 27 reverse, 72 – 27 = 45, key frequency = ½ 144, base of katun cycle, 7200 Kin, 72nd energy dimension complements 18th evolution dimension, as 18 72 determines duration of present cycle of evolution (21/12/2012 = 1872000 kin, ninth octave)

73 Prime key biomass constant (73 x 5 kin chromatic = 365 day cycle), reverse of 37, 73 – 37 = 36, 73 x 8 = 584 day synodic Venuis cycle establishes Earth Venus 5:8 ratio, same as Fibonacci sequence

74 37 x 2, reverse = 47, 74 – 47= 27

75 25 (5^2) x 3, 15 (triangular of 5) x 5, establishes fifth force frequency as triple action force

76 4 x 19, 7 + 6 =13, reverse of 67, 76 – 67 = 9, 76th energy diemsnion complements 19th (Omega) dimension, next stage of human evolution after Omega 2012, vigesimal 3.16 (= 19)

77 11th power of 7, magnitude of liberation by power of 7, perfect self-reflection

12th order of seven

78 triangular of 12, 13 x 6, frequency key to the prophecy of Pacal Votan as inscribed in the 13 seals of his tomb

79 prime, noosphere constant, kin 79 magnetic storm

80 8 x 10, 2 x 40, 4 x 20, 16 x 5, vigesimal 4.0, tenth octave, completes first outermost circuit 441

81 9^2, 27 x 3, reverse of 18 81 – 18 = 63, begins second circuit 441

82 41 (divine interval) x 2 reverse of 28 82 – 28 = 54

83 Prime key, vigesimal 4.3, 43 and 83 connect as the night seer (43) and the command of the night seer (83)

84 12th order of 7, also 6 x 14, 43 x 28, 3 x 21 vigesimal 4.4, 84 is frequency of the 84,000 dharmas – teachings of the Buddha; synchronic matrix has two sides of 84 units each, hence 84 right hand and 84 left hand dharmas

13th order of seven

85 5 x 17, fifth force power of navigation, $6^2 + 7^2 =$ 85, 13 moon calendar frequency interval, number of days in last three moons plus day out of time (280 + 85 = 365)

86 43 x 2, reverse of 68, 86 – 68 = 18, vigesimal 4.6

87 3 x 29, triple power cosmic constant, frequency of 9 Hand, 5th clear sign Pacal Votan's tomb, frequency of Harmonic Convergence 1987 + 26 = 2013

88 8 x 11, 11th octave

89 Prime key, Fibonacci sequence 11 (34 +55), Kin 89 = 11 Moon

90 9 x 10, ¼ of 360° circle, divides circle into quadrants, V20 H11 second gate of left hand unity

91 13 x 7 thirteenth power of 7, key frequency 13:7 wheel of the law of time, triangular of 13, 91 defines term of terrestrial seasons- one quarter (13 weeks) of 364 day year vigesimal 4.11, reverse of 19 , 91 – 19 = 72, reciprocal frequency 10989 (.010989 – = 33 x 37 x 9, or 999 x 11)

14th order of seven

92 23 x 4, measure or form solar cosmic (sunspot) cycle frequency, reverse of cosmic constant 29, 92 – 29 = 63

93 3 x 31, 93, reverse of 39 3 x 13, 93 – 39 = 54, vigesimal 4.13

94 47 x 2, reverse of 49, 94- 49 = 45

95 19 x 5, reverse of 59, 95 – 59 = 36, vigesimal 4.15 (= 19)

96 Complex harmonic: 2 x 48, 3 x 32, 4 x 24, 6 x 16, 12 x 8, 12th octave, reverse of 69, 96-69 = 27

97 Prime key, 97-33 = 64, reverse of 79, 97-79 = 18

98 49 (7^2) x 2, bicameral frequency of dolphins, 98 reverse of 89, 98 – 89 = 9, vigesimal 4.18

15th order of seven

99 11 x 9 reciprocal factor of 11 (1/11 = .999999)

100 10^2, decimal basis of percentage and monetary systems, 10 = ½ of 20, 10^2 = ¼ of 400 (20^2), $6^2 + 8^2 =$ 10^2, vigesimal 5.0

101 Prime palindromic frequency (same written forwards or backwards)

102 51 x 2, 17 x 6, vigesimal 5.2, navigators cube – cube value of 17, hence frequency of the ark

103 Prime key, frequency of Sura 103: By the Time

104 Arcturus Code (13 x 8), 13th octave, 52 x 2 or two castles of four wavespells each

105 15 x 7 = 21 x 5, triangular of 14, vigesimal 5.5, frequency of primal Maldek

16th order of seven

106   53 x 2, Sirian rebirth doubled, frequency of 2 Worldbridger, northern key to tomb of Pacal Votan, first of 10 GAPs, alpha run, Tzolkin matrix

107   Prime key, "primal Adam" (3 Hand), vigesimal 5.7, reverse 701, 701 –107 = 594, 54 x 11

108   9 x 12, 27 x 4, 36 x 3, 54 x 2 Frequency of Galactic Mission – GM108X (4 Star), First heptad gate, First Time Lens codes tones 1, 5, 9, 13 (4th time dimension pulsar) vigesimal 5.8

109   Prime key, reverse of 901, 901 –109 = 792, 72 x 11, V11 H2 second descending gate of unity

110   11 x 10 manifestation of liberation, vigesimal 5.10

111   37 x 3 perfect cyclical recombinant frequency, first order, x 9 = 999 = 27 x 37

112   4 x 28, 7 x 16, 8 x 14, 14th octave, harmony of the wizards

17th order of seven

113   Prime key: Lord of the Dawn (9 Skywalker), Sura 113, Lord of the Dawn (Daybreak), creates recombinant triplet with 131 and 311, 131 – 113 = 27, 311 – 113= 198, 18 x 11, 113 + 131 +311 = 555 (1+1+3 =5)

114   19 x 6, number of Suras of the Quran, vigesimal 5.14 = 19, triplet 114 – 141 – 411 = 666 (1 + 1 + 4 = 6), 141 – 114 = 27, 411-114 = 297 = 27 x 11

115   23 x 5 fifth force of solar sunspot frequency, vigesimal 5.15

116   29 x 4, form of the cosmic constant, vigesimal code, 5.16

117   9 x 13 prophecy code (tomb dedication 9.13.0.0.0, also 13 heavens, 9 hells, etc,) key recombinant triplet 117 (9 x 13) 171 (9 x 19), 711 (9 x 79) 117 + 171 + 711 = 999

118   59 x 2, frequency of Alion planet, advanced evolutionary realm origin of the system of sixes, universal ordering principle

119   7 x 17, 17th order of 7, forms recombinant triplet, 119 + 191 + 911 = 1221 (frequency 12/21/2012) = 33 x 37, 911-119 = 792, 11 x 72, 191-119 = 72

18th order of seven

120   triangular of 15, 2 x 60, 3 x 40, 4, x 30, 5 x 24, 10 x 12, 6 x 20, vigesimal 6.0, 15th octave

121   11^2, analog to vigesimal 1.2.1 or 21^2, first unit 7th or mystic column, tzolkin, vigesimal 6.1

122   61 x 2, reverse of 221, 221 –122 = 99, 11 x 9

123   41 x 3 divine interval triplet, vigesimal 6.3, reverse of 321, 321 – 123 = 198, 11 x 18, key recombinant frequency, reverse of 891(99 x 9) 891 – 198 = 693, 9 x 77, 21, x 33

124   31 x 4, reverse of 421, 421 = 124 = 297 = 11 x 27, vigesimal 6.4

125   25 x 5 , or 5^3 (5 x 5 x 5)

126   7 x 18, 14 x 9, 21 x 6, 42 x 3, 63 x 2 Frequency of Interval of lost time = 126° = 7/20ths of 360° circle representing law of 13:7, Synchronotron principle or wheel of the law of time, vigesimal 6.6 , V2 H11 second gate of right hand unity, frequency of Solar Worldbridger

19th order of seven

127   prime, reverse of 721, 721 – 127 = 594, 54 x 11

128   64 x 2, 16 x 8, 16th octave, 32 x 4, reverse of 821, 821-128 =693 = 63 x 11

129   43 x 3 triple form of the night seer, reverse of 921, 921 –129 = 792 , 72 x11

130   13 x10 ½ Tzolkin

131   prime, see 113 triplet (113 + 131 + 311)

132   33 x 4, reverse of 231, 33 x 7, principle 4: 7, 231 –132 = 99 = 33 x 3, 9 x 11

133   19 x 7, 19th order of 7, mystic mid-point in 19 = 260 code, vigesimal 6.13 = 19. Kin 133 = 3 Skywalker, seal 13, tone 3, = 3.13 Genesis code, supreme sign of the resurrection

20th order of 7

134   67 x 2, vigesimal 6.14 (6 + 14 = 20), 67 (6 +7 =13)

135   9 x 15 reverse of 531, (59 x 9) 531 –135 = 396 ,11 x 36

136   triangular of 16, 17 x 8, 4 x 34, 17th octave

137   Prime key, frequency "Ah Vuc Ti Cab, Lord of the Center of the Earth (7 Earth)

138   23 x 6, 69 x 2, solar frequency cube value 6 solar sunspot frequency

139   Prime key reverse of 931, 931 –139 = 792 = 11 x 72

140   20th order of 7, Telektonon ratio 5 x 28 = 7 x 20, 7/20ths of 400, 126:140::360:400

21st order of 7

141   47 x 3, palindromic middle term in triplet 114 + 141 + 411 = 666, 37 x 18

142   71 x 2, reverse of 241, 241 – 142 = 99 = 11 x 9

143   13 x 11 (143 x 999 = 142857 = fractal of 1/7)

144 12^2, 9 x16, 18 x 8, 18th octave, Mystic Order, reverse of 441, basis of baktun count, number of the elect, forms recombinant triplet 144 + 414 + 441, 414 – 144 = 270, 441 – 144 = 297 (27 x 11), 144 + 414 + 441 = 999, Fibonacci 12th order, V11 H20 second gate of ascending unity, second time lens codes tones 2, 6, 10, 3rd Heptad gate

145 29 x 5, fifth force cosmic constant,

146 73 x 2, reverse of 641, 641 – 146 = 485 = 11 x 45

147 21st order of 7, 49 x 3, 7 x 21, vigesimal (7.7) a "Total" or 1/3 of 441 either one of three bodies (temple destiny, or radiance), or three layers – terrestrial, celestial/noospheric (above), or universal (middle))

First Book Complete – Compendium of the Terrestrial Temple

22nd order of 7

148 37 x 4, reverse 841 (29^2) 841 –148 = 693 = 9 x 77, 33 x 21, 11 x 63

149 Prime key, vigesimal 7.9 analog of decimal 79 –noosphere constant – reverse of 941 – 941 –149 = 792 11 x 72

150 15 x 10, 25 x 6, 50 x 3, 30 x 5, fifth force command frequency, vigesimal 7.10

151 Prime key, palindromic number, vigesimal 7.11, analog of decimal 711- 79 noosphere constant x 9

152 19 x 8 vigesimal 7.12 = 19, 19th octave, completes second 441 circuit

153 17 x 9, 3 x 51, triangular of 17, commences 3rd 441 cuircuit

154 7 x 22, 22nd order of 7, 14 x 11, kin 154 = Wizard 14, Spectral tone 11, vigesimal 7.14

23rd order of 7

155 31 x 5, fifth force supreme gate of unity, command descending, reverse number 551(19 x 29, divine command of cosmic constant), 551 –155 = 396 = 11 x 36

156 13 x 12, 52 x 3, completes third Dreamspell (Blue Western) castle, vigesimal 7.16, 156 (13 x 12) reverse of 651 (31 x 21) 651 – 156 = 495 = 11 x 45

157 Prime key, first kin 13th wavespell, vigesimal 7.17, reverse of 751, 751 – 157 = 594 =11 x 54

158 79 x 2, binary noosphere constant, vigesimal 7.18

159 53 x 3, triple Sirian rebirth frequency, vigesimal 7.19, reverse = 951 (3 x 317) 951 – 159 = 792 = 11 x 72

160 80 x 2, 40 x 4, 20 x 8, 10 x 16, 5 x 32, 20th octave, frequency of kin 160, 4 ahau, long count beginning and end dates of 13 baktun great cycle, 3113-2012, vigesimal 8.0

161 23 x 7, 23rd order of 7, creation frequency of solar sunspot cycle, palindromic number, middle term, 116 + 161 + 611 = 888 (37 x 24), 611 – 161 = 450, 161 –116 = 45, vigesimal 8.1, V19 H11, third left-hand gate of unity

24th order of 7

162 81 (9^2 x 2), note the cyclic recombinant sequence: 126 (7 x 18, 7:13 code)-162-216 (perfect cube)-261 (9 x 29, cosmic constant, reverse of 162)-612 (9 x 68) and 621 (9 x 69) = 1998 (999 x 2, 27 x 37 x 2)

163 Prime key, reverse of 361 (19^2), 361 –163 = 198 = 11 x 18, vigesimal 8.3

164 41 x 4, full measure divine interval, kin frequency (yellow galactic seed) for 7/26/2013, galactic synchronization, vigesimal 8.4, frequency of law of galactic wholes

165 33 x 5, fifth force power of the initiate, vigesimal 8.5, reverse of 561 (33 x1 7, frequency of initiatic navigation), 561 – 165 = 396 = 11 x 36 (396 also 33 x 12)

166 83 x 2, vigesimal 8.6 reverse of 661 – 661 –166 = 495 = 11 x 45

167 Prime key, reverse frequency 761, 761 – 167 = 594 = 11 x 54

168 24th order of 7, 21st octave. 8 x 21, 6 x 28, 4 x 42, 14 x 12, reverse of 861 (287 x 3, 41 x 21), 861 – 168 = 693 = 63 x 11, 21 x 33, 77 x 9, 231 x 3

25th order of 7

169 13^2, reverse of 31^2 961, difference 792 = 11 x 72, vigesimal 8.9, 13th kin thirteenth wavespell, 13 Moon

170 17 x 10, manifestation of the navigator, vigesimal 8.10

171 19 x 9, triangular of 18, middle term in key triplet 117-171 –711 = 999

172 4 x 43, full measure of the Night seer, vigesimal 8.12

173 Prime key, reverse of 371 (53 x 7), 371 – 173 = 198 = 11 x 18, vigesimal 8.13 (logarithmic sequence)

174 29 x 6, cosmic constant multiplied by cube value 6, frequency of the Book, root frequency of Cosmic History Chronicles (number of verses in Quran 6348, 6348 –6174 (14 x 441) = BMU 174)), vigesimal 8.14

175 25th order of 7, 7 x 5^2, resonant power of fifth force

26th order of 7

176 22 x 8, 11 x 16 = 22nd octave, vigesimal 8.16

177 3 x 59, vigesimal 8.17, frequency of the galactic Earth, reverse number 771 (257 x 3), 771-177 = 594 = 11 x 54, first term in triplet: 177- 717 – 771 = 1665 = 37 x 45 = 9 x 185 , V11 H3 third gate of descending unity

178 89 x 2 (11th Fibonacci x 2) reverse of 871 (13 x 67) 871 –178 = 693 11 x 63, 33 x 21, 3 x 231 etc. vigesimal 8.18

179 Prime key, reverse of 971, 971 – 179 = 792 = 11 x 72, vigesimal 8.19

180 90 x 2, 45 x 4, 15 x 12, 9 x 20, 5 x 36, 3 x 60, 6 x 30 ½ 360° circle, vigesimal 9.0

181 Prime key, palindromic number, cosmic interval 441- 260 = 181, vigesimal 9.1

182 26th order of 7, 13 x 14, 91 x 2 (law of 13:7 moved by binary power) vigesimal 9.2

27th order of 7

183 3 x 61 4th coordinate of unity activated

184 8 x 23, 23rd octave 4 x 46, octave of the solar sun-spot cycle

185 37 x 5 frequency of 3 Serpent, initiates cycle of galactic spectra, generator of red electric current Vulom magnetic attraction force field, reverse of 581 (83 x 7) 581 – 185 = 396 = 11 x 36, vigesimal 9.5

186 83 x 2, vigesimal 9.6, reverse 681 (227 x 3) –186 = 495, vigesimal 9.6 = 15, 1+8 +6 = 15, value of the speed of light 186,000 mph

187 11 x 17, reverse of 781, 781 – 187 = 594 = 11 x 54 vigesimal 9.7

188 47 x 4, measure of the prophet, reverse 881, 881 –188 = 693, vigesimal 9.8

189 27th order of 7, 27 x 7, 9 x 21, 3 x 63, vigesimal 9.9, major synchronization of 7,9, 21, and 27, reverse 981 (109 x 9) 981- 189 = 792 = 11 x 72

28th order of 7

190 19 x 10, triangular of 19, vigesimal 9.10 = 19

191 Prime key, palindromic = 11 reciprocal of 9, vigesimal , 9.11 (kin 191, tone 9, Monkey 11), middle term in triplet, 119 + 191 + 911 = 1221 (37 x 33), 911-191 = 720 = 10 x 72

192 64 (DNA code) x 3, triple incarnation frequency, 8 x 24, 32 x 6, 16 x 12, 24th octave,

193 Prime key, reverse of 391 391 –193 = 198 11 x 18, vigesimal code 9. 13, prophetic key to dedication of tomb of Pacal Votan (long count 9.13.0.0.0), V3 H11 third gate of right hand unity

194 97 x 2, vigesimal 9.14, code of the Crystal Wizard, Book of the First Lost Generation, Book of the Throne, note 9.14 = 914 – 194 = 720

195 13 x 15, vigesimal 9.15, code of the Cosmic Eagle, Book of the Second Lost Generation note 9.15 = 915 – 195 = 720 , Book of the Avatar

196 28 x 7, 28th order of 7, establishes 28:7 harmonic matrix creation frequency, 14^2, 7^2 x 4, 260 –196 = 64 DNA code + 28:7 matrix = 13:20 frequency, 9.16 code of the Magnetic Warrior Code of the Book of the Third Lost Generation, Book of the Mystery

29th order of 7

197 Prime key = reverse of 791 (113 x 7, Lord of the Dawn, power of creation) 791-197 = 594= 11 x 54, vigesimal code 9.17 code of Lunar Earth, Book of the Fourth Lost Generation, Book of the Initiation

198 11 x 18, recombinant frequency, second power of 9, simple gematrical frequency of Synchronotron, reverse of 891 (99 x 9), 891 – 198 = 693 = 21 x 33, 9 x 77, etc vigesimal code, 9.18 codes Electric Mirror Fifth Book of the Lost Generation Book of the Timespace

199 Prime key, reverse of 991, 991 – 199 = 792 11 x 72, vigesimal 9.19 (=28) codes Self-Existing Storm, Book of the Sixth Lost Generation, Book of the Transcendence

200 20 x 10, 5 x 40, 8 x 25, 100 x 2, 25th octave, vigesimal code 10.0, Codes Overtone Sun, Book of the Seventh Lost Generation, Book of the Cube

201 67 x 3, vigesimal 10.1, frequency of kin 201, 6 Dragon, Rhythmic Moon out of Time, 2012-2013 (Moon in which old cycle closes)

202 101 x 2, internally balanced frequency, characteristic of all multiples of 101, Vigesimal 10.2

203 7 x 29, 29th order of 7, cosmic constant of cosmic creation, Vigesimal 10.3

30th order of 7

204 4 x 51, 12 x 17, navigator's temple, vigesimal 10.4

205 41 x 4, fifth force order of divine interval (41), vigesimal 10.5

206 103 x 2, vigesimal 10.6, 206 frequency of 11 Worldbridger and10.6 analog 106 frequency of 2 Worldbridger refer to the dissolution of the world cycle of Mars, kin 206 = eve of 21-12 2012, dissolution of terrestrial cycle of history

207 9 x 23, destiny cycle of solar sunspots, frequency of kin 207, Blue Crystal Hand, 21-12 2012 Closing of the Cycle, vigesimal 10.7

208 52 x 4, 104 x 2, 13 x 16, 8 x 26, 26th octave, fourth castle complete, 208th step to Merlin's Tower, 20 Tablets Law of Time: 208th moon, Cosmic Moon 2013, final stage prior to Galactic Synchronization, vigesimal 10.8

209 11 x 19, first stage of the matrix beyond history V11H19 (209) third gate of ascending unity 441, vigesimal 10.9

210 30th order of 7, 7 x 30, 42 x 5, 6 x 35, 21 x 10 vigesimal 10.10, number days in Wuku Balinese ritual synchronization calendar, triangular of 20

31st order of 7

211 Prime key, completes triplet 112 + 121 + 211= 444 = 12 x 37, 211 – 121 = 90 –112 = 99, frequency of 10th clear sign tomb of Pacal Votan, 3 Monkey, vigesimal 10.11

212 53 x 4, measure of Sirian rebirth, vigesimal 10.12, middle term triplet 122 + 212 + 221= 555, 15 x 37

213 71 x 3, rainbow prophecy activation frequency, vigesimal 10.13

214 2 x 107, orginal Adam (107) transformed into new time wizard, vigesimal 10.14

215 43 x 5, fifth force of the Night Seer, all-penetrating vision, vigesimal 10.15

216 supreme perfection of the cube, 6^3, 6 x 36, 3 x 72, 2 x 108, 8 x 27, 27th octave, completes third 441 circuit, third time lens codes tones 3, 7, 11, in traditional Kabbalah 216 letters in name of God

217 31st order of 7, 31 x 7, begins fourth 441 circuit, creation power of supreme gate of unity, coordinating unit (V18 H18) fourth time dimension, Cosmic Cube, and third mental sphere, waking conscious

32nd order of 7

218 109 x 2, reverse of 812 (= vigesimal 2.0.12, 28 x 29, cosmic constant of harmonic standard), 812 – 218 = 594 = 11 x 54, vigesimal 10.18, frequency of kin 218, discovery of the tomb of Pacal Votan

219 3 x 73, activation frequency of the biomass constant, vigesimal 10.19

220 10 x 22, 11 x 20, 44 x 5, 55 x 4, vigesimal 11.0

221 13 x 17, code of the cosmic navigator, Chac Le, midpoint between 1 and 441, in the magic square of 441 221 is the central unit (V11 H11), and all the rows, vertical and horizontal add up to 442 or 221 x 2 or 441 + 1, vigesimal 11.1

222 111 x 2, 37 x 6, perfect self cyclical recombinant frequency, second order

223 Prime key, reverse of 322 (29 x 14), 322 – 223 = 99 = 11 x 9, vigesimal 11.3

224 32nd order of 7, crystal frequency of cosmic creation, = 8 x 28, octave of the harmonic standard, 4 x 56, measure of Start Codon, 16 x 14, vigesimal 11.4, V18 H11 fourth gate of left hand unity and coordinating unit 6th time dimension and sixth mental sphere, subliminal conscious

33rd order of 7

225 15^2, 45 x 5, 9 x 25 (3^2 x 5^2 = 15^2)

226 113 x 2, "Lord of the Dawn commands the Power of Death" vigesimal 11.6

227 Prime key, reverse of 722 (days 7-22 cube journey) 19^2 x 2, 722 – 227 = 495 = 11 x 45, 227 + 722 = 949 = 13 x 73, cyclic order of biomass constant, vigesimal 11.7, pi = 22/7

228 19 x 12 "Temple of God's command", vigesimal 11.8 (=19)

229 Prime key, reverse of 922, 922-229 = 693 = 21 x 33, 231 x 3, matrix of the initiate of the Hunab Ku 21 code

230 23 x 10, frequency of manifestation of solar sunspot cycle, vigesimal 11.10

231 7 x 33, 33rd order of 7, 3 x 77, 11 x 21, triangular of 21, initiatic creation frequency, supreme mystical frequency, in traditional Kabbalah, 231 sephiroths or angels of creation, coordinating unit second time dimension, Cosmic Ascension, fourth mental sphere, continuing conscious

34th order of 7

232 8 x 29, 29th octave, octave of the cosmic constant, vigesimal 11.12

233 Prime key, 13th Fibonacci sequence (144 + 89), vigesimal 11.13

234 13 x 18, corresponds to 234° or 13/20 of 13:7 wheel of the law of time cosmological basis of frequency 13:20, frequency of Cosmic Wizard, 234 inverse of 432 second master time lens, 54th Octave, 432 – 234 =198 = 11 x 18, also 234 is recombinant with 324, 18^2 and with 342, 19 x 18

235 5 x 47, fifth force frequency of the order of the prophet (47), first kin, 19th wavespell, vigesimal 11.15

236 59 x 4, measure of Sirian constant, reverse of 632 (= 8 x 79, noosphere constant) 632 – 236 = 396 = 11 x 36, vigesimal 11.16

237 3 x 79 activation frequency of noosphere constant, reverse of 732 (= 61 x 12), 732 – 237 = 495 = 11 x 45

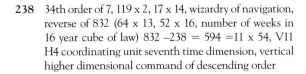

238 34th order of 7, 119 x 2, 17 x 14, wizardry of navigation, reverse of 832 (64 x 13, 52 x 16, number of weeks in 16 year cube of law) 832 –238 = 594 =11 x 54, V11 H4 coordinating unit seventh time dimension, vertical higher dimensional command of descending order

35th order of 7

239 Prime key, reverse of 932 (= 4 x 233, 13th Fibonacci sequence), 932 – 239 = 693 = 9 x 77, 21 x 33, vigesimal 11.19

240 30 x 8 30th octave, 24 x 10, 60 x 4, 40 x 6, 3 x 80, 2 x 120, 5 x 48, vigesimal code 12.0

241 Prime key, vigesimal 12.1 analog of 121 (11^2) , reverse of 142, 241 – 142 = 99 = 11x 9, begins 13th cycle of 20 in Tzolkin

242 121 x 2, 11^2 x 2, binary activation of the mystic code, vigesimal code12.2

243 27 x 9 (3^3 x 3^2) 81 x 3 (9^2 x 3), Heart of Nine, code frequency of Valum Votan (= 9 Night), reverse of 342 , 19 x 9, 342 – 243 = 99 = 11 x 9

244 4 x 61, 122 x 2, reverse of 442 (221 x 2, 17 x 26), 442 – 244 = 198 = 11 x 18

245 35th order of 7, 7^2 (49) x 5, V4 H4, coordinating unit first mental sphere pre conscious and first time dimension cosmic creation, vigesimal code 12.5

36th order of 7

246 6 x 41 cube frequency of divine interval, reverse of 642 (321 x 2), 642 – 246 = 396 = 11 x 36

247 13 x 19, supreme expression of 19 code , 19 = 260, Cosmic Cycle of the Command of God,13 x 19 + 13 = 260, 13 x 20, reverse of 742 (371 x 2, 53 x 14) 742 – 247 = 495 = 11 x 45, vigesimal code, 12.7 (= 19)

248 31 x 8, 31st octave, first unit of 20th wavespell

249 83 x 3, triple command of the night seer, reverse of 942 (157 x 6) 942 – 249 = 693 = 9 x 77, 21 x 33, 7 x 63, vigesimal 12.9

250 25 (5^2) x 10, 5x50, 125 (5^3) x 2, ¼ of 1000, vigesimal 12.10

251 Prime key, vigesimal 12.11, frequency of kin 4 Monkey, signature of 9/11 twin Towers event, –4 sublimating fourth magnitude, sublimated transformer sequence thermic force field (V4 H10) (Holomind perceiver codes)

252 21 x 12, 36 x 7, 36th order of 7, 9th order of 28, 252^3 = interval of cosmic creation = 288^3 – 2808^2 = 252^3 or 144 x 12 x 21 x 441), V4 H11, fourth gate right hand unity, coordinating unit fifth time dimension, fifth mental sphere, superconscious, vigesimal code, 12.12

37th order of 7

253 Prime key, reverse of 352 (11x 32), 352 – 253 = 99 = 11 x 9, vigesimal 12.13, triangular of 22

254 127 x 2, reverse of 452 (113 x 4), 452 – 254 = 198 = 11 x 18, Vigesimal code, 12. 14

255 51 x 5, 17 x 15, navigator of fifth force triple activation, vigesimal code 12.15

256 16^2, 4^4, 64 x 4 completion of four psi genetic space matrix quadrants, master harmonic matrix, 8 x 32, 32nd octave, cosmic crystal resonance, vigesimal 12.16

257 Prime key, master frequency of the planetary navigator, reverse of 752 (16 x 47, harmonic code of the prophet) 752 –257 = 495 = 11 x 45, vigesimal 12.17

258 43 x 6, cube frequency of the night seer, vigesimal 12.18, meditation of endlessness dissolving

259 37 x 7, 37th order of 7, reverse of 952 (17 x 56, 34 x 28), 952 – 259 = 693 = 21 x 33, V4 H18, coordinating unit third time dimension, cosmic synchronization, second mental sphere, subconscious, vigesimal code 12.19

38th order of 7

260 13 x 20, master code frequency of the law of time, 13:20 universal frequency of synchronization, foundation of the Synchronotron 13:7 wheel of the law of time, 4 x 65, 52 x 5 basis of Dreamspell castles, wavespells, harmonics, chromatics, etc., vigesimal code 13.0, , radion value first week 7:7::7:7

261 9 x 29, destiny frequency of cosmic constant, sum of all occult kin pairs, vigesimal code 13.1

262 131 x 2, harmonic balance frequency, vigesimal code 13.2, middle recombinant of triplet 226 + 262 + 622 = 1110 = 37 x 30, 262 – 226 = 36, 622 – 262 – 360 (tun/wheel), vigesimal code 13.2

263 Prime key, reverse of 362 (181 x 2) 362- 263 = 99 = 11 x 9, vigesimal code,

264 33 x 8, 33rd octave (mystic chord), 132 x 2, 66 x 4, 11 x 24, vigesimal code 13.4

265 53 x 5, fifth force frequency of Sirian rebirth, reverse of 562 (281 x 2) 562 –265 = 297 = 11 x 297, vigesimal code, 13.5

266 38th order of 7, 19 x 14, V11-H18, fourth gate of ascending unity, coordinating unit eight time dimension, vertical higher dimensional command of ascending order, vigesimal code 13.6 (= 19)

39th order of 7

267 Prime key reverse of 762 (381 x 2) 762 – 267 = 495 = 11 x 45, vigesimal code 13.7 (= frequency of 13:7 Synchronotron wheel of the law of time)

268 67 x 4, note: 267 + 1 = 67 x 4, reverse = 862 (431 x 2) 862 – 268 = 594 = 11 x 54, vigesimal code 13.8

269 Prime key, reverse 962 (481 x 2), 962 – 269 = 693 = 21 x 33, 11 x 63, 9 x 77, vigesimal code 13.9

270 27 x 10, 9 x 30, 90 x 3, 45 x 6, 54 x 5 frequency 270° = ¾ circle, vigesimal code 13.10

271 Prime key, recombinant 721 (103 x 7) 721 –271 = 450 = 45 x 10, vigesimal code 13.11

272 8 x 34, 34th octave, 17 x 16, harmonic balance frequency of navigators code, vigesimal 13.12 completing unit fourth circuit, 441

273 39 x 7, 39th order of 7, 13 x 21, 91 x 3, cosmic cycle of Hunab Ku 21, vigesimal code 13.13, begins fifth circuit 441, interdimensional phase unit, V17 H17, radial matrix cosmic cube and core galactic channel, beta-beta hyperplasma, radion value second week 7:7::7:7

40th order of 7

274 137 x 2 "The Wizard who tames the center of the Earth", vigesimal 13.14, ESP input unit, core channel Cosmic Cube

275 11 x 5^2, liberating frequency of the fifth force (galactic federation) vigesimal 13.15

276 23 x 12, frequency temple of the solar sunspot cycle, station of the Wizard (Hunab Ku 21 archetypes), vigesimal 13.16, triangular of 23

277 Prime key, reverse of 772 (193 x 4), 772 – 277 = 495 = 11 x 45, vigesimal code 13.17

278 139 x 2, reverse of 872 (109 x 8), 872 – 278 = 594 = 11 x 54, vigesimal code 13.18

279 31 x 9, frequency of the destiny gate of the nine lords of time (bolontiku), vigesimal code 13.19, station of the Pathfinder (Hunab Ku 21 archetypes) V15-H11 fifth left hand gate of unity

280 40th order of 7, 35th octave, 35 x 8, 28 x 10, 14 x 20, 4 x 70, 5 x 56, 40 x 7, 140 x 2, completes Telektonon return cycle, equivalent to first ten moons of the 13 Moon year, vigesimal code 14.0 analog 140 Telektonon code

41st order of 7

281 Prime key, reverse of 182 (13 x 14, ½ 13 moon year), 281 –182 = 99 = 11 x 99, vigesimal code, 14.1

282 141 x 2 (note carry over from previous 14.1 to 141 x 2), station of the path finder, vigesimal code 14.2 station of the Seer (Hunab Ku 21 archetypes),

283 Prime key reverse of 382 (191 x 2), 382 – 283 = 99 = 11 x 9, vigesimal code 14.3

284 71 x 4, ESP input unit beta-alpha core channel Cosmic Ascension, (holomind perceiver codes), vigesimal code 14.4 (decimal analog 144)

285 19 x 15, 3d-4d inter dimensional phase unit, V17 H5, radial matrix cosmic ascension and core galactic channel, beta-alpha hyperplasma, vigesimal code 14.5

286 13 x 22, 26 x 11, radion value third week 7:7::7:7, ESP output unit beta-alpha core channel Cosmic Ascension, vigesimal 14.6

287 41st order of 7, 41 x 7 divine interval moved by primal creation power of 7, radion value fourth week 7:7::7:7, vigesimal code 14.7

42nd order of 7

288 144 x 2, 72 x 4, 36 x 8, 18 x 16, 9 x 32, 96 x 3, 12 x 24, 36th octave, master frequency of polar harmonic, fourth time lens codes tones 4, 8, and 12, station of the Serpent Initiate, red electric circuit gnerator (Hunab Ku 21 archetypes), radion value 7 mystic moons, fourth week 7:7::7:7, vigesimal code 14.8

289 17^2 reverse of 982 (491 x 2) 982 – 289 = 693 = 21 x 33, initiatic matrix frequency of the navigator, vigesimal code 14.9

290 29 x 10 frequency of the manifestation of the cosmic constant, vigesimal code 14.10

291 3 x 97, 2nd heptad gate, the Avatar, station of the Avatar (Hunab Ku 21 archetypes), vigesimal code 14.11, V11 H5 Fifth gate of unity descending

292 146 x 2, 73 x 4, frequency of form and measure of the biomass constant, vigesimal code 14.12

293 Prime key reverse of 392 (49 x 8), 392 – 293 = 99 = 11 x 9, vigesimal code 14.13

294 42nd order of 7, 42 x 7, 49 x 6, cube value of 49, station of the Hierophant (Hunab Ku 21 archetypes), vigesimal code 14.14

Second Book Complete, Universal Order of the Radiant Ones

43rd Order of 7

295 59 x 5, fifth force Sirian Constant, reverse frequency 592 (296 x 2, 37 x 8), 592 – 295 = 297 = 11 x 27

296 37 x 8, 37th octave, ESP input unit alpha-alpha core channel Cosmic Creation (holomind perceiver codes), vigesimal code 14.16

297 11 x 27, master recombinant interval frequency (key example 441 –144 = 297), 3d-4d inter dimensional phase unit, V5 H5, radial matrix cosmic creation and core galactic channel, alpha-alpha hyperplasma, vigesimal code, 14.17

298 149 x 2 ESP output unit alpha-alpha core channel Cosmic Creation, vigesimal code 14.18

299 13 x 23, frequency of cosmic cycle of solar sun spots vigesimal code 14.19

300 20 x 15, 10 x 30, 60 x 5, 50 x 6, 25 x 12, 3 x 100, Station of the Artist (Hunab Ku 21 archetypes),vigesimal code 15.0 triangular of 24

301 43rd order of 7, 43 x 7, resonant creative power of the night seer, vigesimal code 15.1

44th order of 7

302 151 x 2, vigesimal code 15.2, Note: carry-over from prior 15.1 to 151 x 2 to vigesimal code 15.2, reverse of 203, 302 – 203 = 99 = 11 x 9

303 101 x 3, perfect self-recombinant, station of the Compassionate One (Hunab Ku 21 archetypes), vigesimal code 15.3, V5 H11 fifth gate of right hand unity

304 19 x 16, double harmonic octave of the command of God, 38th octave, 38 x 8, 76 x 4, vigesimal code 15.4

305 61 x 5, fifth force of the fourth coordinate of unity, reverse of 503, 503 – 305 = 198 = 11 x 18

306 153 x 2, 51 x 6, 17 x 12, frequency of the temple of the navigator, station of the Healer (Hunab Ku 21 archetypes), vigesimal code 15.6

307 Prime key reverse of 703, 703 – 307 = 396 = 11 x 36

308 44th order of 7, 7 x 44, 77 x 4, 11 x 28, spectral moon frequency of liberation by means of harmonic standard, ESP output unit alpha-beta core channel Cosmic Synchronization, vigesimal 15.8

45th order of 7

309 103 x 3, 3d-4d interdimensional phase unit, V5 H17, radial matrix cosmic synchronization and core galactic channel, alpha-beta hyperplasma, vigesimal code 15.9

310 31 x 10, 5 x 62, ESP input unit alpha-beta core channel cosmic synchronization, vigesimal code 15.10

311 Prime key completes triplet 113 – 131 – 311, reverse of 113 (lord of dawn frequency) 311 – 113 = 198 = 11 x 18

312 13 x 24, cosmic cycle of Velatropa 24 system, 8 x 39, 39th octave 12 x 26, 6 x 52, 3 x 104, Sirius B (52) and Arcturus (104) frequencies synchronize, station of the Magician, blue electric circuit generator (Hunab Ku 21 archetypes), vigesimal code 15.12 = analog 1512 = 216 x 7)

313 Prime key self recombinant palindromic, middle term in triplet 133-313-331, 331 – 313 = 18, 313 – 133 = 180 = 10 x 18, 133 + 313 +331 = 777 = 21 x 37, vigesimal code 15.13

314 157 x 2, reverse of 413 (59 x 7), 413 – 314 = 99 = 11 x 9, vigesimal code 15. 14, corresponds to UR harmonic 103, Channel of command becomes self-evolving

315 45th order of 7, 45 x 7, 63 x 5, 21 x 15, 9 x 35, V11-H17 Fourth heptad Gate of the Initiation, station of the Prophet (Hunab Ku 21 archetypes), vigesimal code 15.15 , fifth gate of ascending unity, UR Harmonic 95, Galactic art whole becomes meditation of reality

46th order of 7

316 79 x 4, form and mesure of noosphere constant = 4 plate psi bank code, corresponds to Ur Harmonic 79, Tree of Cosmic Fiore Generates Planet Mind, vigesimal code 15.16

317 Prime key reverse of 713, 713 – 317 396 = 11 x 36, vigesimal code 15.17

318 3 x 106, 6 x 53, cube value Sirian rebirth, station of the Sage(Hunab Ku 21 archetypes), vigesimal code, 15.18

319 11 x 29, frequency of liberation by means of the cosmic constant, vigesimal code 15.19

320 40 x 8, 40th octave, 4 x 80, 10 x 32, 20 x 16 , 5 x 64, vigesimal 16.0, ESP input unit beta-beta core channel Cosmic Cube, last unit 5th 441 circuit

321 107 x 3, core intergalactic channel beta-beta hyperplasma activates codes of cosmic cube, vigesimal 16.1, V16 H16, first unit 6th circuit 441 matrix

322 46th order of 7, 161 x 2, 23 x 14, 46 x 7, vigesimal code 16.2, wizard's solar sunspot cycle code

47th order of 7

323 palindromic prime, mid term in triplet 233+323+332 = 888 = 37 x 24, vigesimal code, 16.3

324 18^2, 9 x 36, 108 x 3, 27 x 12, 81 x 4 (note 18^2 is also a product of both 9^2 (81) and 6^2 (36), harmonic frequency matrix of 18-dimensional universe, vigesimal code 16.4 (decimal analog 164)

325 13 x 25, 5 x 39, triangular of 25, cosmic cycle of 5th force vigesimal code 16.5

326 163 x 2, V16 H11 sixth gate of left hand unity, sixth unit Dum Duar blue luminic force field vigesimal code 16.6

327 109 x 3, recombinant of 273 (= difference of 54) reverse of 723 (3 x 241), 723 – 327 = 396 = 11 x 36, vigesimal code 16.7

328 41 x 8, 41st octave, octave of the divine interval, vigesimal 16.8, decimal analog of 168, 21 x 8 – parallel frequency to 41 x 8

329 47th order of 7, creation frequency of the prophet, vigesimal code 16.9, decimal analog 169 or 13 x 13, note 13 and 7 factors in this frequency

48th order of 7

330 11 x 30, 33 x 10, 3 x 110, initiatic frequency of manifestation, vigesimal code 16.10, establishes 33rd decimal order, "the initiate"

331 Prime key, V16 H6, core intergalactic channel beta-alpha (beta-nova) hyperplasma, activates codes of cosmic ascension, vigesimal code 16.11

332 166 x 2, 83 x 4, second frequency decimal order of 33

333 37 x 9, 111 x 3, prime self-cyclic recombinant, key integer in decimal order of the Initiate, vigesimal code 16.13

334 167 x 2, reverse of 433, 433 – 334 = 99 = 11 x 9

335 67 x 5 (note parallel with 167 of previous frequency) corresponds to UR harmonic 107, Infinite mind wave illumines space, vigesimal code 16.15

336 48th order of 7, 42 x 8, 42nd octave, 21 x 16, V11 H6 sixth gate of unity descending, corresponds to UR Harmonic 85 Galactic life whole channels time, Vigesimal code, 16.16

49th order of 7

337 Prime key, seventh frequency in 33rd decimal order, reverse of 733, 733 – 337 = 396 = 11 x 36, vigesimal code, 16.17, corresponds to UR Harmonic 69, Firmament divides time

338 169 x 2 (13 x 26), power of 13^2 doubled, galactic time wave frequency, vigesimal code 16.18

339 113 x 3, triple birth Lord of the Dawn, fulfills 9th magnitude of 33rd decimal order, vigesimal 16.19

340 17 x 20, vigesimal code 17.0, frequency of the sacred time of the navigator, Noah (17) (40 days and 40 nights in the Ark)

341 11 x 31, supreme frequency of unity, V6 H6 core intergalactic channel alpha-alpha hyperplasma, activates codes of cosmic creation, vigesimal 17.1 (decimal analog of 171 19 x 9, see next frequency for carry over)

342 19 x 18, 9 x 38, recombinant frequency: 234 (13 x 18 = 234° or 13/20 of 360° circle), 243 (27 x 9 = "Valum Votan"), 324 (18^2, matrix of eighteen dimensional universe), 342 (19 x 18, God's command of 18-dimensional universe), 423 (9 x 47, prophet's power of nine) and 432 (54 x 8, 54th octave and second master time lens, combines 108 (x 4), 144 (x 3) and 216 (x 2)).

343 49th order of 7, 7 x 7^2 or 7^3, master power of creation matrix

50th order of 7

344 43 x 8, 43rd octave, octave of the night seer, vigesimal code 17.4

345 5 x 69, 23 x 15, fifth force triple activation of solar sunspot cycle, vigesimal code 17.5

346 173 x 2, reverse of 643, 643 – 346 = 297 = 11 x 27, recombinant with 364 = 28 x 13, 364 – 346 = 18, vigesimal code, 17.6, V11 H6, sixth gate of right hand unity, sixth unit Dum Kuali red thermic force field

347 Prime key, reverse 743, 743 – 347 = 396 = 11 x 36, vigesimal 17.7

348 29 x 12, 6 x 58, 87 x 4, 116 x 3, 174 x 2, temple of the cosmic constant, vigesimal code, 17.8

349 Prime key reverse, 943 (23 x 41 divine interval of solar sunspot cycle frequency) vigesimal code 17.9

350 50th order of 7, 7 x 50, 14 x 25, 70 x 5, 35 x 10, manifestation of fifth force power of cosmic creation, vigesimal code, 17.10

51st order of 7

351 27 x 13, 9 x 39 triple power frequency of prophetic code 9 and 13, V6 H16 core intergalactic channel alpha-beta hyperplasm, activates codes of cosmic synchronization, triangular of 26

352 44 x 8, 44th octave, 88 x 4, 11 x 32 crystal frequency of liberation, vigesimal code 17.12

353 palindromic prime, middle term in triplet 335+353+533 = 1221 = 11 x 111, 33 x 37, 533 – 353 = 180, 18 x 10, vigesimal code 17.13

354 177 x 2, 59 x 6, cube value Sirian constant, number of days in a 12-month lunar year, vigesimal code 17.14

355 71 x 5, corresponds to UR Harmonic 102, System of commands evolves cosmic space, vigesimal code 17.5

356 89 (11th Fibonacci) x 4, V11 H16 sixth ascending gate of unity, corresponds to UR Harmonic 94 Structure of Reality becomes architecture of space

357 51st order of 7, 51 x 7, 119 x 3, 17 x 21, vigesimal code 17.17, supreme navigators code of Hunab Ku 21, corresponds to UR Harmonic 78 Day and night defines cosmic space

52nd order of 7

358 179 x 2 reverse frequency 853, 853 – 358 = 495 = 11 x 45, vigesimal 17.18

359 Prime key, reverse 953, 953 – 359 = 594 = 11 x 54, vigesimal code 17.19

360 18 x 20, 9 x 40, 36 x 10, 45 x 8, 9 x 40, 5 x 72 , 24 x 15, 3 x 120, 2 x 180, = 360° of a circle, 1 tun (Mayan 360-day cycle), completes 6th circuit 441, 45th octave vigesimal code 18.0

361 19^2, frequency of matrix of divine commands, number of days in 19th month Ba'hai 19 month calendar, first unit in 7th 441 circuit, vigesimal code 18.1, coordinating internal unit, 4th time dimension

362 181 x 2 (carry-over from previous 18.1), binary order of cosmic interval (181),441 – 362 = 79, noosphere constant, vigesimal code 18.2

363 11 x 33, 121 (11^2 x 3), supreme initiatic liberation frequency, palindromic harmonic, vigesimal code 18.3

364 52nd order of 7, 52 x 7 supreme Sirian creation frequency, number of days in 13 moon 28 day calendar cycle, 52 x 7 = 13 x 28, 4 x 91, fulfillment of law of time cosmological ratio, 4:7::7:13, (4 x7 = 28, harmonic standard, 7 x 13 = 91, frequency of synchronotronic wheel of law, 4 x 13, = 52, Sirius B frequency) vigesimal code 18.4

53rd order of 7

365 5 x 73, fifth force perfection of biomass standard, corresponds to 365-day vague solar orbital frequency (364 + 1), vigesimal code 18.5 (decimal analog, 185, 5 x 37 reverse of 73 x5), V15 H11, 7th gate of left hand unity, 7th magnitude Dum Duar blue luminic force field

366 61 x 6, solar cycle with intercalary leap day added, cube value, reverse of 663 (51 x 13), 663-366 = 297 = 11 x 27, vigesimal code 18.6

367 Prime key, reverse of 763 (109 x 7), 763 – 367 =396 = 11 x 36, vigesimal code, 18.7

368 8 x 46, 46th octave, 16 x 23, harmonic order of solar sunspot cycle, vigesimal code 18.8

369 41 x 9, ninth order of divine interval, reverse of 963 (107 x 9) 963 – 369 = 594 = 11 x 54, vigesimal 18.9 (analog 189 parallel frequency 21 x 9), coordinating internal unit, second time dimension

370 37 x 10, manifest order of key recombinant factor, vigesimal code 18.10

371 53rd order of 7, 7 x 53, supreme creation frequency of Sirian rebirth, vigesimal code 18.11, high end recombinant factor = 731 (43 x 17, navigation frequency of the night seer) 731 – 371 = 360, totality of wheel (or tun) of the law

54th order of 7

372 4 x 93 31 x 12, temple of the first gate of unity, corresponds to UR harmonic 112, Infinite mind wave evolves infinitely, vigesimal code 18.12

373 Palindromic prime, middle term in triplet 337 + 373 + 733 = 1443 = 37 x 39, 373 – 337 = 36, 733 – 373 = 360, wheel of totality, vigesimal code 18.13, V11 H7 seventh gate of descending unity, corresponds to UR Harmonic 83, Galactic life whole extends into space

374 187 x 2, 11 x 34, 22 x 17, planetary wizard's liberating navigation codes, vigesimal code 18.14, corresponds to UR harmonic 67, Divine Decree establishes space of second creation

375 5 x 75, 5^2 x 15, 5^3 x 3, fifth force quintessential action code, vigesimal 18.15

376 47 x 8, 4th octave, octave of the prophets, 188 x 2, 94 x 4, vigesimal code 18.16

377 29 x 13, cosmic cycle of cosmic constant, coordinating internal unit 1st time dimension, vigesimal code 18.17

378 54th order of 7, 7 x 54, 42 x 9 18 x 21, 27 x 14, 126 x 3, 189 x 2, frequency of 378-day Saturn synodic loop around Earth, 378 x 29 loops = 28 365-day solar Earth years, vigesimal code 18.18, triangular of 27

55th order of 7

379 Prime key, reverse of 973 (139 x 7), 973 – 379 = 594 = 11 x 54, vigesimal code 18.19

380 19 x 20, 38 x 10, 76 x 5, 95 x4 Command of God as Totality, vigesimal code 19.0

381 127 x 3, V7 H11 7th gate of right hand unity, 7th magnitude Dum Kuali red thermic force field, vigesimal code 19.1

382 191 x 2 (see prior frequency 19.1 for carry-over), recombinant cyclic harmonic 832 = 64 x 13, frequency of 16-year cube of the law, recombinant interval factor 450 = 10 x 45, vigesimal code 19.2

383 palindromic prime, middle term in triplet 338 + 383 + 833 =1554 = 37 x 42, 833 – 383 =450, 10 x 45, vigesimal code, 19.3

384 48 x 8, 48th octave, "hexameride of the octave" frequency range of human experience, high harmonic frequency of the code of life, 8 x 48 = 64 x 6 cube value of DNA code, number of lines in I Ching, binary order of DNA code, 32 x 12, crystal temple code, vigesimal code 19.4 (decimal analog, 194, First Book of First Lost Generation, Crystal Wizard)

385 55 x 7, 55th order of 7, 11 x 35, fifth force liberation of creation frequency, vigesimal code 19.5, internal coordinate third time dimension

56th order of 7

386 193 x 2, reverse of 683 (frequency of the year of the disincarnation of Pacal Votan), 683 – 386 = 297 = 11 x 297, vigesimal code 19.6

387 129 x 3, 43 x 9, frequency of the night seer moved by the ninth power, vigesimal code 19.7

388 97 x 4, 194 x 2, Bode number of the orbital ratio Pluto, vigesimal code, 19.8 corresponds to UR harmonic 100, Union of ascent and descent established as cosmic space

389 Prime key, reverse 983, 983 – 389 = 595 = 11 x 54, V11 H15, seventh gate of unity ascending, 441, vigesimal code 19.9, corresponds to UR harmonic 92, Galactic art whole becomes structure of reality

390 39 x 10, 13 x 30, 3 x 130, 5 x 78, 6 x 65, manifestation of triple order of cosmic time cycle, vigesimal code 19.10, corresponds to UR harmonic 76, Command of cosmic creation engenders firmament

391 17 x 23, navigation of the solar sunspot cycle, vigesimal code 19.11

392 56th order of 7, 7 x 56, 8 x 49 (7^2) 49th octave, 98 x 4, 196 (14^2) x 2, vigesimal code 19.12 final unit in 7th 441 circuit

57th order of 7

393 131 x 3, master palindromic, middle term in triplet 339 + 393 + 933 = 1665 = 45 triangular of 9 x 37, 933 – 393 = 540 = 10 x 54, first unit in 8th 441 circuit, first unit in 9th time dimension, corresponds to hyperparton of secondary luminic cell kemio, light of inner heat, vigesimal 19.13

394 197 x 2, reverse of 493, 493 –394 = 99 = 11 x 9, vigesimal code 19.14

395 5 x 79, fifth force factor of noosphere, vigesimal code 19.15

396 11 x 36, 99 x 4, major recombinant interval factor, fourth power of nine moved by liberating power of 11, V14 –H11 eighth gate of left hand unity, vigesimal code 19.16, station of the Navigator

397 Prime key, reverse of 793 (13 x 61), 793 – 397 = 396 = 11 x 36, see preceding entry, vigesimal code 19.17

398 199 x 2, frequency of the master teachers doubled, vigesimal code 19.18

399 57th order of 7, 7 x 57, 21 x 19, 133 x 3, master frequency command of God moved by power of Hunab Ku (21), corresponds to secondary thermic cell, kum, heat of inner light, vigesimal code 19.19

58th order of 7

400 20^2, Master frequency of totality, 10^2 x 4, 50 x 8, 50th octave, 25 x 16, 5 x 80, 2 x 200 vigesimal code 2.0.0, establishes third order of absolute vigesimal count (Ka'l-tun or 400 count – distinct from relative katun, 360 (18) count where 20 tuns = 1 katun of 7200, whereas 20 x 400 = 1 K'al tun = 8000

401 Prime key, reverse of 104(13 x 8) , 401 – 104 = 297 = 11 x 27, corresponds to UR harmonic 105 octave of infinite mind wave, vigesimal code 1. 0.1

402 6 x 67, 2 x 201, 3 x 134 corresponds to position of hyperneutron of 8th hyperparton circuit, V11 H8, 8th gate of descending unity, vigesimal code 1.0.2, corresponds to UR harmonic 81, Radiogenesis establishes galactic life whole, station of the Yogi(ni), 6th heptad gate

403 31 x 13, numerological correspondence to 3113, beginning of present 13 baktun cycle, vigesimal code, 1.0.3 corresponds to UR harmonic 65, Octave of Divine decree "Be!"

404 harmonic palindromic, 101 x 4, 202 x 2, vigesimal code 1.0.4

405 81 9^2 x 5, 9 x 45 triangular of 9, 27 x 15, vigesimal code 1.0.5 corresponds to primal heat cell hyperparton dum kuali

406 58th order of 7, 29 x 14 cosmic constant of the wizards, 203 x 2 vigesimal code 1.0.6, triangular of 28

59th order of 7

407 11 x 37, master recombinant frequency, e.g., 407 x 351 (27 x 13) = 142 857 (reciprocal of 7), 407 x 27 = 10989 (reciprocal of 91), 407 x 189 (27 x 7) = 76923 (reciprocal of 13), etc. vigesimal code 1.0.7

408 8 x 51, 51st octave, 24 x 17 navigator of velatropa frequency, 12 x 34, 4 x 102, 3 x 136 2 x 204, V8- H11, eighth gate of right hand unity, vigesimal code 1.0.8, station of the Worldchanger

409 Prime key reverse of 904 (113 x 8), 904 – 409 = 495 11 x 45, vigesimal code 1.0.9

410 41 x 10, manifestation frequency of divine interval, vigesimal code 1.0.10 (parallel vigesimal analog 10.10 = 210 = 21 x 10)

411 Prime key, reverse of 114 (19 x 6) third unit in triplet 114 + 141 + 411 = 666 (37 x18), 411 – 114 = 297, vigesimal code 1.0.11, corresponds to primary light cell, luminic hyperparton dum duar

412 206 x 2, 103 x 4 frequency of the temple of the Martian redemption in time vigesimal code 1.0.12

413 59th order of 7, Sirius constant moved by power of cosmic creation, vigesimal code 1.0.13

60th order of 7

414 23 x 18, 46 x 9, 69 x 6, 138 x 3, V11 H14, 8th Gate of Ascending Unity, Fifth Heptad gate, gate of the Timespace station of the Enlightened One, corresponds to hyperelectron, activates South (Darka) pole with double-extended electron, UR Harmonic 90, Galactic Art Whole defined by time, middle term in triplet 144-414-441, vigesimal code 1.0.14

415 83 x 5, reverse frequency 514 (257 x 2) 514 – 415 = 99 = 11 x 9, vigesimal code 1.0.15

416 8 x 52, 52nd octave- Sirian resonance – 4 x 104, 2 x 104, 13 x 32, 16 x 26, final unit in 8th 441 circuit, hyperelectron circuit complete, vigesimal code 1.0.16

417 139 x 3, reverse frequency 714 (7 x 102, 17 x 42) 714 – 417 = 297 = 11 x 27, first unit of 9th 441 circuit, vigesimal code 1.0.17, V13 H13 fifth force coordinating unit fourth quadrant of 441 (beta-beta zone)

418 19 x 22, 11 x 38 frequency of "House of God", vigesimal code 1.0.18

419 Prime key (first prime since 409), reverse of 914 (457 x 2), 914 – 419 = 495 = 11 x 45, vigesimal code 1.0.19, V13 H11, ninth gate of left hand unity

420 60th order of 7, 7 x 60, 5 x 84, 30 x 14, 28 x 15, 10 x 42, 3 x 140, 20 x 21, amplification of 5:7 Telektonon ratio, vigesimal code 1.1.0, totality (20) multiplied by transcendent unity (21), decimal analog of 110 – 11 x 10

61st order of 7

421 Prime key, reverse of 124 (31 x 4), 421 – 124 = 297 = 11 x 27, vigesimal code 1.1.1 (decimal analog 111), V13 H9 fifth force coordinating unit third quadrant of 441 (beta-alpha zone)

422 211 x 2, final term in triplet code 224 + 242 + 422 = 888 = 37 x 24, 442 – 224 = 198 = 11 x 18 (242 – 224 = 18, 422 – 242 = 180, 18 factor triplet) vigesimal code, 1.1.2

423 141 x 3, 47 x 9 power of nine code of the prophet, V11H9 ninth gate of descending unity, vigesimal code 1.1.3 (decimal analog 113, Lord of the Dawn)

424 Palindromic harmonic (same in reverse), 53 x 8, 53rd octave, octave of Sirian rebirth of Quetzalcoatl (Lord of the Dawn), 4 x 106 2 x 212, vigesimal code 1.1.4

425 17 x 25, 5 x 85, fifth force amplification of the avigator, V9 H9 fifth force coordinating unit first quadrant of 441 (alpha-alpha zone), vigesimal code 1.1.5

426 213 x 2, 142 x 3, 71 x 6 cube value 71, first gate of ascending unity (note how all integers of the 61st order of 7 all have multiples of the last digit of each number, vigesimal 1.1.6

427 61st order of 7, 61 x 7 creation power of 4th coordinate of unity, V9 H11, ninth gate of right hand unity, vigesimal code 1.1.7 (decimal analog 117, 9 x 13)

62nd order of 7

428 214 x 2, 107 x 4, frequency of the star form of the primal Adam, vigesimal code 1.1.8

429 13 x 33, frequency of the initiate of the cosmic cycle, 11 x 39, 3 x 143, V9 H13 fifth force coordinating unit second quadrant of 441 (alpha-beta zone), vigesimal code 1.1.9

430 43 x 10, manifestation of the night seer, 5 x 86, vigesimal code 1.1.10 (decimal analog 1110 = 111 x 10)

431 Prime key, reverse frequency 134 (67 x 2) 431 – 134 = 297 = 11 x 27, vigesimal code, 1.1.11 (decimal analog 1111 = 101 x 11)

432 Master frequency, 8 x 54, 54th octave, second master time lens, coordinates first, second and third time lenses (108 x 4, 144 x 3, 216 x 2) , 72 x 6, 12 x 36, 9 x 48, 18 x 24, 16 x 27, vigesimal code 1.1.12, final unit ninth 441 circuit

433 Prime key, reverse of 334, final term in triplet 334 + 343 + 433 =1110 (see above 430 = 1.1.10) 111 x 10, 433- 334 =99 = 11 x 9 (this triplet is governed by 9 factor, 343-334= 9, 433- 343 = 90, 10 x 9) vigesimal code, first unit 10th 441 circuit "Stations of the Ark"

434 62nd order of 7 x 62, 31 x 14, V12 H11, tenth left hand gate of unity, vigesimal code 1.1.14

63rd order of 7

435 29 x 15, 5 x 87, 145 x 3, vigesimal code triangular of 29, cosmic constant, final triangular frequency within 441 base matrix, vigesimal code 1.1.15

436 109 x 4, reverse frequency 634 (317 x 2), 634 – 436 = 198 = 11 x 18, V11 H10 tenth gate of descending unity, innermost gate of descending commands, 436 – 31 (first gate of supreme unity = 405 9^2 x 5), vigesimal code 1.1.16

437 19 x 23, frequency of solar sunspot frequency at the command of God, vigesimal code 1.1.17

438 219 x 2, 146 x 3, 73 x 6, cube value of biomass constant, V10 H11, tenth gate of right hand unity

439 Prime key, final (85th) prime before 441, reverse 934 (467 x 2), 934 – 439 = 495 = 11 x 45, vigesimal code 1.1.19

440 8 x 55 55th octave, 11 x 40 10 x 44, 110 x 4, 220 x 2, 88 x 5, 22 x 20, V11H12 tenth gate of ascending unity, vigesimal code 1.2.0

441 Key Master Frequency of Sirus B and Galactic Hierarchies, 7th heptad gate, 21^2, 9 x 49, 7 x 63, 3 x 147, unification of laws of 3, 7, and 9 V11 H11, 11th Gate of Unity, channel to 11th dimension cube system and dimension of Lordly Spiritual Technological totalities, channel for coordinating hyperplasma Sirius B-52/Element 113 basis of universal fractal of universe of number, concluding unit of 441 Base matrix, vigesimal code 1.2.1 – decimal analog 121 = 11^2

Third Book Complete, Celestial Order of the Mind Lords

Multiples of 441 to 21^3

Seven planes of the Terrestrial Order

441 First layer—Plane of Unified Humanity

882 Second layer—Plane of Universal Spirit

1323 Third layer—Plane of the Dream-time

1764 Fourth layer —Plane of Intrinsic Awareness

2205 Fifth layer—Plane of Universal Kundalini energy

2646 Sixth layer—Plane of Revelation

3087 Seventh layer—Plane of Power of Knowing

Seven planes of the Universal Order

3528 Eighth layer—Plane of Power of Art

3969 Ninth layer—Plane of Cosmic healing power

4410 Tenth layer—Plane of Compassionate energy

4851 Eleventh layer—Plane of Lordly Spiritual Technological Totalities

5292 Twelfth layer—Plane of Universal Wisdom

5733 Thirteenth layer—Plane of Prophecy

6174 Fourteenth layer—Plane of Power of Psychic Force

Seven planes of the Celestial Order

6615 Fifteenth layer—Plane of Telecosmic vision

7056 Sixteenth layer—Plane of All-Penetrating Intelligence

7497 Seventeenth layer—Plane of Synchrognosis

7938 Eighteenth layer—Plane of Cosmic Memory

8379 Nineteenth layer—Plane of Superconscious metamorphism

8820 Twentieth layer—Plane of Supramental Enlightenment

9261 Twenty-first layer—Plane of Galactic Totalalities—Synchronotron—Powers of Universal Cosmic Creation—Hunab Ku 21.

Cube of 21 complete—21^3 = vigesimal 1.3.3.1, analog of 1331 = 11^3

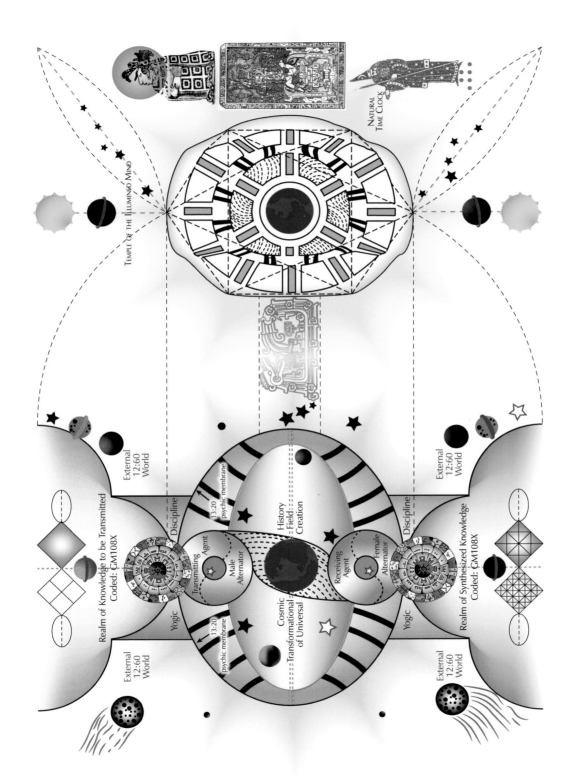

Temple of the Illumined Mind

Natural Time Clock

Realm of Knowledge to be Transmitted
Coded: GM108X

External 12:60 World

Discipline

13:20 psychic membrane

History Field: Creation

Transmitting Agent

Male Alternator

Yogic

13:20 psychic membrane

Cosmic Transformational of Universal

Receiving Agent

Female Alternator

Discipline

Realm of Synthesized Knowledge
Coded: GM108X

External 12:60 World

Yogic

External 12:60 World

External 12:60 World

CALLING FOR
A SPIRIT NATION
TO ARISE AND CLOSE
THE SACRED HOOP